# CHRISTIANITY

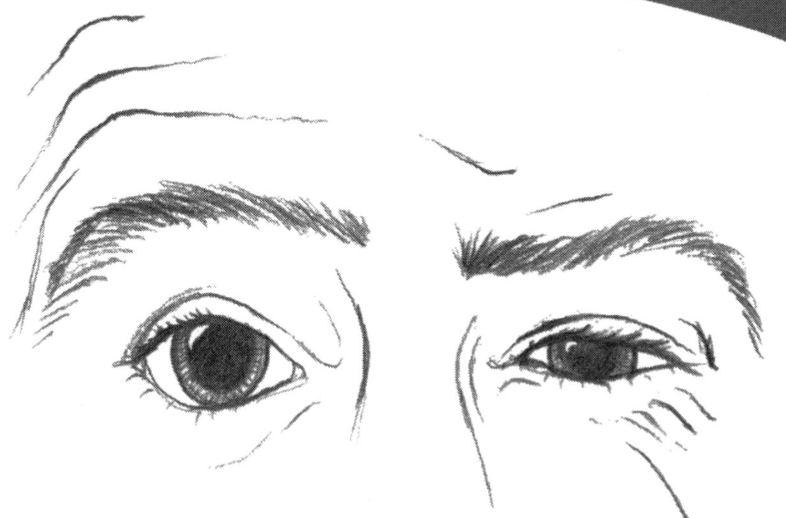

## A Guide for the Thoughtful
## (Skeptic or Believer)

Allen Horstman

Christianity A Guide for the Thoughtful (Skeptic or Believer).


ISBN: 0615777562
ISBN 13: 9780615777566

*For*
*Matt and Fritz*

# ACKNOWLEDGMENTS

This book results from my interactions with many people.

Meeting with the folk in Traverse City Central United Methodist Church and Northwestern Michigan College in classes suggested to me many, many churchgoers did not share the simplistic views portrayed by the media or challenged by the "New Atheists." However, those pewsitters, the Thoughtful believers of the title, were not being given, in their churches, alternative views to the simplistic ones they learned as children. This book is an effort to remedy that void.

My sons helped me, a lot. Matt solved myriad computer problems and Fritz provided the book's cover and the flowchart in the Appendix. Both have been generous in listening to me and, while they know I don't accept the old, traditional views of Christianity, they, like the churchgoers, have no alternative interpretation available; they are the Thoughtful skeptics of the title. This book seeks to remedy that void.

Nan, my wife of my life, has been on the journey with me as we puzzle out what Christians can accept today without "leaving their brains at the church door." A child of the parsonage, she started in a different place than I, a child of fundamentalism, so it has been an interesting joint journey. This book is where I (we?) stand today. As for tomorrow....?

Elizabeth Moran did a wonderful and thorough job of editing the manuscript and made extensive comments.

I thank all and hope this work helps in their questioning.

# CONTENTS

## MISCELLANEOUS

# LIST OF ILLUSTRATIONS

# LIST OF MAPS

# USAGES

The scripture usually cited in this work is the Protestant Bible. While its Old Testament is the same in content as the Hebrew Bible, the book order differs. The Protestant Bible also does not include the Apocrypha or Deuterocanonical materials which are included in the Roman Catholic and Orthodox Bibles and some others as well. Typically the New Revised Standard Version (NRSV) is used because it is an ecumenical and (relatively) non-controversial translation.

Whenever the first part of the Protestant Bible is mentioned, the usage is Hebrew Bible/Old Testament and the second part is Christian scripture/New Testament. Most Christians would use only Old Testament and New Testament but this book is written for more than just Christians.

The dates are B.C.E. (Before the Common Era) and C.E. (Common Era) which reflect, respectively, the same as the older usage of the terms B.C. (Before Christ) and A.D. (Anno Domini). All B.C.E. dates are so indicated. If a date has no identification, it is C.E.

# BIBLIOGRAPHIC THOUGHTS

The interpretations, as well as some of the factually based material, presented in this book are in flux, particularly regarding the meaning of the scripture and the role of religions in the United States today. The footnotes point to some of the recent work, but much more is available. Just don't believe everything you read; a point of this book is to guide you in your reading.

# INTRODUCTION

## Relax!!

Oh ye of little faith, have no fear. At least of Hell. Are you worried? Slightly tense about the afterlife, at least yours? Take it easy. The Hell you worry about is no more. The burning pools described by the fire and brimstone preachers or the wonderfully inventive punishments produced by Dante are not part of the views of many Christians today. Actually that Hell hasn't been around for a century and a half. Mainline Protestant seminaries don't teach it, and in 1999 even a conservative pope, John Paul II, rejected views of Hell as a place, instead saying it is a state of being.[1] Therefore, you may be in Hell now. Hum, a new idea! So, without the threat of Hell, of fire, of fiendishly nasty tortures, what's the attraction of Christianity to those who think about serious things—you, the Thoughtful?

Perplexed? Surprised? Why didn't you know these matters?

## Am I a Thoughtful?

You are if you don't always see things in black/white, yes/no, either/or oppositions. When discussing a topic, you don't have a Truth (capital T) but rather think there might be several truths (small t). That approach applies, whether the issue is politics, religion, zoning, baseball, wine, or any of those other things about which people can get really excited, and adamant. You

---

1 "Hell is getting a makeover from Catholics," http://www.nytimes.com/1999/09/18/arts/hell-getting-makeover-catholics-jesuits-call-it-painful-state-but-not-sulfurous.html?pagewanted=all&src=pm, accessed August 12, 2013.

may have trouble reaching decisions or you may be able to make judgments about some matters but not others; either way, you're a Thoughtful. You have been known, in the face of new information, to change your mind. And you think, but try not to show, your views are superior to being unthoughtful.

You dislike extremes. You accept nuance. It might be a comfort to learn the Bible doesn't often use superlatives about God, creation, and the like. It, in fact, takes a modest, middle route. Perhaps you are tempted by the ideas of the French philosopher/mathematician Blaise Pascal who, in a famous wager, suggested belief in a deity either had an upside (salvation) or was, alternatively, a waste of time but disbelief carried a bigger risk than a waste of time, namely, damnation. Unfortunately, he went on to say a God who authored mathematical truths and the world's order doesn't necessarily have anything to say to the pain of human experience, a standard problem of deism (and creationism?). Where does all these issues leave you?

**Do Christians really believe all that stuff?**

Well, maybe, maybe not. Many Christians, after the emotional release of their conversion experience, are not terribly inquisitive about the details of Christianity (hence unThoughtful). Billy Graham, who preached for more than half a century and became the most famous evangelist of the last half of the twentieth century, fluffed an answer to why Hurricane Katrina (the one that destroyed New Orleans) happened—"The devil might have had something to do with this; I don't know. But God has allowed it ...."[2] Come on, Billy. Why bad things happen to good people is one of the great religious questions. Haven't you thought a bit more deeply about this issue in your 50-year career? Maybe not. Graham reportedly studied theology for a bit but quit because it threatened his faith.[3] It is worth noting, however, Graham, like Pope John Paul II, apparently doesn't accept Hell as a place, though he is a bit vague about it.[4] Exactly what the view are from

---

[2] Jon Meacham, "God, Satan, and Katrina," *Newsweek*, March 20, 2006, 53.

[3] Peter J. Boyer, "The Big Tent", *The New Yorker*, August 15, 2005, 47-50.

[4] Nancy Gibbs and Richard N. Ostling, "God's Billy Pulpit," *Time*, November 15, 1993. See also Billy Graham, *Death and Life After* (W. Publishing Group, 1987).

the pews—those of the average churchgoer—is difficult to assess as most churches are filled with folk whose views are conflicting, and conflicted, and who don't give a lot of thought to most things they hear. And they probably do not know their denomination's basic doctrines.

However, if confronted with a question—say "Is Genesis true?"—many respond "Yes" because they have no other way to handle it. One suspects the view from the pew includes the notion Jesus was God and died for our sins, he gave good moral teachings, the Bible is the word of God, and, for many, Jesus will come again at some end time. Many churchgoers—similar to many Americans—tend to be yes/no people in many areas of their lives so they must accept the Bible as completely true; to do otherwise, they think, would cast doubt on the whole enterprise. The Thoughtful aren't that way.

What's the point of it all—salvation, behavior, accurate beliefs? Why do we have religion anyway? One perspective is to see religion as an effort to explain why the world isn't correct, why things are out of whack. Controlling chaos—bringing order to life—is a common theme in ancient Egyptian, Mesopotamian, and Greek religions (the words for such order are, respectively, *ma'at*, *me*, and *dike*; all mean "justice," the opposite of chaos.). Evil, trouble, and the like could then, and can be still, understood as a result of an angry god, a god made angry by human failings. Simpler folk could, and do, interpret such events as the result to their failure to worship because we are misbehaving, but what is the direct cause of evil and can it be averted? Or maybe it's all just a mystery.

Today's science, while it addresses many things, deals primarily with verifiable facts and uses data, description and mathematics. Religion, on the other hand, is primarily about morality and ultimate meaning by the use of myth, metaphor, poetry, and song. It is one place to look for answers to the related questions "Why am I here?" and "What am I to do?" Early peoples concluded they were here to serve the gods—provide food—because the gods were lazy. Others decided our existence was to entertain the deities. In both cases, one's behavior was directed to finding ways to avoid a deity's wrath which might result in personal misfortune or injury. And beyond that understanding, things have not progressed much. Today, even if any direct involvement by a deity is not seen, one acts in ways to minimize pain to oneself. Are we much different than the ancient peoples?

Science, say some, offers an explanation the past lacked. Ah, comes the retort, there is literalism and fundamentalism, also something the past lacked. For most of two millennia, the Thoughtful did not have to choose between science and literalism (they still don't, but more later) as they took the biblical stories as stories, an effortless assumption, and were never too concerned whether the truths therein were factual or metaphoric. After all, what was the object—salvation, behavior? Today, an unreflective faith is impossible, at least in the United States.

If the Thoughtful will reflect on the matter, for more than 2000 years some of the best minds in the Western world have thought and lived within the Christian tradition, and not all of them could have been hypocrites (though certainly a few were). If the intellectuals of the past could make themselves comfortable with the tradition, perhaps today's Thoughtful should give tradition a hard look. On the other hand, one skeptical philosopher today cannot conceive of a Thoughtful believer.[5]

He's wrong, as you shall see.

**I don't like some of the Christians I know.**

Why? Are they too judgmental? Do they act superior and seem to wear a badge "I'm a Christian and you, schmuck, aren't"? What puts you off?

One possible explanation for this view is you don't know a variety of Christians. Many folk whom this book identifies as Thoughtful Christians are not very expressive—verbally, visually, whatever—about their faith. They aren't inclined to argue about religion, and they don't wear their Christianity on their sleeves. You've met them but may not know their religious views.

---

[5] Daniel C. Dennett, *Breaking the Spell* (Viking, 2006). See Leon Wieseltier, "The God Genome," review of *Breaking the Spell* by Daniel Dennett, *The New York Times Book Review*, February 19, 2006, 12.

The people you're most annoyed with are the unThoughtful Christians, who have certainty about their beliefs and proclaim it loudly and often. These zealots have Truth, and they're on TV, in politics, in all too-public spaces. They seem to be anti-intellectual, self-righteous, and, one suspects, bigoted. This book will delve into the sources and differences of the two groups, the Thoughtful and the rest.

## Quit watching TV

If you're a nonchurch attendee, you probably get your notions of Christianity from TV and the newspaper; we won't go into your childhood experiences. The majority of TV shows of any kind (i.e., regular shows) touching on Christianity take an old-fashioned, often comfortable view or focus on your beliefs (the preacher or evangelical shows). Neither represents Thoughtful Christianity. The regular shows, if religion is touched upon at all, must present something so watered down as to offend as few as possible. Their characters may go to church (denomination unspecified), or perhaps a member of the clergy has a small role (often as one who has been told something important in a detective show). Networks rarely risk a controversial area—child-abusing priests, embezzling church treasurers, doctrines of any kind—and usually ignore the subject entirely. The preacher hours—not just on Sunday any more, as there is a fulltime religion cable channel—speak to the individual believer, not a group. As most watch from their homes by themselves—have you ever heard of a group meeting to watch a TV preacher?—the speaker concentrates on getting the viewer's individual beliefs right. Such a concern for doctrinal correctness is not a major part of Thoughtful Christianity. Reflect!

Newspapers do better, though their need to keep things brief leads them to unsubtle statements. Journalists like to focus on the hypocrites, bigots, freaks—the unusual. Also, letters to the editor come disproportionately from those who know what God wants and are only too willing to share that knowledge with the rest of us. Great!

Overall, the impression is that Christians think Jesus was divine (many do). And certainly that's what nonChristians believe about Christians. As atheists reject a supernatural God, which is what they think most Christians worship, the battle comes down to a supernatural God sending a virgin-born supernatural Son so the Son could die in people's places versus an ordinary man, remarkable in his preaching and healing. It doesn't help the debate when the creeds—fourth-century creations of some Greek-educated church leaders—are introduced. The thrust of this book is both extremes in this dispute are missing the point.

**Why don't I know these things?**

This book attempts to be current with the best scholarly work but, because such information is not widely disseminated, you've missed getting it. Even if you've attended a service in a church given to Thoughtful Christianity, you weren't told the things discussed in this book. Few such congregations or clergy are interested in sermons disparaging or disagreeing with other—i.e., unThoughtful—views. If you went to Sunday school in the church of your parents, you were probably taught Bible stories by a classmate's mother, hardly a source interested in current scholarship. As students often shun history courses, why would a preacher devote much time to Christian history? Even those who take a history course may be confronted with an instructor who is a non-believer (religion is all superstition), or is inept (her specialty is really slavery), or doesn't want to offend anyone (student evaluations or school boards can be murder, or career-destroying anyway). In your circle of friends, religion is avoided because some bug-eyed true believer (unThoughtful) has the capability of bringing any social event to a dead halt, so why go there? Even if you read a lot, either religious themes don't appear or the books are so dense you lose interest.

But you've not been encouraged in this area, either. While learning the history of Christianity is one of the easiest ways to get out of the literalism mode, it often leads to complete disbelief—"I've been misled all these years." And sustained thought on these matters often produces problems, as, for instance, the idea God is all-powerful leads to a conclusion evil exists due to God's will, certainly not a merciful view. If God's will controls all, then why try to change things; if God's will doesn't control, what's the point? Should the Thoughtful avoid or confront these conundrums?

**What you've been waiting for.**

This book is different, of course! The writing is, the author intends, not dense but still factually correct and interpretatively informed. While the book can be read front to back, the organization permits dipping—find a topic, a time, an issue that interests you and go for it. If the reader starts with chapter 1, perhaps the Conclusion should be read next as these two sections place Christianity and Jesus within a perspective that the Thoughtful can understand but need not adopt. Put bluntly, in America today whether one is raised in the Christian tradition or has viewed it from the outside, a sneaking literalism exists, and it is sometimes more than just sneaking. And that literalism is unacceptable to the Thoughtful, whether skeptic or believer. Moreover, with this approach, the Thoughtful might find the first chapter devastating, alienating, because it seems today's Jesus doesn't much resemble the early Jesus of history. After that discovery, a slide into disbelief or unbelief is quite easy. Hence exists the need to read more than one chapter (just like the Thoughtful's educational experience). The first three chapters provide a foundation for the Thoughtful, while chapters 4 through 8 trace the changes altering, maybe even reconstructing, the foundation. The final two chapters answer questions, some often considered—but many not—about about Christianity, and perhaps can be viewed as dessert. This book is not a study of all varieties of Christianity but of Western Christianity, leading to the United States.[6]

The premise of this book is Thoughtful Christianity is not inconsistent with what historians can discover about the past. However, a common response among the Thoughtful who learn biblical stories are often just that—stories, not history—has been to dismiss the Bible as myth and fiction, a form of entertainment perhaps, but not true. That assumption is to throw the baby out with the bathwater. Long ago scholars learned such stories have

---

[6] A broader view, with a British take, is Diamaid MacCulloch, *Christianity: The First Three Thousand Years* (Viking, 2009).

some literal truth in them when Heinrich Schliemann used Homer's Iliad to locate Troy and Mycenae. So at one level there will be some literal truth; the trick is to figure out where it is, and something to which this book gives guidance. (Scholars have known much of this material for a long time but it is usually not found in one place though it has been available to those interested enough to go to a major library.) Where the Bible is fiction, fun reading, the stories often have morals, like Aesop's fables, and themes, like George Elliot's, and should be treated as such. "The Bible as literature" is a common course in education, but there are lots of ways to approach the material. The author is a historian and knows all truth begins with historical understanding, but theological, literary, psychological approaches, among others, to Christianity are included in this book, though not permitted to dominate. These other approaches are, by definition, more speculative and, therefore, open to lots more argument.

Let's be perfectly clear: biblical literalism and its accompanying certitude will not be acceptable to the Thoughtful and will not be promoted in this book. Here, the Thoughtful will discover (or confirm) the knowledge few answers about religion are certain. Thus the goal is to locate questions and devise ways to approach them. In language common today in religious circles, the quest is indeed a journey, one never reaching its destination. The Thoughtful skeptic can observe all these matters while the Thoughtful believer may participate.

The view presented—Christianity explained for the Thoughtful—doesn't advocate any particular dogma or denomination and is not meant to convert the reader, to prompt an altar call.

Nowhere herein is something presented the Thoughtful will find preposterous. Although the Queen of Hearts in *Alice in Wonderland* once said she had believed six impossible things before breakfast, the Thoughtful don't fit that mold. Moreover, this book seeks to present Christianity, or at least aspects of it, in such a light the Thoughtful can see why it is attractive to many other Thoughtfuls. Unfortunately, this approach is largely intellectual and omits what is so important to many: fellowship, community. A church, whether small or large, can provide friends who discuss issues, provide support in difficult times, and generally do what friends do—all without judgment or negativity. Many find these qualities lacking in today's world where one often doesn't know, much less love, one's neighbor and where one's family is scattered throughout the world, suggests why Christianity was attractive in the vast, impersonal Roman Empire. Also, the Thoughtful, reading this book, may focus on belief, not action, although many Christians—especially the Thoughtful ones—don't overly worry about belief; getting beliefs "right" is more a Fundamentalist issue. The approach herein is Christianity can be life itself and the Thoughtful believer enjoys the quest and the questions; the Thoughtful non-believer can see what the attraction of Christianity might be after all. And maybe it makes people better.

Converts are not sought; understanding is. Enjoy.

# FOUNDATION

*The Sermon on the Mount*

# ONE

# *The Main Character: Jesus*

**Did Jesus exist? Yes.**

Can that existence be proved? Not really—there are no eyewitness accounts, no mention by contemporaries, no autobiography—but his existence is as certain as many other figures of his time and before.[1] Numerous people, since the beginnings of Christianity through Bruno Bauer in the nineteenth century and Bertrand Russell in the twentieth century to today, have denied Jesus ever existed. While Jesus can't be "proven" to have existed, the phenomenal effect of his life is very strong evidence in favor of his historical existence. The Thoughtful should not obsess about it, and go on to more worthwhile issues.

So, what do we know about him? Surprisingly little, it turns out. He wandered about in Galilee, preaching and curing. (Even this scenario is not undisputed as one gospel—John's—places him around Jerusalem much more.) He went to Jerusalem, the center of the religion of the Jews (of whom he was one), caused a scene, and was executed. We aren't sure where or when he was born. In the basic sources, the Christian scripture/New Testament

[1] Some believe the fourth gospel, that of John, derives from one of the twelve disciples—from the "beloved disciple"—but among scholars this is a minority view.

writings of Mark, Matthew, Luke, and John (called "gospels"), the details, if not the general theme, of his adult life are conflicting; moreover, they were written 30 to 70 years after his death. And after his death things go up for grabs. Although the search for the historical Jesus has been underway for nearly two centuries, the conclusions are not widely known. And, the search itself is controversial as not all think there is any point in recovering the "true" Jesus.

As the events of Jesus' life are discussed in the following pages, a Thoughtful might consider what is important about Jesus and what is merely interesting. Reserving judgment until the end of the chapter is strongly suggested.

## Who Knows? Early Life.

**Doubtful. Nativity.**

We all know the Christmas stories, which come from the gospels of Luke and Matthew, though the two stories barely overlap (the gospels of Mark and John ignore or have no knowledge of the event). Luke's version is more often used in Christmas services as Joseph and a pregnant Mary go to Bethlehem to register as required by a Roman census, a very doubtful scenario. Do you know where your great-grandparents were born? That gap is the time difference between Jesus' birth and the first writing of it by Matthew and Luke. And the gospels aren't in complete harmony here either as Matthew seems to think the family lived in Bethlehem. While Bethlehem is the common Christmas setting of both gospels, it seems unlikely the event occurred there. For one thing, we can't find any evidence of a general census which was the supposed occasion for Jesus' family visit, though there was a local census in Judea in 6 C.E. Anyway, that sort of thing—registering in some ancestral home—didn't occur in ancient times. And no one would take a woman, especially a pregnant woman, as women didn't pay taxes or otherwise participate in public life. Archaeologists aren't even sure Bethlehem was inhabited at that time.

Early writers also had a strong motive to put the birth in Bethlehem in order to connect Jesus to David, Israel's greatest king (according to the Hebrew Bible/Old Testament, if not history), so the census story was later created to provide a reason for them to be in Bethlehem. In addition a birth in Bethlehem fulfilled a prophecy (Micah 5:2). In John's gospel (7:42) some of Jesus' listeners were surprised he wasn't born in Bethlehem. Just to confuse things, one scholar has located a Bethlehem in Galilee, only a few miles from Nazareth, which retains Bethlehem in the story but doesn't support the Davidic connection.[2] Most likely Jesus was born in Nazareth, where he also grew up.

Besides the census, other aspects of the stories are unsupported historically. If Herod, king of the Jews, ordered all boys under the age of two killed in an effort to head off a possible successor (Matthew 2:13), the Jewish historian Josephus, who was no fan of Herod, would have mentioned it. Also, Luke's gospel is silent on the matter. That Matthew's story parallels events in Egypt during the Exodus story of the Hebrew Bible/Old Testament suggests where and why Matthew created it. (Why would a loving God only warn one family of the impending massacre?) The magi story could be based on a visit by eastern notables to Herod in 9 B.C.E. or by a visit by the king of Armenia with Parthian nobles (sometimes called magi) in 66 C.E. (Matthew doesn't number the magi; that is a later creation.) Perhaps Matthew has the story of the magi in order to connect Jesus' birth with the wisdom of the East, i.e., Babylon. Or maybe to connect it with non-Jews. Magi also turned up when the temple of Artemis at Ephesus burned in 356 B.C.E. so they are not unique to the Jesus story. If the magi followed a star leading them to the young Jesus, it would have to have been about 20 feet off the ground, not high in the sky; most scholars today think the star would more likely be an angel, given the biblical tradition about such things. (A reconstruction of the astronomy of the early first century finds Halley's Comet appearing in 12 B.C.E. and a convergence of the planets Jupiter, Saturn, and Mars in 8 B.C.E.; either one of these occurrences might correspond to the

---

[2] Bruce Chilton, *Rabbi Jesus* (Doubleday, 2000).

star in Matthew—those efforts are misdirected as the star's purpose was to fulfill a Hebrew Bible/Old Testament statement, something Matthew does a lot (Numbers 24:17) and to foreshadow Jesus as a "light unto the world.") The book of Isaiah in the Hebrew Bible/Old Testament may have provided Matthew with some material for his story as it contains images of a suffering servant (perhaps used to describe the later Jesus), maybe even a star, the magi (60:6 – 7), and gold and frankincense (60:6).

The details that today most remember is a conflation of the two gospels: no shepherds in Matthew, no flight to Egypt in Luke, no December 25th birthday. Most likely none of the stories of Jesus' birth as told in the gospels has any basis in historical fact but were written to further the themes of Jesus the two gospel writers were telling.[3]

**Wrong. Time.**

When was he born? The evidence in the tradition, the gospels, and what we know from other historical research creates both conflicts and possibilities.

The dating system we use today originated in the sixth century, when a monk, Dionysius Exiguus (Denis the Little, read "Humble," not "Short"), calculated things by tying various Roman events into the Jesus story. He set Jesus' birth at the end of 1 B.C.E. He seems to have gotten it wrong. If, as the gospels report, Herod was king, a problem arises since Herod died in 4 B.C.E. We have no historical evidence a Roman census was empire-wide at that time—the eason Luke gives for Mary and Joseph to be on the road to Bethlehem—but a census was taken in Judea, which included Bethlehem, in 6 C.E. Forget dating things by the star of Bethlehem; that type of effort rarely works. All in all, perhaps, a reasonable date is about 5 B.C.E.[4]

---

[3] Raymond E. Brown, in *The Birth of the Messiah* (Doubleday, 1993), covers lots, maybe all, the possibilities in over 700 densely and elusively written pages. John Shelby Spong's *Born of a Woman* (HarperSanFrancisco, 1992) presents the possibilities in more accessible form.

[4] For a more complete study of the complexities and mistakes in the dating, see Robin Lane Fox, *The Unauthorized Version: Truth and Fiction in the Bible* (Knopf, 1992), 27-35.

The odds he was born on December 25 are 1 to 365, as we know nothing of this topic either. The Christian scripture/New Testament is silent on the subject but by the fourth century some consensus on December 25 had arisen. There were Roman festivals around that date related to the sun and the longest day which might have provided the connection because some, such as the emperor Constantine seemingly conflated Jesus and the sun god. The worship of the god, Mithras, had a major celebration on December 25; perhaps the early followers of Jesus chose that day to keep people from worshipping both. Additionally, Jesus' followers developed a tradition he had been conceived on the same date as his death, which might have been March 25; thus his birth was nine months later. These traditions all first appear many years after his death, and some of them clearly have theological reasons rather than historical basis.

**Maybe. Parents.**

By tradition, Jesus' parents, Mary and Joseph, weren't married. The church's position has been that Jesus' mother, Mary, was impregnated by the Holy Spirit i.e., God. This is not an explanation historians can use so basically the question is open. Whether Jesus' parents would have been important enough for his followers to have remembered their names is unknown. John Shelby Spong argues their names were chosen by early followers as they were important Hebrew Bible/Old Testament characters. Joseph was a popular Jewish male name and Mary the most common female Jewish name of that era which might make it likely those were their names or, alternatively, a likely choice if the real names had been forgotten. Paul, an early follower and prolific writer, implies Jesus is Joseph's son as does Luke and, finally, John, the chronologically last gospel writer (Romans 1:3 – 4, Luke 4:22, John 6:42). Matthew and Luke give long, and different, genealogies showing Joseph as a descendant of King David. Why include those genealogies if he's not Jesus' father? Want some possibilities with at least a bit of support? Perhaps Jesus was illegitimate; Mark, in his gospel, hints at this position (Mark 6:3)[5].

---

[5] Spong gathers gospel verses that lend support to the issue of illegitimacy in *Born of a Woman*, chs. 6 and 11.

Another: around the time of Jesus' birth a revolt in a city less than five miles from Nazareth was quelled by soldiers who then raped the women of the area.[6] (As to Mary's virginity, no one knows how much peasant Jews observed the rules of the Torah.) Some Jews thought the future Messiah would be a "son of Joseph" so Joseph would be a convenient name for Jesus' father. On the whole, scholars leave the issue open. Finally, *The Second Apocalypse of James*, a second-century non-canonical Gnostic writing, names Jesus' father as Theuda.

**Coincidence? Name.**

"Jesus," as a name is derived from Joshua, a leader from the Hebrew Bible/Old Testament, which means "God saves," "God is salvation," or "God is with us."[7] (The last— "God is with us"—is convenient for those skeptics who think the whole Jesus story is an early fraud perpetrated in the first century.) Jews in Galilee had a renaissance of old names after the second century B.C.E. in reaction to Hellenistic/Greek influence in their national and religious cultures. As a name, "Joshua," would have invoked a champion of the past who overthrew the existing government and gave the promised land to his followers. "Jesus" died out in popular use a few centuries later, though it has reappeared in Latin America.

**Choose. Genealogy.**

The gospels portray Jesus as descended from King David, traditionally considered one of the most powerful kings of the Jews, though Luke and Matthew differ in their list of Jesus' ancestors (Luke 3:223 – 38, Matthew 1:1 – 17). That connection is political and theological, and historians can only say it's possible. There are reasons to doubt the connection though: most importantly its blatant purpose for Jesus' followers describing him

---

[6] Jane Schaberg, *The Illegitimacy of Jesus* (Sheffield Phoenix Press, 2006). Origen, *Contra Celsum* 1.2. A tradition, floating around in the first centuries after Jesus, made him the son of a Roman soldier named "Panther." The Greek for "virgin" is "*parthenon*," which might account for the confusion. Also, a tombstone in Germany contains the name of a Roman soldier named "Panther."

[7] John P. Meier, *A Marginal Jew* (Doubleday, 1991), vol. 1, 206-7.

as "Messiah." As with the term "son of Joseph" some Jews expected the Messiah to be a "son of David," so again nomenclature might merely be convenient.

Both gospels with genealogies show evidence of a structure created to fit a pre-existing theme. Matthew's gospel portends Jesus is the king of the Jews; therefore his genealogy starts with David and descends through kings of Judah. In the nativity story alone, Matthew sees Jesus fulfilling Hebrew Bible/Old Testament verses five times. Luke portrays Jesus as a prophet to all humanity so his gospel genealogy begins with the first human, Adam, and is carried to his birth through a line of prophets.

**Boring? Youth.**

Again, we know next to nothing.

Luke's gospel gives a story of Jesus, as a boy, visiting the Temple in Jerusalem, the center of Jewish religion, and confounding the elders with his knowledge (Luke 2:41 – 9). That view should be dismissed as Docetism or Gnosticism, both of which only see Jesus as God, so of course he knew everything, past, present, and future. Again, not an explanation Thoughtful readers can accept.

In the non-canonical work, *The Infancy Gospel of Thomas,* the young Jesus kills two boys who annoy him during play and is a turbulent student in school. Probably written in the second century, it fits nowhere in the theology of the early Christians. Perhaps, it seeks to show Jesus developing into a "nice" being but the murderous part is a mystery.

The tradition provides no evidence as to whether he was literate (though his teaching certainly implies it) or numerate. (Schools did exist.) He probably spoke Aramaic, but whether he knew Hebrew, Latin, or Greek is unknown. If any of the contacts with the Roman governor Pontius Pilate have a basis in fact, Jesus would have spoken to him in Greek. One of the gospel stories indicates Jesus was able to write: when a crowd is preparing to stone an adulteress, Jesus challenges them with "Let he who is without sin cast the first stone." Then he leans over and writes in the dirt as the crowd melts away (John 7:53 – 8:11). Doodles, words, what? The gospel doesn't say. To make this particular story more difficult to interpret, some of the John's earliest manuscripts do not have this story so it may be a copyist's later addition.

The argument for literacy arises from his familiarity with scripture. However, most Thoughtful can relate the nativity story from Luke—manger, shepherds, etc.—without having ever read it because they've heard it so much. Jesus lived without television, radio, newspapers, and all the other things crowding our minds. The only written material he'd ever have heard was scripture so remembering it would have been relatively easy. The only evidence, other than possibly John's gospel citing his writing in the dirt, of his reading ability comes from a story set in his home village when he may have read from a scroll in the synagogue (Luke 4:16 – 19). However, this story isn't in the other gospels so it may reflect Luke's creation to prefigure Jesus' mission, as the text allegedly read (Isaiah 65:1 – 2) neatly supports Luke's theme. Moreover, some doubt Jesus' village, Nazareth, was significant enough to have a synagogue. Another possibility arises from our lack of knowledge of Jesus' youth; he might have lived with a Jewish group, the Essenes, and become literate as a result. Or maybe, if Nazareth had no synagogue, he walked to Sephoris, a nearby city, where the Pharisees could have taught him, something his followers would not have reported as they considered the Pharisees to be rivals of Jesus in the early days after his death. (In reality Pharisees and early followers of Jesus agreed on most things but were competing for the allegiance of Jews, hence the bad press.)

Mary and Joseph had other children, four sons and an unknown number of daughters (remember, this was the ancient world and daughters clearly counted for less so they weren't counted in the gospels). Roman Catholicism calls these children cousins, the Orthodox tradition says they were Joseph's from a prior marriage—both are theological statements deriving from beliefs about Mary's perpetual virginity—which historians, and doctors, can't accept.[8] (Descendants of Jesus' siblings, called "Desposyni," appear in

---

[8] A fanciful, and amusing, reconstruction of Jesus' youth is Christopher Moore's *Lamb, The Gospel According to Biff, Christ's Childhood Pal* (HarperCollins, 2002).

various writings of the early Church but their importance, or even existence, is difficult to assess.)

At some point Jesus joined the following of John the Baptizer, a charismatic wandering prophet who was living rough and proclaiming the coming end of the world. By tradition, when Jesus left John he was about 30 and various estimates of the dates of his birth and death are based upon that tradition. However, John's gospel has someone telling Jesus he is not yet 50, something not normally said to 30-year-olds.

### Hum.... Marriage.

We know nothing.

The plot of *The DaVinci Code*, includes the notion Jesus and Mary Magdalene were married. Certainly a Jewish man of Jesus' age should have been married. If he weren't, one might expect the writings to mention it to further reveal his uniqueness, if nothing else. Given this possibility, the wedding at Cana, which John's gospel reports Jesus performing his first miracle—turning water into wine—could have been a wedding of Jesus himself. He and his mother give orders to servants consistent with that possibility but other parts of the story don't a support a marriage of Jesus at Cana. Also, the story clearly prefigures John's theme that accepting Jesus makes life like a wedding banquet with endless good wine (John 2:1 – 11). On the other hand, Mary Magdalene does get a lot of press in the gospels. She, and a group of women, followed Jesus and his band of disciples, something an unmarried woman could not have done in those days. She is always listed first whenever a group of women in mentioned. She had the first experience of the Resurrection.

If Jesus followed his father's reputed trade, construction worker or woodworker (not "carpenter" since houses weren't built of wood in that part of the world), he would not have been rich.[9] Joseph himself was poor as evidenced from the family's trip to Jerusalem for Mary's purification for which Joseph couldn't afford a sacrificial lamb (Luke 2:24). We don't know when Jesus

[9] The word usually translated "carpenter," "*tekton*" in Greek, can mean someone in construction in wood, stone or brick or perhaps a general workman.

started following a wandering prophet, John the Baptizer, but that would not have been a lucrative career choice either. One scholar argues Jesus wasn't married because he was too poor.[10] Another possibility is he had been an Essene, a Jewish sect that did not marry.

Why is Jesus' marital status an issue? For one thing, it raises the matter of sex, which has been frequently awkward in Christian history. Also, the church, for much of its history (and Roman Catholicism today), has insisted, for a variety of reasons, on an unmarried state for the clergy, using Jesus as the model. However, Peter, Jesus' lead disciple and claimed by the Roman Catholic Church to be the first Pope, was married, as were Jesus' brothers, who were active followers and, one of whom became a leader of Jesus' followers following his crucifixion.

## Guess. Physical Appearance.

Nowhere in the gospels is Jesus described so subsequent representations varied a great deal. The earliest depictions show Jesus as a beardless youth, often as a shepherd, with strong resemblance to Greek gods such as Apollo, Hermes, and Orpheus. Soon a beard appeared in physical depictions and he took on the appearance of contemporaries. At the Renaissance, artists gave more sensuous, theatrical even, effects. Rembrandt could portray him as a Jew, something the medieval world forgot, or ignored. The English artist Holman Hunt in a heavily symbolic painting, *The Light of the World*, portrays a life-like, fairly well groomed Jesus. Today, the most common image is Warner Sallman's painting, *Head of* Christ, a thin, slightly bearded Jesus with gently flowing hair, gazing away, an image sometimes called Jesus' senior picture. To the contrary, one early tradition described Jesus as ugly, something later ignored.

Jesus was likely an observant Jew so his beard would have been uncut and his apparel fringed. Brown hair and eyes were common in his era though some artists, such as Albrecht Durer, painted him with blond hair and blue eyes. How white his skin varied, often reflecting what

[10] J.D. Crossan, "Why Jesus Didn't Marry," www.beliefnet.com/story/135/Entertainment/Movies/The-Da-Vinci-Code/Why-Jesus-Didn't-Marry.aspx, accessed August 20, 2013.

the artist thought Jews looked like. Portrayals on continents other than Europe and North America have often resembled the locals. A common feature is relative thinness, which would be explained by his wandering life and lack of subsistence; however, a common body type in the area of Palestine today, and perhaps also 2000 years ago, would be short, stout, and balding. On balance, odds are he was about five feet tall and weighed 100 pounds.

**Lots. Things That Didn't Happen.**

Jesus' public activity occurred over a short period, traditionally three years but perhaps as short as six weeks (the gospels disagree). It took place among poor people in a largely illiterate backwater, Galilee, where a mix of Jews and Gentiles lived. This combination of circumstances make knowledge of his early life very doubtful; what was known was passed along orally, a risky technique for accuracy. When the writers of some of the gospels began to compose, they were part of a group of Jesus' followers who were beginning to describe Jesus as divine. That divinity required them, in contemporary thinking, to describe his early life in ways consonant with divinity. Hence, God as a father and the story of the boy Jesus confounding the elders in the Temple.

Matthew directed his gospel to a Jewish audience; therefore, his gospel includes stories intended to persuade that audience about Jesus as the Messiah. Matthew's post-birth narrative comes from the Hebrew Bible/Old Testament as he attempts to show Jesus was part and parcel of Jewish tradition as well as the culmination of it. The return from Egypt has an earlier parallel (Exodus 4:17). The magi/wise men connect Jesus to the font of Middle Eastern wisdom and knowledge, Mesopotamia and Persia. And the star, which they followed, is evidence of a divine plan that included the heavens and also is prefigured in Numbers (24:17)). Their gifts of gold, frankincense and myrrh point to Jesus as a king, and fulfill another prophecy (Isaiah 6:6). All these stories were created to read back into Jesus' life later views of him or to fit some Hebrew Bible/Old Testament ideas about the Messiah.

Luke's gospel includes a story about shepherds attending the birth of Jesus (Luke 2:8 – 18). Thus Luke explains who Jesus is and will be; the shepherds depart proclaiming what they had seen which portrays them as the first missionaries. The spread of Christianity is the theme of the Book of Acts, which Luke also wrote. Shepherds as missionaries are an obvious metaphor about clergy; tending flocks has long been a theme of Christian clergy.

**Summary.**

So what do we know?

- Where was Jesus born? Probably Nazareth.
- When was Jesus born? Probably around 5 B.C.E. The day is anyone guess.
- What did he do before he emerged as a public figure? Probably lived like a typical boy and young man in Nazareth until he hooked up with a prophet.
- Was he married? Who knows?

We really don't know much, though many unThoughtfuls believe a lot more. The date and place of my birth (or yours) are irrelevant to this book; why are those things important when one considers Jesus? Is anything in the foregoing discussion of Jesus' early life vital or necessary to an acceptance of his message or the purpose of his life and death? Does any of it really matter? It may if you want to read things literally, but that idea is the subject in another chapter.

One final problem: the foregoing text assumes the gospels include at least some historical material about Jesus. However, if Mark's gospel is a literary creation, as some believe, then the works of Matthew and Luke probably add nothing. If John knew of the other three gospels, as some argue he did, then the whole edifice becomes shaky. But that position is an extreme distinctly minority view. In the long haul, these issues shouldn't matter to the Thoughtful but would be devastating to many who fear if one detail is false, the structure fails.

# The Big Questions: Jesus' Public Activity.

## Mentor. John the Baptizer.

Jesus began his public activities by following a wandering charismatic known in the gospels as John the Baptizer (aka John the Baptist). John, perhaps a relative of Jesus, was an ascetic—he is described as clothed with camel hair and a leather girdle and eating locusts and honey—who had taken to preaching in the rough country north and east of Jerusalem and along the Jordan River.[11] His efforts produced a group of disciples, and his preaching attracted crowds to the Jordan River valley from Jerusalem. (He still has a few followers, Mandaeans, mostly in the Near East.)

John's title, the Baptizer, arose from his practice of baptizing people in the Jordan to confirm their repentance of their ungodly ways, their sins. His message appears to have been that the present age was coming to a fiery end, soon. His demeanor, practices, and message suggest connections with others in the area, including those living at Qumran, associated with the Dead Sea Scrolls, and Essenes, an ascetic Jewish group, connections that cannot be documented at present.

John's influence on Jesus is debated. John's message to repent because the present age is about to end and a future world begin is called "apocalyptic," which is typical of radical movements, but it is not clear whether Jesus so viewed the world, though Jesus' followers after his death did share such a view. However, unlike John, Jesus did not ask people to repent.

John's baptizing continued after Jesus started his public life, according to John's gospel (John 3:22 – 4, 4:1) though the other gospels do not describe such an overlap. Jesus probably separated from John's group but when and how is unclear. The gospels mark that separation at the beginning of Jesus' public activity, which might have been as early as 27 C.E., when the local ruler, Herod Antipas (son of Herod of the nativity story) decreed John a threat to the public order, arresting and executing him. (The story of Salome's exotic dancing leading Herod Antipas to grant her wish for John's head appears

[11] John's costume looks a lot like Elijah's so maybe the description was borrowed from there (2 Kings 1:8). Or maybe that was the way prophets dressed.

fanciful, though it has inspired some great art and music.[12]) However, the only non-Christian source on John, the Jewish writer Josephus, puts John's execution at 36 C.E., several years after the likely date of Jesus' execution, which suggests he was held prisoner for years, an unlikely event. Perhaps Jesus' early followers and the gospel writers changed events around as they worked out how John was related to Jesus

After Jesus' death, his followers dealt with John by describing him as one who was heralding the coming of Jesus, converting the leader into the precursor by use of some Hebrew Bible/Old Testament verses (particularly Isaiah 40:3 – 5). That John's followers didn't see it that way is suggested by the fact that, instead of ignoring him, all four gospels have material about him, probably seeking to convert those followers to Jesus' group. John's followers survived his execution and still continue as a group today which may be why the gospel of John, written after 90 C.E. addresses his influence.

For subsequent followers of Jesus—the church—Jesus' baptism by John presented a major problem; Jesus was portrayed as sinless so why the need to be baptized? Major gyrations in thinking were necessary to explain this event.[13] In any event, John was important to Jesus, but we cannot be certain about the nature of the influence.

## Whoops! Miracles.

Among the biggest stumbling blocks for the Thoughtful in dealing with Christianity are the miracles, various stories in the Bible fly in the face of how we think the world works. Jesus reportedly, *inter alia*, raised the dead and walked on water. These miracles, and 30 some others attributed to him, offend the Thoughtful's sense of what can be accepted.

Let's be clear: miracles didn't happen in the literal, factual sense. Nature follows laws; God doesn't intervene like a chess player. Had you been there with a camera or camcorder, you could not have caught a miracle for posterity. So, how do we handle the problem? Today's scholars sometimes attack

---

[12] Raymond E. Brown, *An Introduction to the New Testament* (Doubleday 1997), 135, footnote 23.

[13] 2 Corinthians 5:21; Hebrews 4:15; 1 Peter 2:22; 1 John 3:5.

the issue by dividing the over 30 miracle stories reported about Jesus into various groups. For example, one separates them into nature miracles, exorcisms, and healings, while another adds raising the dead as a separate category.

First, a sloppy use of language may obscure clarity on miracles. Today, contemporary miracles are doubtful to the Thoughtful. For example, a man is robbed and shot, the bullet missing his heart by an inch. His relatives proclaim his survival a miracle. Well, maybe it was just probability as a bullet aimed at the chest has x percent chance of hitting the heart. (And what kind of God arranges a shooting in order to perform a miracle?)

Next, as to Jesus' miracles, let's remove their novelty. The Hebrew Bible/Old Testament has miracles, but as the years pass in scripture's composition they become less common and finally disappear. (Most are associated with Moses, Joshua, and Elijah.) In his day Jesus isn't the only reported miracle worker as such stories were not in short supply. They were told about Jews other than Jesus. Hanina ben Dosa, a near contemporary of Jesus, cured a boy at a distance and, to save a town, let a poisonous snake bite him (which killed the snake). Elsewhere in the Roman Empire, also in the first century, Apollonius of Tyana (in Turkey) had a reputation for miracles. Among other things, he is reported to have cured the lame and blind, dealt with demons, and raised the dead.[14] Maybe all holy men had stories of miracles told about them. And the first century was especially rife with miracle-working men.

Scholars are pretty much in agreement Jesus cured people and performed exorcisms, though the exorcisms disappear in John's gospel because some readers thought those references suggested Jesus was in league with the devil. It's how things are reported that muddies the matter. Moreover, memories were supplemented, poetic license occurred, events got "enhanced" to make a theological point. For instance Mark reports the healing of a blind man in a story immediately preceding a story of the disciples, "having their eyes opened," discovering the truth about Jesus, a clear literary construction (Mark 8:22 – 6).

---

[14] Philostratus, *Life of Apollonius,* 3.39, 4.10, 4.45. See Daniel Ogden, *Magic, Witchcraft, and Ghosts in Greek and Roman Worlds* (Oxford, 2002), ch. 4.

Discussions of miracles vary drastically. Some Christians have attempted rationally to explain Jesus' actions. This approach was a major thrust in the early nineteenth century when the issue of scriptural literalism first surfaced in the modern world, and nature miracles were the focus. Thus it is reported Jesus quelled a storm on the Sea of Galilee (Mark 4:35 – 41) where we know storms on that body of water arise and die quickly. So it was a coincidence. As to raising the dead, perhaps these presumed dead were in a coma or merely sleeping, which in fact, is what Jesus is reported to have said before raising a young girl (Mark 5:39, Luke 8:52). The walking on water was an optical illusion when seen from a distance.

Many scholars believe the nature miracles were added by Jesus' early followers and didn't occur during his life.[15] After all, nature doesn't behave that way. The additions were to show Jesus was God and had the power to control nature. And politics played a part as well;, for instance, the nature miracles often emphasize the authority of the disciples (and their successors, later church leaders).[16] Most scholars today think the nature miracles are not historical. But disposing of the nature miracles only takes care of a few miracles, many remain.

Even today many physical conditions are psychosomatic so why might that not be the case then as well? Peter's mother-in-law, cured at Capernaum, perhaps just needed some attention (Mark 1:29 – 31). And exorcisms, driving out demons and devils, can be explained on similar grounds. Most of Jesus' miracles are performed in response to manifestation of faith in him, which lends credence to this idea.[17]

Another approach to the cures involves treating them metaphorically by saying the healing Jesus offered, say, a leper, was care, compassion and willingness to include him in society, which is a healing of sorts, even if the

---

[15] Brown, *Introduction*, 133, footnote 16, for some of the literature. J.D. Crossan, *The Historical Jesus* (HarperSanFrancisco, 1991) 320. Meier, *Marginal Jew*, vol. 2, chs. 20-23.

[16] Crossan, *Historical Jesus*, 177.

[17] If, as seems likely, Jesus was quickly viewed as a miracle-worker, then his followers would be inclined to see miracles. Psychologists call this a "confirmation bias."

skin condition remained.[18] Certainly low-level metaphor might explain the story of Jesus being asked about paying the Temple tax and subsequently telling Peter to catch a fish and pay with the coin he would find in the fish's mouth. Duly done. Or did Peter sell the fish and use the resulting coin to pay? Metaphorically he found the coin in the mouth (Matthew 17:24 – 7).

A final example: the gospels report Jesus feeding large crowds, sometimes 4000, sometimes 5000, with only a few loaves of bread and a few fish. The oldest approach to this story was that a supernatural God intervened and multiplied the loaves and fish in ways contrary to physical laws. A rationalist approach suggests someone volunteered to share his own meal that he had brought along and that act inspired others to do likewise. A metaphorical suggestion would be one that Jesus' life and teachings were spiritual "food" that nourished his listeners. The Thoughtful easily choose the last possibility.

Today most scholars find approaches to miracles, other than the metaphorical, not satisfactory, but even if you do, a lot of miracles remain. Things get dense and murky when the miracle stories are seen as theological interpretations, not historical events. Maybe Jesus did cure people and therefore many of the miracle stories have, at their origin, real events. However, how contemporaries saw and reported them is problematic because theology and perception got mixed.

And, of course, strange things do happen that, even today, with the evidence available we can't explain. In the lifetime of the Thoughtful, Oral Roberts, an evangelical preacher, was known to perform faith healings on television. Watching people declare themselves healed, one had the thought these might be "plants" or "shills." Or else their conditions were psychosomatic. However, studies have shown some of these, and other healings such as at Lourdes, are not explicable by today's medicine. One answer is God intervenes; this solution is Dietrich Bonhoeffer's "God of the gaps," a God still used by some when science has no explanation. The Thoughtful are left

---

[18] J.D. Crossan, *Jesus, A Revolutionary Biography* (HarperOne, 1994), 82.

with the possibility tomorrow's science may have the answer. Or maybe not, and such things will remain a mystery.

Satisfied? Probably not. The miracle stories present one of the hardest parts of Christianity for the Thoughtful. What was a support of faith in Christianity's early years is now an obstacle. The serious person wants to know why these stories were told or included in a gospel in the first place. Today, scholars often use "acts of power" rather than "miracles" in order to indicate these events were included by Jesus' early followers in order to emphasize his power (and perhaps his divinity). However, if Jesus performed miracles, why was he so widely rejected?

On one hand, more miracles stories are told about Jesus than about any of his contemporaries. On the other hand, the earliest surviving writings, those of Paul, make no reference to miracles so they maybe weren't important to all early followers of Jesus. Miracle stories can even be dismissed as completely fanciful, and the world, and Christianity, will go on. But wrestling with them helps the Thoughtful appreciate the charisma of Jesus which led his followers to see, or thought they saw, such things. The Thoughtful can also contemplate how sources can be analyzed to provide multiple insights. Maybe the Thoughtful should look at the miracle stories for their meaning, not their factual reality. Let's leave it at that.

## What'd He Say? Message.

"Kingdom of God," the key term in Jesus' message, is difficult to interpret because he appears to have used it in a variety of ways. (Thoughtfuls beware: none of what follows is uncontested by at least one scholar.) Also the gospel writers and Paul, whose writings are our earliest surviving source, put their own interpretations on Jesus' words. At times it appears the Kingdom of God lies in the future and at times is in the present (Mark 9:1, Luke 17:20-1). As years passed after Jesus' death and no major change in the world occurred, the term began to take on the meaning of heaven, the life after the grave, while sometimes the term referred to earth after the events of the end time. Some use the term today to refer to the life of those in the church. (The word for "Kingdom," *basileia* in Greek, is often interpreted today as "reign,""rule,""dominion," to avoid the sense of a territorial kingdom—something unfortunately, the book of Revelation seems to support. Whatever the meaning chosen, the thrust is the sovereignty of God, not the individual, and that God's will shall dominate at that time, whenever that is; when it happens, an ideal society in the timeless presence of God will occur.)

The gospels all portray Jesus' message as constant throughout his public life, which results from the writers putting their mature understandings into their stories. Any interior development of Jesus' ideas is simply not available to us. It seems more likely they developed as time passed and he talked more and more. One reason Jesus, in Mark's gospel, continues urging his disciples to secrecy might be because he was feeling his way along as to his mission.

In Jesus' day, the term "Kingdom of God" was also used by other Jews, with a variety of meanings, so figuring out what Jesus meant by it is a challenge.[19] One recent effort decides the gospels report what Jesus meant accurately and so our task is merely to understand it.[20] However, most scholars shun that approach, acknowledging we cannot know what Jesus meant in his preaching. What a speaker intends requires access to that person and, even then, a speaker might intentionally mislead (think of "spin" in politics today). What we can attempt is to ask what his followers thought he meant or what we think he meant in terms of our lives today.

At one level Jesus described the Kingdom as a state of existence, not a place, but rather an inward possession. As the Kingdom was everywhere, if you understand, believe, and accept it, it is now, the present. After you accept God's Kingdom, the idiom "today is the first day of the rest of your life" captures the consequence well.

The other approach interpreted the Kingdom as taking place in the future, which may be the very immediate future. Many Jews were apocalyptic

---

[19] Marcus Borg, *Meeting Jesus Again for the First Time* (HarperSanFrancisco, 1994), 92, footnote 29. James P. Mackey, *Jesus The Man and the Myth* (SCM, 1979 ), 126-7.

[20] Garry Wills, *What Jesus* Meant (Viking, 2006), xxviii. Though Wills criticizes the Jesus Seminar group for their historical approach, his overall result of often interpreting Jesus' words symbolically finds him with about the same position as that group as to Jesus' message.

and Jesus might well have been also. Paul thought things would happen soon. The Second Coming, a changed world, Jesus ruling like a king, etc., come from that view. However, by the time of the gospel writers, that hope had faded; the Kingdom of God had receded so much that John's gospel only uses it twice. (John is much more interested in the significance of Jesus himself than in his message.)

If the Kingdom was in the present and it would make a recognizable difference in the world, it increasingly looked like it hadn't happened yet. Therefore, the Kingdom must be found in the believers and their groups, i.e., the nascent church. What we can't tell from this distance is how much, if at all, the behavior of the early followers of Jesus contrasted with the rest of society. If their conduct stood out—say, their charity to the poor—then it is possible to think the Kingdom had indeed begun with the followers. Over the years, however, as the members of the church looked just like all other Romans, it became increasingly common to project the Kingdom as the end time, a heaven. Variations on this solution included a Second Coming, a rule by Jesus and the saints, and lots of other exciting descriptions.

Jesus wasn't explicit in his teaching on the novelty, meaning or demands of the Kingdom. His portrayal of the Kingdom of God was multi-faceted, but not focused. The content of one's life in that Kingdom was described in parables and sayings: love your neighbor, forgive your enemies, turn the other cheek, do the right thing. But often Jesus was vague or paradoxical. The parable of the vineyard workers, which tells the story of three men hired at different times of the day to help with the harvest and all being paid the same sum, offends our sense of fairness (Matt 20:1 – 15). Eating meals with people society deemed outcasts, tax collectors and sinners, clashes with our desire for moral standards and consequences (Mark 2:15). Being rich is a problem, presumably because the riches resulted from greed or taking advantage of someone (Mark 10:21, 23 – 7; Luke 6:20, 24). Sin is forgiven without contrition or penance.

The Kingdom is an outlook, an attitude, producing extraordinary tolerance. The new life was not one of an ascetic, denying worldly pleasures, rejecting the body, as Jesus ate and drank freely and joyfully, with all sorts of folk. The Kingdom clashes with society, then and now, as Jesus was a prophet in the tradition of Hebrew Bible/Old Testament prophets who critiqued their surroundings harshly. Righteousness, justice, and peace will reign in contrast with world of the day. "Love," a word recurring in description of the activities of the "new" individual, meant giving one's self to others, service. After accepting God's Kingdom, one is transformed and desires to live a good (decent, kind, forgiving, caring) life. That life often involves concern and service for others, especially the outsiders, the disadvantaged. The salvation flowing from this position is a healthy spirit, a feeling of wholeness, not a place on a heavenly cloud after death. Or maybe God is the eternal life and followers, by accepting Jesus' message, can partake of that eternity, though not forever.

If Jesus' ideas can be captured in a paragraph, why do denominations today seem to make so much more of his message? The problem is one that the Christian scripture/New Testament sources about Jesus, written years, often decades, after his death, are a mixture of things he said and did and what his followers later attributed to him. Scholars have spent many years trying to separate the two, and, as a result, often the discussion proceeds around the Jesus of history (the man alive) and the Christ of faith (the experiences of him after his death). His followers experienced him in various ways (as the Christ) and wrote about those experiences as though they were part of his life. In addition, like many writings, the gospels have themes and structures reflecting authorial intention as well as Jesus' message. Thus Mark portrays Jesus as being unsuccessful in his early efforts to make the Kingdom of God understandable; therefore, Jesus shifted to talking about his suffering, death, and resurrection. Since his resurrection was not literal but symbolic, any part of his message making reference to it (e.g., the second half of Mark's gospel) is a theological interpretation by the author. Matthew's gospel, written at a time Jesus' followers were competing with the Pharisees and their emerging rabbinic Judaism, sees Jesus also having problems with them, which is unlikely as they had little presence in Galilee during Jesus' life. Matthew's gospel also shows how Jesus fulfilled much Hebrew Bible/Old Testament scripture, which put him squarely in Jewish history. (Matthew used "Kingdom of Heaven" rather than "Kingdom of God" in deference to Jewish tradition of not naming the deity.) And so with other writings, present concerns were, and still are, written into the few details of Jesus' message that survived.

It is a bit easier to say what his message was not. He did not talk about who he was (Son of God, redeemer, etc.); that is the way John's gospel portrays him but John is writing over half a century later with a specific theological purpose and to a certain audience. Jesus did not indicate he would die for the sins of the world; that becomes a way his early followers interpreted his death. Whether he anticipated an early end of this world is uncertain, but he spoke of a Kingdom of God which already existed to those who understood him. In other words, the way many Christians see Jesus today may not be based upon his life but upon how his early followers interpreted that life.

Another view by some sees the Kingdom of God as coming, an end-of-world event. If Jesus thought this about the Kingdom of God, he was wrong, at least so far. In much of the twentieth century, most scholars favored this view, and even today this approach is reinforced by those who focus on the Book of Revelation and such notions as the Rapture. Whether Jesus' views were apocalyptic—thinking the end time is soon—probably can't be determined, but it is worth noting his mentor, John the Baptizer, and his early followers were so it seems likely Jesus was as well.

However, today one can ask if the message is so simple, why is this transformation, this awareness of the Kingdom of God, so difficult for people to accept? It may have been easier in the first century because the end time was thought to be near. ("I can do this for a while.") Also, Jesus was preaching to those who had no power, the peasants, the poor, the average Jew. If the powers-that-be were harsh, a practice works that dealt with them by advocating moving on, getting over it. Remembering injustices done to you is not beneficial or useful. On the other hand, you, the Thoughtful, have at least some power, and as a result know that in your workplace turning the other cheek may mean yet another slap, a missed promotion, etc. Maneuvering, scheming, and gossiping are perhaps necessary to avoid a lifetime in a cubicle. Remembering past injustices might help avoid future ones. Outside the workplace, your jerk brother-in-law or bombastic neighbor strains your ability to forgive, again, and again, and again. Jesus spoke to the powerless; Christianity later became a religion of the powerful. Therein lies a problem, and it accounts, in part, for the additions to and interpretations of his message and his life that Jesus' followers have made since his death, even today.

Jeepers, Jesus' message wasn't all that complex: love your neighbor, forgive your enemies, do the right thing. Have you ever encountered someone who did practice Jesus' message? Such a person can be frustrating as the "usual" means of dealing with folk don't apply. No grudges, just openness. No taking, just helping. It can be enough to make you think and act better, at least for a while. Try those strictures for a day yourself, much less the rest of your life, then we'll talk. Simple, but not easy.

## Jesus' End? Death.

Many others in Jesus' day were teachers, story tellers, miracle workers, so his uniqueness must be found in his last days.

In 33 B.C. (the traditional year though scholars can justify as early as 30 B.C. or as late as 36 B.C.), after preaching and healing in Galilee for a while, Jesus went to Jerusalem, an approximately 100-mile journey. He is reported to have arrived astride a colt, ironic because rulers made triumphant entries on horseback or in chariots. However, this action led credence to a belief he was claiming some sort of power, perhaps on behalf of the poor, or he was plotting a rebellion. Certainly, the event—Palm Sunday—looks staged. And, as a former follower of John the Baptizer, he was a marked man anyway. Additionally, one of his disciples was known as "Simon the Zealot," which would suggest a connection with Jewish rebels (though the term is anachronistic). His arrival coincided with the run-up to Passover, one of the three festivals during which an observant Jew was expected to go to the Temple, and the city, whose normal population as perhaps 70,000, was thronging with around 125,000 Jews planning to celebrate at or near the Temple, the center of Jewish religious practices. The next day he caused a scene in the

Temple (traditionally, disturbing the business of the money-changers and sellers of sacrificial doves), thereby scaring the Temple authorities, who probably profited from those businesses. (John's gospel puts the hostility of the Temple authorities much earlier.) In the following days, he engaged in a ongoing debate with various Jewish religious groups on the Temple grounds, which garnered him much support. He also had a meal (the Last Supper famously depicted) with his disciples. Whatever he actually said at the time, this dinner became the antecedent for the Lord's Supper or Eucharist. Palm Sunday certainly looks like the start of an attempted revolution, though it was intended to be nonviolent. However, a few days later, by the time of the Gethsemane scene, Jesus sees his effort has failed—hence the negative ending in Mark's gospel.

Whatever Jesus' message and actions were, they threatened the stability of those who controlled the Temple, the priestly aristocracy. The Temple was a very rich operation, collecting tithes on agricultural produce and a head tax on all Jews. Besides managing the Temple operations, these people served as leaders of the Jews and cooperated with the Romans to maintain public order (and their own authority). (The chief priest was the most powerful person in Judea, the Roman representative excepted.) They convinced Pontius Pilate, the Roman governor (prefect, actually), Jesus threatened public order (probably not a hard task as the Jews of the day were frequently troublesome and sometimes rebellious). All of the gospels report "King of the Jews" as a charge, one nailed to his cross. The details, many improbable, of his trial are inconsistently reported in the gospels, a hopeless muddle, probably because eyewitness accounts were lacking. The details fit with what we know about Roman trials and fulfill some Hebrew Bible/Old Testament scriptural prophecies. Whatever the charges, the Roman authorities saw him as a threat to the peace and he was executed by crucifixion, a Roman practice. It's worth noting his followers were not persecuted, despite their fears, so they were not perceived as a threat.

An alternative view about his death arises from the execution of John the Baptizer for his crowd-drawing ability. Perhaps that ability led to Jesus' fate too, execution by the political authorities, and the role of the Temple leadership was a later addition to lessen Roman participation (when Jesus' followers were seeking to propitiate Romans).

Did Jesus go to Jerusalem courting death? Probably not. He went to Jerusalem because, as a Jew, that was part of his religious practice. However, the mounted arrival looks like an organized demonstration, showing his popularity and power. (Certainly the authorities were afraid to seize him openly in front of masses of people; they got him at night, outside the city, when he was with only a few disciples.) He planned to continue that demonstration with a scene at the Temple, but no one was around so he postponed that action to the next morning, when there would be crowds. He was clearly up to something. As the week wore on, however, he may have come to realize the danger his actions and words had created. Also, he may have thought he was being successful in bringing about the Kingdom of God so he continued his preaching. Once the authorities seized him, we lack reliable sources on his state of mind; we can't tell if Jesus was surprised, annoyed, frightened, or irate at being arrested (Mark 14:48). While the gospels report varying accounts of things he said during his crucifixion, it is doubtful he said anything much due to weakness and pain.[21] We are left with the possible view Jesus believed he was bringing about the Kingdom of God, and he died because his words and actions threatened civil stability.

Jesus' death was not caused by "the Jews," (a charge leading to anti-Semitism over the centuries), but by a small group of them, the priestly leaders, in concert with the Roman authorities. The list of charges in the gospels includes blasphemy but nothing we know about Jesus supports such a charge. However, Jesus' preaching emphasized the Kingdom of God and he had closeness to God, suggesting the Temple as the intermediary between God and sinner was unnecessary. And, by inference, so were those who supervised and profited from the Temple, the Jewish leadership of the Temple.

---

[21] Steven Pinker, *The Better Angels of Our Nature: Why Violence has Declined* (Viking, 2011), 13, describes a Roman crucifixion. "Tortured to death" might be a better term.

## Don't Sweat the Details. Other Views.

**Traditional.**

The foregoing description, often called "revisionist," is the result of nearly two centuries of research into the "historical Jesus," an effort to recreate his life like any other historical figure. The Thoughtful will not be surprised some scholars hold to another view on the study of Jesus, one labeled "traditional." These scholars ask not what Jesus did but what he meant, or what the Christian scripture/New Testament authors meant. This approach believes Jesus only influenced those around him, but Christianity grew from the writings, the Christian scripture/New Testament. Thus it is the Jesus described in the gospels and the writings of Paul who is important, because the historical Jesus is unavailable to historical inquiry.

This method accepting scripture and not worrying about its historical accuracy has found favor with some theologians, especially those in the Roman Catholic and Orthodox traditions, where commentaries made by early Church thinkers, including allegorical interpretations, and the Apocrypha (writings usually omitted from Protestant Bibles) are used. It is also commonly used in sermons and Bible study throughout Christendom; it coincides with the (unarticulated) views of the majority of Christians both historically and presently. This attitude doesn't reject the search for the historical Jesus so much as ignores it. In short, the words and events of the gospels are accepted, but their actual occurrence not a concern, and they are still interpreted and applied to the present day. As a result, in many denominations of all stripes, listeners, having heard stories about Jesus used as the basis for sermons and homilies their entire lives, assume they are factual though they are not directly told any such thing. In this traditional approach a distinction between truth and interpretation many in the pews never confront and when they do, most have trouble. These are stories, not reports. The unwise preacher who talks of such distinctions will soon observe a congregation with some nodding their heads in agreement and others getting up to leave to find another denomination, one "that respects the Bible." And, after all, if the clergy think their sermons improve parishioners' spiritual lives, discussions of the truth versus the factual may be irrelevant and distracting. One way to frame this matter is through an approach to the Christ of faith whereas the work discussed previously looks for the Jesus of history. To the traditionalist, what the story means, not whether it accurately describes the past, is important. This view builds upon what is reported of Jesus without working out the inconsistencies and additions; instead, it takes Jesus and his later interpreters, the authors of Paul's letters and the gospels, as of a piece and seeks the truth found therein.

A milder version of the traditional view accepts the gospel stories but denies them literal factuality occasionally. Thus the nativity, miracles, the resurrection and the like are not accepted as factual—but exactly what they are is never explicitly stated. The language used feels slippery and vague to the Thoughtful.[22]

For example, in these approaches the gospel authors' use of metaphor is easily accepted; many events may not have happened but are used to capture the essence of a process. The story of Jesus being confronted by the devil with certain temptations after 40 days in the desert may not have occurred but the story exists to summarize a period in which Jesus wrestled with those temptations, "a process is dramatized as an event."[23] If Jesus' early followers added material in order to flesh out the skeleton of a story, it is fine. Thus, if his first followers somehow experienced his resurrection (in whatever form) and the next generation added more events (empty tomb) to create a complete story, a myth, an explanation of Jesus, the process is consonant with the traditional view. Thus Jesus becomes an object of faith and the "truth" is not one of factuality.

Finally, a third traditional view, the one with which the Thoughtful are likely to be familiar, is most often found among fundamentalist Protestants. The gospels are true, factually, every jot and tittle. Inconsistencies are glossed over in a way the Thoughful find unacceptable but which the believer easily swallows. This view merits little discussion as it is unattractive to the Thoughtful.

---

22 The many books of N.T. Wright, an Anglican bishop, illustrate this approach well.

23 Wills, *Jesus,* 19.

All of these traditional approaches will look at the earlier material in this chapter, which might be called "revisionist," note the proponents cannot agree among themselves. By claiming certainty, the traditionalists feel they discredit the revisionists and quell doubts among their followers.

**Minimalist.**

The writings of John Shelby Spong, among others, provide an example of another approach to the gospels.[24] The usual way to look at Jesus' activities is to assume they are historical. However, a minimalist with a vengeance, Spong reverses that assumption and rejects most of the gospel material because it was created by Jesus' followers as they expounded in synagogues about how Jesus fulfilled Jewish scripture. To those listeners Jesus was portrayed as the Messiah who fulfilled scripture and whose Kingdom of God has begun. So, what is left? Outside sources tell us Herod was king of the Jews from 37 B.C.E. to 4 B.C.E., which meets the minimalist test. Pontius Pilate was Roman ruler of Judea from 26 C.E. to 36 C.E., which also satisfies the minimalist.

Another test for some minimalists is considering whether events might have embarrassed Jesus' followers? This approach produces three candidates for historical reality. First, being from Nazareth was to be from the backside of beyond and no respectable movement would situate its founder in such a place. So it is very probable. (Origin stories, a la Abe Lincoln, set in rustic surroundings had no appeal to the ancients.) Second, the baptism of Jesus by John the Baptist makes no sense because a supposedly sinless Jesus didn't need his sins washed away or to repent of anything. Moreover, the founder, Jesus, appears certainly to have been a disciple of John, an awkward relationship. So it is historical. Finally, no major figure would be crucified, a disgraceful way to die.

Beyond these three examples, almost everything else is up for grabs. Mark's discussion of John the Baptist becomes based upon the stories of the great prophet Elijah. Coherent arguments usually in terms of the Jewish

---

[24] See, e.g., John Shelby Spong, *Jesus for the Non-Religious* (HarperOne, 2007).

religion of the day are given for the origins and purposes of the other gospels, but the Thoughtful might ask why "Joseph" and "Mary" couldn't have been the names of Jesus' parents, or if perhaps Jesus did do things that looked like miracles to his contemporaries. And maybe Jesus did, toward the end, come to see himself as the Messiah. With these examples Spong certainly challenges fundamentalist views of scripture.

If Spong looks at reports of Jesus' life to determine what might be factual, Robert Wright, an evolutionary psychologist, goes after beliefs attributed to Jesus. He relies heavily on Mark's gospel, because it is the earliest, and finds Jesus, *inter alia,* ethnocentric as he initially declines to perform a miracle for a non-Jew, likening her to a dog (Mark 7:25 – 30)[25]. Wright also doubts Jesus taught a universal love but rather his "love they neighbor" meant neighbors in the limited sense of fellow Jews.[26] Moreover, Wright, and most others actually, find the command to proclaim the gospel to the whole world (Mark 16:15) to be a later, probably second-century, addition. Overall, Wright, ignoring the later gospels, constructs a minimalist view of Jesus and finds much of Christianity was the work of Paul after Jesus' death. All can agree Mark's Jesus is not the commonly held image; he is unsuccessful in some miracle attempts, his Jesus never gets his message through to the disciples, and he asks, on the cross, why God has forsaken him. Whether the bulk of Jesus' ideas are the product of later followers is more questionable.

The traditional approach to Jesus and the extreme minimalist views of those such as Spong and Wright reach the same conclusion: the Jesus of history cannot be fully recaptured. However, the result of these various approaches is much the same: live life as Jesus proclaimed and get in a right relationship with God. Whether this answer requires the institutional church in some form or not is what separates Protestants from others.

---

[25] Robert Wright, *The Evolution of God* (Little Brown, 2009), 257. Many scholars doubt these are Jesus' words but are Mark's creation as Jesus never claimed a specific mission. See e.g., Robert W. Funk, et al. *The Five Gospels* (Macmillan, 1993), 70.

[26] Jesus may be quoting Leviticus 19:18 which, as Wright asserts, implies love only extends to "your people" but Leviticus 19:33 explicitly includes aliens within the ambit of neighbor.

Finally, the Thoughtful should reflect as to whether it really matters if the gospels are factually true or mainly metaphoric efforts. Can't both convey truth?

**Oh, No, We Don't Agree! The Problems of Interpretations.**

What a story means is obviously a human decision. The Thoughtful remember English literature classes in which a (hypothetical) poem, so obviously about a vine and a tree, really meant something about relationships. Moreover, meanings can change over time as the aforementioned poem might have meant something about slavery in the 1850s, gender relations in the 1970s, and international affairs in the 2000s. When it comes to Jesus, however, scholars and Jesus' followers have, over the centuries, winnowed the choice of interpretations of Jesus' life and words, and traditions have been built up around what his story means, though it is continuously open to new interpretations.

The problem with this approach for some is that certainty can't be found as interpretations can proliferate. But isn't that always true of life? What caused the American Civil War—slavery, federalism, cultural differences, etc.? Why is your brother-in-law so strange—parental upbringing, genetics, brain injury, drugs, etc.? Religion, like all else in life, provides answers; choosing among them is the task. If Jesus' early followers added lots in order to flesh out the skeleton of a story, so be it.

As a general rule, this notion is not the Protestant way, but it has found much favor historically and continues in today's Roman Catholic and Orthodox churches. Even many Protestant scholars, after they've stripped away the later accretions to Jesus, find a mystery, a significance, a truth, that lies outside the historical facts. The tension between these approaches—the Jesus of history and the Christ of faith—surfaces when Christians (Protestants, and largely conservative Protestants at that) assert their faith is based on fact, history, actual events. Being told part of the story is an interpretation, a myth, or it contains later additions doesn't fly with these folk. Their usual response is something along the lines of "If X isn't true, then how can I accept anything else; it might not be true either." This all or nothing, fact or fiction, style of thinking is difficult to counter, and will be discussed later.

But even the Thoughtful, who are comfortable with the techniques of the study of the historical Jesus, have more trouble when the focus shifts to the Christ of faith. Certainty is never possible, even in the quest for the historical Jesus, but those accepting the Christ of faith are asking a lot of the Thoughtful—including leaving some things as a mystery, a probably unsolvable mystery. This traditional approach runs into trouble as the Thoughtful start to ask about the factual basis for a story, something rational people are prone to do. Thus, the Virgin Birth, originally an idea to emphasize Jesus' god-like qualities or to cover "irregularities" of his birth, becomes an obstacle as "things just don't happen that way." Anyway, why does it matter? If it can be so easily jettisoned, why is it retained? Encounters with the creeds and the complex theology of the church that later developed only exacerbate things. The traditional approach often leaves God and Jesus' role as a mysteries, inexplicable and difficult to understand, which those seeking cleaner, more concrete, answers find unacceptable. Traditionalists are content to accept that prior believers understood stories and concepts in a certain way and then to build on them. Also the traditional approach implies, and sometimes states, Christianity can develop, especially with the guidance of the clergy, which doesn't sit well with many Protestants, who, with their "back to the Bible" mentality, don't cotton to that view easily. This whole problem is a variant of the faith versus reason issue.

Can the Thoughtful suspend the use of reason in this area? Should they? Why? Or, is reason still at work? The Thoughtful, usually thinking of themselves as rational and reasonable creatures, come to the crux of the problem. How much of the traditional material about Jesus is one required to accept e.g., miracles? Is this a time, a place, where rationality has its limits? Certainly, many scholars, including some engaged in the quest for the historical Jesus, eventually reach the conclusion some things can't be known, and the answer to the ultimate God question remains a mystery. Also many theologians have come to prefer literary over historical interpretations (perhaps because they think, erroneously, history results in a single answer).

How does one go about this quest? Does one read the Bible to find out what Jesus said or did or to find out what he meant? Perhaps, as Paul wrote, it "surpasses all human understanding," but the search, the process, goes on.

## Who Was Jesus? Thoughts.

The best scholars seeking the Jesus of history, the human being, have worked within the Christian tradition. That search has been largely a Protestant quest, because the basic event of their faith, the Reformation, sought a return to a "purer" Christianity, one not "contaminated" by the medieval church. Until recently much of the work was done in Germany. While two of the present-day scholars seeking the historical Jesus are Roman Catholic, John P. Meier and J.D. Crossan, the general practice of Roman Catholicism has been to stick to the tradition built by the Church in the two millennia since Jesus' death. An example of the Roman Catholic tradition is Garry Wills's book which accepts the gospels as true and yet still often interprets them symbolically and metaphorically, a technique with a long tradition in the Western Church.[27]

Over the centuries various descriptions of Jesus have interested and divided many. Believers have used terms such as "Savior," "Lord," "God," "Son of God," and so forth, terms making Jesus unique and involving articles of faith and theology, not history. He doesn't fit the standard images of Greek heroes or Jewish Messiahs. Scholars have sought to label Jesus in a way that makes him understandable in the context of world history; they have tried to penetrate the "wall" of Easter, the resurrection of Jesus, to discover what Jesus was like before his followers started adding things and interpreting his life. This difficulty is why some believers distinguish between the Jesus of history and the Christ of faith, pre- and post-Easter. The latter idea, the Christ of faith, developed early, already by the year 50 the missionary (and letter writer) Paul was recording parts of it. Soon the gospel authors added

---

[27] Wills, *Jesus.*

more. That ends it for Protestants as they limit their interest to scripture. Roman Catholics, on the other hand, continued developing, and continuous to develop, the tradition. All the while, some scholars seek to identify the "historical Jesus." No wonder the Thoughtful get confused.

The views of Jesus hinge on basically two issues. First, what was his view of the end of time, his eschatology? Did he see a fire and brimstone, militaristic Judgment Day or did he think the Kingdom of God was at hand and thus affected how one thought and acted on a day-to-day basis? Or something else? Second, was Jesus hoping to change society or the individual? Did he have a goal, an ideal world he was working toward; if so, what was it? Was he a preacher of ethics or an apocalyptic visionary?[28]

Much scholarship, back to the nineteenth century and still probably the dominant view today, portrayed Jesus as an eschatological prophet, someone who thought the end time was neigh. The gospels of Mark, Matthew, and Luke easily support this view, and Mark ends with Jesus asking God why nothing happened, which looks like an admission of failure. Most famously, Albert Schweitzer, and most thoroughly, Rudolf Bultmann, interpreted Jesus in this light, an eschatological prophet who got it wrong. Jesus, to these, and many others, thought God would intervene in some dramatic fashion in the world. Consonant with this view, Jesus talked about the destruction of the Temple, the center of Jewish worship, and maybe also about the end time. This interpretative tradition also includes much discussion about the nature of the end time—how soon, cataclysmic—to decide how Jesus was mistaken. One consequence of this view is Jesus was wrong about the end time, unless one interprets his ideas about the Kingdom of God to mean individual, not world, change, which, given the evidence, is an easy interpretation. Even if he was wrong about the end time, his ideas about the Kingdom of God could be valid. If one views him as God who knew everything (a common view from the pew), then the eschatological prophet approach poses problems; however, the Thoughtful might reflect that Schweitzer, who thought Jesus

[28] Another matter—interpretations of what happened after his death—involves faith and history and is discussed in Chapter 5.

got it wrong, went on to be a powerful Christian witness as a missionary in Africa.

More recently, some see Jesus as a Cynic, a term more familiar to students of ancient Greece.[29] Cynics, most famously Diogenes, were philosophers who rejected society and its trappings, preferring homelessness and self-imposed poverty. Jesus fits much of this description as he lived and preached at the bottom of the socio-economic scale and his sayings often resemble those of the Cynics. Growing up in Nazareth, a few miles from the city of Sephoris where Greek thought would have been available, he could have been exposed to the ideas of the Cynics. However, Jesus, during his public activities, avoided the Greek/Hellenized cities of Galilee, which suggests a discomfort with that culture (or a fear of the political authorities). While rejection of family and wealth in favor of the pursuit of virtue was the Cynic practice, they also tended to seek that virtue as individuals, whereas Jesus often involved himself in communities.

With his vivid sense of God, Jesus might be seen as a mystic, a category familiar to history.[30] His time in the desert, his frequent retreats to private prayer, and his hearing the voice of God at his baptism, all smack of mysticism. Maybe his healings were performed while in a state of ecstasy. This approach tends to ignore any issues about the end time in favor of the present. While mystics typically do not found movements—their visions are too personal to communicate successfully—maybe Jesus' charisma made him the exception, though his followers had to alter some things to perpetuate the movement.

Recent views involve seeing Jesus as a prophet, much in the Hebrew Bible/ Old Testament tradition, who challenged the world of his day. In this view he criticized the unequal wealth distribution and many of the contemporary priestly practices. Unlike earlier prophets, Jesus was, if not anti-family, more

---

[29] Burton Mack, *Myth of Innocence: Mark and Christian Origins* (Fortress, 1988).

[30] Scholars differ on whether Jesus' use of "Abba" to address God was unusual or very personal. For a sustained discussion of the mysticism argument, see Marcus Borg, *Jesus* (HarperOne, 2006).

interested in community and egalitarianism. This view can also include a feminist or gay perspective as inclusiveness was his goal.[31]

Related to this view Jesus can be seen as a charismatic who healed the sick and sought to revitalize Israel. Attracting followers and curing people, he attempted to give Jews a vision of a world that combined former glories (of purity, not military greatness) with a compassionate existence.[32]

To the Roman governor of the day, Pontius Pilate, Jesus appeared to be a troublemaker, perhaps a rebel. While fighting Rome was, as we now know, a losing proposition evident from the Jews' unsuccessful attempts at it in the following 150 years; Pilate's view was not unrealistic. As a revolutionary, Jesus was criticizing the powers-that-be while proposing social change and solidarity among the peasants. This view as a rebel explains why he was executed.[33]

Most agree he espoused loving one's neighbor, forgiving one's enemies, and forgetting one's past, but he was not unique in his day in those views. Isocrates, Confucius, and Hillel, among others, had the same ideas.[34] What struck those around him, especially during the last week of his life, were his qualities of self-sacrifice, suffering, and powerlessness; as a result, many decided they had experienced God, they had been in the presence of God. Those experiences, despite his ignominious death on a cross, led to a movement seeking to promulgate his insights. His unusualness, maybe uniqueness, is in the success of the Christian movement after such an inauspicious beginning. While his followers may have changed some things about Jesus—and scholars have less-than-complete sources to study him—the premise of his death and his lasting influence need to be incorporated into any interpretation or analysis of him. This consequence must be captured in an interpretation of his life and his views, especially about the "Kingdom of God."

---

[31] See, for example, Elizabeth Schussler Fiorenza, *In Memory of Her* (Crossroads, 1983). Gary Wills, *Why Priests? A Failed Tradition* (Viking, 2013).

[32] Marcus Borg, *Conflict, Holiness and Politics in the Teachings of Jesus* (Mellen, 1984).

[33] Reza Aslan, *Zealot The Life and Times of Jesus of Nazareth* (Random House, 2013).

[34] Bart Ehrman, *The New Testament* (Oxford, 2000), 95.

His tremendous influence provides the strongest argument he really did exist in first-century Palestine.

## Where Are We? Conclusion.

The more one studies, the less certain one becomes. The letters of Paul mention almost nothing of Jesus' life and the four canonical gospels have such strong theological purposes one suspects the "facts" are not very reliable. For example, a group of approximately 200 scholars examined the gospels and concluded only 15 sayings attributed to Jesus were really uttered by him. Indeed, the gospels may tell us more about the early followers than about Jesus. And they practiced and believed many things, only a few of which survived to become "orthodoxy," so what we have in the canon is only one of several possibilities.

Many of the details of Jesus' life are unrecoverable and many commonly accepted details didn't occur. His message was short, even cryptic. His life took place among poor peasants and their village society (curiously, none of his disciples is described as a farmer). He lived out most of his public life in Galilee, an area the size of the common American county, 600 square miles, and he avoided the cities of that area. Today one might think of communes, the Amish, and other folk who shun the modern world, although Jesus didn't do that—there was no "modern world." He did avoid, or at least not approach, the powerful, the rich, the educated, the urban world. He offered a message to all but his "all" were people barely getting by. To them, a change of attitude could make a difference. Tolerance removes annoyances. Forgiveness enhances village society. Fellowship produces community and deemphasizes the individual. Practicing his message could, indeed, lead to a better place, a Kingdom of God.

How radical was Jesus' message? If, as seems likely, he foresaw an imminent end to the world, he was well within the apocryphal thought of some in his day. The Kingdom of God idea is more difficult to assess. Did he seek to restore some perfect past as radicals and revolutionaries often do? Was it the time of King David? The scriptural descriptions of David's reign are short on information about personal behavior which is usually Jesus' target. His apparent forgiveness of sin without requiring a Temple sacrifice would only mesh with a pre-Solomon time, i.e. David's reign. Or perhaps he had distilled what he considered the essence of Jewish religion tradition: do the right thing and love your neighbor. The latter would produce batter community, whether the local village or the entire nation of Israel. That result would be consonant with scriptural views, especially those of the Hebrew Bible/Old Testament prophets. However, the gospels do not support a view of Jesus as a radical. His healing attracted attention, which led to crowds and Roman interest, but no one seems to challenge his message. Later, followers took pains to emphasize how well his message and the developing church fit within Jewish religious practices, but that that may have been an effort to avoid Roman attention as the Romans tended to be suspicious of anything novel. Whether or not the communities of Jesus' followers were unique in their behavior in Palestine, they did contrast with much of the wider Roman world. However, that contrast was not attractive enough to produce large numbers of converts, at least in the short run. Moreover, the rabbis, in the developing Judaism of the early Christian era were espousing views not inconsistent with those of Jesus. How radical was Jesus' message? Can't be sure.

It does appear that Jesus was wrong about the end time coming soon. He wasn't alone as Paul and much, most, maybe all of the early followers shared the expectation. An individual can be wrong on one thing but right on lots of other things is okay to the Thoughtful. It does point to the individual not being a deity as presumably wrongness is not a divine characteristic, which can guide the Thoughtful to a new understanding of Jesus, one consonant with this book.

Why do we worry about historical accuracy or meshing with scientific reason? And why demand faith in a book? Early followers of Jesus had no books and the accepted canon we know as the Christian scripture/New Testament dates only from the fourth century. Yet people believed something and the early church flourished. One scholar argues being a Christian in the early church was more important than what doctrines one accepted.[35] Perhaps faith should be put in the tradition, the general story and its insights, not in specific details. Thus, the big picture, not the specific details, is the important thing. And we can even argue the word "faith." Instead of interpreting it as "belief," we could substitute "trust." For example, when your parents sent you off to the senior prom, they said they had faith you would behave yourself. (Obviously they didn't have belief; if they did, they wouldn't have had to say anything.) With this interpretation, faith becomes trust and one need not get bogged down in details of what one must believe. Thusly the citation to John 6:29 changes meaning "This is the work of God, that ye believe in him whom he hath sent…" as well as to Mark 5:35 "Be not afraid, only believe." And also Romans 4:3 "For what said the scripture? "Abraham believed God, and it was counted unto him for righteousness."" That view of the word "believe" also harmonizes Galatians 3:20 "For ye are all children of God by faith in Christ Jesus."

As with art, if one looks only at context, all art is seen as a political gesture, and one does not see the beauty or experience the pleasure coming from a study of the form or style.[36] Maybe one can never find the historical figure behind the faith-encrusted Christian scripture/New Testament. Maybe Jesus is the one experienced in the present; the resurrected Jesus is the "real" one. Or maybe it is all an interplay of authorized texts, history, and present experience. So we are left working somewhere between the certainty of the literalists and the nihilism of the non-believers.

Why did Jesus, a poor Jew from remote Galilee, spark a movement that grew into today's Christianity? His message of loving one's neighbors and forgiving one's enemies wasn't unique in ancient times or even in Jewish life. He was a healer, performing acts that came to be seen as miracles, but miracle stories were told about other holy men of the day. Maybe the organizational skills of Paul account for the success. Perhaps the times were propitious with some Jews chafing under Roman rule and remembering a better

---

[35] Keith Hopkins, *A World Full of Gods* (Plume, 2001), 332.

[36] See Wendy Steiner, *The Scandal of Pleasure: Art in an Age of Fundamentalism* (University of Chicago Press, 1995).

past. The Jewish world of his day also was rife with messianic speculation and hope. Whether Jesus saw himself as a Messiah can be debated, though the oldest gospel, Mark's, strongly supports that view. And if he or his first followers thought he was a Messiah, what was the content of that belief? Jesus was charismatic, that seems very likely, though the quality doesn't shine out from the gospels very clearly. When Jesus died, all these themes had not come together to make a story. That confluence required Jesus' resurrection.

But wait. Before we can get to the resurrection, we need to understand a few things that undergird much of the discussion of the rest of the book. So now, let's do something completely different.

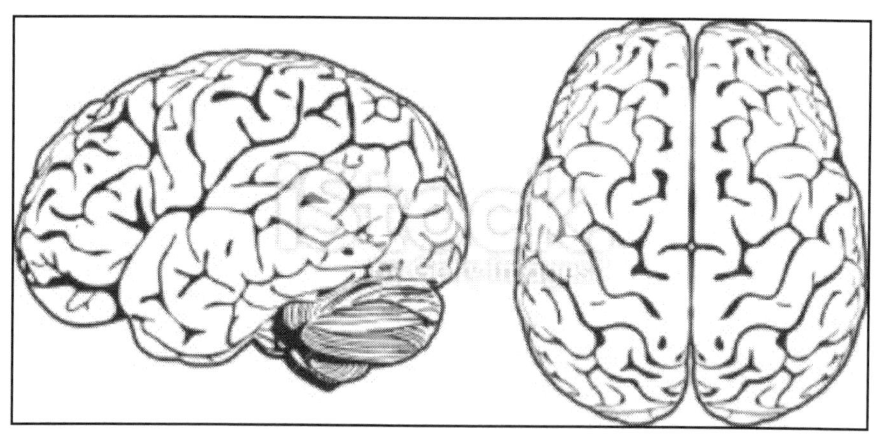

*The Human Brain*

# TWO

# *Ground Rules*

## Non-religious Stuff.

**Those People You Don't Understand. Psychology.**

One of life's frustrations for the Thoughtful, who see nuance in many issues, involves encountering people who have certitude. Those folk know the answers to difficult and complex questions—answers usually of the type "yes/no," or "either/or," never "more or less" or "probably." Why do some people think that way? And why, despite the best efforts of the Thoughtful to enlighten them, do they persist in their certainties, their Truths? These people include many Christians.

Perhaps (note the Thoughtful word) a trip through some developmental psychology will help. Psychologists who study the human personality have long noticed many, perhaps most, children go through a series of stages during which they can deal with some events but not others, yet a few months later can deal with the others as well. Jean Piaget, a Swiss psychologist, is the most famous scholar of this phenomenon. His observations of infants found that between months 8 and 12 the tyke discovers causality and knows that a certain noise means a bottle is about empty, that after 18 months the game of peek-a-boo loses its surprise, and that after age 2 and before age 7 a tall, thin glass holds more liquid than a short, fat one even after watching the equal amounts being poured into them. Perhaps to parents the most frustrating situations in the 2 – 7 year-old period, involves the focus on intentions; the concept of "accident" covers everything one didn't intend to do even when the result is foreseeable. Anything found not to be true is a lie, regardless of the speaker's intention. Piaget has lots more observations and the Thoughtful can try them on toddlers. (It's fun to watch their developments.)

The Thoughtful probably recognize these developmental issues in themselves. Consider the example: two students write about a book they read. The first writes a report describing a rich family with five daughters, whose mother wants to get them married and whose dad is unpretentious. A rich guy moves into the neighborhood, with an even richer friend. A clergyman arrives and asks the eldest two daughters to marry him. A whole bunch of mistakes and offenses occurs, as they do in middle school. Finally the heroine and the rich man get together. The second student focuses on the relationships seen in the book and discusses how our opinions can stand in the way of people getting together or understanding one another. Opinions about looks, wealth, jobs, personality, and our own lives are the problems confronted. However, eventually the heroine Elizabeth realizes her pride and prejudices were wrong and so lands her Prince Charming, Mr. Darcy. Which paper gets the better grade? Does knowing the theme help integrate the various anecdotes better? Can the first student ever become the second?

Another instance of developmental psychology is called "formal operations" and may develop after age 11. These include those wonderful logic problems from the standardized tests, such as dog is to hair as bird is to ____ or if A is less than B and B is less than C, is A more or less than C?[1] Another aspect of this period is making judgments logically but not taking into account the "real world" e.g., "Thou shalt not kill" and the death penalty, abortion, and war all involve death intentionally inflicted but that issue is often ignored. Formal operations, studies suggest, are

---

1 Answers: feathers, less.

developed by only about 50 percent of the U.S. population.[2] Explains a lot, doesn't it?

Armed with this knowledge of developmental stages, let us turn to religion. In the 1960s William G. Perry, Jr. worked with Harvard undergraduates to throw light on our issue of religion and the problem of certitude.[3] Perry observed students typically moved through four stages in the handling of new material of any kind, not just religious.

Initially, they sought certainty, clear dualistic answers, mastering the facts (dualism):

- "There's nothing more annoying than a question that may have more than one answer." (64)
- "If teachers would stick more to the facts and do less theorizing, one could get more out of their classes." (67)

Next, students discovered there might be many ways of looking at a problem but aren't always comfortable with that knowledge (multiplicity):

- "I'd like to teach an English course sometime, just for people who would like to read some good books and not know anything about Melville's complexes." (74)
- "You're reading a book ... and the lecturer is just reading things into it that were never meant to be there." (79)

Third, they accept there are multiple answers but don't think any one is better than another (relativity):

---

[2] D. Elkind, "Quantity Conception in College Students," *Journal of Social Psychology* 57 (1962) 459-65. L. Kohlberg and R. Mayer, "Development as the Aim of Education," *Harvard Educational Review* 41 (1972) 449-96. D. Kuhn et al., "The Development of Formal Operations in Logical and Moral Judgment," *Genetics Psychology Monograph* 95 (1977) 115. I.Q. tests also value abstract thinking, something that can be encouraged. James Flynn, *What is Intelligence"* (Cambridge, 2007).

[3] William G. Perry, Jr., *Forms of Intellectual and Ethical Development in the College Years* (Holt, Rinehart, 1968). All psychology textbooks discuss development and a lot of work has occurred since Perry's. Nevertheless, his insights correlate well with people's views on religion today.

- "I think everyone (in economics) that writes or everyone that speaks has their opinion and they, they see one meaning to it, but that's why they assign different writers with different opinions." (103)
- "Well, the problem I was talking about last year was "What am I going to do, and what shall I think about this?" So now I say that, well, I'm going to just have to choose. I'll read the topic for a paper and then I'll choose a side." (106—7)

Finally, they choose one of the multiple answers because it works for them but don't deny other answers might be valid for other people (commitment):

- "You can't expect these internal evolutions to just develop and then suddenly bloom, you've got to work at it, I think." (138)
- "You just have to jump into it, that's all, before it can have any effect on you. And the farther in you force yourself to get in the first place, the more possibilities there are, the more ideas and concepts there are that can impinge on you and so the more likely you are to get involved in it." (139)

Some students move through all four stages—dualism, multiplicity, relativism, commitment—and some stop at one, never continuing. Moreover, dualism may last longer in one subject than another, e.g., chemistry versus history.

The Thoughtful can now recognize themselves as either relativists or committed and often have little patience for those back at dualism. The knowledge perhaps 50 percent of Americans are dualists doesn't make it any easier to understand others. Perry's categories help one make sense of such things as politics and religion. As so many people are dualistic, either/or, yes/no kinds of folk, politicians and preachers pander to them by refusing to acknowledge nuances and complexities. What makes it worse; there is evidence the more certain someone is, the more likely it is flawed thinking was involved.[4] Scary, huh?

---

[4] Deanna Kuhn, "How Well Do Jurors Reason," *Current Directions in Psychological Science* 5 (1994) 289-96. Another version of these approaches is Isaiah Berlin's metaphor of "The Hedgehog and the Fox." Psychologists call the certainty of the less informed the "Dunning Kruger Effect."

As F. Scott Fitzgerald wrote almost a century ago in *The Crack-Up*, "the test of the first-rate intelligence is the ability to hold two opposed ideas in mind at the same time and still retain the ability to function."[5] Dealing with multiple truths, which may be inconsistent, is not for everyone. It's good, but frustrating sometimes, to be Thoughtful.

The relevance of these ideas to Christianity is obvious. Some people cling to a literalism about the Bible and desire absolutes in morality which indicates they are, in the above vocabulary, dualists. Moreover, they are not in a position to accept the idea people who do not share their views can possibly be right.

## Making Up or Making Sense? Patterns.

Researchers have concluded there is something innate about the human brain that causes people to see patterns in life. We resist the idea events occur randomly.[6] Perhaps that manner of interpreting the world developed to protect us against predators. Alternatively, if it isn't nature, it might be nurture as evident from the time the ancient Greeks began looking for universals, constants, laws even, among all the confusion of the real world. As we can see in today's Western culture, we're intellectual descendants of those Greeks. The ability to see patterns also lets us see patterns where perhaps none exist—a noise in a summer storm need not be a god telling us something. And believing there is a pattern in that storm increases the chances you'll find one. In other words, a feeling for religious experience, the supernatural, might be a pattern we seek.

Studies have also suggested a correlation (not necessarily a causation) between schizophrenia and religious feeling.[7] Families (since schizophrenia has a genetic component) with people who hear voices, a common

---

[5] *Esquire* (Feb. 1936). F. Scott Fitzgerald, *The Crack-Up, with other Uncollected Pieces, Note-Books and Unpublished Letters*, ed. Edmund Wilson (New Directions, 1945), 69.

[6] Martin Plimmer and Brian King, *Beyond Coincidence* (St. Martin, 2005). "Apophenia" is the terms psychologists use.

[7] Most famously in the work of Seymour Kety.

schizophrenic phenomenon, are more likely to be religious. Once this information is stated, is it any surprise? Religion is, therefore, genetic?

Most pewsitters never appreciate the notion scripture was written to show patterns and themes. The knowledge that many hands wrote and sometimes changed the Hebrew Bible/Old Testament to make the facts conform to a theme is a surprise. If it contains "truth," why any need to alter it? The idea there might be two major themes is an even bigger surprise.

**Think so? Memory.**

When dealing with the past, the Thoughtful bring a certain humility to its reconstruction. Many think a memory is like a book, a dictionary perhaps: one takes it off the shelf, looks at it, returns it, and the next time it is consulted, the word will have the same definition. However, memories change every time they are examined. The view of memory by neuroscientists today is that reactivating a memory destabilizes it, making it flexible and capable of being changed. Each time you access a memory, you change it. The fewer times you use a memory, the better (more accurate) it is. Aunt Betty contributes a detail or you realize a memory has a darker side or people's actions aren't without motive. Hence, a memory moves, by stages, to a different place, one more fitting with the history one is constructing of oneself. Inconsistent details, perhaps entire memories, must be erased.

Moreover, a memory can be even created. A series of well-known criminal prosecutions around 1990 occurred when people recovered, or thought they recovered, memories of witnessing a murder or being abused. Some of these "memories" became so fantastic it is a wonder anyone would accept them, much less prosecute because of them.[8] However, many psychologists have the notion one can, and will, suppress an unpleasant event so one doesn't remember it. The knowledge many of the recovered "memories" were assisted by psychologists with leading questions and suggested

---

[8] For one particularly outrageous case, see Lawrence Wright, *Remembering Satan* (Knopf, 1994). That repressing memories might be a feature of time and place, see Harrison G. Pope, et al. "Is dissociative amnesia a culture-bound syndrome? Findings from a survey of historical literature," *Psychological Medicine* 37 (2007) 225-233.

facts only makes the mess messier. The moral of those prosecutions and later studies surrounding events is that memory is a dodgy thing, capable of creation and manipulation.

Today, researchers have cast doubt on eyewitness testimony and police lineup identifications, both based on memories. Additionally, our memories tend to forget the length of an event and emphasize its best moments (duration neglect, peak-end rule, the terms researchers use). They have also produced lots of other understandings suggesting humans don't fit the "rational man" model.

The relevance of memory to Christianity arises because certain aspects, e.g., Jesus' sayings, histories of Israelite kings, depended on people's memories. While the foibles of memory are real, that knowledge doesn't make those sayings and histories wrong, but it does create a hesitation to take them as fact; however, the probabilities often favor them.

## Are You Sure? Probabilities and Surveys.

"Figures lie and liars figure."

Usually, one can base an informed opinion on some evidence, often statistical. Thus, politicians make decisions when a pollster tells them a certain position is popular with, say, 63 percent of the electorate. However, any survey is open to potential problems.

The question "Should abortion be allowed as a means of birth control?" will produce negative answers from perhaps 80 percent of the respondents whereas the question "Should abortion be available in certain circumstances?" will find positive support of about 60 percent. Both can be (mis)used to argue 80 percent of Americans oppose abortion or 60 percent favor it. Neither is correct as close attention to the questions reveals. The questions asked and even the sequence in which they are asked can skew results.[9]

Pollsters report results sometimes with a footnote to the effect "The margin of error is plus or minus 5 percent." Several years ago the voters of Ohio were asked to approve the hunting of doves. A few days before the

---

[9] For clear explanations of many of these issues, see Joel Best, *Damned Lies and Statistics* (University of California Press, 2001).

election the results of two polls were released. One found voters approved the proposal 55 percent to 45 percent while the other determined they opposed it 55 percent to 45 percent. Figures lie? No, both polls had a margin of error of 5 percent which means maybe as many as 60 percent or maybe as little as 50 percent supported or opposed it. The way to make the two polls jibe is to realize the voters were split 50 percent-50 percent; both polls were correct though apparently inconsistent.

Darrell Huff's wonderfully entertaining book *How to Lie with Statistics* (Norton. 1954) examines, in easily understood short chapters, the many ways the collection and presentation of data can mislead. In an age when so many policy arguments about moral issues are driven by statistics, the Thoughtful do well to be aware of pitfalls.

How is statistics and the like relevant to Christianity? When certainty is elusive, the Thoughtful can survive with some probabilities. For instance, we have no direct evidence Jesus ever lived, but taking all the surrounding evidence into account, the probabilities clearly favor the proposition he did live. And when the Thoughtful consider contemporary issues that have Christian aspects—abortion, homosexuality, female clergy, et al., the discussion can be advanced without certainty but with numbers bolstered by surveys. However, statistician Joel Best observes "Never underestimate the understanding of an innumerate public."[10]

Historians, whose work is the basis for part of this book, rarely do sampling—not enough data available—so their results might be called the available sample. The number of Christians in the Roman Empire or of abortions in the nineteenth century, however, is a figure advanced by some but is doubtful to the point of being dismissed. Not all numbers are valid.

While the Thoughtful skeptic or believer can't be certain, it is still possible to lean one way or the other, based upon the probabilities. Most of this book is written on that assumption. Thus, *inter alia*, the probabilities

---

[10] Best, *Damned Lies,* 82. This book also has good examples of the misuse of statistics. See also Charles Wheelan, *Naked Statistics* (Norton, 2013). Another explanation for the parties to the abortion debate talking past each other is that they use different kinds of reasons. Charles Tilly, *Why?* (Princeton University Press, 2006).

favor the existence of Jesus but do not support the story of the exodus of the Israelites from Egypt.

**Your Basis. Authority.**

In discussions people often must go beyond an opinion or justify it somehow. The solution is to cite an authority, something or someone others might accept as more informed, better argued, etc.

For many, an authority will be a person. A parent, a member of the clergy, or instructor will be trotted out as having said something supporting one's position. Of course, one wouldn't use a preacher's statement in a chemistry class or a physics instructor as a Holocaust denier. The experts are only experts in their field, and maybe only a subpart of that field

Books often become authorities, especially if they're authoritative. The Bible is perhaps the most common example of an authority as it can be cited on divers matters such as homosexuality, alcohol consumption, pacifism, and child raising. Not too long ago, the works of Karl Marx (1818 – 83) were authoritative for many around the world. Many Americans are ideologues about the value of the marketplace though few have read Adam Smith's work, a source of that idea. And any history instructor will tell you many students worship a textbook and often loathe essay questions.

Logic can provide answers and serve as an authority. Syllogisms and the like are fun though not always useful. Juries have to (or are at least supposed to) accept logic as they puzzle out whether the defendant committed the crime. But the Thoughtful all know the problem with logic involves the assumptions upon which the edifice is constructed. Syllogisms are easy, but as soon as someone says "All human beings are selfish," an argument begins as most know the premise—in this case selfishness—contains the conclusion, say, why capitalism is the "true" economic way.

History is often appealed to as an authority. "Munich" and "appeasement" and "Vietnam" and "swamps" routinely appear in political speeches. The argument the empires of Rome and Britain fell because of divorce and class snobbism, respectively, bring up counterarguments that the causes were instead militarism and racism. These attitudes are based upon a widespread belief history can be used to predict the future. Not true. Or some historians should be very rich, having predicted stock market trends. (For the curious, history tells us how we got to where we are, not where we're going. And it's fun, all that sex and violence.)

The most difficult authority to question is personal experience, a subset of history. If something happens to someone, that event takes on the aura of truth. For example, if a driver escapes from a burning, wrecked car and believes if she'd had her seatbelt on, she would have died, no amount of research or number of studies will convince her of the utility of seat belts. The anecdote trumps the generalization every time.

It is difficult to challenge an authority. One can often cite another authority as scholars often disagree. Or one can investigate the field oneself and seek to become an authority. Knowing someone is using a certain authority is, for the Thoughtful, useful because it helps in acceptance or denial of the position advanced. Christianity, both historically and at present, is rife with problems of authority. Unfortunately, often the less one knows of a topic the greater one's trust in and adherence to an authority, and Christians often exhibit that trait.

**Your Answer. Opinion.**

"Everyone's entitled to their own opinion."

Besides being grammatically wrong (with the word "everyone," the purported antecedent is "he," "she," or "one" not "their"), the statement itself is flawed. It is anti-intellectual and a rejection of education and study. One may have opinions about music, but if one never studied music seriously or doesn't have a good ear, why would one think one's opinion is as good as one of a professional musician?

"People believe what they want to believe." True, but what makes an idea acceptable to one person but repulsive to another? Why does the notion of a free market find a home in some minds but not others? At base, one's circumstances have a lot of do with making an idea attractive. If you are well off, the idea that hard work—merit—got you to that condition is attractive whereas a hardworking, impoverished person will attribute your success to luck, or parentage. Both the poor and the well off are in that condition because of choices they made. In the case of the poor, some would attribute it to choices such as dropping out of school, having children too early, drinking, gambling, throwing money away—everything but the acknowledgment they started off poor and did not have the means to change their status. Undoubtedly some folk accept ideas running counter to their circumstances—a Jew is occasionally found among Nazis—but, even then, a resort to psychological interpretations can often account for the bizarre. Yes, people choose what to believe but circumstances have a great influence of what they will accept.

"There are opinions, and there are informed opinions." Certainly the first statement is true—all have opinions—but it can't be used in a scholarly or logical argument. The average person in a pew is not equally thoughtful or even informed about, say, biblical content as is a scholar. And knowledge of science in our culture is lousy, yet those least informed are most likely to accept such idiocies as creationism. Certainly, experts can be wrong and consensus knowledge does change but, for most of us, we listen to what those we deem the brightest and best say about a subject.

Researchers have found all sorts of things affect opinions other than objective reality. An anecdote—e.g., my aunt would have burned to death if she'd been wearing her seat belt in that accident—will trump the statistical finding seat belts save lives. This is known as the "anchoring effect." Another example: we overstate benefits and understate costs—the planning fallacy—and we fear losses more than we value gains—loss aversion. All make the Thoughtful wonder if anything can be known. Yes, but with humility.

And some opinions are flat wrong. Historians disagree about the causes of the American Civil War: slavery, federalism, and industrialization surface as chief contenders. But all agree it was not caused by the invention of the automobile. One consequence of the "we all have opinions" idea is a reluctance to tell someone an opinion is flat-out wrong. This book doesn't suffer from that incapacity.

Educated discussion is also thwarted by the opinion idea. Presumably one can produce evidence or make logical arguments to buttress one's position, but all is lost if that position can be countered by someone who responds "That's my opinion and we're all entitled to our opinions." Grr.

People would never tell a chemistry instructor that in one's opinion mixing an acid and a base will not combine to produce a salt and water but they are perfectly willing to opine, dogmatically, about religion. While the certainty of knowledge in the two areas—chemistry and religion—differs, there is still value in knowing more rather than less, in having an "informed opinion." Study is good.

## Myth. A Problem Word.

Like truth, myth is a story that satisfies the need to have an explanation for something. It is the imaginative use of material to describe something beyond human experience. Unfortunately for discussion purposes, "myth" is used in several ways, even by the Thoughtful. Something once thought true but now is recognized as untrue, such as the earth is flat, is a myth. Also "myth" is used to describe something clearly known always to have been untrue, e.g., Santa. But the word can also be applied in the sense of the first sentence above to science, a construct that explains. Most often, however, it is (and has been) used in a religious or quasi-religious sense of a story about the world, usually involving gods. Mesopotamian myths included how the world was created, why it rains, and reasons for one's personal misfortunes. Egyptian and Greek myths shared those qualities but often seem to offer little more than entertainment. Scholars have long noted parallels, maybe borrowings, between Mesopotamian and Israelite traditions, but many Christians hang on to Genesis as factually accurate and enduringly unique.[11] Today, the Thoughtful might look at a story described as a myth to see if there might be a core event within it; on the other hand, the abstract way in which scholars address myth studies often cause the Thoughtful to lose interest.

---

[11] See Alexander Heidel, *The Babylonian Genesis: The Story of Creation* (University of Chicago Press, 1951).

Separating historical fact from something created to explain things, the word "myth" need not be a dichotomy. The story of Abraham, traditionally seen as the founding father of the Israelites, presents an example. If he existed, he was alive before 1500 B.C.E., but there is no historical proof of his existence in the usual sense of the term. A Thoughtful can treat all the stories about him as a myth, as a metaphor, created to explain something to the Israelites or a Thoughtful can accept his existence as real with semi-legendary additions to a basic story. Whatever the approach, the result is pretty much the same, a story of the foundation of a people with some interesting details.

In the absence of scientific explanations for events, people relied on myth. Thunder meant a god was unhappy, not the clash of weather systems etc. The Thoughtful haven't seen either the god making the thunder or a low pressure area, so what's to choose?

Did ancient people believe their myths? Yes and no. It seems they were inclined to think there was a core historical event with "stuff" added to give it a moral and maybe merely to make it more interesting. In fact this approach is, for most of Christian history, how believers have treated the Bible. Only with the appearance of Fundamentalism in the late nineteenth century did literal truth become an issue. To Fundamentalists, if not to the Thoughtful, "myth" means "made up," "created," and therefore untrue. The Thoughtful, however, realize a myth, whatever its origin, can convey a truth without worrying about the factuality of it.

Most, if not all, religions are based on myth—acts of faith incapable of proof or disproof. However, Christianity claims a basis in historical fact, not myth. Hence the outrage when someone claims to have found the possible tomb of Jesus, or questions the virgin birth, or points out the narrative inconsistencies in the Bible. In Christianity the greatest act of faith, taken as historically factual by many, is the bodily resurrection of Jesus. Scholars, scientists and historians cannot accept that explanation which often results in them being lumped with nonbelievers, heathens, or pagans. To the Thoughtful, potentially satisfactory explanations of the Resurrection are available but a physical, bodily reappearance is not among them. The

Resurrection, therefore, is the prime example Christianity is based upon a myth rather than a lie.

## Who're You Talking About? Religions.

Three faith traditions—Christianity, Judaism, and Islam—grew out of the religion of the Hebrew Bible. Is it not at all ironic that at various times these religions have despised and hated one another because many adherents think, the other two traditions got it wrong? But which two? The Thoughtful might also ponder whether any one religion, any one view, is God's only message to humanity or therefore provides humanity's only understanding of the great mysteries of life.

**Christians.**

So who is a Christian? The most basic definition is someone who accepts Jesus as Christ. However, that definition doesn't settle things because what "Christ" means is much debated. "Christ" is Greek, a translation of the Hebrew word "Messiah," which means "the anointed one." In the Hebrew Bible/Old Testament, the term is applied to some kings, a few priests, the nation of Israel, and even a Persian emperor. Generally however, a ruler in David's line is the object. Calling Jesus "Messiah" doesn't narrow the usage, therefore, a Christian who accepts the claim Jesus was the Messiah may mean lot of thing to lots of people. (The study of the word "Christ" is called "Christology" and fills many a volume.)

Any definition making Christians of those who are members of a Christian denomination runs afoul of the fact a significant number of Americans call themselves Christians though are not members of a denomination and maybe never darken a church door. From the other extreme there are folk who call themselves Christian but deny that designation to anyone who has different beliefs or practices from their own. In contrast with Judaism and Islam, Christianity has many, many groups, and many,

many denominations (probably over 30,000 worldwide). In some cases, Christians from different denominations get along and in others they loathe each other heartily. Chapters 6 and 7 discuss how so many parts came to exist and chapter 8 looks at Christianity in the United States. If people read this book to find out which group is true, right, or legitimate, this book will disappoint. Tolerance and understanding, not conversions or heresy-hunting, are the goals herein.

The chart in the Appendix lays out the historical development of Christianity and indicates some of the significant groups within it. In the United States, a major division has historically existed between Roman Catholics and Protestants. Roman Catholics are those members of an institution headed by the pope in Rome. Protestants long ago rejected that structure but are not unified under any one alternative. Orthodox make up a third, smaller, part, often consisting of immigrants, and their descendants, who came from the Balkans, Greece, and Russia. Scholars analyze these and other Christian groups in various ways—ethnically, sociologically, politically, etc., but this book will address the major divisions between Roman Catholics and Protestants and, within Protestantism, denominations described as mainline and fundamentalist. A big issue here is whether to see the Bible as literally true, but other differences include denominational governance, openness of services (especially communion) to non-members and requirements for becoming a member. Evangelicalism, an approach found in both mainline and fundamentalist groups, though more heavily in the latter, seeks a more emotional approach. These demarcations are confusing, and confused, so an entire book—this one—must be directed to sorting things out.

**Jews.**

When someone is said to be a Jew, several possible interpretations of the word exist. Nazis had a definition, the state of Israel has another, and conversions are controversial, so no single definition describes Jews in the past or now. At its narrowest, a Jew is someone who practices the religion

Judaism. The broadest usage would involve someone who was born of a group of people historically known as Jews even if that person had no interest in Judaism at all. A famous example of the latter is Benjamin Disraeli, a British Prime Minister in the nineteenth century. Born to a father who had converted to Christianity from Judaism, baptized as a child as a Christian, married in a Christian ceremony, he was nonetheless often referred to as a Jew. "Jews" is therefore an imprecise term which has cultural and ethnic qualities, in addition to religious aspects.

Three words are used in scripture to refer to this group. "Israelites" are the descendants of Jacob, who was renamed "Israel." The language of the Israelites was "Hebrew," in scripture, other peoples—not the Israelites—use the term "Hebrews." The most common usage of the term "Jews" refers to the members of the group who returned to the area of Jerusalem in the sixth century B.C.E. following the Exile; it has remained the most common term since. The singular "Jew" is and has been often used offensively to refer to certain characteristics unique to members of the group. The Thoughtful should remember Jesus was a Jew.

Historically, "Jew" has been loosely used but, as laws and practices of society limited and isolated Jews as a group, a people have existed over centuries whose adherence to Judaism was their chief, but not only, characteristic. As we shall see in chapter 5, Judaism and Christianity emerged by 100 C.E. from a common background. Never unified or controlled by an institution such as the church, Jews and Judaism were guided by rabbis, men schooled in the tradition and dedicated to continuing it.

In addition to the religious dimension, ancient Jews had a political identity which led them to revolt, though unsuccessfully, against Roman rule. In the First Jewish Revolt, the Temple, the center of Judaism, was destroyed in 70 C.E., and never rebuilt. After suppressing the Second Jewish Revolt of 132 – 5 C.E., Rome ordered all Jews out of Jerusalem, the traditional center of both religion and politics for the Jews. Jews were already scattered around the eastern Mediterranean and Mesopotamia and the resulting dispersion ("Diaspora") increased their presence. The cities of Alexandria and Antioch in particular became major centers, and, by and large, Jews were city folk, not farmers, except maybe in Palestine.

Christianity, as it moved away from Judaism, began to develop ideas of Jews' separateness and difference. Sometimes this position led to anti-Semitism and, after the Roman Emperor became a Christian, disabilities, though forced conversions were rare. As city dwellers Jews practiced their various trades and eventually they seemingly came to dominate the slave trade in Western Europe. (Christianity hadn't declared slavery evil, much less even a problem.)

As the medieval church in the West began to establish more control of society in the tenth and subsequent centuries, distaste for money-lending became a doctrine of the church. A good Christian should give or at least lend interest-free money to someone in need, rather than take advantage of someone's poverty; lending at interest was "usury," and considered sinful. This concept only applied to Christians; therefore Jews continued practicing usury and became identified with money-lending. Since few people are fond of their creditors, Jews suffered for this role. The first Crusade, in 1096, became an opportunity for what was perhaps the first attack on Jews, a pogrom, in the Rhineland. ("Why go to the Holy Land to kill non-Christians when we have some right in our midst? And I owe them money.") Eventually rulers expelled Jews from most of Western Europe, and areas to the east (especially modern Poland and Russia) became home to the Jews. While Jews were permitted to return to Western countries centuries later, their numbers there never were as significant as in Eastern Europe.

Jews, like others, emigrated, and in the years after 1890, many headed to the United States. Again, they settled largely in the cities and yet again, the religion and practices kept them apart. Not a proselytizing religion (though converts are usually welcome), Judaism today in the United States has several strands, including Orthodox, Conservative and to Reform (the differences largely existing in practices). Estimates of numbers in the United States are in the area of 6 million.

**Muslims.**

Mohammad (571 – 632 C.E.), an Arab merchant, had a series of revelations after age 40 which provides the basis of Islam, meaning "submission to the will of God." These revelations became the Qu'ran (Koran in older usage) and constitute Islam's holy book. Not divine in any way, Mohammad was a prophet in the tradition of the Hebrew Bible/Old Testament and claimed his revelations were a continuation of that work. Claiming the faith was descended from Abraham, he included Jesus as a prophet.

Compared to Christianity, the doctrine and theology of Islam are simple and relatively unambiguous. Allah, the name usually given the deity, means "God" and is monotheistic—no issues of the Trinity here. The life of the believer is built upon five pillars: belief in Allah, prayer five times a day while facing the holy city of Mecca, fasting during daylight in the holy month of Ramadan, giving alms to the poor, and undertaking a pilgrimage to Mecca. Various dietary rules, prohibitions on gambling and drinking, restrictions on the dress of women, and the absence of representational art are perhaps the most noticed aspects of the faith by non-Muslims. Holy wars are sanctioned and seen as a way to gain entry to a heavenly afterlife.

Lacking an organized priesthood and therefore any strong institution like the church in Christianity, Islam fragmented early in its history. A dispute over who should rule the faithful after the death of Mohammad produced the Sunni and Shi'a groups. These two groups then divided further over other issues; today approximately 90 percent of Muslims are Sunnis. Sufism is a mystical aspect of Islam, and other subgroups exist, such as the Saudi Arabian Wahhabi who practice a strict version of the Sunni tradition. Just as various parts of Christianity became identified with certain countries, e.g., Italians and Irish as Roman Catholics, Swedes as Lutherans, Greeks as Orthodox, the various branches of Islam have ethnic identities. For instance, most Shi'a are concentrated in Iraq, Iran and Bahrain.

Islam's success began immediately. Within a century of Mohammad's death, Islam had spread by military conquest across Africa west to Spain and south to the sub-Saharan areas. Also central Asia and parts of India became Muslim. Today more than one billion people, about 20 percent of the world's population, are nominally Muslim, and they make up 1—2 percent of the U.S. population, i.e., between one and five million people.

## Interpretation. Again?

### What Does It Mean?

Once the issues of sources, copies, and translations are analyzed as seen in Chapter 10, the Thoughtful are still left with the question of interpretation. The idea scripture needs interpreting is by no means accepted by all Christians. After all, God's word is accessible to everyone, an attitude especially prominent among conservative Protestants. However, the Thoughtful know no text is self-interpreting, and various approaches have been developed over the years to understand scripture.

One metaphor to help understand various approaches reading the Bible is to visualize a blue summer sky with patches of white cumulus clouds drifting by. History is the blue sky and the other approaches are the clouds. Without the blue sky, the clouds make things overcast and indistinct. Each cloud therefore is part of the big picture, a picture given dimension and depth by the sky. So with scholarship. Sociological and literary criticisms, for instance, provide insight but all only make sense because of history. (Yes, the author is a historian.)

However, even historical explanations are interpretations. Facts are chosen; facts are omitted. Events are connected as causes. Motives are assigned. While historians are limited by the reality they uncover, the resulting historical writing should not be seen as scientific in the same sense as the law of gravity is scientific. Historians, like scientists, approach their material systematically and logically, but they are constantly dealing with unique occurrences, unlike most scientists. How events are mingled with probabilities and psychological understandings becomes the historian's product which, in essence, is a work of art. Certainly, it is a truth but whether it ever rises to Truth is doubtful. The Hebrew Bible/Old Testament and Christian scripture/New Testament don't even purport to be histories, though they contain history, so they can be variously interpreted.

Beyond a historical approach, analyses of the biblical text take many forms. An initial issue involves examining the myriad copies of a text we have, seeking the earliest and the best source of information: textual criticism. Given the variety of sources, copies, and translations, the task is considerably larger than those in the pew imagine. Once a scholar realizes how much variation there is in the texts, the possible interpretations become numerous; hence the search for the best.[12]

When the best text is settled upon, interpretation begins. Source criticism seeks to find written sources behind the text we now have. For instance, as discussed in Chapter 10 scholars have long thought the early books of the Hebrew Bible/Old Testament are composed from four earlier writings—writings identified by the name used for the deity, nature of the subject, place names, etc. Then redaction (editing) set in with numerous editions. In the Christian scripture/New Testament, the gospels of Matthew and Luke rely on Mark's gospel and Q, a collection of Jesus' sayings that hasn't survived in manuscript form, so these texts can be studied for their differences. For example, why are the beatitudes and the Lord's prayer separate in Luke (chs 6, 11) and joined in the sermon on the Mount in Matthew (chs 5, 6)? Matthew presented Jesus as the Messiah to a Jewish audience while Luke has Jesus as savior to all, including Gentiles. Different audiences, different themes, both using Mark and Q.[13]

Exegesis, the term scholars use for close analysis of a text, takes several forms, including thematic analysis, which is common in other reading the Thoughtful do regularly. Thus Luke, whose gospel's audience is the Gentile world, continues his story in Acts with a theme moving from Jerusalem to Rome, local to universal. Exegesis is, more or less, the literary criticism the Thoughtful have practiced in classes. While you thought the poem was about a vine on a tree, you learned it really was about relationships. The

---

[12] See, e.g., Christopher Tuckett, *Reading the New Testament: Methods of Interpretation* (Fortress, 1987), ch. 2.

[13] Bart Ehrmann, *The New Testament* (Oxford University Press, 2000).

Christian scripture/New Testament book of Revelation is really a metaphor about dealing with life under Roman rule in the years after 60 C.E., though today many Christians mistakenly interpret the book as one addressing the future. Genre analysis, also encouraged by the study of literature, means learning Huck Finn was a picaresque, not just a good story. Once a story is located in a genre, the interpretation follows easily, though not without contest. For instance, Genesis is filled with myths but they can be interpreted differently, depending on the theory used to analyze myth.

Form criticism, another method of closely examining text, particularly the gospels, involves looking at a small unit of text, the form it takes, and the type of situation in which it is used. The unites in the writings about Jesus, for instance, are categorized as miracle stories, pronouncement stories, parables, sayings, and so on. This approach lets the scholar look at structure and by comparing various gospels tease out possibilities of authorial "creativity."[14] Related to this is contextual work, putting a person or event in the historical setting of the day. For example, miracles became something done by charismatic individuals generally in the first century C.E.

Other literary approaches examine organization styles. Mark often uses a sandwich style (intercalation) to make a theological point. He starts with one story, interrupts it with a second which he tells in full, and then returns to finish the first. (e.g., 3:20 – 35; 11:12 – 21) Luke stops to show how an event fits a divine plan (e.g., 4:43; 24:7; Acts 1:16.)[15] Foreshadowing, a favorite literary device, occurs in Luke 4:1 – 13 when Jesus' destiny is laid out before he started his public life. This organization was also a common style in ancient biographies.[16]

Metaphor has long been a favored interpretation. As early as the third century Origen (c.185 – c.254) used it extensively and his approach was very popular in the Middle Ages. In the parable of the Good Samaritan (Luke 10:30 – 7)—a traveler is mugged and two religious leaders walk by him but a despised foreigner provides help—here the obvious theme is a person should

---

[14] Gerd Theissen and Annette Merz, *The Historical Jesus* (Fortress, 1998), 288.

[15] Robert W. Funk et al, *The Five Gospels* (Polebridge, 1993), 276.

[16] Funk et al., *The Five* Gospels, 278.

help those in need regardless of nationality or religious differences. Origen had no difficulty with that interpretation but he provides an allegorical one that may amaze the Thoughtful:

> The man who was going down is Adam. Jerusalem is paradise, and Jericho is the world. The robbers are hostile powers. The priest is the Law, the Levite is the prophets, and the Samaritan is Christ. The wounds are disobedience, the beast is the Lord's body.... And further, the two *denarii* mean the Father and the Son. The manager of the stable is the head of the Church, to whom its care has been entrusted. And the fact that the Samaritan promises he will return represents the Savior's second coming.[17]

Later, in the Middle Ages, interpretations were formalized in what was called the *quadriga* referring to the literal, allegorical, tropological (moral) and anagogical, which allows lots of possibilities. Since the Reformation, most scholars have been more restrained. The Thoughtful should be thankful.

More recently sociological approaches have been used, with mixed results. Thus, Paul's letters convey the wide social makeup of the Corinthian group: slaves, women, the wealthy, etc. The risk of relying too heavily on these sociological approaches, which look at groups, not individuals, arises from the assumption people are basically alike despite the 2000 year separation. Looking at religions today, the wealthier are more skeptical today, ergo, it was so in the first century. But cults attract the wealthier and as Christianity early on was a cult, it actually prospered among the prosperous.[18] The knowledge the evidence for early membership is too sparse to support any conclusion at all is irrelevant as the theory is in place. Sociological analysis, moreover, often fades into the historical.

---

[17] Homily 34 found in Joseph T. Lienhard, *Origin: Homilies on Luke; and, Fragments on Luke* in *The Fathers of the Church* 94 (Catholic University of America Press, 1996), 138.

[18] Rodney Stark, *The Rise of Christianity: A Sociologist Reconsiders History* (Princeton University Press, 1996), 37, 46.

An example of all these possibilities comes from the Exodus story which has received lots of attention from scholars who limit themselves to the ancient writings and ignore archaeology. They divide the epic into parts, according to different writings from different periods. Form criticism further breaks down the story into more basic elements of folk tale, myth, ritual rules, songs, and so on. Thus, Moses, found in a basket in the Nile, corresponds to stories elsewhere; remember Romulus and Remus? And Sargon, a Mesopotamian king in the third millennium, had a similar origin.[19] The reality of the Exodus story may clash with an image the Thoughtful have from the 1950s movie epic *The Ten Commandments*, in which the Israelites pour through the Red Sea by the thousands, a veritable army. An alternative image might show a handful of escaping slaves scampering across the desert. This interpretation does not deal with the possibility the story is "really" about escape from bondage, pure metaphor.

With this background the Thoughtful can begin to appreciate the big themes of the Bible. The final editors of the historical and quasi-historical books of the Hebrew Bible/Old Testament—Joshua through Nehemiah in the Christian scripture—produced a grand synthesis, called the Deuteronomistic history, which covers the period from the appearance of kings to their failure in the face of foreign conquerors. The theme is kings prospered, as did their kingdoms, when they obeyed and honored God; things went badly when they didn't. All very rational. With the destruction of the southern kingdom of Judah and the transportation of many, perhaps most, of the Israelites into Babylon—the Exile—a new theme emerged. During the time in exile, priests constructed a story set in the period before the kings, beginning with Saul and David, that seems to be tragedy after tragedy: the expulsion from Eden, the Problems of Cain and Abel, the failure of the Tower of Babel, the exile in Egypt, the 40 years of wandering, and much more, ending at the edge of the Promised Land. However, these tragedies are mitigated; the focus remains on God demonstrating continued concern by providing the Israelites with a means to show their loyalty by practicing various ceremonial laws,

---

[19] Carol A. Redmount, "Bitter Lives: Israel in and out of Egypt," in Michael D. Cogan (ed.), *The Oxford History of the Biblical World*, (Oxford University Press, 1998), 82-6.

purity regulation and dietary rules, all under the guidance of (who else?) the priests.

The Christian scripture/New Testament is, like the Hebrew Bible/Old Testament, a collection of several varieties of writings: works that look like biographies but aren't, letters to early followers of Jesus, miscellaneous writings, and an apocalypse. They present several views of Jesus, his message, and the consequences of his death. Large numbers of contemporaneous writings are not included so the selection itself was a matter of interpretation.

Within the Christian scripture/New Testament the gospels receive the most focus. Each evangelist wrote his story of Jesus for a different audience, with a different intention, in the different context, and using a different understanding of his subject. Mark, believing the end time was near, wrote for a non-Jewish audience, and saw Jesus as a man, a suffering man. Matthew wrote for a Jewish audience, showing how Jesus fulfilled much of Jewish scripture; Matthew presented Jesus as the Messiah (something Jesus probably would not have done—too dangerous) and the culmination of Jewish tradition. Luke's audience was non-Jewish, therefore, pagan-like aspects such as the virgin birth and the Holy Spirit fathering Jesus were acceptable. For Luke, Jesus resembled a Hebrew Bible/Old Testament prophet. By the time John wrote his gospel, Jesus had become divine for many, which John addresses. Moreover, Jesus' followers were excluded from the synagogues which led John to include some anti-Jewish sentiments. The exorcisms stories had faded from John's writing since they could be seen as putting Jesus in league with the devil. The world changed over the decades when the gospels were composed: a Jewish revolt failed, the Temple was destroyed, the end time didn't occur, maybe persecution happened, and Jesus' message had more appeal to Gentiles than Jews. Each gospel responded to some or all of these changes and presumably so did Jesus' followers. The view of Jesus moved from a martyred man to a divine figure.

These interpretations are not universally accepted and myriad other possibilities exist, some very basic, some not. If the Bible recorded Jesus sat at a table to eat, it is possible the witness to that event got it wrong (people usually reclined on a couch to eat) or a copyist or translator made a mistake.

However, sitting or reclining doesn't seem significant to Jesus' life or message, or Christian history. Likewise, when Jesus used the term "Kingdom of God," problems arise for us. "Kingdom of God" had several meanings to his fellow Jews at the time, but as Jesus spoke Aramaic, it comes to us translated first to Greek, then to English, and in both languages the choice of word rendered "Kingdom" has several possibilities including kingdom, rule, reign, and sovereignty. Moreover, each of these words has different connotations to every reader/listener, which may change over time and in different cultures. For Protestants, attempting to recover Jesus' meaning is paramount, whereas Roman Catholicism and Orthodoxy also accept tradition in thinking about the same term; both approaches are valid, and maybe partial.

Interpretation unites and divides Christianity and is contentious. As traditions have emerged, perhaps participating in, and furthering, a tradition is all the Thoughtful believer can hope for. To many Christians—particularly Roman Catholics spring to mind—the tradition encapsulates the Truth. That tradition might change; it is different today or a year ago or a millennium ago is acceptable as it has a kernel that endures even though that kernel may be indefinable. Similarly for those in the Orthodox tradition. The difficult group is the Protestants. With their constant reference to the Bible, not any accumulated tradition based upon the Bible, Protestants are seeking an individual Truth but one they want to share with, or impose on, others. Their Truth is essentially individual, not corporate, and like political Truth, it is always debatable.

Within the last two decades, at the same time the search for the historical Jesus has been a major activity, others have turned to a literary search. Scholars have looked for the big themes, examining metaphors for personal understanding. This approach has the same rewards, and risks, the Thoughtful experienced when studying a novel or poem. Reflecting on the work of developmental psychologists, the Thoughtful can understand the believer takes away various truths—truths applicable to the individual and the group. How to live one's life, dealing with ups and downs, belonging to society, are all insights Christianity offers. All these interpretations do not necessarily challenge faith, but they may challenge belief in certain aspects of that faith. The idea a Thoughtful believer suspects other traditions, not just Christianity, offer the same results need not be unsettling but liberating.

Those in the pews are largely unaware of all these matters because the sermon or homily they hear doesn't delve into such matters. Rather, scripture is used differently. A common approach, especially for dealing with non-scholars—begins with Jesus' words and their historical context, distills the gospels for common themes and ideas, brings in history and philology, then hermeneutics and exegesis.[20] Along the way this can result in a text that means one thing to an author and a time and another thing to us today. This is a common preaching device where a biblical story is told and then retold in order to apply to the person in today's pew. It also lets the preacher avoid the problem of whether the story factually took place. The idea the Bible has some big themes is rarely discussed, at least explicitly, and most who have read the Bible straight through (more people than the Thoughtful can imagine) did not read it with an eye to discerning those themes.

## The Thoughtfuls' Obstacle. Literalism.

Now, armed with the foregoing, let's beat up on literalism as it is so popular—and annoying—today. Literalism takes on the look of an ideology in that it overrides whatever facts challenge the belief. Moreover, when a Thoughtful points out a problem with literalism, an inconsistency, biblical or otherwise, the response of the literalist typically is "Oh, that's different." Analogies and slippery slope arguments are beyond the comprehension of some.

A major problem confronts all readers, not just literalists (but literalists are more likely to be ignorant of or choose to ignore) which is there is no "original" text, as discussed in Chapter 10. Our oldest full text of the Hebrew Bible/Old Testament, the Masoretic, dates from about 1000 C.E. We also have copies of the Greek version, the Septuagint, but they differ among themselves, and the Samaritans have their own version. The 1940s discovery of the Dead Sea Scrolls, which date from 225 B.C.E. to 70 C.E., revealed

---

[20] Preaching isn't as complicated as this sounds. It is a common saying among preachers that preaching is all story-telling.

significant variety in the texts of the Hebrew Bible/Old Testament. How to be certain in face of so much uncertainty? Many, perhaps most, literalists in the United States focus on the King James version of the Bible, published in 1611. In that translation, the Christian scripture/New Testament portion was based on earlier, but inferior, versions. And we now know the Masoretic Text of the Hebrew Bible/Old Testament differs from the Septuagint and Samaritan versions. Today, the earlier scholars find the more variety in both sections of the Bible; put simply, there is no "original" Bible.

Many learned Bible stories in Sunday school taught by someone's mother or a nun who had in turn learned them as a child in a similar manner. Thus many cling to stories that introduced them to Christianity as children. (At about the same time as learning about the Bible many children were also taught that reproduction involved a stork. Later learning other possibilities existed means no one ever had to say the stork story was hooey.) As this example shows, early in their lives Christians developed an adjustment to explaining information according to the knowledge level or age of the listener—accommodation—and the practice continues. Every Sunday many pastors and priests talk about many topics; however, listeners usually pay no attention to what is being omitted: the stories are not literally true in a factual sense.

The preceding discussions of psychology have suggested why some people find literalism attractive. However, nothing in the Bible itself claims a literal reading is necessary, and even the idea the human writers of the Bible were "divinely inspired" is not biblical.[21] While some language such as "Thus says the Lord" can be found, usually in the prophetic books, its purpose was to lend authority to the speaker, not imply everything was from the Lord's mouth. The strongest scripture that might support literalism is 2 Timothy 3:16: "Every scripture is inspired by God and is useful for teaching, for showing mistakes, for correcting, and for training character…."(CEB) While that epistle is attributed to Paul, it is almost certainly by someone else, ironically; moreover, the Greek for that verse is awkward.

---

[21] James L. Kugel, *The Bible as It Was* (Harvard University Press, 1997), 22.

Within two centuries of Jesus, Origen wrote in his *First Principles* literalism was sometimes impossible. A "spiritual truth was often preserved …in the material falsehood."[22] To him, and others such as Tertullian, who also wrote in the third century, the Bible is the *word* of God, not the *words* of God; clearly metaphors are included. The emphasis on "belief" might be misplaced; perhaps it should be equated with "truth" "or faith" (the Greek can be translated either way). Literalists' worship of the Bible verges on idolatry, so venerated is the text.

Words can be ambiguous, not only in the way discussed above as changing meaning over time but in that listeners hear different things. Funeral services often include a phrase such as "She's with the saints now." Some listeners hear she's in heaven, others hear she's just like all other dead people and will soon be pushing up daisies. As another example, the Thoughtful know well children hear words differently than parents, to the frustration of both. And with some creative reading, things can be discovered the Thoughtful would never have thought were there, as when the Trinity (an idea the church developed in the centuries after Jesus) was found in Genesis, hundreds of years after it was written.[23]

Customs vary across cultures. Literalists often assume the past is just like today. Christian practice today portrays Jesus as dying on a Friday with the resurrection occurring on a Sunday. By some texts, Jesus predicted he would rise on the third day, by our reckoning this day would be Monday. Literalists should have a problem here but don't. (Jews counted both the first and last day when they said three days, hence Sunday.)

Inconsistencies in the Bible pose the greatest problem for literalists; of course with some really creative wriggling they ignore these contradictions, at least to their satisfaction. The internal inconsistencies are most prevalent in the Christian scripture/New Testament where four authors tell more or

---

[22] Origen, *Commentary of John*, 10.4.

[23] Finding the Trinity in Genesis involves some dubious reasoning about the name of the deity, Elohim. Some find this to be a plural, hence the Trinity, whereas most scholars think it can be singular or plural and need not even mean "God" but also angels or holy ones.

less the same story. But problems exist throughout the Bible. What follows is only a sample of the many problems:

- Exactly how did the world get created? Was it by God's word (Genesis 1), by God's actions (Genesis 2), or after a fight between God and sea-dragons (Psalms 74:12 – 7)?
- Was Adam created from a clay doll and Eve created from his rib (Genesis 2:7 and 21)? Or were they created simultaneously in some vague way (Genesis 1:27)?
- When Noah took animals into the ark, did he take them by twos (Genesis 6:19 – 20) or by sevens (Genesis 7:2 – 3)?
- Who killed Golaith? 2 Sam. 21:19 says Elhanon.
- The genealogy of Joseph, Jesus' father, differs in two gospels (Matthew 1; Luke 3). Why does it matter if Jesus was not conceived by a human father?
- The names of the twelve disciples are reported differently (Matthew 10, Mark 3, Luke 6).
- Did Jesus throw the moneychangers out of the Temple at the beginning of his public life (John 2) or near the end (Mark 11, Matthew 21)?
- Did Jesus heal a blind man before entering Jericho (Luke 18:35, 19:1) or after entering Jericho (Mark 10:46).
- Did Jesus die on Passover (Mark, Matthew, Luke) or the day before Passover (John)?
- Did Jesus ascend into heaven on Easter night (Luke 24:50 – 1) or forty days later (Acts 1:3, 9)? Luke wrote both his gospel and Acts.

Literalists are aware of these problems and have worked long and hard to reconcile them. For instance, they posit when two stories conflict, aforementioned in the first two points above, the first states a general principle and the second provides an example. The name problem of the disciples is solved by giving men two names; that was not the Jewish practice of the day, but literalists would answer one cannot be sure until you know the names of every Jew alive then. (Thus, enters the old problem of proving a negative.) Jesus cleared the Temple two or maybe three times.

Literalists often know some science and history but do not use them like the Thoughtful would. The idea DNA "deteriorates" over the generations explains why today we do not live the long lives of hundreds of years like some of the Genesis characters. An occasional Philistine might have lived on the Mediterranean coast in 2000 so the patriarch Abraham could have dealt with him (Genesis 21:32) even though most scholars think the Philistines arrived much later and also doubt Abraham is a historical figure. Archaeological excavations at Jericho have shown the location was deserted or was populated or was deserted when the Joshua stories are set (each dig improves on its predecessor) so one picks the dig that supports tumbling walls.

A related problem arises when literalists apply the Bible to contemporary times. Thus, some read Revelation to foretell the end of the world, which will be connected to a cavalry of horses. This part of the work has required constant reinterpretation as those horses have been seen as metaphors for the Chinese, the Russians, and most recently, Muslims. (A significant number—one in five—of Americans think Jesus will return within 50 years. Millenarians usually think the end will occur in their lifetimes—fairly arrogant, some would say.)

A curious effort to deal with some problems in Genesis produced a view called "Pre-Adamite." As Genesis frequently makes reference to humans who have not been mentioned or even created yet (Whom did Cain marry? The mark put on Cain protected him from whom?), the solution posited people existed before Adam, and the Bible only describes Jewish history. This solution helped explain the beginnings in Genesis; there were two creations, one for Jews, another for Gentiles. This view was popular after the seventeenth century when scholars began providing troublesome evidence of early peoples.

External inconsistencies, when the Bible disagrees with what we know from other sources, are a bit rarer.

- The Queen of Sheba came to visit King Solomon from a faraway land, a story found in 1 Kings 10:1 – 13 and 2 Chronicles 9:1 – 12. That land is usually identified as Yemen, but that country did not exist until the eighth century B.C.E. whereas Solomon' existence is dated to the tenth century.

- Mary and Joseph were on the road when Jesus was born because they were responding to a command from the Roman Emperor Augustus that all people in the Roman world should be registered, a census (Luke 3). Historians can find no evidence that Augustus ever ordered such a census. A local Roman official, Quirinius, did order a census but it was ten years after Herod's death. Anyway, it was not the practice to report to one's ancestor's home. And who would take a pregnant woman?
- Geography poses some challenges. When Jesus casts out some demons at Gerasa (Mark 5:1 – 20), the demons move into some pigs which run down the hill to the Sea of Galilee, which in fact is 30 miles from Gerasa. Tired pigs.

These external inconsistencies prove less difficult to literalists because they can simply say historians haven't learned enough rather than accept the notion the Bible got it wrong. Turns out there were dinosaurs on Noah's ark, according to some. At the extreme, some make God into a trickster by arguing what appears to be an inconsistency is simply material created to test one's faith, i.e., God expects you to accept something your reason rejects. On the other hand, such folk find confirmation of their approach whenever the Bible does agree with external events, e.g., the fall of Nineveh in 612 B.C.E. exists in the Bible and other records. They get to have it both ways.

Another solution to addressing these inconsistencies is to pick and choose texts to make a point—quarrying. For example, regarding women preachers, shows the willingness to strain to get to the result one seeks. From the beginning of Christianity, the leaders of the church did not permit women to be ordained as clergy. One basis for this practice is Paul's letter to the group at Corinth where he writes "Let your women keep silence in the churches" (1 Corinthians 14:34 – 5). Pretty clear. However, if a woman seeks to preach, she cites the Hebrew Bible/Old Testament woman Deborah as a leader (Judges 4:4 – 5). How are literalists to settle the conflict? The woman pastor says Paul was only directing the Corinthians, which would mean, unfortunately for Christian history, all of Paul's writings could be dismissed as directed to local issues of his day. Another solution would be to say this part of Paul does not govern today, just as biblical injunctions prohibiting divorce and remarriage do not prevent many from divorcing and remarrying, but that solution raises the problem of deciding what does govern today. (The Thoughtful might say Paul was a creature of his time and place, when men had all the public roles; as society changed, his words continually need to be interpreted in new settings.) This particular instance has produced some irony. The Roman Catholic Church and the Church of England, churches which contain many of the theologians who have moved the farthest from literalism, cling hardest to the tradition of not ordaining women, whereas the more fundamentalist Protestant churches, which are the biggest defenders of literalism, often have women pastors.[24]

Homosexuality offers another instance of literalist selectivity. For those who see homosexuality as wrong the accepted basis is Leviticus 18:22 and 20:13. (Other anti-gay cites are Genesis 19:5, Romans 1:26 – 7, 1 Corinthians 6:9.) First problem: this text doesn't deal with lesbianism. Secondly, bundled with this statement in Leviticus are others banning the trimming one's beard (19:27), getting a tattoo (19:28), and mixing fabrics in a garment (10:10).

And literalism occasionally goes out the window when the Hebrew Bible/Old Testament book entitled "The Song of Solomon" must be confronted. Scholars see it as a love song between a man and a woman, perhaps for a wedding, and puzzle about why it was included in the sacred canon anyway. Literalists have to stretch a bit and describe it as an allegory about

---

[24] Terms in this discussion are often used loosely. Literalism and fundamentalism are not identical ; the basics of fundamentalism are the virgin birth, factual accuracy of miracles, substitutionary atonement, the bodily resurrection, and a second coming. Not all fundamentalists are literalists but probably most are. When approaching scripture, many use the term "inerrant" to describe it. However, that word has many levels of usage: some say scripture contains no errors in statements of faith and practice, others say it has no false statements on anything, still others argue that any errors are human in origin due to copying and translation.

Jesus' love for the church. The language is, well, risqué. The Anchor Bible translates part of chapter 7 as follows:

> Your curvy thighs like ornaments
> Crafted by artist hands.
> Your vulva a rounded crater:
> May it never lack punch!

Steamy stuff, huh? Doesn't really sound like an allegory about Jesus' love for the Church, does it?

Sometimes the literalist imagination seems to have no bounds to justify present desires. When drink became a major social problem in nineteenth-century America and temperance reformers sought biblical support, they developed the "two-wine theory" by which all positive references were to grape juice and negative ones to wine. Another example is when the book of Acts describes several times the sharing of goods in common (Acts 2:44 – 5, 4:34 – 5:11) and the latter citation has a nasty end for those who do not share. Not much support for capitalism there. And, finally, how can literalists reject the earth as the center of the solar system when the Church long supported that idea based upon Genesis 1:14 – 8 and Ecclesiastes 1:5?

What's going on here? Literalists have several fears. The strongest, is once any part of the Bible is decided not to be literally true, where will it all stop? If the Flood did not occur, did God not create the world as told in Genesis? And Jesus did not exist? If parts of the gospels are inaccurate, can we trust anything reported about Jesus? Also people need rules to guide, control, their behavior. If we open up the Bible to questioning, where will it all end? Moral chaos will break out.

Another concern connects with science. Much "old-time" religion isn't all that old; it actually gathered much of its force in the nineteenth century when people reacted to the discoveries of science (and much more than just Darwin's theory of evolution). It was (and still is) easier to reject science that one doesn't understand, than lose the cherished biblical Truth, literalism.

Not surprisingly, literalism today correlates with lower social class and less educational achievement. The Thoughtful suspected as much.

As literalists are typically dualists, as discussed above, and think they have Truth. It is not a big stretch for some of them to believe they are "superior" to those who don't share their Truth. This attitude has been part of the force behind overseas missions, bringing Truth to benighted (usually nonwhite) heathens, and at home may let those further down the socioeconomic scale feel above their "betters." ("We have Truth, and heaven, and you, sorry millionaire, don't.") This feeling of superiority is captured satirically in a song by the Austin Lounge Lizards, "Jesus loves me, but he can't stand you."

Rabbinical Judaism has never worried much about literalism. While children studied the Torah, they moved on to the Mishnah and eventually the Talmud, both interpretative overlays of the Torah. Similarly Roman Catholics have not worried the issue, letting the tradition of the church deal with the problems. It is only Protestants, and certain Protestants at that, who are exercised by the matter.

## Details, Details.

### Dates.

Putting events and people in sequence is relatively simple and agreed upon by scholars. Exact dates can be a bit more problematic though not terribly important. Nothing is certain before 1250 B.C.E. as no other culture or literature mentions biblical events or Israelites. The Exodus, if it occurred, happened around 1250 B.C.E., and David and Solomon ruled in the tenth century. After 900 B.C.E., scholars, relying on the Hebrew Bible /Old Testament and some records of other cultures, have pieced together a relatively complete chronology. Nevertheless, the dates should not be taken as precise.

For instance, in the 1980s and 1990s Martin Bernel published in two volumes, *Black Athena*, arguing for greater Egyptian influence in the Eastern

Mediterranean than other scholars accept. According to his dates, events often occurred three quarters of a century earlier than the conventional chronology, but his dating is not widely accepted.

As we move to the period after Jesus' birth—called the Common Era (C.E.)—the dates used today originated in the early seventh century. Dionysius Exiguus correlated Roman events with Christian origins. He seems to have gotten it wrong by a few years. Thus the flap a few years ago over Y2K because some thought great things would happen 2000 years after Jesus' birth was misplaced; the two millennia anniversary had occurred a few years earlier.

While some dates in early Church history are less than firm, the sequence is generally agreed upon, and after, say, 1000 C.E., historians are comfortable with both dates and sequencing of events.

In other words, don't get excited about this matter. (See Chronology in the Appendix.)

**Names.**

In the Hebrew Bible/Old Testament various names are applied to the deity. Early on "El," an ancient Semitic name, was soon joined by "Yahweh," an extrapolation of YHWH (Hebrew used no vowels in writing). Yahweh was not to be said aloud so circumlocutions appeared: the Lord, the Holy One. Elohim, a variation of El and God of Abraham (an early figure), and other similar titles appeared as well. In the sixteenth century C. E. "Jehovah" became a common usage. This is the deity Christians call "God" and Muslims "Allah." The deity, in the Hebrew Bible/Old Testament, used "I am" as the name (Exodus 3:14) which can be interpreted many ways. "God is" would suggest being or existence or the root is the verb "to be"—the Thoughtful who have studied a foreign language recognize the centrality of that verb in its many permutations.

Today, most Thoughtful give thought to names only when a baby's birth is imminent, and the original meaning of names is lost. No one hears "Renee" and thinks "reborn" (though hearing "Allen" might bring to mind "handsome"). Similarly in the Bible, many names have meanings lost on the modern listener's ear. "Adam" probably means "human being" and also sounds a lot like "ground" (from which he was made). "Jacob" means "heel" as he was a twin, born holding his older brother's heel. "Moses," in Egyptian means "son of" and in Hebrew it is related to the phrase "he who draws out," as in Moses "drew out" the Israelites from Egypt or he was "drawn out" of the water as a baby.. And so it is with the origins of many names in the early parts of the Hebrew Bible/Old Testament. (Maybe if translators left these names in their real meaning, people would be less likely to take the stories literally.)

"Jesus," a Greek variation of Yeshua or Joshua, was a given name, meaning "he shall save" or "God is with us." In life he was referred to as "Jesus of Nazareth." After his death, the appellation "Messiah" ("Christ" in Greek and meaning "anointed") was added and became virtually a last name. "Lord," "Savior," "Son of man," "Son of God," "Lamb of God," and others which have theological content have also been used.

**Geography.**

The bulk of the events in the Bible occurred in Palestine, an area less than 200 miles north to south, and 50 miles east to west, approximately the size of Vermont or the metropolitan San Francisco Bay area. Egypt, which sometimes ruled the area and was the source of the Exodus story, was 300 miles away. Once Christianity reached Rome, it had traveled 1500 miles. The medieval events, popes, kings, monks, occurred from Ireland to Poland to the Mediterranean, an area only a little larger than the United States east of the Mississippi.

"Palestine" came from the Greeks who named the area after the Philistines who occupied the coastal plain in early times. Today, the state of Israel controls most of the area involved in the scripture stories. Palestine's terrain is hilly, mountainous by some definitions, and was a bit more verdant in biblical times. While the Mediterranean coastline appears prominently in maps, that body of water played little part in the Hebrew Bible/Old Testament or Jesus' story. The southerly flowing Jordan River is the eastern boundary of much activity with lots of the action in the hill country immediately to its west.

When the action shifted to Europe, Italy was separated by the Alps from the plains of northern France and Germany. The waters of the English Channel and the Irish Sea isolated the rolling countryside of England and Ireland from events on the Continent.

Things moved slower in the past. Water travel, perhaps riskier in terms of weather, was faster and easier; hence the importance of the Mediterranean and the great rivers, Rhine, Rhone, and Thames. Land travel and the movement of armies were slow enough rebellions and heresies had time to do their mischief before the authorities could react. The geographically isolated peoples hindered effective government and also meant famine could occur near abundance. The geography is a backdrop to the story of Christianity but rarely important.

*The Trinity*

# THREE

# *Basics*

This chapter grazes the surface of some very deep questions. Some of the issues would qualify under the title "theology," but so to label them can be intimidating to the Thoughtful. After all, thinkers have been discussing Christian theology for at least 1700 years and haven't reached consensus (and never will). That information should be a hint to the Thoughtful that many of the issues in this chapter have several answers. What follows, therefore, is an overview that hints at the complexities.[1] That "introductory" theology textbooks easily run over 400 pages indicates how much one could easily write about such matters. Many find theology, the study of God, to be irrelevant, wishing instead to focus on obedience to God; even then, however, arguments that are theological can break out. To each his or her own.

In matters theological, the main eras were the years from 300 to 500 C.E. and the Reformation of the sixteenth century.[2] The years 300—500 C.E. saw the integration of Greek thought into the Jewish religious outlook of the early followers of Jesus. Most of that blending occurred in the

---

1 "Theology," the study of God or gods, has expanded in Christianity to embrace the totality of Christian doctrine. It is not clear that things have progressed much; maybe the best definition of God is that of the eleventh-century monk, Anselm.

2 Christian theological debate didn't really get underway until the Roman Emperor Constantine converted in the fourth century. Before that, Christians, while not constantly persecuted, had other matters with which to concern themselves.

eastern Mediterranean where Greek culture was stronger. Slowly, the eastern and western areas of the Mediterranean diverged, not only politically after Diocletian established a two-emperor governance system, but also religiously as the East was more philosophically inclined than the Latin West. Eventually the differences resulted in a more formal division, often dated to 1054 C.E., when the Western, Catholic tradition and the Eastern, Orthodox tradition parted ways.

The early period hammered out numerous creeds, minimal statements of beliefs, that still form the basis of Christianity, although disagreements over those creeds led to the formation of several religious traditions, traditions that still exist today. The Reformation of the sixteenth century did not revisit those creeds but, as the various groups (which become called "denominations") struggled over truth, they composed "confessions" which are much longer and more detailed than the creeds. (The Nicene Creed is a little over 200 words, while the Belgic Confession of many Reformed denominations runs more than 9,000 words.)

## The Big Question. God.

### God's Existence.

Let's get this one out of the way right away.

Can you prove God exists? No.

Can you prove God doesn't exist? No.[3]

And it's not for lack of trying that both questions have negative answers as logicians and theologians have tackled the matter century after century. To confuse things further, are we talking about a creator God, a vengeful God, a loving God, a judging God, all of the foregoing, or something else? The Thoughtful will recognize this is an area where premises are the important thing in the argument as a conclusion may be forced by the premise. So, beware.

---

[3] Richard Dawkins in *The God Delusion* (Houghton Mifflin, 2008), ch. 4 seeks to show that the existence/nonexistence issue is not 50-50 but heavily in favor of nonexistence.

Non-believers point to the lack of proof of the existence of God, further supporting their argument by listing all the evils and horrors that have occurred, and still exist, as well as the atrocities committed in the name of God. These facts might be evidence a loving God doesn't abide anywhere though it would also be consistent with the existence of a nasty deity.

Believers have answered the question with a variety of arguments. The oldest comes from Anselm, a French monk who later became the Archbishop of Canterbury, in the eleventh century whose argument is called an "ontological" one. He proposed God is the greatest, biggest, most powerful, most everything thing we can think of ("that than which no greater can be conceived") because if we could think of something greater, bigger, more powerful, that thing would be God. The Thoughtful will recognize this problem may be a matter of semantics: we can think of God so God must exist. Does the argument also apply to unicorns? An *a priori* argument, the conclusion proceeds from the premise.

A somewhat related argument derives from the empirical observation that people everywhere and at all times have believed in a deity or deities. *Ergo* a deity or deities must exist. Easy objection: if people all thought the world was flat, would that position make it true?

Today, an argument with traction, especially among the unThoughtful, is based on examining the wonderful way the world fits together. The various constants of equations in physics have to be exactly as they are or the world couldn't exist. Living things, including people, are so complex and interrelated so a master designer had to be at work to make them. Called "creationism" in one of its variants, this argument has a potential problem in that it looks like deism, in which a deity designs the clock, winds up the machine that is the world, and then takes a hike. Jesus as Christ fits awkwardly into this schema. Again, the premise—things are too complex to be "accidental"—contains the conclusion.

"First cause," also known as the "cosmological" argument, the name given to another approach, argues since the universe exists, something caused it. (Warning: that conclusion need not be true though the Thoughtful do tend to see cause and effect everywhere.) While, in Christian terms, this solution gives a creator God, it doesn't address the issue of a loving or judgmental deity.

A fourth argument proceeds from the existence of morality. If there are rules about right and wrong, then something had to make them. Presumably dogs and cats don't worry about morality, they just do dog-like and cat-like things: kill other animals, steal food, attack strangers, etc. So the existence of human morality argues for a God. The Thoughtful can easily suggest maybe we are just like dogs and cats and moral rules are evolutionarily advantageous for us to observe, just like parenting behavior is for animals.

Others give up on logic and declare God can only be experienced, not proven. Thus, many people believe they have personally felt God and they have seen how that experience changed them or others. Exactly what that experience was and whether others can participate is often an open question. To these folk logic is irrelevant; they know, because it happened to them. Whether real or delusional, the experience trumps logic. If reality is created by us, then God can be created, too?

Some might argue the Thoughtful have never seen a low-pressure area, in weather terms, but they accept the existence of same. Believers in such an area see swirls of clouds on radar, notice the arrow on the barometer heading down, and feel the rain on their parade—but a low-pressure area, no, they've never seen it. They just noticed the world seems to be better explained using low-pressure areas than an angry Olympian god hurling thunderbolts. Similarly with God: look at the effects, so the argument goes. (This is pretty much the position of the Roman Catholic Church in a catechism approved in 1990 by Joseph Cardinal Ratzinger, later Pope Benedict XVI.)

Obviously this section could run on, and on, and on, as people have spent their lives studying the topic and libraries have been filled with writings on the existence of God, but no idea has ever swept the field. Maybe it should be left that whatever or whoever produced the universe and living beings is beyond human inquiry. The Thoughtful will find some solace in knowing no one knows whether God exists or not, at least in ways the Thoughtful find definitive without personal experience.

**Thinking About God.**

The big trick when thinking about God is to escape our culture which relentlessly portrays God as a grandfather in the sky. Curiously, that image first appears in the Hebrew Bible/Old Testament in the Book of Daniel (7:9), written only a few hundred years before Jesus' birth. What probably sealed the image in many minds is Michelangelo's Sistine chapel ceiling depicting the bearded old fellow reaching out to give Adam life. Today, the most common location of such an image is in the comics pages of newspapers.

God's qualities are limitless, but a few have dominated Christian thought. An advertisement for a Roman Catholic Bible called it the Word of "the all-knowing, all-loving, all-powerful God," and perhaps the most common divine attribute is omnipotence, all powerful. After all, that quality and immortality are most common historical descriptions of gods. Omnipotence becomes problematic when the Thoughtful realize it means everything that occurs is ordered or permitted by God. Moreover, mercy is often a characteristic Christians ascribe to God which, when combined with omnipotence, makes evil and suffering incomprehensible. Omniscience is often an attribute of God. Again, when it is paired with omnipotence, God causes everything and knows everything, so we humans become creatures without true free will because God knows everything we're going to do (and maybe even causes it).

A possibility few Thoughtful have encountered is called "process theology," an idea associated with Charles Hartshorne and Alfred North Whitehead, two twentieth-century thinkers. In this view God is not immutable, omnipotent, or omniscient, but changes constantly in response to everything else. This approach is difficult for the Thoughtful but repays investigating, something beyond the scope of this book.

When these ideas are combined with the idea Jesus was God, things get murky. Did Jesus know everything? For instance, did he know modern science? Could he speak Japanese? Scholars are uncertain if he could even read as only one passage (Luke 4:16) reports him reading; remember, he was a peasant so schooling might be unlikely. If Jesus knew everything, he was God, not really a man. Since at least the fourth century, Christianity has taught he was a man. To believe he knew everything and was God only is called "docetism," Unfortunately for some, to pursue this line of argument leads to the conclusions Jesus did not know he was divine or he was the Son of God. This view comes close to seeing Jesus as a man who had especially strong and frequent experiences of the divine, and nothing more. When a theologian who accepted this approach was named the Archbishop of York and lightening promptly struck the transept of his cathedral, some saw the hand of God. The issue of Jesus' divinity greatly complicates thinking about God for Christians.

By now the Thoughtful are beginning to see the problem in definitions of God. Perhaps that result is why theologians write things such as "the ground of all being," "the beginning of creativity," "transcendent and immanent," "the mystery at the center of things," and so forth.

**Atheism.**

Today a literary debate rages between atheists, non-believers, and some Christians, largely conservative ones, about the existence of God.[4] The atheists' position is advanced by educated, many well-educated, people, often scientists. These are folk whom the Thoughtful find comfortable so their ideas get taken seriously. Unfortunately, their characterization of Christianity does not resemble what is being discussed in this book; as a result, such atheists seem to think it is impossible to be a Thoughtful believer.

Many atheists have had a passing relationship with Christianity, often as a child, so their vision is often a bit childlike or simplistic. One asks "What is the use of a God who does no miracles or answers no prayers."[5] Thus, God created the world (even if not in the Genesis version), controls things today, and later rewards (and maybe punishes). He (yes, it's usually he) sent his only son Jesus to Earth (shades of Zeus on Mt. Olympus or Yahweh on Mt. Sinai),

---

[4] The atheist authors include, among others, Daniel Dennett, Richard Dawkins, Sam Harris, and Christopher Hitchens. Philip Pullman, *The God Man Jesus and the Scoundrel Christ* (Canongate Books, 2007), 251, has an interesting take of the Jesus story by a self-described lapsed Anglican and a "thoroughgoing materialist."

[5] Dawkins, *The God Delusion,* 342-8.

called the "Incarnation," Jesus performed (unbelievable) miracles, died on the cross to save humanity from sin, and rose (bodily) three days later. Isn't all of this approach intellectually mediocre? While many Christians accept all these things, the Thoughtful realizes this book posits a Christianity that looks at these issues differently, often metaphorically, and most non-conservative Christian thinkers today pursue an unknowable deity, don't seek a set of dogmas, and engage in practice, not arguments about belief. (It is small comfort Islam takes lots of hits from atheists because of the violence of some of its followers. However, Christianity, historically, has sanctioned a fair amount of violence.)

Certainly most, perhaps all, denominations have people in the pews who are fundamentalists or literalists even if the pastor and hierarchy are very progressive, non-literalists. All comes back to the yes/no, either/or mentality discussed in chapter 2. What the religions (probably inadvertently) provide is a scripture that can be (selectively) read to permit or encourage extremism, such as murdering an abortion provider or bombing an abortion clinic. The Thoughtful would do well to consider this argument. Thoughtful believers, who are clearly not attracted to extremism, might ponder to what extent they are providing "cover" for actions they would find reprehensible.

**Evil.**

Why do bad things happen? And to good people? In a world controlled by a beneficent deity? These are questions every religious tradition seeks to answer but none ever disposes of to the complete satisfaction of all, especially those outside that tradition. Don't hold your breath for a resolution here either.

The basic problem raised by skeptics over the centuries involves the nature of God. As we don't want evil things happening, at least to us, we look to a deity for explanations of murder, disease, disaster, *etc.* In other words, God and evil are linked. If the deity can't prevent evil, then it is not all-powerful; if a deity is all-powerful but will not prevent evil, then how can that deity be good and just? Thus, evil's existence challenges the common notion of God. For instance, the seeming randomness of the incidence of evil was a major cause of the loss of faith in a Christian God by educated Europeans. When a gigantic earthquake destroyed Lisbon in 1755, many concluded that was just the way nature is. God had no part in it.

Maybe evil exists because humans have free will, the power to choose between right and wrong. One exit, therefore, from the problem of evil is predestination, the idea we do not have a choice because the universe is organized so that it just unfolds as fate would have it. This line of thought says while we think we are making choices, in reality we are merely acting out what was foreordained. Intellectually, the Thoughtful might find predestination attractive—it was popular for several hundred years after the Reformation—but we all act as though our choices do matter.

Another approach has been to redefine evil. Thinkers, over the years, have sometimes divided evil into natural (tsunami, cancer, hurricanes, etc.) and moral (lying, murder, theft, etc.) but that division only removes some of the evil from the equation and maybe even then not neatly. (Is a factory layoff a human issue or not; maybe it's a law of economics.) Watching a television nature show, the viewer gets to see lions catch and eat a zebra. Evil? While the viewer may cringe or offer sympathy to the zebra, the idea this is how nature works explains things. Why doesn't that logic apply to humans? Well, for one thing, we doubt zebras have a loving God to care for them. But then what evidence makes humans think they themselves do? However, to remove the all-good portion violates what many, perhaps most, people see as the benefit of Christianity.

Some religious traditions assert evil grows out of earlier lives while Christians often explain it as due to the disobedience of Adam and Eve or, in other words, human nature. While moral evil, the result of human choice, remained, it was explained as the result of ignorance, a part of history, economic law or psychological problems, *inter alia*. Events such as the Holocaust, Cambodia, and 9/11, continue to make Christians forced to deal with the problem of evil, but no satisfactory explanation has emerged.

As to God being all-powerful, a common divine quality, ancient Mesopotamians decided their gods were nasty folk. Lazy, the gods created humans to serve them. Suffering arose when the gods got to drinking and one made people with various deformities and others then decided to make a competition out of creating problems for humans. Not an attractive view but one that accounts for bad things and their irrational distribution among humanity. A Mesopotamian couldn't avoid evil but nevertheless attempted to placate the gods with sacrifices. And it keeps the gods as all-powerful.

Once a culture, such as the Israelites, settled on having only one God, religious life got better and worse. God, the guardian of their culture, meted out deserved punishments; God was judge, a just judge. Therefore, if evil occurred, the victim had done something to deserve it. Perhaps one failed to worship God correctly or transgressed some rule or law. This approach is the contract view of religion: you behave, you get rewards; you misbehave, bad things happen. And even if you behave, maybe one of your ancestors didn't, so vengeance comes down on you. Find the sin, repent, and all will be well, or at least better.

Unfortunately, bad things still happened to good people, and the Book of Job in the Hebrew Bible/Old Testament explored the issue. A piece of fiction written sometime between the sixth and third centuries B.C.E., the story of Job tells of a prosperous man in the tradition of the patriarchs with 7,000 sheep, 3,000 camels (that probably dates the story after about 600 when scholars think domesticated camels appeared), 500 yoke of oxen, 500 donkeys, and many slaves. Job becomes the unwitting victim of a discussion between God and Satan. God, meeting with his council of lesser gods (monotheism hadn't triumphed yet), brags about Job as a blameless and upright man. Satan, one of these lesser gods (not yet the name given to the devil) argues Job is good only because he has been so materially blessed. To prove Satan wrong, God proceeds to have Job's children killed and his possessions carried away. Job remained steadfast so he was then afflicted with sores all over his body; Job persevered. Next, three friends visit Job and tell him he must have done something wrong and therefore deserves his punishment. Job denies wrongdoing and eventually is reconciled to the unknowability of the divine. The moral of the story? Evil happens even when there is a just God, but Job continued to have trust in his incomprehensible deity. It's a mystery.

When priests began narrowing the panoply of gods into just a few, a god of evil usually survived. Mythologies often have a primeval struggle involving good and evil—in Egypt the bad god kept winning. For Augustine, a Roman Christian writing in the fifth century, evil was the absence of good but he did not explain why God permits such a void. A common response has been to conjure up an evil spirit or god, a Satan, a devil. (The idea God permits this rival, lesser though it is, is not easily explained. The argument all this evil is created to test an individual's worth is unsatisfactory; how would you view a parent who operated this way—beneficent, merciful, sadistic?) In the Christian tradition a god of evil keeps popping up despite officialdom's doctrine of monotheism. Satan, the devil, Lucifer, Old Nic are not very present in scripture but the creation of medieval minds and writers such as Dante and Milton. In standard Christian theology, only one God exists so a god of evil is out-of-bounds.

In 1710 C.E. Leibniz suggested God created the best of all possible worlds and evil is somehow necessary; other Deist thinkers argued God withdrew irrevocably from intervention in life as part of granting people free will. A more mysterious proposal, perhaps God permits evil as a means toward perfection of humans.[6] However, ordinary churchgoers have difficulty reconciling a God of love with bad things happening in life so the devil keeps reappearing. For instance, Billy Graham, a popular evangelical preacher but not a deep thinker, mentioned Satan in discussing why hurricane Katrina happened.

When it comes to the individual, the notion of personal salvation becomes very important. Obtaining this salvation wasn't always easy though it usually meant following the will of God—something a bit difficult to discern, hence the multiplicity of denominations—or else waiting for God to tell you that you are among the elect—something that seems to happen to almost everyone who thinks God acts this way. And some see the hand of God in many activities—rain, medical cures—though they are thrown back on Satan to

---

[6] Rejection of all these explanations by a philosopher working in the Christian tradition can be found in Marilyn McCord Adams, *Horrendous Evil and the Goodness of God* (Cornell University Press, 1999).

explain drought and disease, all of which trivializes both events and God. Jesus, in this view, often becomes a personal savior, almost a personal God.

Salvation is often connected with notions of an afterlife, and the idea of heaven provides one response to the problem to the complexities of evil. God is still loving but an afterlife extends things so a later reward compensates for present suffering. This notion developed at various times in various places. Ancient Egyptians had an afterlife based on a morality test as did Persian Zoroastrians. When Job's friends talked with him, none offered heaven as a solution because, as of the writing of Job, that concept hadn't been developed in Hebrew religion. When it did develop later, the Christian tradition picked it up early on. Besides helping deal with the issue of evil, it also had the advantage no one could show it was false so hope was there and evil mitigated.

Within this tradition, your problems—illness, death, job loss, etc.—could become a test. How well you endured or dealt with it helped determine your destination. Also, your example would help others understand things better, which has some logic to it but may not make you feel any better. It builds character. Or, it's a mystery. This line of reasoning led Marx to describe religion as "the opiate of the masses," the drug that keeps people from destroying their oppressors. The Thoughtful may not find this answer satisfactory but heaven gives hope, and endurance, to millions.

To take another tact, most of these arguments and problems are based upon the idea the world is about you, the Thoughtful. Perhaps it is about God. The ancient Mesopotamians thought they were put on Earth to serve the gods so evil and suffering were just the gods entertaining themselves. All one could do was try to bribe the gods with gifts and sacrifices in the hope one could avert disaster. Both the Hebrew Bible/Old Testament and Christian scripture/New Testament contain the idea that humans should seek to serve God. For instance, Calvinists, from the sixteenth century on, saw the purpose of life being to honor God, to do God's bidding in all things. Thus the fate of the individual was irrelevant—bad things do happen to good people—in the same way the death or injury of an ant or bee, while it may benefit the group, is of no concern. That idea doesn't explain suffering and evil so much as make them irrelevant. We play the cards we're dealt and that's all there is to it. We can try to obtain salvation—spiritual health, wholeness—but it will only help us roll with the punches, not avoid them. However, such a notion of salvation makes the punches a bit less painful as we're not trying to figure out "why me?" Satisfied? Perhaps not.

Shifting away from God as judge, Christianity often gives God loving, merciful, and compassionate attributes. However, Job's problem remains. How can a loving God permit evil and suffering? A loving parent's comfort and hug doesn't reduce the pain or blood of a skinned knee but does help the child feel better and the parent suffers also with the child. The image of a loving God doesn't avert evil but lets the sufferer know something or someone cares and also suffers when evil occurs; God doesn't cause suffering but can redeem it. For the Thoughtful, that idea is a big step away from the traditional image of God in the sky, supervising the world. (It also removes concern about sin as an offense to God as the source of evil; rather it is an offense to oneself and the world at large.) Often God's loving care is found in the response of other people to the sufferer, just as a parent's response is to a child. But even when no human comfort comes forward, the Thoughtful can reflect that a child's skinned knee can be endured a bit better knowing a parent, though not present, cares.

Satisfactory? Not entirely. Understandable? Yes. Got a better solution? Probably not, as no religion or philosophical system has a good answer. The knowledge the Thoughtful can't control the incidence of evil is a frustration but also a reality, just as zebras have no control over lions that hunt. With that knowledge, the Thoughtful can shift to concern with the response to evil and suffering, a response maybe made better if one is part of a group, be it family, club, or congregation.

## Truth. Thoughts Thereon.

### Truth With a Capital "T."

Truth is a complicated thing to the Thoughtful. Philosophers have made, and still make, a living from discussing "truth." Many hairs have been split and the results are difficult for the Thoughtful to understand or even attempt to follow. And, to make it worse, philosophers today have no agreed-upon definition of truth.

Christians confronted the problem when the gospel of John had Pontius Pilate, the Roman who ordered Jesus' execution, ask "What is truth?" (John 18:38) For purposes herein Truth (capital T) means one of those statements people always and everywhere accept as valid, probably because they think it conforms to reality. The Thoughtful will recognize this view of Truth in much of Christian history. All this talk reminds the Thoughtful of Plato and his "myth of the cave" in the *Republic* wherein the "real world" is "out there" and we poor humans merely perceive its shadows. And, in fact, in the early centuries of Christianity, the leaders—increasingly men educated in the Greek tradition—began interpreting their various understandings about God and Jesus in Platonic terms. A Truth is an absolute, existing at all times and places, never changing.

Today, and historically, most folk retain those Platonic ideas of God and Jesus as such Truths. The church has seen its role as one leading the faithful to understand and appreciate both God and Jesus, and many other things religious. In terms of *The Myth of the Cave*, Christian leaders seek to unshackle believers so they can perceive the ultimate reality of these things, Truth. Other notions flow from the influence of ancient Greeks and especially Plato on Christianity, such as the dichotomy of body and soul, life here and now versus life hereafter, abhorrence of moral relativism, and more. (Even today's scientists, Aristotelians at heart believing sensory experiences are everything, seek after laws and grand unified theories, a Platonic quest.)

Unfortunately, the church has had, and still does have, many branches, many denominations, most claiming their doctrines to be Truth. The Thoughtful have noticed conversations with a religious Truth-holder (or, for that matter, a Truth-holder in any area, say, economics) are difficult. One soon learns failing to accept the Truth gets one labeled ignorant or evil. After all, as it is Truth, if you don't agree, perhaps you don't fully understand it. Alternatively, you do understand it but you willfully oppose it for some nefarious reason. This approach tends to be offputting to the Thoughtful.

Marcel Duchamp's painting, *Nude Descending a Staircase*, offers an example of studying Truth. To a Thoughtful unfamiliar with this work (and to one who is but who can ignore that fact), many possibilities spring to mind. Is the nude a man or woman? What kind of stairs, asks the woodworker? How the leg muscles are portrayed might be an issue for an exercise physiologist. To a novelist, metaphors about descending into sin come to mind, and an actor might try to imagine inhabiting the role. And so it goes. Can there be one Truth for this painting? (Now go look at a copy of the painting.[7])

Perhaps seeing Truth as the sun in the solar system helps. Someone standing on Mars sees it easily and as quite large while a viewer on Neptune has to try harder as the sun would be a fairly small object in the sky. Everyone is looking for the same thing but some must work more to see it. This example is simply a restatement of Plato's cave. In religion many people, and not just Christians, believe they have Truth but as others don't agree, the Thoughtful are left to contemplate the possibility there may not be just *one* Truth.

## Can Truth Change?

If Truth be true, can Truth change?

Not if you think like Plato. For a Platonist a Truth is "out there" and is eternal; our job is to try to understand it. It is immutable, but our grasp may be partial or incorrect so we can still argue about it. This approach probably is the view of most faithful Christians today.

Today, Truth, for many, must correspond to facts; people even say, redundantly, "true facts." Historically, such a narrow usage did not hold the field as Truth was a general quality and every detail need not have happened precisely as described. Even today some people might say, after a long, confused criminal trial in which odd details kept popping up., "But, in the end, truth was served." Others reject the fact-based definition of truth and only ask a story to cohere with a general system of belief. Indeed, until the Enlightenment, truth often meant this coherence instead of a

[7] www.philamuseum.org/collections/permanent/51449.html, accessed August 20, 2013.

correspondence with facts, a difficult idea for the modern mind to understand. A real can of worms can be opened when truth is defined to include metaphor. Can a novel contain a truth about the human condition? Does a myth explain religious truth? For instance, today's focus on the historical Jesus, while not inconsistent with the early Trinitarian views, may end up forcing the believer to think more metaphorically than literally.

Could Jesus' message mean one thing to a first-century Palestinian peasant, another to a thirteenth-century pope, and yet something else to a twenty-first-century suburban parent? Does that seem likely? If Truth is "out there" and eternal, changed circumstances can't change it. On the other hand, the Thoughtful can think of many examples where something used to be wrong and now isn't, at least for them e.g., certain curse words, premarital sex, gambling. And those things are absolute wrongs for many people.

History did play out along the lines of a progressive discovery of Truth, albeit with some irony. Thus the early followers of Jesus hadn't really thought much about the consequences of describing Jesus as God e.g., his relation to the God of their religious tradition, so it was up to later thinkers to harmonize those views in the doctrine of the Trinity. The early church thinkers soon added other overlays to whatever Truth they accepted and were soon interpreting things allegorically, literally, morally, and mystically. Later when the conclusions of reason about the world began to conflict with the dictates of faith, thinkers in Christianity (and Judaism and Islam) came to accept the "double truth" idea; both reason and faith (think science and religion today) were true even if inconsistent. Maybe Indians have a better explanation of this matter in the story of the ten blind men describing an elephant (which is presumed to exist) based upon the part they feel; one feels the side and thinks of a wall, another a leg and imagines a tree. The deity is a great mystery experienced by all and sundry in many and sundry ways. Actually, the quest for the historical Jesus, the changing views of him over time, suggests this answer.

An approach to God that rejects the eternal absolute of Platonism while keeping the notion of change is called "process theology." While the deity remains an abstraction, with such qualities as love, goodness, etc., change occurs over time as the world changes. The understanding of God becomes one of progressive growth—a "living God". This idea began by at least the nineteenth century, became very popular in the 1950s and still influences many pastors and theologians of many denominations, though not the pewsitters. Process theology conforms to the Thoughtful's suspicion that maybe Truth, or God, isn't always known and static; it is something that happens in time and space. Thus, Truth changes, though perhaps some of its qualities do not.

Some call this approach to Truth "moral relativism," what is "right" depends on the circumstances. Like it or not, most of us are moral relativists at various times. We accept "Thou shalt not lie"—as a good principle, but in order not to hurt Aunt Bertha's feelings, we evade her invitation to a (horrible) dinner by "discovering" a prior engagement—a white lie. And "Thou shalt not kill" causes all sorts of problems when wars, capital punishment, abortion, even vegetarianism, are raised.

The problem with Truth changing is it makes it nearly impossible for all of us to agree on what Truth is. (Not that we can readily agree on a static Truth.) Certainly modern physics presents some serious problem i.e., is an electron a wave or a particle? (The answer is in how you test for it.) Maybe this problem connects with the ancient Greek issue of the separation of "being" and "becoming." (The Thoughtful remember Parmenides and Heraclitus.) Is it time to throw up our hands?

**Practical Truth.**

Might it not be easier to assume not all questions have answers? We're used to this solution in the mundane, e.g., child raising practices, why not religion? We can say beating children is a bad idea but historically it's been done, a lot, and even today "normal" people emerge from such treatment. But, on balance, we think it's a bad practice. (Probabilities again, see Chapter 2.) In religion, including Christianity, perhaps some issues are too deep, too unknowable, to have answers. Or maybe future millennia will find some answers.

Herein, therefore, a "truth" is an understanding that satisfactorily explains something to you; this is not Truth (with a capital "T"). At the youngest, a child is content gifts come from Santa, babies are brought by storks, and Grandma was taken to heaven (not she died of cancer). Later, other explanations are required.

At another level the Thoughtful have even accepted explanations they know were false because that explanation worked. When measuring a room for carpet, a flat earth theory works just fine. Airline pilots, on the other hand, need a round earth to plot their flight plan from New York to Tokyo. And rocket scientists need a still more subtle description of the earth's shape to insure an intercontinental ballistic missile will hit a military target and not a farmer's cattle 1,000 feet away. What is "true" depends on its use.

In a religion, all the sources of authority—book, person, experience, reason—are used, albeit often by different people. Many experience God in some direct and personal way; their faith is unshakable and, often it produces admirable changes in them, but their understanding is difficult to convey to others. For others, faith flows from another individual, a parent or preacher, while yet others find their faith in their personal history, the faith in which they were born and raised. For Christians, a major source of authority is a book, the Bible, but interpreting it has been an occupation or an avocation for over two millennia. Truth remains elusive.

### Faith and Reason.

Do we really want to go there?

No one has proved God exists to the satisfaction of all. And if it could be done, what would become of faith? If God can't be proven, how can the Thoughtful, grounded in reason, accept the notion?

These questions have exercised minds for a long time. In the Middle Ages, at the latest, the idea of two truths existed, though perhaps they conflicted. Indeed, one definition of the twentieth century involved the ability to hold inconsistent truths.

Whether the various views of the Duchamp painting, *Nude Descending a Staircase*, are inconsistent or merely different is an open question. If someone insists one particular view is the correct one, what to do? Maybe just say the views conflict and leave it at that. So it is with faith and reason. This topic gets wrapped up in philosophy and theology; safe to say, no consensus exists among the practitioners of those disciplines. The Thoughtful, therefore, can rest easy, knowing there is no answer. Those who claim there is, either all faith or all reason, are not Thoughtful.

**Other Religions.**

If Christianity has truth, why isn't the whole world Christian? Are other religions valid and do they have Truth also?

One response suggests non-Christian traditions can be valid because God wishes everyone to find salvation, spiritual health. In essence, this approach comes down to an observation about behavior. If someone exhibits traits such as love of neighbor, then that person has experienced the truth about God without realizing it is the Christian God.[8] Since the Enlightenment, many have argued all religious traditions are variations on a single theme, all religions are paths to the same ultimate reality. By analogy to the discussion of Truth, God is the center, like the sun in our solar system, and like planets revolving around the sun, all religions revolve around that deity. This solution, however, raises the question of the role of Jesus, especially the Resurrection.

Many Christians, however, are convinced all the other faith traditions are false and their followers cannot achieve salvation and may even be condemned to hell. Thus, Muslims, Buddhists, and all other world faiths are not capable of achieving positive results, in the ultimate sense. Judaism is a special case, but it generally gets lobbed in with the other "false" religions. The denominations the Thoughtful might be attracted to usually don't address these issues. If forced, the leadership would say the answers are open;

---

[8] An example is the Roman Catholic writer Karl Rahner in *Content of Faith* (Crossroad, 1993). Rahner is not recommended reading for the Thoughtful as his thinking is typically German, e.g., dense.

those in the pews might disagree. Perhaps other religions are valid or at least not wrong (unless they lead to behavior we find abhorrent).

Things are not a lot better within the Christian fold. There is a strong urge to think your denomination, just like your college sorority, political party, or sports team is better, not just for you but for all and thus leading to the conclusion others are lesser, probably wrong. After all, why choose this denomination if it isn't preferable to the others? And lots of Christians refer to the scripture passage that people will be divided into sheep and goats; while God knows which is which, things get complicated regarding whether one's denomination is filled with sheep and whether there are more outside the fold than inside. Pope Benedict XVI strongly suggested the Roman Catholic Church was the only way and, while he didn't pronounce all others damned, he left that impression. And some Baptist denominations reject mission work seeking converts as they believe God will make certain the right people are in the church when the final trumpet blows. Many Christians believe unless one has been "born again" there is no hope for that person's salvation. At the other extreme, are Unitarian Universalists, strictly speaking not Christians, who believe salvation is available to all and will be obtained by all.

The Thoughtful, realizing Christianity has over 30,000 denominations world-wide, cannot accept the argument any one denomination, sect, or maybe even Christianity as a whole has a monopoly of religious truth. How various religions connect or relate to one another is a complex study but is not critical to an understanding of the Christian tradition.

As the Thoughtful are discovering in this book, an afterlife is not a required aspect of Christianity but how one gets through this life is. World religions all deal with this problem, and the Thoughtful can understand Christianity offers one set of solutions. Exclusivity is not claimed. The easy out that all worship the same God is not taken, but not denied. Is Christianity God's only connection with humans? Christianity is unique. So are the others. Maybe this situation is a place the Thoughtful decide not to decide. Leave it at that.

As Christians, however, are still trying to convert the world, stay tuned.

## Matters Christian.

The "science of God," theology, in Christianity means investigation of the faith, and it provided grist for the mill of the Greek-educated leaders of the early church, medieval scholastics, and a few academics today. Unfortunately, it also often means "I'm right and you're wrong." Historically that idea could determine if person A or person B became bishop of a community, and sometimes the loser in this competition was accused of heresy. Since at least the fourth century, it has also been the cause of denominational divisions of the church. Over time, divisions within the study of theology appeared, such as moral theology, natural theology, contextual theology, womanist theology, black theology, etc. If the Thoughtful think acts, not beliefs, are the important component of Christianity, theology becomes irrelevant. The Thoughtful can also take heart that perhaps theology isn't all that important as the church had no systematic theology for the first two centuries, until Irenaeus wrote *Against Heresies* (c. 180 C.E.) and Origen, *On First Principles* (c. 215 C.E.).

A preliminary problem arises as many assert their particular beliefs are true, and certainly belief has commonly been a test of orthodoxy. However, many reject a test of faith based on belief and argue instead for a faith based on trust. Thus one trusts God exists, one is saved, etc. in the same way children trust parents are looking out for their best interests. The Thoughtful should know most theology is irrelevant to the lives of most Christians. Oh, some take great comfort (and often inordinate pride) in feeling they have grace and are already destined for heaven, but on a day-to-day basis, theology rarely intrudes. Today's growing Christian groups emphasize worship, life, and work over theology.

The Thoughtful can continue these examinations of Christianity without worrying about the nuance of doctrines. However, for those who can't resist splitting hairs, several major topics are discussed hereafter.

### Simple Beginnings. Message.

Matthew's gospel (5:3 - 7:27) describes Jesus' Great Sermon—the Sermon on the Mount—which ranged over many topics. It begins with the

Beatitudes (nine statements promising blessings for the people in God's favor: "Blessed are the meek, for they will inherit the earth" etc.) and includes the Lord's Prayer, also known as the "Our Father." The Great Sermon comprises material Jesus likely said, sayings common in his day, and creations by Matthew which fell in line with his theme. His gospel is in the tradition of creating speeches the writer thinks the speaker would have given (think Thucydides, *The Peloponnesian War*). Moreover, the Great Sermon covers far more material than any one speech could, or should have, so it represents a summary of Jesus' ideas as understood by his early followers. It provides a handy place to look for the beliefs of the early followers of Jesus.

**Love.**

"Love your neighbor" "God loves you." Perhaps some of the most common ideas the Thoughtful hear about Christianity involve the word "love." What does this word mean?

First, put away the idea "love" means the emotion mostly commonly used in relationships today. Although many Christians seem to take the notion that might be expressed as "I'm like a puppy and God, my master, loves me," the Thoughtful will want to disregard this approach. In other words God's "love," as used in Christian history and theology isn't the same as the most common usage today.

The Christian scripture/New Testament was written in Greek, the lingua franca of the eastern Mediterranean. At least four Greek words are used we would translate as "love": *agape*, *philos*, *eros*, *storge*. *Agape* is probably the most common and often translated as selfless love, charity (as in "the most charitable take on her words is …."), and, in the case of God, a self-sacrificing love for humanity. "*Philos*" is best translated as friendship and "*eros*" as sexual love. "*Storge*" is affection, the fondness found through familiarity. In some views *agape* might encompass all the others.

The gospels tend to use *agape* and *philos*, and John uses these terms most often. In John's gospel, love is not an emotion (as what one feels for a life partner), but a living for others, often a set of behaviors, reciprocal loyalties and commitments. Today, the Thoughtful might use this sense of love to describe a parent's response to a child; situations might arise when the parent would even sacrifice herself for the benefit of her child. (This approach is akin to the popular view of Jesus' death; he atoned for humanity's sins.)

For Paul, the great letterwriter, love meant group solidarity and interpersonal commitment; in his later letters love became a cosmic force for giving salvation. In those later letters, called "pastorals," (not authored by Paul) love emphasizes submission and subservience, not group solidarity. (The Thoughtful might observe the development of the church as an organization with its attendant leaders can be followed in the letters of Paul and shifting understanding of "love.")

To conclude: "love," in the Christian scripture/New Testament can mean a reciprocity of feeling and action, even of one's enemies. It can also mean a group solidarity of helping follow believers. Or, the gift of salvation from God. And, lastly, the submission to one's superiors. This book concludes love means service, in the sense of helping others, particularly the less fortunate. The idea such a love might bring a sense of spiritual health, which some call salvation, would be a fringe benefit.

### The Main Goal? Grace.

An important term in Christianity is grace. "Grace" is considered an act of God, once given grace helps the believer along the faith journey. The arguments come when the mechanisms of grace are examined. Does God give it freely or do humans earn it in some manner? Further refinements have included "prevenient grace," "irresistible grace," "efficacious grace," "habitual grace," "actual grace," and such.

Jesus is the way grace reaches humans according to Christian thinking and is a distinctive feature of Paul's writings where it is related to "justification," which is God's acceptance of people as free from the guilt of sin. Theologians address the issue of grace as it intersects with other complex issues, such as the incarnation, sin (original and other), will, faith, salvation and so on, issues of only some interest to the Thoughtful, though discussed later in this chapter (just in case such interest is growing).

Put simply, grace is how the human condition, however sinful, is overcome. Grace is not earned, but freely available. It may be an idea unique to Christianity. .

**Changing the Future. Prayer.**

To the average believer, the crucial question is "Does prayer work?" To which, Christian folk have long answered "Yes .... and no."

To begin with, if you define the deity in terms of power and knowledge—and many do—so that God is all powerful and all knowing, logically prayer cannot work because you are seeking to change the course of the world God controls and foresees. If you can accomplish such a change through prayer, sacrifice, or whatever, you are more powerful than God. This problem surfaced long ago with the ancient Greek Aristotle and has never been solved.

Nevertheless, for many believers, the hope or trust is, if they are good, deserving, whatever, God will act in response to the request. If they are asking for someone else—e.g., "Help my mother get better."—it is intercessory prayer; if for the prayer is for their own well being—e.g., "Help me hit a homerun."—it is petitionary prayer. These approaches are based upon a belief in a higher power, perhaps the God portrayed on the Sistine chapel ceiling, and assumes one can change God's mind about how the world is unfolding. On a personal level, nearly one in five Americans prays for material things and another one in four seek personal success (job, base hit, love, etc.)

Prayer for the sick is a common form of both intercessory and petitionary prayer. In a study of 1802 hospital patients with coronary bypass surgery—the latest and largest study of prayer and the ill—researchers divided the patients into three groups: 1) those not prayed for, 2) those prayed for but not told of it, and 3) those aware they were being prayed for. Groups 1 and 2 had no significant differences in recovery, but group 3 was slightly worse off, perhaps due to stress and performance anxiety.[9] Prayer doesn't work.

Yet, many people will testify they know someone who was cured of terminal illness by prayer. Well, they've been cured, whether by prayer or just

---

[9] Herbert Benson et al., "Effects of Intercessory Prayer...."*American Heart Journal* 151 no. 4 (April 2006), 934-42.

statistical probabilities depends on one's view of things. (Such folk usually don't keep track of when prayer fails to alter the prognosis.) But to the Thoughtful, the argument is over; intercessory and petitionary prayers don't work.

So why do Thoughtful believers pray?

Some pray as a form of meditation, with all the results practice can provide. Others pray for an understanding of God's will, of what to do, how to co-operate with God. Thus, the object is to change the one who prays, not to change God. Prayer can change one's internal reality, but not the external reality.

Some thinkers believe prayer might work though some mysterious process—energy flows among people praying. Certainly my attitude—cheerfulness, depression, pessimism, etc.—can affect another when I encounter that person, so perhaps my prayer can do that as well. This solution is helped along if your definition of God is in the relationships that bind us together.

A final possibility comes from process theology, a view God changes in response to the world's events. In other words, God isn't a transcendent constant, but process theology hasn't caught on with those in the pews.

After one decides to pray, the Thoughtful might be surprised to know controversies aren't over. In particular, should prayer always be the same or can the worshipper be spontaneous? The eighteenth-century poet, Christopher Smart, was once confined to an asylum for his practice of public, spontaneous prayer (although his behavior was clearly on the edge of seeming insanity, given his propensity for accosting strangers in London and demanding they kneel and pray with him). Various denominations take various stances on the issue although most recite the prayer called the Lord's Prayer or Our Father. As a general rule Roman Catholics and Episcopalians are more given to standardized prayers while Pentecostals prefer spontaneity.

Curiously, perhaps, scripture never relates the fact Jesus prayed publicly.

## Why Did I Do That? Predestination and Free Will.

In Western Christianity, grace, free will, and predestination have been intertwined as theologians have tried to work out the roles of God and people in life. A matter of theology that matters to the Thoughtful, at least on a theoretic level although no one seems to find it relevant when doing a particular act, is the predestination/free will problem. Predestination is the idea God knows the fate of the individual before that individual is born, the destination: heaven or hell, as it were. The Thoughtful viscerally reject the idea because it seems to run counter to desires to control one's destiny, be "captain of one's fate," to be rewarded because of what one accomplishes. Lots of believers talk of "God's plan for you" without seeing the predestination aspects of the phrase.

The source of the idea of predestination in Christianity comes from two places. Paul, the great Christian scripture/New Testament theologian and letter writer, posits it. (Ephesians 2:8 – 9; Romans 8:29 – 30), but it can arise in any religion where the deity is all-powerful and all-knowing, common characteristics given to deities. (If God knows everything, then your destination is known. Nothing you can do will change it because if you can change God's mind, you're more powerful than God.) In philosophy this is related to the issue of determinism and dates back at least to the ancient Greek Aristotle.

While Paul's writing underlies all Christian thought, various denominations have tackled predestination a bit differently. Roman Catholicism's most recent catechism has no entry for "predestination" or "free will" but the thrust of the argument is in favor of free will. An earlier catechism started with Paul's idea of predestination, but then the role of the Roman Catholic Church is inserted as a means to salvation.[10] Protestants, from Martin Luther on, have long more openly admitted believing in predestination with John Calvin the source of this idea. Calvinism, in its many manifestations, most notably in American history in the Puritans, long guided Protestantism and appeared in the creeds of all Protestant denominations. The Orthodox tradition similarly followed predestination.

To the Thoughtful, the idea of predestination is distasteful. However, the issue might be posed differently: what is the purpose of life? If gaining individual salvation is one's goal, predestination sucks. But if honoring God is our purpose, then we are mere ants in the great universe and our destination

---

[10] *Catechism of the Catholic Church*, (Doubleday, 1995). John Hardon, *The Catholic Catechism* (Doubleday, 1975), 80, 236, 234, 36.

is irrelevant. With strict Calvinism, one could not know one's fate, but various writers, including the American Jonathan Edwards (1705 – 58)—he of the famous sermon about God holding "you over the pit of hell, much as one holds a spider, or some loathsome insect over the fire" fame—worked out what a believer could know. Most decided they were predestined to go to heaven. (Surprise!) After Calvin, a weaker version of Calvinism also soon appeared in the work of the Dutch theologian, Arminius (1560 – 1609) who inserted some free will into the equation (in ways the Thoughtful don't care to worry about). That's where things tend to stand today: some say we have free will, others believe we have some choice about matters, and a few rigid Calvinist predestinarians still linger. For many, predestination is more attractive later in life because as one looks back over life, many events seem not to have been within one's control.

The Thoughtful might find a way out of the logic trap of predestination by concluding maybe one can define the deity as something other than all-powerful and all-knowing. Say, love. Or by disregarding the notion of an afterlife (though that decision really doesn't solve much as it throws the question back to why some are believers). Such thoughts would ruin lots of literature and art, like the image on the Sistine Chapel ceiling, but that's a small price to pay for relief from the nasty grip of predestination.

Just to stir the pot a bit studies of the brain are reducing the role of what we think is free will or choice. We think we generate a plan to do something but, in fact, the brain is way ahead of us because it constructs representations of all possible actions with the world we face and then starts tamping some down to reach the one we do. Another study suggests we do something, and then, a nanosecond later, our brain provides the reason. None of this science changes the feeling we have we're freely choosing to do something, but it is a bit eerie to think we just acting out a scenario created at the Big Bang.[11]

---

[11] Psychologists are amassing significant evidence that much of our life is not controlled by our conscious mind, despite what we think. In fact, neuroscience is producing lots of material that challenges how we think we operate in the world. For an entertaining take of some of those studies, see David McRaney, *You Are Not So Smart* (Gotham Books, 2011). A more detailed discussion of these insights and their ramifications is Daniel Kahneman, *Thinking Fast and Slow* (Farrar, Straus, and Girous, 2011).

While this whole topic may not interest the Thoughtful, the same issues arise in connection with the criminal justice system. If the perpetrator could not help what he (and it's usually a "he") did, how can he be punished? Our society is beginning to wrestle with that issue in connection with sex offenders; it seems they can't be deterred or cured so we hate to let them out into society. But is it fair to punish them? Hmm....

## What Not To Do. Sin.

Okay then: what is sin? Certainly, one of the things that is off-putting about some denominations to the Thoughtful is all the talk about sin. Sin, with a capital "S" is, at its broadest, estrangement or alienation from God. Sins, with a small "s" and plural, are the actions that evince that estrangement. Those actions can be thoughts, words, and deeds, or any of them, and therein lies the rub. Which thoughts, words, and deeds are bad? For instance, some find drinking alcohol, dancing, or gambling to be legitimate activities, recreations, while others condemn them totally.

Religious leaders, rather than leave sin at the generality of estrangement, decided certain rules needed to be obeyed and failure to do so, especially if that act was deliberate, was a sin. Moreover, very early on in history, many people decided bad things happened because the individual had offended a god, sin. Thus in the Hebrew Bible/Old Testament, pages are filled with prohibitions and commands. Besides the famous Ten Commandments, rules about food, beards, slaves, and so forth, totaling 613. The standard procedure of dealing with the commission of a sin was to be sorry and make a sacrifice.

Christianity started out in a different direction, for a while. The letter writer Paul claimed "the Law" (by which he meant the laundry list of Jewish prohibitions) had been swept away by Jesus' death and resurrection; Jesus had saved people from the consequences of sin by his death. However, the developing institutional church soon began developing its own lists of prohibited actions. Believers, or at least many of them, came to a position not unlike the earlier times as they worried more about the details of behavior than the big picture. Sins, in the plural, began to multiply.

By at least the third century Christian leaders had developed the idea of penance. A believer, who had committed a sin (presumably serious), was denied membership in the local group. When the sinner repented, the local leader set a period of prayer, fasting, and charitable work, and eventually the sinner was readmitted. This approach was all fairly arduous so sometime in the early Middle Ages the notion developed of confession and absolution, followed by a relatively light penance. The confession has to be sincere but penances began to be quite varied—pilgrimages, for example—and could be shortened (commuted) by money. Also the church developed a gradation of sins into mortal and venal; mortal, the serious kind of sin, involves, as a generalization, a denial of God, blasphemy, and maybe other things while a venal sin is of lesser quality.

With the Reformation, Protestants, motivated at least partly by anti-clericalism, abolished the idea of the confessional but did not replace it with any institution or action that enabled believers to feel their sins were forgiven. Today, Protestants tend to divide into denominations that worry about sin and those where the word is never mentioned. The former are those pushing for various laws that will "improve morality" and tend to have codes of conduct that the Thoughtful find a bit strict. As an aside these folk also seem to worry a lot about the sins of others and often exude an air of self-righteousness, which can be off-putting to the Thoughtful. Also the Thoughtful tend to be moral relativists in many situations—a lie, a white lie, might be okay to avoid hurting someone's feelings—and so a list of absolute prohibitions seems a bad idea.

Many have seen the notion of sin, or more often sins, as a device for control, to make a better society. The leaders of the faith, from ancient priests to modern pastors, have emphasized sins in order to induce a feeling of guilt in the believer. This guilt, in turn, might be expunged by some act, such as vowing not to repeat the sin, which made for a better society. The act of expunging the sin might be of material benefit of the temple or institutional church, and therefore indirectly to the leaders of the faith. As those leaders specified the nature of that act, they had a means to control the believer, perhaps for the leaders' benefit. Or is this answer too cynical?

The seven deadly sins—pride, covetousness, lust, envy, gluttony, anger, sloth—were deadly because according to medieval thought they could destroy grace, thereby leading to eternal damnation. Not mentioned in the Bible, the sins in this list have varied a bit over time. The writers Dante and Chaucer, among others, used these sins for literary purposes and artists, especially in the later Middle Ages, portrayed them often.

One more complication in the area of sin is the doctrine of "original sin." Not an idea found in Jewish religion, it popped up in Paul's letters (Romans 5:12 – 21; 1 Corinthians 15:22). Thus, sin came into the world when Adam disobeyed God and has been with us ever since. (Partly this idea was used to combat the Gnostic view all matter is, and always has been, evil.) Augustine, a major Christian thinker in the West, developed the idea that original sin is transmitted by sex, so everyone has it. Others tended to equate original sin with human nature. Many believed the purpose of baptism was to wash away original sin and, without baptism, the individual was damned. Related to all this notion is the issue of baptizing infants. As they are not in a position to "choose" Christianity, many question the validity of such a baptism. Infant baptism is still controversial and is one idea separating denominations. No one idea ever dominated the subject of baptism so the Thoughtful can move on to other concerns.

Where does all this talk about sin leave the Thoughtful? The confessional appears to be a nice idea as it provides release from worrying about sin but has the side effect of the necessity of keeping track of one's sins in order to confess them. Progressive denominations focus on leading a better life, without detailing the consequences of failure, which is a more positive, if vaguer, position, and, for some, a side effect is a nagging unease about the uncertainty of it all.

Try not to do bad things—you know what they are—and when one happens, be sorry and resolve not to do it again. Whether that makes you feel more or less religious is an individual matter. Oh, and the only unforgiveable sins is to deny God (Mark 3:9).

**The Big Picture. Atonement.**

"Jesus died for our sins" became a common statement in the early days of Christianity—a statement the Thoughtful have trouble comprehending.

Jesus died because the Roman governor thought he might pose a risk to public order. And he might have—think of Palm Sunday as a political demonstration. The Temple authorities probably urged the governor in that Jesus' teachings threatened the role of sacrifices at the Temple (and therefore their livelihood)

Why did Jesus die and nothing happened, no new world begin? His followers sought explanations for his death. Paul, whose writings are the earliest we have in the Christine tradition, was all over the board in discussing Jesus' death, but eventually a theme emerged related to Jesus' teachings. With sacrifices at the Temple no longer necessary (and after 70 C.E. and the destruction of the Temple, these sacrifices were not even possible), people's sin and presumably, God's anger had to be handled differently. Jesus' death stepped into that void. In some way that death had to be connected to the abolition of the Temple system.

Related to the matter of sin, atonement (at-one-ment) is the religious term for getting right with God for one's disobedience, or sin. While various human actions—sacrifices, confessions—are a step, the church also developed an overarching schema. The initial position was Jesus died for us to make things right with God. Paul knows this argument by the fifth decade C.E.. One consequence of that approach was Jesus had to be divine in order for the sacrifice to be sufficient. Of course, once Jesus became God, things got really complicated, but that was what Greek-trained churchmen have always loved, complications. Early on this answer was seen as paying a ransom to the devil for us, a bribe if you will; this remains the position of Orthodox denominations today—the "ransom" interpretation of Jesus' death.

The Archbishop of Canterbury, Anselm, wrote in the eleventh century Jesus' death appeased God, paid our debts, by being a ritual human sacrifice, like a Temple sacrifice, a position held by Roman Catholics today. Conservative Protestants, who often juxtapose a Christian scripture/New Testament God of love onto a Hebrew Bible/Old Testament God of wrath, see Jesus' death as a substitution, a payment to God, for the rest of us so God will be appeased and therefore merciful ("penal substitution" theory). A final view, found among liberal Protestants, sees Jesus' death as an example to his followers to die for one's convictions and those convictions survived the worst things that worldly powers could inflict: torture, suffering, and death ("moral" theory). Alternatively, perhaps Jesus died "because of" our sins (Paul's Greek can be translated either way), "our" being the nasty world of which we are a part.

The Christian scripture/New Testament is shot through with the issue of atonement. This vocabulary accounts for the constant reference to Jesus as a "Savior," in that he saved humanity, or maybe just his followers, from the consequences of their sin. Liturgies and hymns using "lamb of God" and "blood of the lamb" are related to the Jewish rite of Passover, when in the Exodus story the blood of lambs was smeared on doorposts in Egypt so the angel of death would pass over that household. (This ritual may account for the gospel of John moving Jesus' death a day sooner than the synoptic gospels; Jesus was killed the same day the lamb was for the Passover meal.) This explanation also suggests the prevalence of the crucifix, the dead Jesus on the cross, in the art of Christianity.

The irony of all this development does not escape the notice of the Thoughtful. Jesus probably sought to deemphasize the focus of Jewish religious practices of his day on sin, sacrifice, and the Temple, but his followers quickly replicated the general theology of the old practices. All this discussion of how Jesus as God can also deal with God is a wonderful example of the educated mind at work; the Thoughtful might observe and decide to ignore it all. Moreover, very little of this material is in the gospels but rather in the other writings of the Christian scripture/New Testament.

**Salvation.**

For many Christians, salvation is the goal, which in theory leads to admittance to an afterlife for an eternity—in heaven, a nice place. For many, obtaining that goal usually means having the right beliefs, but for some it means leading a good life. However, things can be a bit more complicated.

For many progressive Christians, heaven has disappeared, or at least become hazy, and salvation means spiritual health, being in a right relationship with God, something that may entail trust more than belief. Moreover, such folk see salvation as a lifelong process, not a sudden event, and one's certainty about it may be quite uncertain.

For many Christians, Jesus' life or death or both made for a world in which human salvation became possible; hence the description of him as "Savior." Salvation, however, is not exclusively a Christian notion, as it permeates the Hebrew Bible/Old Testament with the Exodus story being the primary model—the escape from slavery in Egypt becoming the figurative escape of all from bondage of some sort. Scripture sometimes seems to use salvation for groups or the nation of Israel and sometimes for the individual, sometimes beginning now, sometimes only at the end time.

Part of this salvation thinking confusing the Thoughtful arises from Christian vocabulary describing Jesus as a "Savior" "who died for our sins." This idea of salvation smacks of an ancient scapegoat, an animal symbolically loaded with the sins and then killed or one became a Temple sacrifice. One, not the only, solution to this issue is to see sin as alienation from God (sins are a result of that alienation). Thus, if one accepts the understandings of the life and God Jesus taught, one comes into a correct relationship with God, that is salvation. Hence Jesus "saves" us, and his death, while remaining loyal to his understandings, was "because" (synonymous with "for") of society's (then and now) being alienated from God.

### Really? The Afterlife.

Many, including the Thoughtful, associate religion with ideas of an afterlife. For lots of Christians the object of believing, doing good, whatever, is to obtain a pleasant afterlife, to enter heaven. It doesn't seem to register this goal is no different from a Mesopotamian peasant in 2000 B.C.E. offering a sacrifice to Enlil to get water for his crops and to have his next child to male. To many today, the former is valid, the latter silly superstition. Yet both are forms of "contract religion" whereby the human does something and the deity rewards it. Much like a dog rolling over for a treat. (Theologically, a problem exists here in that it appears humans control the action; God is bound to reward the virtuous.)

The people of the Hebrew Bible/Old Testament, early on, had little notion of any afterlife, though other cultures around them did. The Mesopotamians thought, upon death, everyone went to some sort of cave where they ate mud and drank dirty water, an eternal school cafeteria. No sense of reward or punishment was involved. The Egyptians developed views of an afterlife that seems to have been a continuation of the better parts of this life, which accounts for all the items buried with a deceased, especially the king (pharaoh). This afterlife, initially limited to the king was extended to the nobles and then to everyone. Somewhere along the line, a morals test was instituted whereby the deceased's heart was weighed against a feather. Failing that test meant instant devouring by an animal; nonexistence, not punishment, was the result of an evil life. (The list of things the deceased had to be innocent of was sufficiently detailed that one suspects the animal was well fed.) Some describe the afterlives of these two cultures, Mesopotamian and Egyptian, as the polar opposites; the former invented hell and the latter heaven.

As late as 500 B.C.E. the people of the Hebrew Bible/Old Testament had not conceived much of any notion of an afterlife. Miscellaneous passages here and there speak of ghosts and talking with the dead, but generally there was no heaven though Sheol was a place of the dead, much like the Mesopotamian afterlife. ("Shoel" might translate "unland.") Described as a "land of gloom and deep darkness ... where light is like darkness" (Job 10:21 – 2), Sheol also looks a lot like the Greek Hades, with no rewards or punishments (2 Samuel 12:23). Although Enoch and Elijah were taken alive into God's presence, that hope was not realistic for all. The Book of Job, discussed above as a story of the sufferings of a pious man, also is relevant to an afterlife discussion. At no point is Job told, though he suffers now, he will be rewarded in the afterlife. Job, in his awful condition, hopes for annihilation (Job 3:13 – 9).

The Jews, during their exile in Babylon, came in contact with Zoroastrians (Greek: Zarathustrians) who lived in Persia (Iran) around 1000 B.C.E. That religion had a series of texts but they weren't written until after

300 C.E. and most of these texts have not survived so, like Christianity, lots of accretions make finding the "pure," "original" ideas difficult. The religion was monotheistic and its disciples were known as magi (yes, the three wise men of the nativity story). The supreme god, Ahura Mazda, begat twin spirits of good and evil, which explains how a god of good can co-exist with worldly evil. Over time Zoroastrianism absorbed many of the time's polytheistic elements and became too complicated for this book. One upshot of all this reasoning was that a heaven existed for the just and a hell for the rest, and all of these ideas had developed by 600 B.C.E. so the exiled Jews would have encountered them. Whether this view had any influence on those Jews is debated.

A push that developed Jewish ideas of both an afterlife and the resurrection was the revolt of the Maccabees (beginning in 167 B.C.E). Jewish martyrs were dying and so a hope had to be found for them. The lack of justice in this life for such folk meant there had to be some justice of some sort in the future so Zoroastrian concepts appealed (2 Maccabees 7; Daniel 12:2).

By the first century B.C.E., many Jews looked forward to an afterlife and a bodily resurrection of the dead. (In some ways a general resurrection made concerns with an afterlife less urgent.) This knowledge was in the background as Jesus went about his activities. One interpretation of his life involves Jesus preaching a message he believed would change the world and, when he discovered change wasn't occurring, he shifted his focus to a belief in the general resurrection. What happened next resulted from followers' reactions to his message and death. What is odd, in terms of Jewish ideas of the day, is they had him resurrected before the general resurrection promised to all. (Jews had little notion of souls going to heaven; that idea comes from the Greeks, particularly Plato, and would have been known in Jesus' day. The Greek view meant no resurrection occurred.)

The early followers of Jesus believed the end time was soon, immediate even, and when it did not occur, they had to rethink the end time they had anticipated. Paul, already in the fourth and fifth decades C.E., had to deal with the problem some of Jesus' followers had died before the end of the world. He fashioned a resurrection belief that included a body, different from our present bodies but beyond that things get fuzzy. Matthew, in his gospel, used the term "kingdom of Heaven" rather than "kingdom of God"; Jesus and other gospel writers used this term out of deference to the Jewish practice of not speaking the name of the deity; however, heaven, in the sense of an afterlife, soon eclipsed the idea of the kingdom of God in the here and now. Finally, the author of the Book of Revelation gives a vision of heaven the Thoughtful recognize today: angels, harps, singing, lights, recognizable friends and family, etc. By the end of the first century C.E., an afterlife was firmly set in many Christian minds, an afterlife recognizable today.

Heaven also occupied the attention of early Christian thinkers. Irenaeus thought heaven would be like this world, only perfect—people have children, etc. (who presumably would be well behaved!). Augustine, heavily influenced by Greek thought, believed the soul united with God in a continual mystical ecstasy, and he disregarded the resurrection. But the Thoughtful should not believe the church ever came to a clear conclusion about heaven. Ideas of a heavenly city, a garden of Eden, everlasting contemplation, mingled with confused notions about rank (are we all equal?), appearance (all will be 33, the age of Jesus at his death?), and love (eroticism lurked). This approach continued into the Middle Ages which is rife with visual representations of an afterlife but it is not clear if the peasants had any hope in that very hierarchical time where rewards flowed to the clergy.

Since the Reformation of the sixteenth-century, thoughts of the afterlife occupy the minds of believers much more than of Protestant and Roman Catholic leaders. Discussion of heaven are often elusive as many denominations preach about "salvation" and leave it at that. The preachers, Protestant or Roman Catholic, probably mean a condition of spiritual health, of wholeness, here and now, while many in the pews are thinking of a heavenly afterlife. To disabuse the followers of their ideas is to risk the question "So what's the good of going to church?"—the age-old contract version of religion. Already by the eighteenth century intellectuals rejected heaven and hell but thought this rejection would upset the masses so said little, a situation that has prevailed among many clergy up to today.

For those Christians who think of heaven as a "place up there," the goal of life is to gain admission upon death. For most Roman Catholics the ticket is good behavior. Hence the common image of St. Peter, the gatekeeper for heaven, as a bookkeeper tallying up good and bad deeds. Most Protestants, and especially the more evangelical Protestants, argue correct beliefs are necessary to enter the pearly gates. Both groups, therefore, portray God as setting a bar, a standard, and, if individuals surmount the bar, meet the standard, God has no choice but to admit them, thereby reducing God to a powerless onlooker.

The most elaborate construction of an afterlife today emanates from those who believe in dispensationalism. Reading scripture to find a sequence of ages which lead to the coming end, these folk have composed an elaborate scenario, helped by the "Left Behind" series of fictional books, with a Second Coming, lots of fighting, wonderful rewards, and so forth.

People who believer in a heaven tend to think of it as a "better place," a perfect world, without ever confronting the consequences of those ideas. The author Mary Anne Evans (published under the name George Eliot) said she couldn't imagine a heaven she'd want to inhabit. Dante wrote about heaven but who's read the part of the Divine Comedy when the part about hell is so juicy? Julian Barnes, in *A History of the World in 10 ½ Chapters*, examines a heaven and concludes it would be pretty boring.[12] In short, heaven exists in people's minds as an improvement on today but, if closely examined, may be an unattractive concept. For instance, the people with dementia or Alzheimer's have no sense of the present and, often, little of the past. They worry not at all about the future so life goes on day after day, week after week, with no ups or downs. No cares, no worries, but also no joys, no happiness. This is life stripped of its ills.

Nonetheless, lots of folk have turned their imaginations loose on the subject. Some think they will be as they are at death (I'm going to spend eternity in a wheelchair and diapers?) or age 33, the age of Jesus at his execution (Grandma is a hottie!). In the Middle Ages knights and others were portrayed

---

[12] (Vintage, 1989).

on their tombs as skeletons (after earthly processes had taken their toll) and at age 33. Today, the Mormons have perhaps the most completely developed descriptions of heaven. And Pat Robertson, the TV evangelist, detailed some of his thoughts in *The Inspirational Writings of Pat Robertson,* writing heaven will not be a democracy (rank remains), there will be animals there (Fido goes with you), and you "will be assigned to watch over a planet or two." [13] Once you get started down this road, the complications are endless.

Hell has attracted less attention.[14] The Greek philosopher Plato had ideas of eternal punishment as did the Zoroastrians and these were perhaps picked up by Jewish thinkers and expressed mainly by the Pharisees. It was reinforced when Greek-educated church thinkers contemplated the problem in the first centuries of the Christian era. The Book of Revelation has some startling images, and hell got more infernal in the Middle Ages as preachers, especially the mendicants, wanted to frighten their hearers into better behavior.

It is Dante, in his Divine Comedy, who gave the definitive description of devilish punishments. The Englishman John Milton also contributed a bit. The problem, early Christian leaders had quickly realized, is ideas about hell distract followers from ongoing human injustices, so hell has survived as much to satisfy the faithful the bad guys will get theirs as from any desire by church leaders to promote it. Certainly, few encourage thoughts of it outside some fundamentalist denominations, who are still promoting the same fear of the medieval preachers.

About 300 years ago some doubts began to enter the minds of a few and by the end of the nineteenth century, hell was no longer a reality in the minds of a growing number of people; what kind of God would permit such a place? And niggling details bothered some: are all punishments the same, does a small sin merit eternal punishment, etc. In the last century hell has disappeared from the curriculum of most mainline seminaries. And Pope John Paul II announced in 1999 that hell was certainly not a place but a

---

[13] (Inspirational Press, 1989), 295.

[14] The notions of hell we have today are mostly from the Middle Ages. John J. Pilch, *A Cultural Handbook to the Bible* (Eerdmans, 2012).

state of being. Sometime during the twentieth century heaven followed hell into oblivion, at least in progressive seminaries. Sermons, however, didn't reflect this new state of affairs so those in the pews remain firmly attached to a hope, sometimes an assurance, of a rewarding afterlife. After all, it's very satisfying to imagine those one dislikes in some fiendish hell while one basks in the eternal light of heaven.

Today, some religious thinkers accept a heaven but think bad people are simply extinguished, not punished by a hell. There's nothing new in the world as ancient Egyptians had a morals test for the afterlife and one who failed was simply eaten by a dog and was gone.

Or maybe those ancient Mesopotamians had it right. In the Epic of Gilgamesh, the heroes prepare to enter a forest in which a monster resides. "Some call the forest "hell" and others "Paradise.""[15] For the Thoughtful an alternative to accepting an afterlife but still leading a good life would be to live as though you're going to have to answer for what you've done (even if you won't).

Writers have had a field day with both heaven and hell. Dante (*The Paradiso*), Goethe (*Faust*), John Bunyan (*Pilgrim's Progress*), William Blake (*The Marriage of Heaven and Hell*), Mark Twain (*The Bible According to Mark Twain*), and C.S. Lewis (*The Great Divorce*) are some of the more popular. Films also explored the topic.

Perhaps underlying the thoughts of an afterlife is the notion of individualism. How can this wonderful personality called "Me" ever be allowed to just be extinguished? Surely something of me has to survive. And surveys reveal most people who believe in heaven also think they will get there. And they think they know someone, usually a relative, who will go to hell.

"Eternal life" is a more slippery term and is more often used in progressive denominations. It is the fullness of life the believer gets here and now by becoming part of God's group, which will never end. (Reread that sentence to see how subtle or ambiguous it is.)

---

[15] Herbert Mason, trans., *The Epic of Gilgamesh* (Mentor, 1972), 35.

Not all religions envision an afterlife, and many Christians don't either. Perhaps the Thoughtful realize they should take care of the here and now and let the deity take care of the hereafter. Let's leave it at that.

## Oh, Come On. Purgatory.

While the good folks get to heaven, few are sinless. Should the perfect saints and martyrs be accompanied by the run-of-the-mill sinners? Also, where is everyone in the period between death and the Last Judgment?

The early church had some inchoate ideas which the early universities made a bit more concrete in the twelfth century. The general theme was sinners had to spend some time working off their sins before they were pure enough for heaven. Manuals appeared that connected sins with time served. (In one version, a monk, copying manuscripts, who got careless had to spend 4,000 years in purgatory for his mistakes—makes proofreading a bit more important, doesn't it?) Pope Innocent III (1160 – 1216) championed the idea of Purgatory and Dante (1265 – 1321) created the lasting image in his Divine Comedy.

Shortly after the clearer formulation of purgatory, indulgences appeared. Essentially forgiveness of sins, indulgences could be obtained by certain actions. Inducements to get the nobility to go on crusade included forgiveness of sins while gone. In 1300 Pope Boniface VIII proclaimed any pilgrim who went to Rome that year would get a plenary indulgence, a complete pardon of sins.

By a process the Thoughtful can appreciate, indulgences got commercialized. For instance, if a knight took a vow to go on crusade and then got injured so he wasn't an effective fighter, he could pay for someone to take his place and he still got the indulgence. The next step was to pay money to the church to hire someone and get the indulgence. A further step: the church keeps the money, but the knight gets the indulgence. It is beginning to look a lot like money will buy forgiveness of sins. When, in the fifteenth century, indulgences were sold for souls already in purgatory ("when a penny in the coffers rings, a soul from purgatory springs" was a German saying), some Christians, including Martin Luther, thought things had gotten out of hand.

At the Reformation, reformers tended to reject the idea of purgatory but the problem of the treatment of the worthy and less worthy was never settled. With the slow disappearance of an afterlife in progressive circles in the nineteenth and twentieth centuries, the whole matter became irrelevant, which is just fine with the Thoughtful.

If baptism is necessary to get into heaven, what to do with the good folk, including babies, who never went into the water? Medieval thinkers developed the idea of Limbo, a destination for those people, a place without the punishments of hell but also without the full joys of heaven. Never an official doctrine and without scriptural basis, Limbo was an easy mark for Reformation reformers. In 2007 Pope Benedict XVI seemed to endorse a report that Limbo isn't doctrine. Like purgatory, Limbo became irrelevant when the afterlife vanished, something the Thoughtful consider likely—indeed acceptable.

### Monotheism? The Trinity.

The deity in Christianity is referred to as the Trinity: one God that exists in three persons, Father, Son and Holy Spirit (or Holy Ghost) but only one substance. The Thoughtful can be excused for not understanding; few do.

While some Christians find the Trinity in the Hebrew Bible/Old Testament, it is in fact not there and may not be mentioned in the Christian scripture/New Testament either.[16] Most scholars see the idea developing in the days of the early church from problems that arose when believers began converting Jesus into God, probably because of the way they viewed the Resurrection, but it is first mentioned in the second century.

Battles were fought in the third and fourth centuries, creeds were written, and jobs, especially episcopal jobs, were lost. By 400 C.E. things were pretty much hammered out in what came to be known as the Nicene Creed:

> We believe in one God the Father Almighty, Maker of heaven and earth, and of all things visible and invisible. And in

---

[16] Older versions of the Bible include a mention of the Trinity in 1 John 5:7, but scholars now accept that this, the "comma Johannen," is a fourth-century addition.

> one Lord Jesus Christ, the only-begotten Son of God, begotten of the Father before all worlds, God of God, Light of Light, Very God of Very God, begotten, not made, being of one substance with the Father by whom all things were made; who for us men, and for our salvation, came down from heaven, and was incarnate by the Holy Spirit of the Virgin Mary, and was made man, and was crucified also for us under Pontius Pilate. He suffered and was buried, and the third day he rose again according to the Scriptures, and ascended into heaven, and sits on the right hand of the Father. And he shall come again with glory to judge both the quick and the dead, whose kingdom shall have no end. And we believe in the Holy Spirit, the Lord and Giver of Life, who proceeds from the Father <u>and the Son</u>, who with the Father and the Son together is worshipped and glorified, who spoke by the prophets. And we believe one holy catholic and apostolic Church. We acknowledge one baptism for the remission of sins. And we look for the resurrection of the dead, and the life of the world to come.[17]

That so much energy and time was spent to settle an issue of no particular relevance to a believer might puzzle the Thoughtful. However, when it is pointed out the chief use of a creed, especially in the fourth century, was to destroy the careers of opponents (and thereby open their positions to one or one's followers), things become clearer. Also, many of the groups pestering, and ultimately conquering much of, the Roman Empire (barbarians, Germans, whatever) held a view of the Trinity that didn't carry the day so opposing them was a religious, as well as patriotic, virtue.

On the other hand, some scholars have argued the definition of the Trinity mattered. One problem was the developing worship of Jesus as God; if he remained merely a man and was worshiped, the believers might

---

[17] The West inserted the "and the Son" (filioque) clause underlined above in the sixth century, which was another cause of the eventual split of the Eastern and Western Christians.

question why they should worship another man. Also if Jesus was really God, and if he suffered and died, then Christianity would have more appeal to the masses—God went through something worse than you do.

All this development was facilitated by the term "Son of God" which was rooted in the Hebrew Bible/Old Testament. Davidic kings, upon their coronation, were "Sons of God" (Psalm 2:7; 2 Samuel 7:14), and Jesus was seen as part of that tradition. Maybe it can all be seen as an attempt to express biologically what is really something else. If Jesus taught and acted like God or how God would if human, then is he God? Hmmm... Ultimately, the doctrine of the Trinity lacks any clear explanation, which probably accounts for the seemingly interminable struggles over the term.

### The Big Stumbling Block? Resurrection.

Jesus was executed about 30 C.E. Already by the fifth decade C.E. Paul, probably quoting an early creed of the church, referred to Jesus as "being raised" (1 Corinthians 15:3 – 5) on the third day. This is a core, perhaps the core, conviction of the Church. What do the Thoughtful make of this?

When the idea of resurrection first appeared in the Hebrew Bible/Old Testament, it seems it meant the revival of the nation of the Jews, not necessarily a bodily resurrection of individuals. This notion of resurrection appeared about 160 B.C.E. as a result of concerns about martyrs during the Maccabean revolt. (Several writings, not in the canon, elaborate this matter: Wisdom of Solomon, 2 Maccabees, 4 Ezra.) When Paul started writing about it, that background caused him difficulty because he wanted to show Jesus, as an individual, had been resurrected but this image clashed with the traditional assumption that all of the people of Israel would be raised. Moreover, Paul thought things were going to end soon—the time was neigh; in fact, Jesus had started it—and he concocted a "spiritual" body for that event. Things have been no clearer since though church folk have run with the idea and created lots of possibilities.

The broadest statement is God vindicated Jesus after his death. The real question is how did his followers perceive this vindication? Paul's language, cited above and in other places, is translated Jesus was "seen" by others.

This language appears to mean people suddenly, sometimes in groups, realized, saw, understood what Jesus had taught, much in the same way the Thoughtful have "seen" what a teacher was trying to convey (though usually after the exam). The "Aha! moment." This view, so to speak, is probably most pronounced among progressive Christians, who can be heard to say "the resurrection of Jesus still happens" as new believers come into the fold.

Later writings after Paul, the gospels, have the resurrected Jesus appearing in Jerusalem and Galilee, though the details vary and no single appearance is reported in two gospels. Indeed, for such an important event, the gospels deal with it sparingly. Mark ends his gospel before any Resurrection appearances can occur.[18] Matthew and Luke each have one chapter (out of 28 and 24 respectively) and John has two (out of 21).

The bulk of the appearances of the resurrected Jesus are consistent with an interpretation of a discovery of an idea not previously appreciated. And they all occurred to followers, not the general public. The most popular appearance story is the road to Emmaus, when two of Jesus' followers are walking from Jerusalem to the village Emmaus on the third day after Jesus' death. They are joined by a third walker (who is Jesus, but they do not recognize him) and the three of them talk about recent events. At Emmaus the two invite the third to stay with them and, as he broke bread at the meal, they realized he was Jesus, though he promptly vanished. The Thoughtful readily see the metaphor here: offering hospitality, in terms of room and board, to a stranger, giving oneself to another, being of service, was the essence of Jesus' message, and when the walkers realized this, they "saw" the resurrected Jesus.

However, the gospels also suggest other possibilities, possibilities that will trouble the Thoughtful as the laws of science are violated. For instance, the gospels have an empty tomb, something not mentioned by Paul. John's gospel (20:19) also suggests a ghost-like resurrection as Jesus can pass through doors. Also, John, in the doubting Thomas story (20:24 – 8) has

[18] The gospel of Mark has two endings after chapter 16, verse 8, a shorter and a longer. Both conflict in style with the bulk of the gospel and are generally considered later additions. Resurrection appearances do occur in them, though not in the original parts of the gospel.

a disciple, Thomas, say he won't accept the resurrection until he can touch Jesus. The resurrected Jesus duly appears and Thomas proclaims his belief (although the text never explicitly says Thomas touched Jesus). Luke had Jesus eat a piece of broiled fish (24:43), implying he had bodily functions—a human body.

There you have it. Most of the appearances are consistent with the "Aha! moment" interpretation but a few suggest something involving a more material event occurred. Certainly many believers throughout the common era have treated the Resurrection as a material event; whether the Thoughtful over the ages have also treated the Resurrection as such is an open question as the language used is so slippery.

### Call It What You Want. Eucharist, Mass, Communion, Lord's Supper, Divine Liturgy.

Jesus' early followers gathered weekly for a meal and to talk about his life and death. By 50 C.E. the use of bread and wine as part of that meeting, increasingly thought of as worship, was mentioned by Paul in his first letter to the Corinthians (11:23 – 5). The bread and wine represented Jesus' body and blood, but exactly what that language meant was uncertain. (Whether the Last Supper, the alleged basis for this practice and its wording, actually occurred as the gospels claim, is doubted by many scholars.) In 1215 C.E. a medieval council used the term "transubstantiation" to assert the bread and wine were changed into body and blood. At the Reformation, leaders fell to squabbling about this issue and eventually various doctrines appeared: transubstantiation (Roman Catholic), consubstantiation (Lutheran), a memorial (Reformed), and virtualism (other Reformed). (In the sixteenth century, your position on this matter could get you killed.) Some denominations have this event in weekly worship while others use it monthly or quarterly.

The overall view is that ritual is related to Jesus' death and often portrays death as a sacrifice, much like lambs and doves were sacrificed at the Temple during Jesus' time and before. Which leads to the question: what was Jesus' death all about? Back to the Atonement discussion.

## Joining Up. Baptism.

Using water in a religious ceremony goes back to the misty past. Uncleanliness, in a religious sense, results from a violation of a rule, taboo, whatever, and as a result the individual is less pure, dirty, etc.; water will wash away the problem. (Germs were irrelevant until the late nineteenth century.) Baptism, as used in Christianity, may have originated with John the Baptizer, who used the waters of the Jordan River on those who had repented of their sins. This position is probably what brought about his execution because Temple authorities wanted people to sacrifice at the Temple to expiate their sins. Jesus was baptized by John, which became a difficult matter to explain when later Christians decided Jesus was God. Why the need for a baptism? Whether Jesus baptized is uncertain, but his early followers certainly did, and it became the rite by which a new Jesus follower would be admitted to the circle of believers. Language about new life and washing away one's prior sins quickly became part of the event. The general procedure was to immerse the would-be member in water, perhaps three times (in the name of the Father, the Son, and the Holy Spirit). Baptism soon became a key sacrament in the church.

What is a simple event became, and remains, fraught with issues. Very quickly, the issue of baptizing infants became contentious. The historical origins of the practice are uncertain. Obviously one had to be an adult in order to make the decision to become a Jesus follower. Moreover, in the early days the future Christian had to fast for two days, which probably eliminated infants. However, at some point, at least by 200 C.E., infants became baptized, perhaps when a rich individual had an entire household baptized. In the Middle Ages, all infants were baptized soon after birth.

Since the Reformation, a major squabble has been over infant baptism. Some, called "Anabaptists," believed the sacrament must wait until adulthood and, if one was baptized as an infant, one needed to be rebaptized (the meaning of "Anabaptist") as an adult. Today, denominations that practice infant baptism usually have another rite, confirmation, whereby the baptized child, now at adult or at least adult-like (i.e., teen) undergoes a course of study and is then united with the denominations.

By the third century disputes arose when a baptism was performed by someone who was himself (and it was "himself" by then) impure, due to sin or even heresy. Can a clean event come from a soiled performer? For sake of the institution, the answer had to be the ritual was effective regardless of the purity of the baptizer. Otherwise everyone would be in doubt as later evidence might surface that would invalidate the baptism and arguments would be endless. No way to run an institution!

Baptists and Orthodox are also separated from other denominations by the procedures of baptism as they practice total submersion. Most denominations sprinkle a few drops of water on the head (called "affusion").

**The Rites. Sacraments.**

In the early church the word sacrament was broadly used as "outward and visible manifestation of an inward and invisible grace," a means by which believers actively participated in the benefits of Christianity. The Thoughtful can rest easy about this topic as it is one primarily for clergy. During the early church period the idea developed that certain events in religious life were special; the origins and causes of this attitude are unclear. Over time, several such events emerged, and, in the thirteenth century, the Western church, following the work of Peter Lombard (c.1100 – c.1160 C.E.), settled on seven specific acts as sacraments: baptism, confirmation, Eucharist, marriage, penance, extreme unction (anointing the dying), and holy orders. Protestants, at the Reformation, usually discarded all but some kept baptism and the Eucharist, also called communion or the Lord's Supper.

As with most theological issues, sacraments were debated. Did Jesus originate them all? Probably not, but that interpretation was a widely held view for their existence. During the Eucharist, the words about bread and wine becoming Jesus' body and blood are used; the interpretation of those words led to bloodshed in the Reformation: were they literal, symbolic, commemorative, something else? Today, various denominations hold various views on the matter; sacraments are said to convey grace, strengthen one's faith, enhance church unity, or convince the believer God cares, and

Protestants especially tend to be all over the boards about what these events "really" mean.

For people who are literalists, i.e., many conservative Protestants, the metaphoric nature of sacraments is troublesome but not enough to eliminate the word completely from usage. Hence "the sacrament of marriage" in the gay marriage (but not in heterosexual divorce) debates, even though marriage is not a sacrament in their denominations.

### The What? The Incarnation.

To the Thoughtful, this idea translates to "Ugh!" Jesus was God who took flesh when he was born of Mary and thus became fully God and fully man. This union diminished neither Godhead nor manhood. Those Greek-educated Christian leaders worked this matter out, to their satisfaction at least, and provided a creed that reflected it. Of late, progressives see all this as metaphor. Perhaps the Thoughtful need not concern themselves too much as it is a theological matter of little relevance to everyday life. In ancient times, the pharaoh, the ruler of Egypt, was the incarnation of Horus, so such notions were not just the wild creation of some Greek Christians.

If a solution is really necessary here, some thinkers suggest seeing Jesus as the face of God, the man who best captured what God is about; Jesus embodies God, is the Word as he is what God has to say. Thus God is fully in the world, a world whose processes are the means through which God works; the stories of Jesus reflect that view. This answer is consistent with such things as the Nicene Creed and shifts the entire discussion away from God being in the sky. (A hiccup here is Jesus might not be unique.)

## The Organization.

### Titles and Names. Christ, Messiah, Christian.

"Christ" is the Greek word for "Messiah," which is Hebrew for "the anointed." In the Hebrew Bible/Old Testament the term was applied to several men, including Cyrus, the Persian emperor. Around the time of Jesus, the Jewish world was looking for a Messiah—or perhaps more than one. (Whether that individual was to be a political figure who would lead the Jews to greatness or a religious one varied across the Jewish world, and such a distinction was probably pretty much irrelevant anyhow.) The term was quickly adopted by Jesus' followers as they saw he had shown them a new way to greatness. The term "Christian" was in use at least as early as the year 60 C.E. to refer to those followers who accepted Jesus was "the Christ." The term has always been vague because no definition of Messiah was ever widely accepted. The bulk of the Jewish population of the Mediterranean did not accept Jesus as a Messiah, which led to his followers eventually separating themselves, or being separated, from Jewish religion. At base, a Christian must accept Jesus as Christ, even though that term is wide open for interpretation.

**The Group. Church, Churches, Sects, Denominations.**

Vocabulary in this area—what to call a collection of believers—is not always precise. For instance, "church" means the Christian community, for the world or locally, or a building. The former category, the community of believers, can be defined by membership ("The Methodist Church admitted me.") or can be invisible ("Only God knows who are in the church, the true believers.") When someone refers to "the church," context is very important; in the Middle Ages, that term usually meant the institution otherwise referred to as "the Catholic Church." Today, a woman in a Minnesota town talking about "the church" is probably referring to a local community of believers belonging to the Lutheran denomination. Members of all these entities will refer to the building specifically used by them, as "the church." ("I'm going to a meeting at the church tonight.")

Okay, what's a "denomination" then? A group of congregations associated together, usually with a common set of doctrines that differ from those of other groups, makes up a "denomination," all in a society with no state church. Thus, in the United States, Presbyterians, Roman Catholics, Episcopalians, and the like each makes up a denomination. Some congregations are unconnected with any other even though they all use a common title, such as "Baptist."

The word "sect" has a traditional usage whereby a group split from a church that was the official church of a state. In England, the government supported the Church of England and those who thought the established church erred and set up their own groups, which were called sects. Early on, the Puritans were a sect; later, when Quakers, Baptists, and others refused membership in the Church of England, they were labeled sects. In the United States, the term is also loosely used to describe a group that leaves a denomination but retains many of its characteristics. In the nineteenth century, groups left the Methodist Episcopal church over issues such as slavery and lifestyle and established sects that later became denominations, including the Church of the Nazarene and the Free Methodist Church.

A "cult" might be seen as a subpart of Christianity, and it varies from a denomination only in numbers i.e., a popular cult becomes a denomination.

## The Staff. Clergy, Pastors, Preachers, and Others.

By 100 C.E., the followers of Jesus had organized themselves in groups that were developing the characteristics of an institution. As the church adapted to more members, persecutions, and eventual adoption of Christianity as a state religion, various offices and titles appeared. And, for the record, most were held by men, and still are.

Early on, the followers met in small groups in someone's house and needed a person to take care of organizing things, coordinating the food, helping the poor, and the like; such a person came to be called a "deacon" (or "deaconess," a rare place women had a role). Another person in the small group was a leader, presbyter, the antecedent of priest. Bigger groups or groups of groups had a leader called a "episcopus" (a bishop), who communicated with his peers around the Mediterranean. Those titles still exist, though "priest" is replaced by "pastor" or "preacher" in most Protestant denominations; "minister" is a very general term usually referring to someone performing functions in a church. (Some congregations have a "parking-lot ministry" that helps traffic on Sundays.). The medieval church also developed a hierarchy with a leader at the top (pope) with a group of advisers (cardinals).

Another term, "apostle," was an early, and very vague, term which included Jesus' original disciples (to which in later times the term was restricted) as well as missionaries. A "vicar," having various meaning in various denominations, usually means, and meant historically, a priest who represents another, usually higher ranking member of the clergy. The root of "elder" is someone older, and historically would have been the leader of the tribe, group, etc. Ditto, the early believers. Thus an elder would have functioned as a priest or teacher and still does in some denominations. While a "curate" technically had the charge ("cure") of a parish, nineteenth-century English novels and paintings made him out to be an over-worked and under-compensated member of the clergy, exploited by all.

"Clergy" are the group ordained to do religious services although in many denominations the leaders have gone through no special ceremony before embarking on their careers (and might object to being called clergy). As Protestantism has proliferated, many of these titles have disappeared or been applied to job descriptions little related to their original meaning. As a result a Thoughtful, when meeting or writing a leader of a denomination or its local unit, should inquire as to what title, if any, the individual prefers.

Oh, and "Reverend" is an adjective and should be preceded by "the," hence "the Reverend Jones," not "Reverend Jones."

### The Real Issue? Governance.

The Thoughtful, upon reflection, shouldn't be surprised religion might be about who runs things, not just what to believe and do. After all, much of the workplace is about promotion and success, and the ideas, programs, strategic plans, what not, are merely vehicles to achieve those ends. Why should religion be different? Every organization has to have someone run it and how that decision is made is political (in the broadest sense of the word). While it seems obvious to the Thoughtful that regarding as the task of the church is to tend to its members, organization should be a no brainer. Isn't there a way, one way, to do this? At the two poles are the ideas, as Truth is at stake, all should agree and coalesce into an organization with a single leader versus all believers should govern. Monarchy versus democracy. In reality, most denominations are aristocracies, governance by a few.

Certainly the Hebrew Bible/Old Testament lends itself to that interpretation. The very first chapter of Genesis, the creation, can be seen as giving a reason we rest on the seventh day, the priests' day. Similarly much of the Exodus story is devoted to explanations for why a particular group will inherit the priesthood of the Israelites. The elaborate rules set out in Deuteronomy and elsewhere mean transgressions were common and so atonement, a sacrifice (by a priest, who had to be paid) was also common.

And the priests guarded their monopoly zealously. The Christian scripture/New Testament offers the possible interpretation the troubles and deaths of the three major characters—John the Baptizer, Jesus, and Paul—resulted from conflicts with the Temple authorities. John, with his practice of baptizing for remission of sins, offered an inexpensive alternative to Temple sacrifices, something the priests could not abide. [19] Jesus clearly ran afoul of the Temple authorities when he went to Jerusalem. Upsetting the tables of the moneychangers and animal sellers, he also preached a message that obviated any need to sacrifice at the Temple. The Temple authorities quickly pressured the Roman governor Pilate to execute Jesus as a political threat even though his real threat was to their position. Paul continued what by then was a tradition of hostility to the Temple organization. Known for rejecting "the Law," Paul interpreted Jesus' death and resurrection as a one-time sacrifice, which rendered further sacrifices superfluous.

Additionally Paul included Gentiles in his mission which further distanced the nascent Jesus movement from the Temple. In 57 C.E., Paul took money he had gathered from his various groups to Jerusalem to help support the Jesus people there. Led by Jesus' brother, James, that group maybe practiced community of property and was certainly impoverished. Exactly what happened is unclear. He probably had a dispute with James about the Gentiles (again), he may have taken a Gentile into a forbidden area of the

[19] The traditional explanation of John's death comes from Josephus who recorded that Herod feared John's ability to generate large crowds which might presage political revolt.

Temple, or he may have been attacked in the street by Jews offended by his work among Gentiles. Or maybe all three of these possibilities occurred. The Jewish authorities were unsympathetic and that attitude was the beginning of the end of Paul. The threads running through the fabric of this story is the Temple priests can be found involved in the deaths of all three figures and all three provided rationales and opportunities that bypassed the Temple and its role in Jewish life.

Things didn't go any differently in the Christian era. Much of the squabbling about which texts to include in the canon of the Christian scripture/ New Testament was also a squabble about who decided such things. As the early church came together, bishops, one to a city, became the governing reality. They corresponded and met to iron out wrinkles in the developing fabric of Christianity. Over time, a few bishops became more important, usually because of the importance of their city. Rome, Constantinople, Antioch, and Alexandria were the most influential, with Jerusalem, site of few Christians, sometimes included. By the fifth century at the latest, the bishop of Rome, sometimes called the "pope" claimed eminence, partly due to the importance of his city and a (disputed) claim to be the spiritual descendant of Peter, Jesus' lead disciple. Political and military events conspired to leave the pope alone in the Western church, and by the twelfth century, a relatively clear hierarchy reported to him, from priests in their parishes, to bishops who supervised priests in their dioceses, to the headquarters in Rome—a tiered wedding cake, if you will with the pope on top. The Eastern church remained run by bishops, as it is today.

However, the pope's claim to run the Western church did not go uncontested. The Middle Ages is rife with conflict among popes, kings, and emperors about who was in charge. And within the church, things were not always peaceful as, for example, the time there were two popes, and during times when the bishops and cardinals got particularly assertive, forcing popes to respond quickly.

With the Reformation, chaos broke out. The remnant of the medieval church that remained loyal to the pope in Rome kept the wedding cake organization. Protestants, on the other hand, went many ways. The Church of

England, formed when Henry VIII broke with Rome, put Henry atop the wedding cake but kept everything else. Lutherans, swept the pope away, but tended to keep the bishops as their governors. Reformed groups swept away the pope and the bishops in favor of local congregational rule but under the leadership of the congregational "betters." Anabaptists were democratic, often to the point of having no ordained clergy and structure. Today, such diversity continues, though, like most organizations, a few people end up with more power and responsibility than others, regardless of titles. While every denomination has its own governing structure, or lack thereof, non-denomination churches, often quite large, tend to be run by one individual, the pastor. The Thoughtful can only marvel at such variety in the organization(s) devoted to God's Truth.

**Worship Styles.**

The white Thoughtfuls, especially if raised in a church tradition, tend to equate worship with a certain formality, traditional hymns, and sermons that evoke little (public) response. Black Thoughtfuls, on the other hand, may have been exposed to a service that more directly engaged the worshipper with its rhythmic clapping during music and "Amens" during sermons. Another style that often links whites and blacks has evolved in Pentecostal churches. During the service, some congregants get excited and jumping up, speaking in tongues, and other inspired activities.

Recently, many churches have developed a third alternative, often called a "praise service" or a "noisy service" or "contemporary service." These services attract a younger congregation with non-traditional music of simple melodies and low range provided by a live band, the lyrics projected electronically on a screen. Traditional worshippers are often put off by this type of service (to put it mildly) for reasons known only to them.

**The Calendar.**

While the Thoughtful go about their lives, watching January 1 become July 4, then December 25, and finally January 1 again, the Western church has its own calendar the liturgical year. This calendar begins with Advent, the runup to Christmas, and is counted by Sundays thereafter. The four Sundays of Advent lead to Christmas; next is Epiphany (January 6) which tradition says is when the magi (wise men) visited the baby Jesus. Then some time passes between Epiphany and the beginning of Lent, the precursor to Easter. Lent, the 40 days before Easter (not counting Sundays, who knows why), leads to the really big day of the Christian year, Easter, which is a moveable feast (i.e., it changes all the time. For those interested in such things, Easter is the first Sunday after the first full moon after the spring equinox (roughly, therefore, March 21 to April 25). From Easter to Pentecost (the day when tradition says the gift of preaching to the world in many languages came upon Jesus' followers) is 50 days. Finally the long stretch from Pentecost (in April or May) to Advent finishes the Christian year.

Each season has a specific color and a lectionary is published with the suggested scripture readings for the year. Thus the entire year is organized to tell the Christian story.

Why count by Sundays? Why not by Saturdays, the traditional day of worship for Jews? (The Jewish Sabbath corresponded to the Roman Saturday.) Early on, the tradition developed that Sunday was the day Jesus rose from the dead. It did not become a day of rest until the fourth century when the Roman Emperor Constantine forbid urban (but not rural) work on Sunday. Also Constantine may have confused Jesus with the sun god Sol so Sunday became a natural day for worship.

In the nineteenth century Sabbatarianism (the Sabbath being Sunday, go figure) appeared in Protestant countries, and most work and business ceased on Sunday, a development slowly reversed in the last half of the twentieth century.

The Thoughtful can take solace in their ignorance of all this material as few in the pews are aware of these things either, like much else in this chapter.

# HISTORY

*Moses*

# FOUR

# *Israel—The Background*

A brief sketch of the history of the Israelites will help the Thoughtful work their way through the rest of the chapter. The Appendix has a timeline for what follows.

By tradition (the Genesis story), the Israelite patriarch Abraham migrated from Mesopotamia. Stories of subsequent patriarchs follow until the Israelites find themselves enslaved in Egypt. Moses leads them to the Promised Land and Joshua conducts a series of military campaigns to conquer the area known as Canaan. Then, the Israelites settle down into twelve tribes and eventually produce a monarchy, uniting those tribes, under Saul, David, and Solomon. Solomon built the first Temple in Jerusalem, which became the focus of Israelite religion. After Solomon's death, ten tribes formed the northern kingdom of Israel and the other two became Judah, the southern kingdom. (Note to the Thoughtful: "Israelites," a vague term, covers people before and after the kingdom of Israel, and Israelites also lived outside that kingdom as well. Herein the terms "northern" and "southern" will be used for the two kingdoms rather than "Israel" and "Judah.") Prophets abounded, usually criticizing the kings. Insignificant as the two kingdoms were, they eventually fell to outside empires, Assyrians for the northern kingdom, Babylonians for the southern. In both cases some of the population were transported, to an unknown location for inhabitants of the northern kingdom and those people disappeared from history, Babylonia for those from the southern kingdom, a time referred to as the "Exile." Eventually, the southerners were allowed to return to Jerusalem where they rebuilt the Temple and conducted their affairs while ruled from elsewhere by, successively, Persians, Ptolemies, Seleucids, and Romans, with only a brief period of independence under the Jewish kings, the Maccabeans. How much of this story is historically reliable is the subject of what follows, but for Jewish religion the Exodus and the Exile are extremely important. The Thoughtful should keep in mind writers of the Hebrew Bible/Old Testament were more interested in the theological interpretation of the past than in getting the details right. Also, a brief look at the literature these folk produced that is not directly historical/religious—myths, sagas, law codes, prophetic utterances, court tales, apocalyptic visions—is included. If the Thoughtful have difficulty seeing how things hang together, refuge can be taken in the knowledge the works examined have too much diversity in topic, time, and style to provide a unified interpretation. Also, the ancients spoke metaphorically much more than we do, which may mislead us.

This chapter proceeds with an overview of developments as seen by scholars today, followed by an examination of the first five books of the Hebrew Bible/Old Testament, the Pentateuch, particularly Genesis. Finally, a closer look at the story as developed in the period when "doing history" is possible.

## Borrowing and Separating. Beginnings.

### Origin.

Where were Americans in 1200 C.E.?

Well, they didn't exist yet. Yes, people inhabited the lands later known as "America," but they didn't call themselves Americans. Historians now think the idea of being "American," as opposed to "English" emerged among some of the colonists in the years between 1750 and 1776. In other words this identity didn't always exist—the settlers of Jamestown thought of themselves as English—and was developed partly as a result of unpopular policies of the government in London as well as warfare on the North American continent. Not everybody thought immediately of themselves as American, but the Revolutionary War furthered the idea, which continued to grow in the nineteenth century.

Where were Israelites in 3000 B.C.E.? Or 2000 B.C.E.? Or 1500 B.C.E.? They didn't exist, yet. Scholars date civilization back to about 3000 B.C.E. as at least by that date people in several places on the planet lived settled lives in cities with writing and some division of labor and governments. Conquests, empires, buildings (the peak of pyramid building was over by 2400 B.C.E.), writings (the epic of Gilgamesh was committed to writing before 2000 B.C.E.)—all the accouterments of civilization had existed over a millennium with no mention of the Israelites. They had yet to come into existence.

How was the notion "Israelite" created? In Genesis the Hebrew Bible/Old Testament gives the story of people from the creation of the world on down, a kind of history of the Israelites, but the bulk of that story is folklore, legend, myths with perhaps a bit of memory mixed in. For scholars, the first inkling that Israelites exist in history appears in the thirteenth century. However, these scholars disagree over exactly when and how that people came to be.

The events leading to the creation of the Israelites occurred in a little strip of land east of the Mediterranean, though not on the coast. To oversimplify, this land consists, moving west to east, of a coastal plane, a hill country, and a river (Jordan) valley. Continuing east is desert. The central hill country, where the bulk of the action occurs, lacks good soils and abundant water (winter is the rainy season) so the prospects for prosperity were meager. The highlands were sparsely settled before 1200 B.C.E. and probably forested. Archaeology suggests a rather sudden settlement after 1200 B.C.E. and the appearance of egalitarian villages, events that correspond to the beginnings of the Israelites. Additionally, the Merneptah stele, a carved stone plaque dating to 1207 B.C.E. that contains the victories of the Egyptian pharaoh

Merneptah, includes the statement "Israel is laid waste and its seed is not."[1] By 1200 B.C.E., if not before, "Israelites" existed.

**Location.**

As peoples have moved around and ruling entities succeed one another, writers of the day changed what they called this little strip of land at the eastern end of the Mediterranean. Less than 150 miles north to south and 60 miles east to west (an area smaller than Rhode Island), the earliest name was Canaan, and its inhabitants were a mixed bag of people called Canaanites. After the subjects of the Hebrew Bible/Old Testament came into existence, that book calls the area Israel although not all inhabitants were Israelites. ("Israel" was the name given Jacob, the folkloric founder of these people; the name means "he wrestles with God.") Rather, the landscape was spotty with Israelites here and there and other peoples also living in the same general area; various names for these inhabitants were used, leading the Thoughtful to ignore them all. Political events made life more complex after approximately 922 B.C.E., when the people lived in two kingdoms, in the area previously called Israel—a northern kingdom called Israel, the southern kingdom called Judah. By the time of Jesus, the area was often called Palestine because a group, Philistines, arrived about 1200 and dominated the coastal area so Hellenic writers extended the term to the entire area. Today most of the area is part of the state of Israel. The important thing here is that the land was never occupied or ruled, by a single racial or ethnic group and other religions long survived alongside that of the Israelites. Indeed, the Israelites themselves worshipped other gods for a long time.

**Settlement.**

As to Israelite origins, the oldest view of scholars, derived from the book of Joshua in the Hebrew Bible/Old Testament, described the peoples later

---

[1] Some scholars interpret this line, with its predecessor, to mean the area called "Canaan" was also called "Israel." The dispute is whether the people were nomads, or so well established that the area carried their name, or something in between. In essence, were they recent arrivals or not?

called Israelites as nomads in the Sinai who conquered the settled areas and cities of what was then called Canaan (and later became Palestine). (The Exodus story, which puts the Israelites as slaves in Egypt, while important religiously finds little support among scholars; this version of the Exodus would push the existence of the Israelites further back in time but without any clear cause for their origin.) By this scholarly scenario, the Israelites, led by Joshua after Moses' death, quickly conquered the area around 1200 B.C.E., destroying many major cities, including Jericho. Besides the Bible some Egyptian literary evidence can be construed to support this interpretation; however, the archaeological evidence generally does not support the idea Israelites overran the area in 1200 B.C.E., or at any other time. For instance, Jericho wasn't destroyed then because no one was living there. Furthermore, this version lacks support from archaeologists and other scholars. What is clear is around 1200 B.C.E. many peoples were in movement around the eastern Mediterranean world.

A less warlike version of the appearance of Israelites imagines nomads settling down in the sparsely populated highlands, not needing to conquer anyone, a peaceful infiltration, if you will. While consistent with some of the archaeological evidence and not inconsistent with the biblical narrative, this view runs afoul of much of the archaeological evidence that suggests the settlements in villages, occurring fairly suddenly after 1200 B.C.E, were agricultural from the beginning, not a slow transition from the nomadic traditions.

A third view finds less need for movement of outsiders to explain the appearance of Israelites in Canaan. Rather, the existing locals revolted from their urban lords, which fits better with the biblical book of Judges and the archaeological evidence. City-states along the coast collapsed and chaos ensued; in other words, the people who came to be called Israelites were already there, though mostly as nomads, but it seems doubtful their numbers were augmented by settlers leaving the Canaanite cities. The stories of conquest by Joshua, which better fit activities in the seventh century, were written, "created," later and then put into the account of the earlier age in order to justify military control of a "Promised Land" and make the Israelite deity into a conquering god worthy of comparison with neighboring gods.

Merging the second and third views above, the current scholarly position, called "ruralization," posits events occurring during the general economic troubles in the eastern Mediterranean around 1200 B.C.E. As a result, according to this view, pastoralists shifted to some farming and contributed to the village culture of the highlands. The decline of political authorities, be they Canaanite city-states or Egyptian pharaohs, contributed to the problem. This sort of collapse, not the result of military defeat, is more understandable to the Thoughtful since the peaceful disappearance of the U.S.S.R. in 1991. So city dwellers took to the hills. Thus the area of the future Israelites came to be populated by a diverse mixture of peoples who were forged into a unity by later events. Even though people thinking of themselves as Israelites existed, they lived among other Canaanite peoples, and one theme of the Hebrew Bible/Old Testament is the constant tension and temptation connected with the gods of these other peoples. These interpretations have been in flux since about 1980 in academic circles so stay tuned for future developments.

**Judges.**

Settlement alone, however, wasn't sufficient to create an identity of being an Israelite. Around 1200 B.C.E. peoples were on the move in the eastern Mediterranean, and the Hittite and Mycenaean empires collapsed. (The Trojan War, occurring around 1200 B.C.E., was part of this chaos.) Scholars have found many groups changing locations and have posited reasons from earthquakes to new military techniques. As to our story, one group, later called Philistines, settled after 1185 along the coast just west of the highland peoples. These Philistines, also part of a group called the "Sea Peoples," came from the Aegean Sea area and are known there as Mycenaeans. They lived in five cities after they arrived and soon put military pressure on the highland peoples.

At the same time as the Philistine menace appeared, population growth occurred in the highlands, due to either natural reproduction or outsider migration, perhaps including those fleeing the successful Philistine conquests along the Mediterranean. The numbers surged, growing from maybe 20,000 in 1200 to 50,000 in 1000 (or 50,000 to 150,000, take your pick)[2] This growth brought stress in terms of resource control (think land squabbles) that, combined with Philistine military pressure, produced political changes in the highlands.

This polyglot group, some families, some clans, some regional peoples, somehow developed a bit of government, a bit that resembled others at other times and places in history. Elders, an aristocracy—clan leaders, don't think wealthy nobles—provided leadership in the events that defined the day—war, religion, and justice—and probably came from clans dominant in a given area. Many of the stories of these individuals, called "judges" in the Hebrew Bible/Old Testament, are old hero tales somewhat domesticated. (They didn't "judge;" they led, sometimes—the stories are a mixed bag.) Lots of good scenarios occurred surrounding idolatry, violence, trickery, farce, and the like, but the general drift is a more chaotic land emerged (which therefore required a king).

These stories were later edited to produce a theme: breach of the covenant with Yahweh was the source of the troubles. They fill the gap of history until monarchy appears. The "judges" dealt with the loosely divided tribes in a variety of ways. (Twelve tribes, with stability, is anachronistic—tribes were very, very loose groupings at this time; even their names change, and not all were originally present in the highlands, e.g., the story of the tribe of Dan has hints of arriving later (Judges 5:17, 18:1). Only subsequent history causes us to see them as an entity called Israel.) They were not clearly demarcated units with the territories found in biblical atlases, so tribes had no strong sense of membership and continually absorbed other groups, slaves, and those related by marriage (though kinship probably predominated in tribal membership). Tribes fought one another and sometimes joined to fight outsiders. During all this chaos, the position of judge seems to have increasingly passed by birth, not merit. The period of the elders, the judges,

---

[2] The conflict numbers are available in one book. Michael D. Coogan, ed., *The Oxford History of the Biblical World* (Oxford University Press, 1992), 134,194.

which included at least one woman, Deborah, culminated with Samuel, a *de facto* leader of all the tribes.

The pressure of the Philistines threatened, indeed defeated, the Israelites and a single leader emerged—Saul—who was succeeded by a bandit/warlord, David. Social scientists describe tribal societies' passage to monarchies involving an intermediate stage, chiefdom. Centralization is one key to the change and, in Israel, this organization fully emerged with Solomon, David's successor.[3] The building of the Temple in Jerusalem wonderfully symbolizes that process. From Samuel to Solomon, kingship had replaced aristocracy; a king, not a group of elders, governed, but the extent of the power of that king is unknown.

**Religion.**

Canaanite religion looked like many religions of the day, polytheistic, focused on natural phenomena, myths and rituals connected with the events of daily life. El, the father of the gods, was a distant ruler of the cosmos and is one of the names the Israelites used to describe their god. Baal, son of El, was the chief god who was killed and reborn, reflecting the yearly fertility cycle of agriculture. Goddesses included Asherah, consort of El, Anat, wife of Baal and instrumental in his rebirth, and Astarte, another wife of Baal. All are mentioned in the books of Joshua and Judges and were worshipped by some of the early Israelites. (A cult pole, found among Israelites, was called an "asherah.")[4]

---

[3] Archaeological support for David and Solomon is slight. A 1993 discovery of some pottery from c. 850 B.C.E. that mentions the "House of David" (not everyone reads it thusly) suggests David did exist. The Hebrew Bible/Old Testament hints that David ruled vast lands but, as it was during a kind of Dark Ages, records of other political entities are slight and make no mention of same. The dating of some the ruins of the period is controversial and, on one reading, moves much that is attributed to David's time to another period, about a century later which makes kings Omri and Ahab more important. The Jerusalem Western Wall, long attributed to Solomon now is thought to be the work of Herod in the first century B.C.E.

[4] A goddess named Asherah and a similarly named sacred pole make for confusion and difficult scholarship. The goddess seems to decline in importance in Israelite religion after 1000 B.C.E. but the poles last longer, maybe.

Monolatry, the worship of one god without denying the existence of others, described the religion of many peoples of the day. The First Commandment "Thou shall have no other gods before me" (Exodus 20:2) requires Israelites to treat one god as chief but with numerous other gods around. Even polytheistic Egypt had a brief episode of monolatry when the pharaoh Akhenaten (1352 – 36 B.C.E.) decided Aten, the sun disk, was supreme. Whether this attitude was monolatry or monotheism, only one god, is unclear. In any case the practices did not survive Akhenaten's death.

Into this religious milieu, a god perhaps from the south appeared and contributed to the emergence of the Israelites as a unified people. They called this god YHWH. (Israelite writing didn't use vowels but later interpreters expanded YHWH to Yahweh, which becomes the name throughout the Hebrew Bible/Old Testament. Although it was a name, like Zeus or Osiris, it became holy and "Adonai"—Lord—was substituted. Would the Thoughtful be bothered if the Hebrew Bible/Old Testament deity was addressed as "Yahwah?" Probably not, but Yahwah is a name so the deity could be named "Jennifer." Change your opinion?) Here, support for immigrants as part of the story of the settlement can be found. Scholars have long thought the notion of Yahweh came with people to the south from what is today northern Saudi Arabia, in particular the area just east of the Gulf of Aqaba. These events occurred before 1000 B.C.E., maybe before 1200 B.C.E., and is traditionally associated with Moses. Presumably this little group merged with others in the Canaanite highlands and Yahweh joined the band of gods being worshipped there. A council of gods is mentioned several times in the scriptures, (e.g., Psalm 82), and Yahweh had a consort at least as late as the eighth century. Exclusive worship of Yahweh, monotheism, was far in the future, maybe well after the end of the Exile in the sixth century B.C.E. Why Yahweh emerged as the first of the many gods and later the only God for Israelites is still a difficult question. Criticism of Baal appeared about the same time the Israelite monarchies were taking shape, and, a bit later, King Josiah's "reforms" in the seventh century focused on eliminating non-Yahweh forms of worship as he ended cults of the sun and moon, defiled cultic sites, removed or destroyed idols (including some of Baal and Asherah in the Temple) (2 Kings ch. 23). Josiah, however, was soon killed in battle, and his changes failed.

Other explanations abound. Some see Yahweh as one of the Canaanite gods who slowly emerged as dominant, probably due to the actions of political leaders, or maybe Yahweh is a son of El who rose to dominance as El became more remote. The possibility that Yahweh was a god of people in the southern part of Israel while El was worshipped in the northern part also is attractive. When the two areas were united by a king, El took the name Yahweh; this view has dominated since the late nineteenth century. Non-Israelites, the Kenites, also worshipped Yahweh (1 Samuel 30:29). Or perhaps Yahweh is a name given to Baal at some point. Finally Yahweh announces himself and says he previously used a different name (Exodus 6:2 – 3).

At any rate, Yahweh starts out as one god among many, perhaps a warrior god (Exodus 15), and looks like other gods. He had sons who bred with human women (Genesis 6:1 – 4) and a council. He walks in the garden of Eden, sews garments from skins for Adam and Eve, asks Cain what became of Abel, and the like, and even had a consort, Asherah, who was worshipped in the Temple as late as the seventh century B.C.E. (2 Kings 23:6). Over time the other gods lessened in importance and maybe transformed into angels. The connection of monolatry, and maybe monotheism, with monarchy is very likely. Certainly, Joshua centralized all worship of Yahweh at the Temple, destroying other shrines in the countryside, and brought the priests into his court. However, the common folk appear to have continued honoring the old gods as the ruins of Jerusalem after the destruction by the Babylonians in 586 B..C.E. contain small clay figurines of several gods. (Like today's religious folk, not everyone was at the same stage of religious understanding at the same time.)

Although a Yahweh-only group may have existed early on within the larger group of Israelites, maybe before 1000 B.C.E., only worship Yahweh, didn't prevail until after the Exile and perhaps even as late as 300 B.C.E. Pure monotheism was written back into the history after the Exile, although some scholars cling to an older position that monotheism was a theological innovation of an unnamed, pre-Exile prophet . (The Greek Xenophanes developed the idea of monotheism at about the same time, so perhaps it was "in the air".) Scholars today reject the older evolutionary idea of Israelites progressing from primitive polytheism to a more advanced monotheism. How Yahweh emerged as the winner was a messy business involving some Israelites using Yahweh to distinguish themselves from their neighbors, kings using Yahweh to buttress royal power, and, in a story not yet told, priestly factions competing for supremacy.[5]

At some point, possibly after the Exile, various practices were enunciated which, to many Thoughtful today, represent the distinctive aspect of Jewish religion. Sacrifices changed from being done by anyone anywhere to the Jerusalem Temple and done only by priests; centralization of religion accompanied centralization of political power. A tax on all men 20 and older to support the Temple apparatus appeared. Purity became a focus as many events created a need for special attention and perhaps a later cleansing action. Food practices—most famously the avoidance of pork, and a concern with blood—became the norm. Whether all of these things were in fact observed by ordinary Jews or were instead results of what scripture writers thought should occur isn't known.

And the story is not all one of love and mercy as these early stories have some pretty nasty events. Abraham is ordered to sacrifice his son though Yahweh is really only testing him (Genesis 22:1 – 18), and Job, though clearly fictional, is made to suffer because Yahweh and one of his minions have a bet as to whether Job will remain faithful to Yahweh. The Israelites are ordered to attack the Amalekites and "kill both man and woman, child and infant, ox and sheep, camel and donkey" (1 Samuel 15:3). The prophet Jeremiah describes the terrible things that will occur to Babylon when the Exile finally ends and the Jews head back to Palestine (Jeremiah 50 - 1).

## Exodus.

The Exodus: did it happen? Well, certainly not in the manner depicted by Cecil B. DeMille in the epic movie *The Ten Commandments*. Today,

---

[5] Robert Wright, *The Evolution of God* (Little, Brow, 2009), chs. 5-7 restates the idea from the perspective of an evolutionary psychologist.

most scholars don't believe a people known as Israelites even existed in, say, 1300 B.C.E., much less they were slaves in Egypt. One source for this story is the Hyksos, a people who did invade, and control, a portion of Egypt in the second millennium (1800 – 1550 B.C.E.), a story that was reinterpreted to get the Israelites into Egypt. (Many of the early Israelite names, such as Jacob, are Hyksosian.) Another part of the story involves slaves, nomads, criminals, etc. who occasionally fled Egypt, ending up in Palestine; their descendants would have preserved the story of their escape and could have been the basis of the Exodus. And Egypt had, for much of the second millennium, controlled the coastline of Canaan, so the end of that control could metaphorically become liberation from slavery. (Indeed, if the Exodus is dated to the thirteenth century, the most common dating, the Israelites were fleeing Egypt only to end up in Egyptian-controlled Canaan.) When early Israelite writers—no earlier than and probably much later than 1000 B.C.E.—came to compose the story of their people, their god Yahweh, and their land, these various oral traditions were available. Also, the (fictional?) escape from slavery to the Egyptians and the later conquest of Canaan legitimated the possession of the land. Some details of the story are specific to the time of Ramses II which might mean that is when the slaves escaped or only mean an Egyptian scribe in Palestine was present when the story was written included these stories from his folk memory.

Using Exodus 12:37 – 8 as a basis, the Thoughtful can for fun calculate that between 2 and 3 million people participated in the Exodus, an impossible number because that was about the total population of Egypt at the time. Also the logistics of such a group would stagger the abilities of even a modern government and would have left their tracks all over the Sinai and archaeologists cannot find such evidence. Moreover, Exodus 1:15 says two midwives serviced the population, which suggests a very small group. Scholars suggest, at most, a small group left Egypt and later merged with the other peoples in the highlands of Canaan.

Exodus, over the centuries, became the story of the liberation of the Israelites from oppression and the beginnings of their covenant, their agreement, with Yahweh. Did it "really" happen? Not in the sense it could be captured on, say, film. Is it true? Yes, in the sense it conveys a truth about life and discusses theologically valid issues.

### Israel Emerges.

The highland people, coming from several sources as well as being indigenous, slowly coalesced into some sort of identity as a result of these events. The Philistines, hated so much their love of pork caused the Israelites to shun it, were a constant threat. (The Israelites also practiced male circumcision, but that action was not particularly unique at the time.) As many groups of the day had a chief god, similarly the Israelites adopted Yahweh, which also served as a means of separating themselves from the Canaanites. Internal and external events forced the highland people to "join or die," and political leaders slowly gathered power until kingship was either the preferred or imposed result. However, worship of other gods was constantly a part of Israelite life.

This is the state of scholarly interpretation today—a story much less coherent than the timeline and the stories contained in the Hebrew Bible/ Old Testament. So, where's all the stuff about Adam and Eve, Noah and the Flood, the Tower of Babel, the whole of Genesis?

## The Core. The Pentateuch or Torah.

### The Early Myths. Genesis.

What about Adam and Eve? Noah? The other Genesis stories?

The Thoughtful have long had doubts about all of that material. What to make of such things? Those stories are a mixture of myth, folk memory, and fiction, all wrapped together to provide explanations to those who heard or read them. The early parts of Genesis look like myths around the world—creation, the first people, etc.—while later stories of the patriarchs might have a kernel of real events buried in them. It is never fruitful to seek the origins of these things; rather, their function, how they worked, why they were told, can be approached. How all this material was assembled into one continuous story is found in Chapter 10.

At the earliest, these first books of the Hebrew Bible/Old Testament were created as a compilation from several sources. One reason for producing this continuous story was to give those in the Babylonian Captivity, the Exile, a sense of their corporate identity and help their culture survive. When someone put together the materials, bits and pieces were merged. The various names in Genesis often have significance in Hebrew that isn't apparent in English, and there is a fair amount of word play that is also lost in translation. The Thoughtful really should learn Hebrew to appreciate the richness of this writing.

By tradition the ancestors of the Israelites lived in Mesopotamia.[6] As civilization originated there and in Egypt, and early Egypt was isolated from the rest of the world, the stories of the Mesopotamians provided the material for many people's myths. The writing the world began as water makes sense for those in the flood plains of the Tigris and Euphrates Rivers, but not for those living in the highlands of Canaan. The story the first human would be made from a clay doll ("adam" means "man", "adamah" means "earth" or "soil") also fits silt-laden Mesopotamia, not rocky Canaan. In the beginnings the world of the gods was polytheistic and so were the Israelites; the Hebrew Bible/Old Testament, compiled after 600, presents a monotheistic religion and has moved that monotheism into earlier days. (It's not fair to compare the Hebrew Bible/Old Testament of 500 with Mesopotamian stories of 2000 or 1500 B.C.E.; by 500 B.E.C. those folks had also moved to monotheism, as had the Greeks who may draw on this background.) Some older myth survived in the Hebrew Bible/Old Testament including the story that world created was after a fight between God and sea dragons (Psalms 74:12 – 7). The creation stories are probably a response to the Mesopotamian story called Enuma Elish (which suggests they were written during the Exile). Even with the editing, however, two

---

[6] This tradition may originate as late as the Exile when the writer identified as P put Abraham in Ur so his movement to Palestine would parallel the Jews' movement back after the Exile.

creation stories survive in the Hebrew Bible/Old Testament, chapters 1 and 2 of Genesis. They weren't unified or harmonized which suggests the editor recognized them for what they were: interesting, metaphorical, but not literally true. And throughout the Hebrew Bible/Old Testament the compilers had a high tolerance for tension and contradictions.

Chapter 3 of Genesis reveals the origin of sin and provides an explanation for why life isn't perfect and why people misbehave. (And why snakes crawl.) As educated people, the Thoughtful can be troubled by the idea of learning as a bad thing. (The tree of knowledge has the forbidden fruit.) However, one theme of Genesis is everything people do estranges them further from God and knowledge is the first step. Perhaps "ignorance is bliss" after all.

A second aspect of the tree of knowledge segment relates to women. In Genesis 1 God created male and female simultaneously (or maybe the first human was a hermaphrodite) (Genesis 1:27). However, Genesis 2 describes the woman created from the man's rib. The woman, in Genesis 3, succumbs to the serpent and becomes the cause of human sinfulness, though this interpretation of her actions did not occur until 200 B.C.E., hundreds of years after the writing. This story became fodder for the argument woman is a lesser creature—fodder still prevalent in some religion today. The Thoughtful remember one function of myth is to explain something current so if women were second-class citizens back then, when the Hebrew Bible/Old Testament was being compiled, and long before, it is reasonable to have a myth explaining the origins of that status. To argue the myth is truth and is the creation of woman's condition is to turn myth interpretation on its head. At the same time, there are T-shirts asserting "Adam was a rough draft," turning the myth on its head in another direction.

Following the creation story is what those versed in psychology recognize as sibling rivalry: Cain and Abel squabble. The easy explanation here is the bad feelings between farmers and herders. God prefers the herder's sacrifice, mirroring the role of blood sacrifice throughout the Hebrew Bible/Old Testament. The murderer Cain then goes on to build a city, which is part of a minor theme in Genesis of hostility to urbanization; it's a book for nomads.

(Curiously, the phrase "Am I my brother's keeper," frequently used today to explain lack of knowledge about someone, was uttered by the murderer. So why do we use it?)

A flood story comes next—an unlikely occurrence in Palestine and one leading scholars to believe it also originated in Mesopotamia. This story reads a lot like the Mesopotamian story of Enuma Elish, which dates to the early third millennium. Thus, the Noah story is a myth; the only factual basis being the presence of big floods in Mesopotamia. There, in the world's oldest epic, Gilgamesh, which predates the Hebrew Bible/Old Testament by centuries, a flood occurs and became the basis for a story written down at least by 1700 B.C.E. (though its hero dates about a millennium earlier). In the Genesis version, some oddities occur, because, like the creation of people story earlier, two versions have been blended. Are the number of animals, two or seven (6:19 – 20 vs. 7:24) and how long did it rain, 40 or 150 days (7:12 vs. 7:24)?

The final story in this early part of Genesis is the mythological explanation for the variety of people and languages—Noah's sons spread across the map after the Flood and the tower of Babel was built. Yet again, people's actions alienated them from God. Genesis, chapters 1 – 11 therefore include the stories of creation, sin, purification, and sin again tracing a course that will be repeated, often, in Israelite writing. These myths resemble those of many cultures in that they try to explain why people exist and what they should (but don't) do—the two universal questions of humanity.

Extra-scriptural stories are legion. The Adam and Eve story makes no mention of sinlessness, the devil, or the "Fall of Man," while the "Rock" in Jerusalem, the historical site of the Temple, became the scene for Abraham nearly killing his son Isaac, the garden of Eden, the burial spot of Adam and Eve, and, for good measure, Mohammed's ascent to heaven on his night journey.

### The Patriarchs.

The rest of Genesis is devoted principally to the actions of Abraham and Jacob, who are portrayed as the ancestors of the Israelites. While historical reality might lie behind these stories, they have been molded by theological concerns. The individuals, if ever they existed, are probably composites of many ancestors, with some creative writing thrown in, and the stories were told by and integral to nomadic clans.

Scholars have attempted to put dates on these people's lives, but the Hebrew Bible/Old Testament's reliance on formulaic descriptions of time make any probability, much less certainty, improbable. Also no correlation with other cultures is possible so, if dates must be found, the Thoughtful can place the dates in the second millennium and leave it. After all, the context of the stories doesn't require any particular year or era. Why worry about it?

The stories are a composite. While Abraham, Isaac and Jacob are portrayed as three generations of one family, they were of no relation, certainly not grandfather-father-grandson. The Abraham story mentions places in southern Canaan; the Jacob northern. Thus it appears two clans, each with its old traditions and tales, have been combined, and some writer had to, and did, concoct a relationship

A theme running through these stories is the covenant, the contract, between God and his chosen people: Abraham will have lots of descendants who will prosper. (A sign of the covenant is circumcision so this story explains why this practice occurs; in reality, it was not uncommon in the area at the time.) The Abraham story proceeds with ups and down, tests and rewards, all illustrating the covenant and Abraham's faithfulness to it. The story of Jacob includes sibling rivalry (again), trickery, lots of blessings, and confrontations with God. Recurring themes in both also include childless women suddenly becoming fertile, odd brother-sister relationships, female rivalries and other timeless stories found in the world's literature.

Finally, Joseph and the amazing Technicolor Dreamcoat appears at the end of Genesis. Another story of sibling rivalry gets Joseph sold into slavery in Egypt by his brothers. Rising through the ranks of the pharaoh's government, he is given the opportunity to avenge himself on his brothers but forgives all and they move to Egypt. Nice story. Treachery, rags to riches, forgiveness—it has it all. Any basis? From c. 1650 to 1550 the Hyksos a (nomadic) group controlled the northern part of Egypt, but as Israelites didn't exist yet, it is difficult to equate the two. More likely, the story is a vehicle to get the Israelites into Egypt so they can later have the Exodus out of Egypt.

## Why Genesis?

Wowsers. From the creation to the beginnings of the Israelites in one easy book. Lots of excitement with murder, incest, redemption, forgiveness, and the other components of a good story. Much like a term paper written by a committee (see Chapter 10) with the shifts in style and inconsistencies, Genesis is a confused result, much as the Thoughtful would expect. Myths like those of other cultures and a unique God who works through history might seem inconsistent. People write with a purpose, and the editor(s) who put all this material together about the time of the Exile had one: provide a story to keep the scattered Israelites together, today called nationalism. The covenant provided hope for the future as well as explanation for past and present problems. Any book, including this one, should do so much.

Because the editors of the Hebrew Bible/Old Testament chose the interpretative motif of finding God acting through history, Christians had the opportunity to continue that theme. And they did. As history, in the popular mind, is definite, factual, and settled, it has been an easy transition to see the scripture, both Hebrew Bible/Old Testament and Christian scripture/New Testament, as definite, factual, and settled i.e., literally true. The authors of scripture thought they were writing interpretative pieces of history, not factual ones, a notion which has had little impact on many of the unThoughtful.

## Finding Support for Biblical Events.

Since 1800 Christians have sought to support the biblical stories by finding evidence, usually in the ground. In the nineteenth century in both England and the United States groups founded and supported archaeological work explicitly expecting it would confirm the old stories. Thus it was great news for them when a flood story was unearthed and early excavations at Jericho supported the Joshua invasion. As time wore on, the confirmations were few and the divergences many, with the result being most of the old stories are not supported by archaeological findings and a few, such as Jericho, are actively disputed by archaeology. As of now the first person named in the Hebrew Bible/Old Testament who is also known from historically factual sources is Shishak, an Egyptian pharaoh of the tenth century B.C.E.

Other folk have turned to explanations that sought to make natural events the background, and a cottage industry now exists trying this approach. The crossing of the Red Sea was made possible by a great wind that temporarily pushed back waters for the children of Israel; then the wind ceased, letting the sea drown the pursuing Egyptians. Recently the flood story has been linked to the Black Sea. This theory suggests that body of water was originally landlocked and considerably lower than today. The Mediterranean eventually broke through, raising the level dramatically and destroying the inhabitants along the shoreline.[7]

The ten plagues that afflicted the Egyptians and led the pharaoh to let the children of Israel leave have produced modern explanations also. The Nile turned red because an earthquake released a gas or iron oxide or else some small red thing grew rapidly and colored the water. Next, frogs fled the red, presumably toxic, Nile, followed by gnats, fleas, livestock disease, locusts, and boils, all resulting from poisonous waters. Hail and lightning, the seventh plague, and darkness, the ninth, are easily explained after the others. Only the death of the firstborn is a bit tricky. Or, instead of an earthquake, perhaps it was the volcanic explosion on the island of Thera (today's Santorini) which set things off.[8]

Most biblical scholars find this need for historical confirmation unnecessary (ignoring whether it is ever successful) as they find other reasons for the stories, myths really. Scholars today see those plagues as representing Egyptian deities, e.g., Hapy, god of the Nile; Hokafe, frog goddess; Apis, a

---

[7] Valentina Yanko-Hombach et al, *The Black Sea Flood Question: Changes in Coastline, Climate and Human Settlement* (Springer-Verlage, 2007).

[8] Sigmund Freud described the whole story as a fake but scholars have resisted that term, finding metaphorical value instead.

bull god; Hather, a cow goddess; etc.[9] However, many believers, keeping the stories factually based so the nature explanations suffice.[10]

Even though the stories reach back to the beginnings of time, the Thoughtful should keep in mind that all of this material was not finally assembled until late, perhaps as late as the fifth century B.C.E., hundreds of years after the events purportedly described.

## The Rest. More Like History.

Once the story gets out of the books of Genesis, Exodus, Joshua, and Judges the timeline begins to resemble modern history, except Yahweh is far more active than any contemporary historian would dare posit. Some of these writings, though perhaps originally dating from the tenth century B.C.E., were significantly reworked during and after the Exile in the sixth century and perhaps even later. Today historians suggest the Hebrew Bible/ Old Testament was created after the Exile and themes then projected back into the earlier writings. (In the past, people didn't think about or write history like we do; our style is the product of the Renaissance.)

### The Glory Years? David and Solomon.

David, in many ways the hero of the Hebrew Bible/Old Testament, probably began his career as a bandit/warlord in the services of the Philistines. He was chosen king of a portion of the Israelites upon Saul's death. Or maybe he seized power—warlords do. (The text works hard to show David was far away when Saul died; the lady doth protest too much?) David eventually became king of all the Israelites and reduced the power of the Philistines. (The Goliath story metaphorically shows the power of the Philistines.)

---

[9] Douglas A. Knight and Amy-Jill Levine, *The Meaning of the Bible* (HarperOne, 2011) 15.

[10] In *The Genesis Enigma: Why the Bible is Scientifically Accurate* (Dutton, 2009), a book with a misleading subtitle, Andrew Parker urges acceptance of science and the use of metaphor to explain the implausibilities.

As king, David created a new capital in Jerusalem, a site not previously identified with any subpart of the Israelites. The ark of the covenant, a wooden box containing the seat of Yahweh, was brought to his Jerusalem palace. Later writers gave David the theological endorsement of Yahweh who promised that David's descendents would rule Israel forever. (Hence Christians' later need to connect Jesus, as Messiah, to David genealogically.)

David's personal life became the subject of later writers' moralizing. Adultery, rape, murder, arranged death, multiple wives, father son rivalry—the soap opera, maybe largely fictional, played out until one of his sons, Solomon emerged as his successor. This extraordinary detail about David's life suggests a contemporary of David, close to the action, wrote a court history that later writers incorporated into their stories.[11]

Solomon, David's son who survived the carnage of the succession, understood the two things any regime must provide: defense and justice. His construction program included arsenals and gated cities. In Jerusalem he built his palace and the Temple, thereby centralizing Israelite worship in his capitol. His opulence and many wives demonstrated the grandeur of the monarchy. All these developments cost money, and Solomon's taxation was heavy, something he countered with a campaign emphasizing his wisdom and justice. How much of the material about these qualities is contemporary or even true cannot be determined, but the overall effect was to produce a monarch doing his jobs and firmly linked to Yahweh.

How powerful these two monarchs were in the larger world of the day is difficult to assess. The period 1200 to 900 B.C.E. is one of the ages historians label "Dark Age" because writings were scarcer than the years before and after, big political empires didn't exist, and monumental construction was curtailed. Perhaps David conquered or controlled indirectly an area roughly the size of the modern state of Israel, though with different boundaries, and Solomon had, among his many wives, a (nameless) daughter of a pharaoh.

---

[11] The problem with a contemporary author of a court history is that archaeologists have not found much evidence that there was writing in the area at the time of David. Moreover, the stela found at Tel Dan in 1993 that mentions a "House of David" dates to about 850 B.C.E., several hundred years after David's purported reign.

Neither king is mentioned in the archives of neighboring entities which might be a freak of archaeological survival, the absence of well-organized regimes nearby, or the insignificance of the Israelite kings. The worship of Yahweh might not have been as dominant as portrayed, something hinted at by the names of Saul's son, Ishbaal, and grandson, Mersbaal, both containing the name of the Canaanite god, Baal. Whatever the situation, these two kings, David and Solomon, became symbols of the best years in Israelite history and were encrusted with so much legend and myth that locating reality can be difficult.

**Downhill.**

Upon Solomon's death in 922, his son was unable to keep all of his father's lands, and it was split into two kingdoms—one in the north and consisting of ten tribes (confusingly called "Israel") and one in the south of the other two tribes, ruled by Solomon's (and David's) successors (called "Judah"). From this year on, the dating is reasonably secure and some biblical events can be correlated with non-biblical sources. Neither kingdom was of great significance internationally and both soon fell under the influence and ultimately control of the Mesopotamian-based empires of Assyria and Babylon. Those regimes frowned upon revolts and when the northern kingdom rebelled and was defeated in 722, the population, or at least its leadership, were moved somewhere else in the Assyrian empire. There they lost their cultural identity as Israelites and disappeared from world history. (The "lost 10 tribes" have been the object of speculation ever since, and claims of their rediscovery somewhere in Asia surface periodically. They are also a part of Mormon history.) The southern kingdom grew in population, according to archaeologists, which suggests an influx from the northern kingdom. A problem with the sources arises from the disappearance of the northern kingdom. As a result, all writings were ultimately edited by someone from the south, someone hostile to the northern kingdom, and the story of the north suffers accordingly.

Not learning from their northern neighbor's mistake and misjudging how much support Egypt would provide, the southern kingdom revolted in 586 against the Babylonians, successors to the Assyrians as the dominant empire of the area. The leaders of these Israelites, perhaps numbering 2,000, were also uprooted and moved to Mesopotamia, although probably 70 percent of the population remained; some scholars, however, see a larger number of people transported and the area around Jerusalem deserted during this time. Thus began the "Babylonian Captivity" or "Exile" which lasted until 538, when they, or their descendents, were allowed to return to Palestine. Returning to a devastated area, these Israelites, who may have numbered 10,000 in Judah never achieved political importance.[12] Even the Davidic line of rulers disappeared. Persian domination was followed by the successors of Alexander the Great, and finally Rome ruled the roost. The Israelites rebelled occasionally, but only once successfully, and that single independence only lasted about a century, from 167 to 63 B.C.E..

**Prophets.**

From the eighth to sixth centuries Israelite religion was often characterized by individuals called prophets. They arose (or their speeches were recorded first) at that time because literacy was more common than before and a major power, Assyria, began expanding into Palestine. These men (as they most often were) only occasionally predicted the future but always spoke for Yahweh. Sometimes they supported a king, sometimes they criticized; the latter are more interesting: they spoke "truth to power." Their general theme was religious unfaithfulness of some sort and often they connected that quality to temporal troubles, especially for rulers. Excesses of monarchial power, problems of the poor, worshiping gods other than Yahweh—all brought prophetic denunciations, and sometimes reforms. As other peoples lived among the Israelites, the temptations to worship their gods arose and were more than occasionally succumbed to. A southern king, Josiah, attacked the worship of Asherah, Melech, the sun and other "foreign" gods around 622 B.C.E., but the worship of Baal was a continuing problem[13]

---

[12] Coogan, *Oxford History of the Biblical World*, 384.

[13] 2 Kings 33

Other cultures and other gods had prophets. Monarchs surrounded themselves with diviners, sorcerers, and the like as well as "spin" masters, who parroted the official line ("Our god approves of our king.") Israelite prophets were often known as miracle-workers, a sign of a genuine prophet. Many had followers, which accounts for survival of their activities in writing. While they spoke to their time and place, later readers applied the words to their own situation, the development of a tradition. The books of the prophets in the Hebrew Bible/Old Testament probably originated as a compilation of an individual's words and actions. It is even possible some prophets, such as Jeremiah, are creations of a later time.[14] Subsequent editing, perhaps multiple times, added material to make the prophet's activities more relevant to an audience different from the original. All of this story resembles Jesus' activities which helps explain why many of his contemporaries saw him as another prophet in the long line of prophets, a line which had ended several centuries earlier.

## The Intertestamental Period.

The Hebrew Bible/Old Testament does not contain anything written much after about 160 B.C.E. However, some written material from subsequent years is included in some Christian Bibles as Apocrypha and Pseudepigrapha. In addition, the discovery of the Dead Sea Scrolls in the 1940s added greatly to our knowledge of ideas swirling in that age as well as producing (sometimes variant) texts of most of the books of the Hebrew Bible/Old Testament. ("Intertestamental" is a Christian term as the writings, chronologically, fit between the Old Testament and the New Testament.)

For the Thoughtful, two things from this period are important, both related to the political life of Palestine. Alexander the Great conquered Palestine in 333 B.C.E. After his death, the area came under the rule of one of his generals (Ptolemy) and his successors, located in Egypt. (Cleopatra was the last ruling Ptolemy.) In 198 B.C.E. the descendants of another of Alexander's generals, the Seleucids, headquartered in Syria, took control of

---

[14] Frank Frick, *A Journey Through the Hebrew Scriptures* (Harcourt Brace, 1995), 401.

Palestine. One of this line, Antiochus IV Epiphanes (175—163), sought to eliminate traditional Jewish religion. A pig was sacrificed in the Temple and a statue of Zeus introduced. Observance of Jewish religious customs was banned. In 166 B.C.E., the Jews successfully revolved under the leadership of Judas Maccabeus (hence the Maccabean Revolt). An independent Israel, under Maccabean kingship, lasted to 63 B.C.E., when the Romans conquered Palestine.

During the rule of the Maccabeans internal strife among Jewish aristocratic factions became intense, and the Maccabean king eventually decided to become the high priest to stop the squabbling. Other factions included the Sadducees who helped run the Temple and the Essenes, a group that rejected the Temple priesthood as corrupt. Pharisees concentrated on holy living.

During the rule of Antiochus IV Epiphanes, the sufferings and sometimes torturing of Jewish rebels led to notions of an eventual resurrection so justice would prevail. After all, such martyrs should not have died in vain. While there had been hints of this attitude to an afterlife in the Hebrew Bible/Old Testament (Daniel 12:1-3), the Intertestmental writings brought it out vividly. Also, some earlier writings of the Hebrew Bible/Old Testament (e.g., Ezekiel) were reinterpreted to include the idea of a resurrection. While no one view prevailed, it appears the resurrection would occur at an end time and all would be resurrected at the same time. Alternatively, the resurrection might be of Israel as a nation rather than of Israelites as individuals. Notions of a resurrection or salvation were more usually political or physical than spiritual; that notion came later from the Greeks.

A second idea, with an ancestry in the Hebrew Bible/Old Testament, experienced great growth: a Messiah. The word, translated into Greek as "Christos," meant "one who was anointed" and had been applied to several men in the Hebrew Bible/Old Testament, including a Persian emperor. A Messiah was endowed by God with unusual powers; other than this definition, the word meant many things. One interpretation was a Messiah would lead Israel to greatness, presumably political independence and perhaps moral reform. The Dead Sea Scrolls even envisaged two Messiahs, one military, one priestly.

Both the resurrection and Messiah concepts were responses to the search for deliverance, salvation, redemption. This interest, this hope, in the future tended to focus on an exciting end time, an apocalypse. The book of Daniel, the only such writing to make it into the Hebrew Bible/Old Testament, was written about 165, in the midst of the revolt. Not only did apocalypses appear, but the book of Daniel has the only unequivocal statement in the Hebrew Bible/Old Testament of an afterlife involving rewards and punishment (12). Other apocalyptic writings not included in the canon included 1 and 2 Enoch, Baruch 2, 4 Ezra, Jubilees. The followers of Jesus continued this tradition with Revelation (the only apocalyptic writing the Christian scripture/New Testament) and, inter alia, the apocalypses of James, Paul, Peter, Stephen, Thomas, and the Virgin. And Mark, in his gospel, reveals Jesus speaking about an apocalypse. Thus Jesus and his early followers lived in an age when many expected things, exciting things, to happen, and these ideas were incorporated, perhaps by Jesus—certainly by his followers—into the emerging view that beccame Christianity.

**Other Writings.**

In addition to reading the Hebrew Bible/Old Testament to study Israel's religious and political actions, the Thoughtful can find much other writing, most of it created in the time around the end of the Exile.

Grouped as poetical and wisdom literature, many only tangentially touched the themes of religion and politics; nevertheless they were included in the Hebrew Bible/Old Testament as they were used in worship or expressed interesting sentiments. The book, Song of Songs (Song of Solomon), is love poetry, often with explicit sexual language and imagery.

> 1.2 Let him kiss me with the kisses of his mouth!
> 7:1-3 Your rounded thighs are like jewels,
> the work of a master hand.
> Your navel is a rounded bowl
> that never lacks mixed wine.
> Your belly is a heap of wheat,

encircled with lilies.
Your two breasts are like two fawns,
twins of a gazelle.
8:14 Make hast, my beloved,
and be like a gazelle
or a young stag
upon the mountain of spices!

The Thoughtful will not be amazed to learn this book is controversial, not only for its sexual language, but because it never mentions God and often has a clearly female voice. It made it into the canon partly because it was attributed (wrongly) to Solomon and because it was read allegorically as Yahweh's love for Israel. Christians subsequently interpreted it as Jesus' love for the church.

Two other canonical books, Ruth and Esther, though located in the historical section of the Old Testament (but in Writings section in the Hebrew Bible) are fictional, even more so than the other historical books. Both books feature women which shows the Thoughtful, yet again, that in real life patriarchal men dominated; only in fiction could women have important roles, at least as far as the writers/compilers of the Hebrew Bible/Old Testament were concerned. The story of Ruth features a loyal, widowed, daughter-in-law ("Where you go, I will go...where you die, I will die." 1:16 – 7), who despite being a foreigner, ultimately honors the rules of Levirate marriage, taking as her second husband a relative of her first, which conveniently continues the line that eventually produces King David. Along the way, a bitter mother-in-law, scenes of sexual predation (first by field workers, then by Ruth), and clever dealing about land keep the ancient listener and modern reader entertained, all while showing how Yahweh works in mysterious ways. Some scholars see the book as a counterblast to efforts of the day to restrict Jews marrying non-Jews. (After the Exile, some sought to limit assimilation by developing rules relating to food, apparel, etc.) For the Thoughtful, the story has also fascinated scholars whose (over?) interpretation can occupy one's spare time.

The Book of Esther purports to tell the history of a Jewish woman, who became queen of Persia during the Exile, protected her fellow Jews from a persecution. This activity explains the origins of the Jewish festival of Purim, which celebrates deliverance from danger and death. Once again scholars have had a field day as the story involves a women (whose independence is one of the debated issues), actions against Jews qua Jews, and court intrigue. Curiously, the book also never mentions God. One footnote that is rarely the subject of scholarly disagreement but Thoughtfuls, especially men, should note is that in both the Ruth and Esther stories alcohol plays a significant part in the men's problems.

The books of Proverbs, Job, and Ecclesiastes are collectively called "wisdom literature," and relate to similar writings in other cultures of Mesopotamia and Egypt; the thrust is meditation on the meaning of life for the individual. (The stories about Jesus often resemble wisdom teachings.) Job, a fictional book, explores why bad things happen to good people and comes away with no answer. Ecclesiastes is so pessimistic the Thoughtful can puzzle over why it was ever included. Proverbs provided advice for aristocrats. Indeed the Hebrew Bible/Old Testament may have a bit of something for everyone, violence, sex, advice, fiction, adventure.

## Conclusion.

While practices—worship at the Temple, dietary restrictions—evolved, the religion of the Israelites never had a central authority—a king or priest—who could enforce uniformity and punish deviants. The religion was much like U.S. Christianity today in which some followers adhere to particular sects or beliefs while others are content with the vague label "Christian." Or it was like today's Judaism with followers who range from orthodox with distinctive clothing, hair and work schedules to those who acknowledge a Jewish ancestry but never partake of anything smacking of that heritage. Even the point at which Israelites are monotheistic is difficult to ascertain with some scholars seeing it emerge with the eighth-century prophets and others only in the time of Second Isaiah, c. 530 B.C.E. If it occurs at the latter time, the Thoughtful will observe the Greeks had also postulated one god behind all the diversity of the world at about that time.

The Thoughtful shouldn't see Israel's religious history as a stream, gradually flowing through twelve centuries before Jesus' time. Rather it is part of the history of a group that managed to cling to its identity despite its political insignificance. In antiquity every group had a god but it is rare in history for the worship of that deity to survive the political destruction of the group. The single thread of Israelite worship of Yahweh is the covenant, but the nature of that relationship changed, a lot, and was probably written back into the earlier stories by later writers. Yahweh ruled the world and history and that the Israelites were Yahweh's chosen people are about the only constants in the story, but those ideas weren't established early. The roles of ritual, ethnicity, rulers, prophets, people, foreigners—all were integral at various times. Moreover, this scripture was written from the eighth (maybe tenth) century down to the second. One consequence of these diverse influences and lengthy time was a literature rich in possibilities, possibilities that rabbis and Jesus' followers mined and still mine.

To further grasp the timeline of Christianity, the Thoughtful might note Jesus, an observant Jew, was operating in a religious tradition that did not come into existence in the second millennium B.C.E., and that remained unchanged thereafter (although that is pretty much the impression given by the final version of the Hebrew Bible/Old Testament). Rather, Jewish religion hadn't settled down by his time, with apocalyptic writings and messianic hopes keeping things interesting. Judaism, which this book dates to about100 C.E., appeared about the same time as Christianity when the two movements rejected each other. And both continued changing even after those dates. Jesus was, for the Thoughtful, just another strand in a faith tradition, Jewish religion, that changed a lot over the years. The Hebrew Bible/Old Testament may not have a single Truth although many seek to find such. It is, after all, the works of authors, not an author, and a collection of books, not a book.

*Paul*

# FIVE

# *The Early Followers of Jesus*

Jesus was executed. Then what happened?

## The Beginnings of Christianity. Maybe.

### Uh Oh, Part II. Resurrection.

If the Thoughtful find miracles difficult to accept, the Resurrection comes no easier. Jesus, executed on Friday, was raised by God three days later, Easter Sunday—the official position.

Let's dispose of one trivial issue right away, the three days. Assume, for sake of the argument, these were factual events. The Thoughtful do not count Friday afternoon to early Sunday morning as three days. However, Jews in Jesus' day counted any part of a day as a day so parts of three days were involved.[1] To complicate things a bit, when Jesus, as reported in the gospels, said he would reappear in three days, he may have been using an idiom of the day which meant eternity or long time. Subsequent interpreters

---

[1] Someone, to help with understanding this, said Jews counted days like luxury cruises do today. An "eight-day cruise" will actually begin with embarkation late Monday night and end with disembarkation early the following Monday morning. That's eight days to the cruise line, six to the passengers.

of these stories give us the view often held today: the Resurrection occurred on Sunday shortly after Jesus' death.

Resurrection was not a common topic in the Hebrew Bible/Old Testament, and, when it appears, it usually referred to a national, not an individual, resurrection, the future of Israel. Ezekiel's dry bones is a prime example. Jesus' choice of twelve disciples might have reflected this desire for a national restoration (or did his early followers expand the number of his core group of 3 or 4 following the same reasoning?).[2] The idea of an individual resurrection started appearing after around 200 B.C.E. The book of Daniel, an apocalyptic work, first mentions an individual resurrection, but the clearest statement is in the Apocrypha, in the second book of Maccabees, where a mother and her sons were executed because they won't give up their Jewish religious practices. In 167 B.C.E. Antiochus IV Epiphanes, the Syrian king who controlled Palestine, set out to eliminate Jewish religion, its customs and practices. These Maccabean martyrs all talked about being resurrected at the end of time. While people getting killed is not an unknown topic in scripture, the Maccabean executions are something new, the result of religious persecution. This development made the issue and the literature relevant to Jesus' followers. After the dam broke, resurrection was discussed, and lots of passages of the Hebrew Bible/Old Testament were reinterpreted to foretell resurrections, e.g., Psalms 16, 49, 73. By Jesus' day, many, perhaps most, Jews would have known about the idea of an individual resurrection, though not all accepted it (especially Sadducees). To add a complication, Jews who had been exposed to Greek thought, such as Plato, would have rejected a bodily resurrection in favor of the soul moving immediately to an afterlife. One detail that posed a problem was the resurrection which was to occur at the end time; Jesus' resurrection didn't fit that expectation, which helps explain why his early followers were sure the Final Trumpet was about to sound.

---

[2] The gospel lists of the 12 disciples are not identical and at least half are not mentioned again after their initial selection.

To get at the real issue here, the gospel narratives have little agreement about the Resurrection, which no one actually witnessed.[3] Two independent traditions of post-death appearances exist, some happened in Galilee and others in Jerusalem, and attempts to harmonize them fail.[4] No one appearance is reported in more than one gospel, and the issue gets further complicated for the Thoughtful by mention of the empty tomb in the gospels. Perhaps most significantly, Jesus never appeared in a public arena after the Resurrection; he only appeared to believers.

In the context of the times, the listeners to the gospels would not have had any difficulty with all this story. It happened elsewhere in the ancient world and not infrequently, although Jewish believers in a resurrection thought it would occur at the end time. And language may be an issue here, as the three days might be a Jewish expression about salvation; think about that—all metaphor.[5] Still, however, the Thoughtful have trouble with all this. What to do?

Historically, attacks on the Resurrection involved accusations of fraud, excessive credulity, and the influence of pagan stories, i.e., the lack of factual basis, but the issue is more complicated.[6] As the Thoughtful have discovered, a story may be true but not factual.

Jesus himself probably thought his public activities (largely in Galilee) would be successful, and the world would change. But he later came to realize it wasn't happening and he was beginning to offend the authorities, something that might make for a bad end. When his death appeared eminent, he

---

[3] A second-century writing, the Gospel of Peter, has the Resurrection witnessed by soldiers and elders. The story includes two figures whose heads reached to the sky and a talking cross, which might explain why it isn't included in the canon.

[4] Raymond E. Brown, Joseph A. Fitzmyer, Roland E. Murphy, eds., *The New Jerome Biblical Commentary* (Prentice, Hall 1990), 1375.

[5] Edward Schillebeeckx, *Jesus: An Experiment in Christology* (Seabury Press, 1979), 526-32.

[6] Charles Freeman argues that Jesus' body was stolen by agents of the chief priest and a man placed in the tomb to tell the disciples to meet the risen Jesus in Galilee. All was part of a plan to get Jesus' followers out of Jerusalem and avert political turmoil which would upset the Romans who would cause trouble for the chief priest. Charles Freemen, *A New History of Early Christianity* (Yale, 2009), 32-3. In John's gospel, Mary Magdalene and Peter both initially think the body has been stolen.

resisted. When he concluded it was probably inevitable, he sought refuge, took solace, in the faith of the Jews of the day that he would be raised up, resurrected, at the end of time.[7] But that's not the story his followers later told.

Today, one can pose several possibilities:[8]

(1) A bodily resurrection occurred in the sense one awakens from sleep with the same material body and personality. The world doesn't work that way for the Thoughtful.[9]

(2) A spirit, a ghost, appeared, which could move through walls, travel quickly over long distances. The world doesn't work that way for the Thoughtful.

(3) Jesus appeared to people as a vision. Visions of the deceased still happen today and are considered by some to be a normal part of the grieving process, something the Thoughtful can understand.

(4) Followers realized what Jesus had meant by his words and deeds. Okay, maybe they realized what he meant. The Thoughtful have taken classes in which, perhaps weeks after the final exam, they have the aha moment: "That's what the instructor meant." Jesus' disciples, who had deserted him, came to understand he had shown them the way to transform their lives, how to die to the old ways and how to be reborn to the new. His life and ideas took on new meaning.

The Christian scripture/New Testament offers illustrations of all these possibilities. The earliest Christian scripture/New Testament writer, Paul, wrote he "saw" Jesus (1 Corinthians 9:1, 15:8), possibility 1 or 4 above and, when describing the general resurrection of the dead, used the term "spiritual body" (1 Corinthians 15:44), which might mean possibility 2 or 3. Writing 20 years later, Mark, in the earliest gospel, always identified the event with

---

[7] As part of the changing views of Jesus—the descriptions of him that made him divine—the later gospels portray him as calmer, more in control of events, than does Mark's gospel.

[8] Geza Vermes in *The Resurrection* (Doubleday, 2008) finds 8 categories. A discussion of Resurrection appearances and culture is John J. Pilch, *A Cultural Handbook to the Bible* (Eerdmans, 2012).

[9] N.T. Wright, *The Resurrection of the Son of God* (Fortress, 2003) in over 800 pages, makes this argument from within the Christian, in this case Anglican, tradition, although he is a bit vague about the nature of the resurrected body.

the words "he appeared"—this satisfies all four possibilities—most fully 3 or 4 (Mark 16:9, 12, 14) (none of these occurred in Mark's original gospel but appeared as a later addition.) Matthew's gospel reported the disciples "held (Jesus) by the feet," which implies 1 unless the language contains a metaphor about how to worship a ruler (Matthew 28:9). Luke let Jesus "vanish" (Luke24:31) which points to possibilities 2 and 3 and describes his "flesh and bones" while eating, suggesting 1 (Luke 24:39, 43). In John, the last gospel written, Jesus may tell Mary Magdalena not to touch him (or not to hold onto him) (John 20:17), and he passes into a closed room, twice (John 20:19, 26), implying possibility 2. In the doubting Thomas story, John never described Thomas as touching Jesus. In John's next chapter Jesus "showed himself" (John 21:1) and leaves the impression he ate bread and fish (John 21:15), so all possibilities fit.

Jesus' post-death appearances were always to the faithful. In the book Acts of the Apostles, the second volume of Luke's work, Jesus "shows himself," rather than "the apostles saw him." This story resembles the visions of mystics at other times and places. While, from this distance, we can't tell exactly what the faithful thought, it seems probable at least some of them thought they had experienced the reality of the risen Jesus. And the ambiguity of language is an issue here; the Thoughtful can read the descriptions of Paul's experience on the road to Damascus and easily draw differing conclusions.

Whether the Resurrection of Jesus was unique or not is questionable. Mark's gospel reports dead Jesus followers were seen in Jerusalem, and the concept of resurrection along with some examples, existed during Jesus' time. To the modern mind, perhaps the Resurrection meant God brings life, spiritual life, out of death, spiritual death. Thus metaphors that Jesus' followers used to help explain him also help the Thoughtful interpret the many Christian scripture/New Testament stories of Jesus' post-death appearances. Basically, the Thoughtful can go with the third or fourth of the possibilities above and accept the fact the world still operated by the same rules today as then.

As to the empty tomb, Paul, in the earliest writing in the Christian scripture/New Testament, doesn't mention it, so perhaps that tradition hadn't developed yet i.e., added later; that happened, a lot. Today, several scholars doubt that part of the empty tomb story entirely and think the Romans threw Jesus' body in a common grave, like others they executed.[10]

## What Did/Does It All Mean?

Jesus' followers had to find a purpose in his death, and his being a threat to civil order didn't satisfy. Their earliest views included one that Jesus suffered the fate of many previous prophets, martyrdom. Later, his death became a part of God's plan of salvation, and, finally, his followers interpreted his death as a sacrifice to reconcile God and people.[11] Other views of Jesus' death include one in which his life and death represent a conquest over the powers of the world that make life miserable. Or maybe his death called attention to his life and showed the importance of his message and his devotion to it.

Over the years, the theological interpretations of Jesus' death and resurrection proliferated, and as theological, not historically factual, interpretations, they are open to argument, since these assertions cannot be proven. Followers explain the Resurrection in many ways—as a conquest of death, as a validation from God, as proof he was not wrong in his announcement of the imminent rule of God and he was becoming one with God. Introducing the term "salvation" helped little as it could mean triumph over evil, an understanding the notion of forgiveness, some version of eternal life, or something else. Today the most popular view in the churches and the pews, if not among scholars, is Jesus died as a sacrifice for our sins. This view, God created a world where forgiveness of sin could only occur through the death of his son means, well, divine child abuse. It makes little sense.

On a more cynical level, Resurrection appearances validated the disciples as the ones who would begin (and control?) mission work. In this vein, Paul, not one of the original 12 disciples but a significant missionary, also

---

[10] Scheelebeekx, *Jesus,* 332. John Dominic Crossan, *Jesus: A Revolutionary Biography* (HarperSanFrancisco, 1994), 154. Luke Timothy Johnson, *The Real Jesus* (HarperSanFrancisco, 1996), 135, dismisses the issue of the empty tomb as unimportant.

[11] Schillebeeckx, *Jesus,* 274.

felt it necessary to have a Resurrection appearance. What better way to work than with the founder's imprimatur?

What can the Thoughtful accept? The disciples, who had deserted Jesus at his death, came to understand his public activity and their desertion was forgivable, and forgiven. To see Jesus in that way means one's present and future, not past, are what count. And the understanding can occur over and over, a part of the Kingdom of God. Thus, for the Thoughtful, the best explanation of the Resurrection encompasses a view that for Christians the Resurrection becomes the continuing experience of Jesus as a reality, both then and today, something the early church had come to believe.

**Spread the Word. Missionaries.**

The Thoughtful can observe the religion *of* Jesus, what he understood about God, became the religion *about* Jesus and he became God. And, in many traditions, so it remains today. How did that change happen?

Jesus' followers, after his death, continued to think of Jesus as something special, and they wanted to share that belief. Almost immediately after Jesus' death, his followers started missionary work to spread knowledge of him, his life, death and resurrection; this effort was directed especially at Jews as Jesus' followers thought of Jesus as an integral part of Jewish history and religion. The Christian scripture/New Testament records the efforts primarily of Paul in Asia Minor and Greece but others existed, particularly in Egypt. A hint to the number of these people (perhaps including women) comes in a first-century manuscript (one not in the Christian scripture/New Testament), the *Didache*, which lists rules for a community of Jesus' followers. Besides instructions on baptism and eating habits, the manuscript told them to host these traveling missionaries and assist them on their journeys.

In the next 50 years or so, the Jesus movement underwent several changes, in theology, organization, and practice, as diverse groups eventually coalesced, or separated, into "Christianity," or "Christianities." During this first half century, Jesus' followers remained a part of Judaism, same as were the Pharisees, Essenes, Sadducees, and others. (Just as Christianity includes Methodists, Roman Catholics, and Baptists today, divided in practices and theology but united in accepting Jesus as Christ.) They met in the synagogues and used the same sources (Hebrew Bible/Old Testament). In other words Christianity as a separate religion did not exist; the movement was referred to as "the Way" as it promoted the way of God of traditional Jewish religion. Even as non-Jews began joining the Jesus movement, the majority of Jesus' followers were Jews, not Gentiles, well into the first century.

As an aside, it can be mentioned these missionaries, including Paul, often had miracles reported about them. Exactly what went on in the meetings of the early followers is hinted at by Paul, in his first letter to the Corinthians, when he discusses people speaking in tongues, prophesying, and healing (1 Corinthians 12:8 – 10). In fact, the issue of miracles never completely died out as, for instance, even today, the Roman Catholic Church demands evidence of miracles before someone can become a saint.

## The Second Founder? Paul.

Very soon after Jesus' death, perhaps 3 to 5 years, a fellow named Paul, who had not known Jesus alive, came to accept Jesus' Resurrection.[12] Paul may have been a Pharisee who persecuted the Jesus people, but, while travelling from Jerusalem to Damascus, he experienced a vision of the risen Jesus that changed his life. Luke so describes Paul in Acts; Paul did not describe this himself in his own writings.[13] Paul then became a missionary for this new movement. His writings, mostly from the 50s, are the oldest we have in the Christian tradition. They became a major portion of the Christian scripture/New Testament, and his interpretation and actions shaped and enabled the movement to spread beyond Jerusalem and Galilee.[14] Because Paul's work came to form much of the basic interpretation of the Resurrection,

---

[12] Paul was known as Saul prior to his conversion experience.

[13] J.D. Crossan and Jonathan L. Reed, *In Search of Paul* (HarperSanFrancisco, 2004), 379. The Book of Acts is a doubtful source; it has been called a "theological novel." Gary Wills, *What Paul meant* (Viking, 2006), 30.

[14] Scholars doubt that all the scriptural writings that bear Paul's name were actually written by him rather than someone later using his name, a not uncommon practice in the ancient world. The doubtful works are Ephesians, Colossians, Hebrews, Timothy and Titus, at a minimum.

many see him as the second founder of Christianity. Paul himself didn't see it that way; he thought he had a new understanding of his old tradition, Jewish religion, an understanding that would lead him to clash with other Jesus people.[15]

In the 30s and 40s, Jesus' followers appeared wherever Jews had settled in any numbers but the group in Jerusalem functioned de facto as the home base with leadership provided by Peter, one of the disciples, and James, Jesus' brother. However, diversity abounded and many think Antioch, where Paul started, focused more on Jesus' death and resurrection while Jerusalem paid attention to his life and teachings. To oversimplify, which issue, Jesus' life or death, dominated in importance? The dispute survives today.

Paul's work involved moving to a city, and while earning his living possibly as a leather worker or tentmaker, trying to convert others to his understanding of Jesus. His travels took him through Asia Minor and into Greece where he left "house churches" of followers of Jesus.[16] However, once he had departed, the locals had questions and problems so they sought his advice, and Paul responded with letters, which eventually came to make up a substantial portion of the Christian scripture/New Testament. As he wrote to answer specific questions or deal with particular problems, his theology, ad hoc, changed over time. What he taught in person cannot be known so we are ignorant of how much the locals knew about Jesus' life and teachings. Paul's letters, however, focus heavily on the death and the Resurrection; he mentions Jesus' view on divorce (which he modifies) but very little else about Jesus' teachings. Finally, some of his ideas about the relationship of the risen Christ and the individual believer are essentially mystical and difficult for the Thoughtful to understand.

After Paul's conversion experience—his vision of the resurrected Jesus while traveling to Damascus—he, an educated Jew, brought that

---

[15] For the view that Paul broke with Jewish religion, see Reza Aslan, *Zealot The Life and Times of Jesus of Nazareth* (Random House, 2013).

[16] No record exists that Paul went to Babylon, home to many Jews after the exile. Perhaps Judaism was better organized there under the emergent rabbis. Doron Mendels, "Why Paul Went West," *Biblical Archaeological Review* 37 (2011). 49-54, 68.

education into his interpretation of Jesus, particularly his crucifixion and the Resurrection. Paul's view of Jesus used the word "Christ," Greek for "Messiah," a term from Jewish history often referring to kings, sometimes prophets. Paul almost always wrote "Jesus Christ," as though Christ had become Jesus' last name. (In some circles today, in times of stress or anger a middle initial "H" is added, as in "Jesus H. Christ.") In Jewish history, Messiah meant "the anointed" and denoted a person invested by God with a special mission; most commonly kings had the title. By Jesus' time the use of Messiah usually meant someone, descended from King David, who would lead the Jews out of their Roman bondage; by implication, the Messiah means a military figure. (Other men claimed to be a Messiah, such as Theudos (c. 45) and Menahem (c.66), usually in connection with a revolt against Rome.) Remember, at Jesus' execution the Romans nailed a sign, "King of the Jews," a Messiah-like expression, on his cross. With Paul, use of this term took a different turn, connected with the end time. God chose Jesus and resurrected him to start that end time. In other words, Paul's view of the end time was not the one favored in Jewish religion: no militarism. Moreover, he had to deal with the Jewish belief the resurrection would come for all at the end time but it had already occurred for Jesus. His solution was the end time is neigh, which colors much of his writing. Over time, he had to address the fact some believers had died and questions arose about their future; he combined his Jewish view of the general resurrection with some Greek notions and produced an end time resurrection at which believers would have "spiritual bodies." The Thoughtful may not find this answer a good solution, and the church has never dwelt overly much on the matter.

For Paul, if one accepts Jesus as Christ, one is saved, has salvation, though the meaning of that concept remained vague. Paul proposed a doctrine of "justification by faith," ("faith" probably meaning "trust," not "belief"). This justification opened the Pandora's Box of faith versus works. (To a considerable extent this matter became the nut of the Reformation theological debates 1500 years later.) The consequence of Paul's idea meant one could not earn salvation by doing good things ("works") but must trust one has it. This trust, or belief, came to separate the Jesus people and, ultimately, Christianity from other religious traditions where belief was not an issue.

This notion of faith being all important became part of the debate Paul had with other of Jesus' followers over "the Law," the rules of Jewish practices. Over the centuries, Jews had developed food laws, today called kosher, as well as beliefs and practices about the Sabbath, circumcision, clothing, hair, etc. If one failed in some aspect of this tradition, a sacrifice or purification at the Temple in Jerusalem made things right again. Paul rejected this approach in his interpretation of Jesus, particularly the Resurrection. For Paul, Jesus, as a part of God's plan, had fulfilled scripture so all the old understandings became irrelevant. Jesus' death, therefore, ended "the Law" and the need for Temple sacrifices. As the end time for everyone approached rapidly, Paul focused on what would happen then, not how to behave now.

This matter of traditional practices, the Law, came to a head, probably in Antioch, because Paul converted non-Jews, Gentiles. It appears synagogues, besides being places of worship and study for Jews, attracted Gentiles who liked the monotheism and ethics of Judaism. These people are called "God fearers," and they may have constituted a substantial number of Paul's successes. The question arose as to whether they needed to follow the traditional Jewish practices because, after all, the Jesus movement still situated itself firmly as a part of Jewish religion. Food might be one thing, but circumcision would something else entirely; not surprisingly, Paul may have had more success converting women than men. For Paul, Jesus had fulfilled scripture and so the end time for all was soon, hence the Law's irrelevancy. In an effort to get uniform practices in the new movement and to ratify his work with Gentiles, Paul went to Jerusalem in 49 to meet with the leaders of the Jesus people there. That group practiced traditional Jewish religion; indeed, James, Jesus' brother, was so observant of Jewish customs he earned the nickname "the Righteous." They reached a working compromise that later fell apart and Paul continued his conversion of Gentiles without requiring them to follow traditional practices. While he did his missionary work, a "truth squad" followed him, advocating traditional Jewish practices for the followers of Jesus. In the long haul, by the 90s at the earliest, Paul's position won out but did so at the cost of Jesus' followers being excluded from the synagogues, finalizing a separation that led to Christianity and Judaism as distinct religious traditions, both growing from a common seed, ancient Jewish religion. For the future of Christianity, the decision to abandon Jewish practices, especially circumcision, was the most important development after Jesus' death and before Constantine's conversion.

The people whom Paul converted didn't always get along. In particular, discontent reigned at Corinth in Greece. Lots of discord occurred over lots of issues. For example, the Corinthian Jesus people took Paul's ideas to mean equality for all with faith, all Christians counted the same. As the group included slaves and women, one can imagine the uproar when such second- and third-class folk claimed their place in the sun. Hence, Paul had to write and tell them to behave in the traditional manner, but not to worry, he told them, it won't be for long as the end time draws neigh. When the end time didn't occur, Paul's words became one cornerstone in perpetuating in church history the inequalities of the Roman world. However, in a letter to the Galatian group of Jesus people, he made a ringing affirmation of equality for all, Greek, Jew, free, slave, male, female, so with so much scripture, lots of possible interpretations exist (Galatians 3:28).

In an aside, it can be mentioned that some portray Paul, who never married, as homosexual. Certainly his interest in a slave, Onesimus, and a Greek boy, Timothy, lends itself to the possibility, but that is as far as this interpretation can go. However, modern ideas about homosexuality don't fit ancient mores so any interpretation, in absence of more evidence, remains dodgy. One scholar suggests reading Paul's letters as though he were gay brings new understandings.[17] Let's leave it at that.

Paul emphasized the Christian life was to be lived out in a community and his letters contain lots of admonitions about folks' behavior. The new life of the believer is to include love, joy, peace, patience, kindness, generosity, faithfulness, gentleness, self-control, and so on, and the greatest of these is to be love (by which he usually meant service to others) (1 Corinthians 13:13).

---

[17] John Selby Spong, *Rescuing the Bible from Fundamentalism* (HarperSanFrancisco, 1991), 116.

Thus it appears he had learned the Kingdom of God material Jesus taught, even though he uses the term as few as eight times.

In addition to the focus on Christ, the Messiah, rather than Jesus' life and teachings (a focus that made the cross an important symbol), Paul left a legacy in his writings that influenced the future of the movement, even to today. (However, no gospel writer seems aware of Paul's writings so the effect would come after the first century, maybe as late as the fourth century.) One can debate whether he saw Jesus as divine, but subsequently people such as Marcion found that idea in his writings; the issue of Jesus' divinity had a great future. Paul also had no argument with the political role of Rome, for a couple of reasons. When the end time occurred, Rome would be irrelevant. Moreover, if he had Roman citizenry (a status not held by all, but only some, in the Empire), he reportedly took advantage of that status when he got into trouble with Jewish authorities during a trip to Jerusalem. His attitude to Rome led him to counsel patience with the world's authorities, another position that led the church over the centuries not to be obstreperous in the face of oppression and corruption by governments. Finally, his attention to his converts as a group led him to see them as a body, the body of Christ, which is how the church later came to see itself also. All these issues grow out of Paul's conviction the end time approached rapidly; when it didn't happen, followers read his words as applicable to their situation, something Paul never envisioned. And, without doubt, he was instrumental in creating the understanding his religion was about Jesus, not his teachings or life. That view of Jesus and the argument about the Law, Jewish traditions, contribute to the view of Paul as the second founder of Christianity.

## Variety, Diversity, Confusion? Christianity or Christianities?

What happened in the centuries after Jesus' death is difficult to reconstruct as few of the writings deal with history of the early movement. To a considerable extent, the materials were written by the "winners" in the many contests over beliefs, practices, indeed, just about everything.

By 100, Jesus' followers, excluded from the synagogues, found their membership increasingly non-Jewish. From this point on, they will be called "Christians" and Christianity will be treated as separate from Judaism. The organization developed under the aegis of bishops, but the theology, especially about the relationship of Jesus and God, remained in flux. From the perspective of today, the major writings that came to be the Christian scripture/New Testament all existed but, at the time, Christians had no agreement about that matter, the canon had not been developed.[18] There is little documentation about practices available for this period, though it is clear baptism was the most important ritual. While sometimes subjected to persecution, Christians had de facto toleration for about 40 years after their persecution in 260; churches could own property and build buildings. Christianities, not Christianity, better describes the first few centuries.

### Why Did Christianity Prosper?

Maybe God knows! Ever since Edward Gibbon's famous fifteenth chapter in *The History of the Decline and Fall of the Roman Empire* (1776) on the matter, scholars have posited explanations.

It was not because Christians had Truth; history doesn't work that way. In contrast with many, though not all, religions and cults of the day, Christians proselytized. Like Jews and a few other groups, they sought to spread their faith. And that faith grew in membership at a rate of perhaps 40 percent each decade; accurate numbers are not available.

The future resurrection of the individual might be a very attractive idea in a Roman Empire, beleaguered by external threats of Germans and Persians and torn apart by periodic clashes among generals. Also society increasingly stratified into a few rich and multitudinous non-wealthy. The combination of the economic division, a worsening of effective governmental control of the countryside, and the changing structure of government

---

[18] Much of what follows comes from Robin Lane Fox, *Pagans and Christians* (Knopf, 1989).

creating many more bureaucratic openings for aristocrats which lessened the political cohesions of the cities. Whereas the rich and the rest had once taken pride and ownership of their locality, the rich increasingly looked to the Emperor and the rest looked out for themselves. Christianity provided a community that replaced the former political community.[19]

This new community, now called the church, mostly comprised the "humble free class" rather than slaves or aristocrats and provided charity for its poor, especially widows and children. This work had previously been a role of the rich but the collapse of local patriotism led to its abandonment. So far as we know, Christian charity was nearly unique in this period. Besides filling a societal need, this charity helped convince non-believers of the power of the Christian message.

Followers highly prized membership. Baptism into the group came after a several year apprenticeship during which one received instruction in the faith and one's behavior was observed. Once in, if one got excluded, subsequent readmission might be denied until the deathbed. Adultery and denial of membership during a persecution seem to have been major foci for exclusion. Bishops developed the power of excommunication, by which a member was expelled from the group (and benefits of membership, both now and in the hereafter). Denial of reenrollment combined with more talk of a nasty hell helped control potential miscreants.[20] Christianity appears to have been a group worth joining for reasons the Thoughtful today might not appreciate.

### Jesus Changes. The Divinity Issue.

Jesus, or the description of him, changed over time. He moved from man to deity to deity/man but not without a lot of arguing by his followers

---

[19] About 250 the church in Rome was caring for over 1500 widows and persons in distress. Eusebius, *Ecclesiastical History,* trans J.E.L. Oulton, (Harvard University Press, 1964), Book VI, xlii, 11-12.

[20] Whether the development of a professional class, the priests and bishops, was a "good thing" has been debated since their emergence. Sixteenth-century reformers had a strong anti-clerical bent, and recently Garry Wills, a loyal Roman Catholic, has questioned the value of a priesthood. *Why Priests? A Failed Tradition* (Viking, 2013).

along the way. Also the debates over Jesus pushed followers into taking other positions, e.g., his birth from a virgin with the Holy Spirit as father, which strain credulity today. Beware! The Thoughtful should know few things in Christianity will provoke the same degree of heated responses as those raising the possibility Jesus was not divine. Most pewsitters seem to see Jesus as God who came down to Earth (called "high Christology" in scholarly speak and is based on John's gospel); most scholars, however, see Jesus as a man who through his intense feeling and understanding about the deity, came to look like God (called "low Christology"), a view comporting with the modern, and Thoughtful, mind.

Jesus, even in his lifetime, was occasionally described as the "Messiah," the anointed one (the Greek word is "Christ"). When he preached about the Kingdom of God, his ambiguity about its time, now or future, led some listeners to connect him with a prevailing understanding of Messiah, an understanding involving political power. The general political conditions of Palestine produced many who looked for an individual, a Messiah, to lead the people to freedom from the Romans. In 66, after Jesus' death, one group, the Zealots (who were not Jesus' followers), revolted, though unsuccessfully. This notion of a Messiah, a king with a divine commission, was somehow connected to the past, the reign of King David, and to an apocalyptic future. The Davidic aspect accounts for two of the gospel writers putting Jesus' birth in Bethlehem, the city of David, and including Davidic genealogies leading to Joseph (although they then didn't make Joseph Jesus' biological father). Also the creation of Mary's annunciation of her coming pregnancy with Jesus buttressed this connection.

For the Thoughtful, if one accepts the idea of the Kingdom of God, a new understanding by the individual results in a different notion of "right" thinking and action. Then the Messiah aspect of Jesus flows easily. If a general societal change—political or cultural—is necessary for the Kingdom of God, then the Messiah description is a problem as nothing much happened.

Another term applied to Jesus was "Son of God." This term pops up in Mark's gospel and is applied to Jesus after his baptism. This view, called "adoptionism," means Jesus was a human whom God selected as special.

Whether Mark got this idea from the Roman world is unknown, but Roman emperors often adopted someone as son so as to provide for a smooth imperial transition. Augustus adopted Tiberius and Tiberius adopted Caligula so the practice was known. As the emperors were gods, the adopted individual became a "son of god," different from Christianity's "Son of God." Mark's decision, therefore, was more than imitating the imperial practice, it smacked of treason as he was proclaiming Jesus, not the Roman emperor of the day, as the Son of God. That understanding got lost over the years, and Jesus became "Son of God" without any Roman connection.

Jesus died. Why? Scholars see the combination of Temple authorities and Roman officialdom as the cause of the crucifixion. His followers, however, needed a stronger, more cosmic, reason and quickly decided Jesus died to bring about forgiveness of sin. Certainly Jesus did not just die to placate an angry God; that smacked of paganism. And political regimes had long used scapegoats when things went badly. The entire Temple organization had it basis in the idea that sacrifice removed sin. If Jesus taught sin was unimportant, then it was easy to see his death as a sacrifice for others since this position easily fit into the day's mentality. So important was this connection to sin the fourth gospel writer, John, put Jesus' trial, etc., a day sooner so his death would correspond to the killing of the Passover lamb, an event Jews celebrated as revealing God's goodness and protection. In the Exodus story the blood of the lamb protected the Jews from the angel of death; if Jesus' death took away the sins of the world and gave eternal life, it then also protected against the angel of death. Exactly why someone had to die to bring God and people together is a theological conundrum the Thoughtful can be excused for ignoring. It won't be the last thing either.

The nature of Jesus, the union of the divine and human, and the incarnation occupied thinkers, too much. Their heresies detail some of the machinations. A few basic issues lay at the root of the disputes. The tendency was to make Jesus all God, no man, because if he were a man, the problem of sin raised its ugly head. If being human, sin was inevitable, then did Jesus sin? Could his death then free all from the powers of sin? One outgrowth of this problem was the virgin birth because to be born as a result of normal human intercourse would give Jesus original sin. Even if Jesus is given two natures, the argument continues as to whether he had one will, or two, a heresy called "monotheletism."

After Jesus' death and his appearance to his followers (i.e., the Resurrection), one can watch the progress of interpretations that made Jesus a part of God. The switch from charismatic prophet to superhuman being may come as the Jesus movement shifted from Palestine to the larger Greco-Roman world. In the first century, the period of composition of the bulk of the Christian scripture/New Testament, Jesus carried numerous titles after his death—Son of Man, Savior, Son of God, Word, king of kings, servant, and others. Perhaps the most common, "Lord," described the followers' allegiance and dependence on Jesus; they could honor and worship him while also serve him by their life's work. (Paul frequently used the term "in Christ" to mean followers were united mystically and ethically in a fellowship, which quickly became known as the "church.") Christian scripture/New Testament portrays Jesus as changing not a bit; after all, a god would be perfect from the get-go.[21]

By the end of the first century, the *Didache*, a manual of practice for the early movement has no redeeming Christ, no Word, no Son of God, a very low Christology. On the other hand, John, in his gospel, written slightly earlier, is close to portraying Jesus as entirely divine and suggests Jesus had existed since creation or even before creation. He also described him as the Word, *Logos,* a Greek word with many meanings but which probably meant the face, the countenance, of God by which the followers know the deity. By about 120, the *Epistle of Barnabus*, a non-canonical work, sees Jesus as quasi-divine. But things didn't end there. Clement, writing about 200, could argue Jesus was divine and merely looked like a man. However, that position did not hold although it took many centuries of theological debate before various groups decided to go their own ways about the nature of Jesus.

---

[21] Two texts hint at Jesus changing but they appear to be throwaway lines, not biographical observations. Luke 2:52; Hebrews 5:7-8.

## Out With the Old? Jewish Traditions.

The disputes between Paul and other early Jesus people about the relationship of the Jesus movement to Jewish religion didn't end with any clear settlement, but over time, Jews declined in numbers among the Jesus people, although issues of Jewish history didn't go away. Ironically, Christianity was traditionally, begun on a Jewish holiday, Pentecost. The Jesus people and the other Jews slowly drew apart from each other, partly because Jesus didn't fit the usual views about a Messiah. When his followers started speaking of him as divine, many Jews reacted negatively because their religion was strictly monotheistic. The rabbis were, in the Mishnah, moving their faith from Temple sacrifices to family rituals, the practice of Judaism today. A standard prayer, dating to the Hellenistic era, was interpreted as being directed against the followers of Jesus[22] By the fourth century, church scholars were ignoring (or ignorant about) the Jewish practices and lore the rabbis had developed.

To summarize a complex argument, the Thoughtful need to understand many future Christian ideas hinged on Jesus' death. If Jesus gave salvation to all by his death, he fulfilled the understandings of Jewish history and practices. His death, in other words, broke the power of sin and the past, so Jewish practices became irrelevant. (Matthew's gospel suggests rejecting Jesus is to reject a correct understanding of Jewish religion.)

Despite Paul's position, the early movement was riven by this issue, and some of the missionaries who followed Paul to his early conversion groups, caused considerable dissent (Galatians 16:6 – 7). Eventually a group emerged among the Jesus people who adhered rigorously to Jewish practices. This group, the Ebionites, claimed to be followers of Jesus' brother James. And Matthew, in his gospel, argued Jews among the Jesus people had to keep the Jewish Law, though Gentiles didn't.

At the other extreme was total rejection of all Jewish history and practices. A second-century Roman from Asia Minor, Marcion, rejected the God of the Hebrew Bible/Old Testament as too harsh, but accepted the God of love

---

[22] Birkat ha-Minim, the 12th benediction of the Amidah. At one time this was thought to have been created in 70 C.E. to deal with Christians; now it is thought to be much older.

of the Christian scripture/New Testament. He and his followers used Paul's letters and a modified version of the gospel of Luke. Groups of Marcionites could be found all over the Empire.

Other things alienated the Jesus followers and Jews. When the revolt against Rome began in 66, Jesus' followers sat it out. In fact, Symeon, said to be Jesus' cousin, led his followers out of Jerusalem before things got nasty with the Romans. The fall of Jerusalem and the destruction of the Temple were viewed by many Jesus followers as God's judgment on a people who didn't accept the true belief, theirs. Also, this event—the fall of Jerusalem—probably scattered the group that had formed around James and who had been most loyal to Jewish traditions. Increasingly, the Jesus folk began to see Jewish religion in terms of supersessionism, which means their beliefs override those of the Jewish past; one result of this development was to call the Hebrew Bible the "Old Testament" and the developing canon since Jesus as the "New Testament," the old and new ways of looking at the relationship of God and people.

**Other Views.**

A more pervasive approach which surfaced in some Ebionites and Marcionites, as well as others, goes under the broad title of Gnostic, an intellectual current that peaked in the second century though it appeared earlier. Covering a wide variety of approaches, Gnosticism was not a single religious view within Christianity (we can identify, inter alia, Valentinian, Sethian, Orphic Eucratitic strands) and also had non-Christian dimensions (Manichaeism being the most popular). In Christian and other views, the premise included secret "special knowledge" (*gnosis*) limited to only a few; even the gospel of Mark has episodes where Jesus tells the multitude a story and then explains its real meaning to the twelve disciples (Mark 4:11, 34). Gnostics developed an elaborate mythology of how the world came to be, an overarching cosmological system, and saw it as a dualism of good and evil, spirit and matter. Jesus, being good, was wholly spirit and had appeared among humans to explain the deeper meaning of life. As Gnostic writings were highly symbolic, multiple interpretations were easy. By the end of the first century, writers were dealing with the Gnostic issue. The later writings in the Christian scripture/New Testament are filled with warnings against "false teachings," and the later gospels include stories about the resurrected Jesus inviting people to touch him and eating food (something a Gnostic "ghost" wouldn't do). Within the Christian tradition, this view appealed to many, especially Egyptians, and can be discerned among the Corinthians (1 Corinthians 6:12 – 20, 8:1 – 13). Because it was eventually eliminated, probably by the end of the fifth century, the details of Gnosticism remain obscure, though the discovery of documents at Nag Hammadi in Egypt in 1945 gave us a lot of information about their views.

Still another approach appeared in some of the above groups, and others, and falls under "Docetism." It addresses whether Jesus was human or divine. Many had trouble with Jesus' death so a solution was to see him as only appearing to be human while he really was a divine being or a human into whom the divine lodged temporarily (leaving before his death). Even the gospel of Mark lends itself to this view as he writes the divine entered Jesus at his baptism by John the Baptizer and had left him before his death on the cross when Jesus asks why God has forsaken him. The Thoughtful might note the influence of Plato (remember the myth of the cave?) in both Docetism and Gnosticism.

All these groups—Ebionites, Marcionites, Gnostics, Docetists, and many others—had their own scriptures. Today, scholars have found parts of at least 30 gospels, writings about Jesus, his life, and his death. The "problem," if a problem it was, arose from the fact no individual or group had sufficient control, stature, or authority to hammer out a single view. Moreover, as a relatively tiny group within the Roman Empire, Jesus' followers didn't attract much attention. Over time, however, the debates and confusion began to produce a view that came to be called "orthodox," but the Thoughtful should be aware that during the early days, for centuries even, the Jesus movement was a diverse group, very diverse.

Mystery religions, though not involving followers of Jesus, had many qualities and practices which looked similar to the Romans and made for relatively easy conversion to Christianity. (Called "mystery" because they usually involved an initiation and some information only available to those initiates.) Followers of Mithras, Cybele, Isis, and others might find Jesus more attractive as he had been a real person, not a creature of myth, and his followers offered a community in which charity and love predominated.

The Jesus movement arose in the wing of apocalyptic Judaism that included John the Baptizer, the people of Qumran, the community that wrote the book of Enoch, and the like. Even within the Christian scripture/New Testament various strands appear as Mark's gospel attempts a narrative of Jesus' life whereas the collection known as Q was only interested in his teachings. Add in the divisions Paul deals with—the role of the Law, antinomianism, the sexual behavior of some early believers, the presence of Gnostic ideas—and the early Jesus movement begins to look so diverse as to be formless. Many groups have left no trace so their ideas, practices, or size cannot be determined today. Some may have coalesced around a leader, others may have existed in only a few congregations, but whatever the situation, variety was the rule. Mysticism, sex, attitudes to any church hierarchy, elitism of some believers, attitudes to Jews, vegetarianism (Ebionites), continuing revelation, Mary Magdalene—all were important to differing factions of the early Jesus movement. Already by 100 or so the need for better order and more discipline was evident in a writing (wrongly) attributed to Paul (1 Timothy).[23]

## The Winner. Orthodoxy.

The term "orthodox" only means the view that ultimately prevailed, not one that is true (unless "true" is defined by winning). Arguably the views that won represented compromises, middle grounds, among the many possibilities available. Along the way did anyone notice many of the resulting doctrines are, to the Thoughtful, paradoxical, perhaps even inconsistent? How did this history occur?

Perhaps the strongest reason for the success of the winner was the strong reliance on the notion the leaders all had been decided, ordained,

---

[23] Hegesippus, about 170, lists nearly a dozen Christian sects, and the fourth-century writer Epiphanus has dozens of groups.

commissioned by previous leaders who had all been decided, ordained, commissioned by people in a direct line back to the original apostles. This "apostolic succession" apparently gave the leaders credibility in disciplining members and in claiming the truth of their particular interpretations. Congregations did not just spring up spontaneously but as the result of the work of a missionary, the claim had plausibility. Ultimately, the apostolic succession would be broken if the group had a later internal split, as one of the resulting leaders would not have been created in the manner claimed. However, the force of this argument for orthodoxy is somewhat blunted by the awareness Ebionites, Marcionites, Gnostics, and others probably made the same claim.

The focus on monotheism had great appeal to the educated of the day and despite the Trinity issue, was vigorously defended by the orthodox. Greek philosophers had centuries earlier concluded only one god could be behind all things, and increasingly the leaders of the Jesus movement were Greek-educated. And Jews had long maintained belief in one God, although it is not clear if they thought there were others, subordinate, for non-Jews. This belief in one deity separated the orthodox from the Marcionites, who had a Hebrew Bible/Old Testament God and a Christian scripture/New Testament God, and the Gnostics, who had many gods. The matter of the Trinity, not part of Jesus' ideas but apparent among Christians at least as early as the second century, was an interesting compromise for those who wanted to but couldn't quite give up the notion of multiple gods; how it was understood by the masses is unknown. Whether the Trinity and monotheism are a paradox or are genuinely inconsistent is left to the Thoughtful to ponder. (Curiously, another paradox, the nature of Jesus—divine, human, or both—didn't get much traction until the fourth century when orthodoxy was pretty much dominant.)

Greek philosophers had also developed the argument that certain ideas were "right" while others were not. This approach was not a view held by the pagan religions as no creeds were demanded of anyone before a prayer or a sacrifice. Paul's emphasis on the death and resurrection of Jesus, not his life or teachings, also meant his version of Christianity had a "right" idea. Scholars believe the early Jesus people held a variety of beliefs and engaged in diverse practices as discussed earlier. Thus in the areas where Paul had worked the Jesus people had worked out a different view of the meaning of "Christ" than those followers in Jerusalem, Antioch, or Alexandria.[24] Other differences included expectations about the end time and the nature of church leadership. In the early second century, baptisms involved reciting of creeds of belief. This development probably separated the orthodox from the Gnostics because every individual Gnostic could have a unique interpretation as special knowledge had been imparted to that individual. Also creeds had a useful quality in that they enabled leaders to discipline members, and creeds developed in the second century in which groups sought to define themselves (and exclude others).[25] Over time, the leaders met and corresponded with one another to develop a network that began to bring the theology and practices of the various groups into harmony, though uniformity remained a long way in the future, if ever it occurred.

Organization played a part, but we can't tell if the orthodox structure was unique. Even before the disputes over the Law led to the Jesus people being excluded from the synagogues, they met in the homes of members, presumably rich members with large homes. These "house churches" often had disagreements internally as we know from the letters of Paul written in the 50s. House churches evolved an organization by designating certain members to arrange meetings and perhaps provide the food for the group's meals (elders, deacons). As a group got bigger or as a city contained more than one group, one individual emerged as a fulltime worker, the bishop (or *episcopus* in Greek), a development visible by the end of the first century. Bishops also emerged in response to disputes among elders.

With the deaths of the first generation of Jesus people, these bishops were left to their own devices about answers to new questions, so more and

---

[24] Arland J. Hultgren, *The Rise of Normative Christianity* (Fortress, 1994), 9.

[25] Hultgren, *The Rise of Normative Christianity,* 84, citing Epiphanis, *The Panarion of Epiphanis of Salamis,* Eusebius, *Ecclesiastical History,* 4.22.5, and Justin, *Dialogue with Trypho,* 35.

more, bishops corresponded with one another about issues and practices, and a meeting of some bishops (a practice with a great future) early in the third century is recorded and maybe such meetings occurred earlier.[26]

## Women. What Women?

The Jesus movement and later Christianity, as they developed, became a religion, with its attendant institutions, staffed and run by men. Was it always such?

In addition to the 12 male disciples, we know of several women, most famously Mary Magdelene, who were followers of Jesus. We do not know how Jesus and his ragtag group supported themselves—he lived among and talked to the poor—and it is more than possible his finances were "provided for him" by females—again, perhaps Mary Magdalene (Mark 15:41).

Jesus certainly didn't ignore women in his public life. Stories include ones in which he praised a poor widow's generosity to the Temple (Mark 12:42), used bridesmaids as examples of both foolishness and wisdom (Matthew 25:1 – 13), and saved the life of an adulteress (John 8:3 – 11). To the extent Jesus proposed an "upsidedown world," where the poor would be rewarded, women also would be elevated from their second-class status in Jewish society.

At his death, the women remained the most faithful, watching from a distance (Matthew 27:545, John 19:25, Mark 15:40) and the first Resurrection experience occurred to Mary Magdalene and other women (Mark 16:9, Matthew 28:9, Luke 24:10, John 20:15). Reading between the lines, the Thoughtful might well conclude Mary Magdalene was quite important as she keeps appearing. Her name, "of Magdala" probably refers to her hometown but also might point to her importance as in Aramaic "magdalla" means "great." (Her identity as a prostitute comes 500 years later when someone translated Magdela to mean "curly hair," an attribute of prostitutes.) Exorcised by Jesus (Luke 8:2), she followed Jesus in his travels. This devotion was unusual, given the customs of the day that women

---

[26] Fox, *Pagans and Christians*, 512.

did not travel without family supervision. She did follow him which supports the idea she was traveling with her husband, *The De Vinci Code*. Alternatively, she may have been a widow which would have given her a bit more freedom (and perhaps money) in patriarchal Palestine. Writings such as Pistis Sophia, the Gospel of Mary, and the Gospel of Thomas, not included in the Christian scripture/New Testament, give her a much larger role in the Jesus story.

Then along comes Paul, and his writings send a mixed message. He mentions the presence of many women in his letters: Phoebe as a deacon (Romans 16:1 – 2), Junia as the foremost among the apostles (Romans 6:7). To Paul gender was irrelevant (Galacians 3:28), but he also, in his two letters to the Corinthians, espouses traditional views about the subordination of women. However, his strongest statement, one in which he tells wives to obey their husbands, may result from his outlook the end time approaches so one need not rock the boat. More likely, a copyist added this later as it doesn't fit the flow of the letter (1 Corinthians 14:34 – 5).

Though Paul's letters suggest women as both missionaries and leaders were important to the movement, later writings included in the Christian scripture/New Testament in the first century are less supportive of women's roles. The letters entitled Titus and Timothy define bishops and deacons as male (1 Timothy 3, Titus 1:5 – 9) so it appears Jesus' followers conformed to the usages of Jewish and Roman society by 100. Montanism, one of the varieties of Christianity in the second century, centered around three individuals who engaged in ecstatic prophesying. Two of them were women which might have contributed to other Christians' rejection of their insights. On the other hand, during the persecutions, women constituted a very significant percentage of the martyrs, and the emphasis on virginity gave women moral superiority, even to bishops. Whatever the case, by the second century, whatever roles and power women had ever held in the new movement disappeared. And so things remain, in most parts of Christianity today. Whether this development helped or handicapped the development of orthodoxy cannot be determined.

## Apologies. The Gospels.

The development of a canon, an accepted set of writings, helped the orthodox maintain unity, although other groups (e.g., Marcionites) also had canons. At the same time Paul was writing, collections of Jesus' sayings were floating around so some Jesus people, *contra* Paul, interested themselves in Jesus' public activity rather than just his death and resurrection. Many of those writings have not survived, and some that did are not included in the Christian canon, the Christian scripture/New Testament. Nevertheless, they shed light on the developing church and its diversity. The most famous writing that didn't survive is "*Q*," short for the German *Quelle*, meaning "source." A collection of Jesus' sayings, not a narrative of his life, *Q* probably originated in Galilee where Jesus engaged in the bulk of his public activity. Another collection of Jesus' sayings, labeled *The Gospel of Thomas*, may have been made in this period also, though scholars argue over its date. Other possible writings, which didn't survive, include collections of Jesus' parables and miracles, and stories of his death. In addition oral traditions abounded.

As the first generation of Jesus' followers died, writings appeared seeking to interpret Jesus' life for his followers. Today called "gospels" (the word means "good news," as in the message about the Kingdom of God that Jesus taught), these writings do not fit the category of history or biography because they do not seek completeness and have strong themes, reflecting their authors' intentions and their audience.

Between 65 and 75, someone, traditionally called Mark (we don't know the name or anything about the author), composed a story of Jesus that included his life and death. Mark probably wrote in the city of Rome and addressed Gentile, not Jewish, Jesus followers (his Galilean geography is often wrong). By Mark's time, one group of the Jesus' followers saw Jesus as "Lord," "Son of God," and "Savior," and Mark read this approach back into Jesus' life and words. He interpreted events to show that Jesus preached about the Kingdom of God, but his followers did not get it; his followers, especially the disciples, received harsh treatment by Mark. Also Mark sided with Paul in terms of the inclusion of Gentiles, something probably opposed by the original disciples. Thus in Mark's telling, Jesus, failing to enlighten his followers, turns to emphasizing his coming death as a martyr to his ideas. Mark probably wrote after Nero's persecution of the Jesus' followers in Rome from 64 to 68 and maybe after the failure of the Jewish rebellion in Palestine against Rome from 66 to 73. Given these events, Mark probably wrote to explain the costs of following Jesus.

Mark dealt with the Resurrection very, very briefly. In some ways Mark provided the first part, the life and death of Jesus, of the story, and Paul picked up with the consequences, the Resurrection and beyond, even though Paul wrote earlier.

Next, around 80 – 5, came two authors, traditionally called Matthew and Luke (again, we lack exactitude in these identities), who produced two more gospels, using Mark's gospel and some other materials, now lost to us, and a collection of Jesus' sayings. (See *Q* above). If Mark wrote to or on behalf of Gentile followers of Jesus, Matthew, probably living in Antioch, wrote to Jewish followers of Jesus. For example, in deference to Jewish tradition of not naming the deity, Matthew changed "Kingdom of God" to "Kingdom of Heaven." With Matthew, we get the nativity story and many more post-death appearances. Also. he was the only gospel writer to include the Sermon on the Mount and named Peter as the chief disciple (which makes his the favorite gospel of Roman Catholics, or at least the pope's favorite). Matthew repeatedly showed Jesus fulfilling Hebrew Bible/Old Testament prophecies so that the Jesus movement was a continuation of the Jewish tradition, even though it now had lots of non-Jews in it. Thus the emergent church of the Jesus people, the new Israel, carried forward and replaced the old Israel of the Hebrew Bible/Old Testament.

At the same time as Matthew, but independent of him, Luke, living either in the city of Rome or Greece, produced a gospel. His, also, like Matthew's, relied on the gospel of Mark and other materials, including Q. This gospel is part of a two volume set that includes Acts of the Apostles, another writing later included in the Christian scripture/New Testament. To Luke the Jesus people movement had become the new or true Jewish religion. Luke also confronted the problem of why the end time had not occurred and extended it into the indefinite future. Luke emphasized, more than the other gospel writers, Jesus' interest in the poor, the sinners, the outsiders. The nativity story usually used at Christmas today along with many post-death appearances are found in Luke's gospel.

The Book of Acts, the other part of Luke's work, described the church after Jesus, by tracing the movements of missionaries, especially Paul, and the spread of the movement in the Roman Empire. A corollary of this expansion was an effort to show the church did not conflict with Rome. As part of this accommodation with the Empire Luke excused the Romans and blamed the Jewish leadership for Jesus' death.

Then, along came John. In the 90s, the final canonical gospel, which was attributed to John, appeared. Where he lived is anybody's guess; tradition says Ephesus. By now the synagogues excluded the Jesus people because of their insistence of equating Jesus with Christ, the Messiah. As a result John came down particularly hard on "the Jews."[27] This gospel, probably written without knowledge of the earlier three, has a completely different style. Theology being the aim, Jesus is portrayed making long speeches telling who he is—The Word, Lamb of God, Son of Man, Messiah, and so forth—and how he carries out God's tasks. Believers, not possible converts, constituted the intended audience, and John sought to show what God had done for them in Jesus. This gospel provides the saying, common in creeds, "That God so loved the world he gave his only son." The "Son of God" usage dominated more than it did in earlier writings and points to the developing issue of Jesus' divinity.

The gospels, collectively identified as "apologies," a term meaning a justification or defense, were written for believers and those interested in joining the movement. Mark, Matthew and Luke have a common story line and are referred to as "synoptic," because they are so similar (viewed with the "same eye"). However, no gospel constitutes a biography in the modern sense. The four gospels have much more than this brief summary indicates,

[27] This use could also refer to Jewish Christians, the old issue of adherence to the Law still being alive.

and their overall interpretation divides denominations today. Moreover, if a Thoughtful grew up in a Christian tradition, one learned the overall story without any concern about which gospel was the source, so it is difficult to appreciate the significant differences among them.

## Moving on. After 100 C.E.

### Problems. Rome.

The Empire in which Jesus lived changed, often dramatically in the second and third centuries. After the period described as the Good Emperors (98 – 180), all sorts of problems beset the land. The frontiers were challenged in the north by peoples variously described as Germans or barbarians and in the east by a new Persian empire. One northern group got inside the empire and sacked many of the cities of Greece. Eventually, the city of Rome itself had walls built as fears of these roving groups grew. Persia and Rome fought continuously with the eastern border of the empire moving back and forth for several centuries.

Economic issues are harder to analyze in the absence of good numbers, but it appears the population dropped perhaps 50 percent as a result of plagues and didn't recover, which would hurt productivity and reduce the tax base. With military demands increasing, taxes also increased, often causing aristocrats to flee the cities (and the easy reach of tax collectors) for country estates. As government became less able to police the empire, brigands and pirates made life less safe so those estates came to be walled (think medieval castles). When the government debased the coinage as one response to its problems, inflation surfaced as an issue. In 212 all the inhabitants of the empire were given Roman citizenship, a long coveted status; at the same time, the inheritance tax on citizens was doubled. The general drift of the society was the rich got richer while the rest did not, so stratification became more severe. In some cases, things got so bad peasants fled their land, but those remaining had to pick up the taxes and pay the rent left unpaid; sometimes people were forbidden to leave their land (think medieval serfdom).

Politically, the stability that had characterized the rule of the Good Emperors vanished as 26 emperors ruled in the years between 180 and 284. The emperor's body guard, the Pretorian Guard, auctioned off the emperorship late in the second century, and the army was openly in control of the government. The Pax Romana (the peace of Rome) that had characterized the previous era was no more.

Things changed in 284 when Diocletian (284 – 305) seized control and generally stabilized life, though doubling the size of the army was necessary. In essence, the entire society was organized to supply the military. He created a co-emperor so one could concentrate on the northern border and the other the eastern; each had a deputy and helped supervise the growth of a professional bureaucracy of perhaps 30,000 people. The division of responsibility in eastern and western areas foreshadows a permanent division that became apparent later in the fourth century. The Rome that resulted from Diocletian's changes was the same Rome as existed when Jesus was alive in name only; it was dramatically different, especially for the old aristocracy, and considerably less safe for most of its inhabitants. Even the two emperor system had problems as often the emperors engaged in civil war when the frontiers were pacific. At the end of one such war Constantine (324 – 37) emerged as dominant; he adopted Christianity, the first emperor so to do.

## Tragedy. Persecutions.

To the Romans, offering a sacrifice to the emperor, who was interpreted as a god, was a simple act of patriotism; therefore, when Christians refused to treat the emperor similarly, they were much as we might treat traitors today.[28] Assessing persecutions challenges scholars and students. Not that they weren't horrid and gruesome, but the questions of number and geographical reach remain puzzles. The first persecution occurred in the city of Rome from 64 to 68 under the emperor Nero. (Traditionally, the explanation for the cause was that he used Christians as scapegoats for a fire that burned

[28] The analogy to patriotism is well illustrated in U.S. history when members of the Jehovah's Witnesses denomination declined to say the pledge of allegiance. Disturbances and even a Supreme Court case resulted.

city center. Scholars doubt that account as they doubt the legend of Nero's playing the fiddle during the fire.) Between Nero and Diocletian in 303, numerous, sporadic, and usually local persecutions occurred but are not well recorded, if at all, so the big picture does not focus well. The first empire-wide persecution erupted in 250, and the biggest, and last, persecution—the the "Great Persecution" in church history—occurred in 303 under the emperor Diocletian, allegedly ordered when a general, a Christian, crossed himself in the presence of the emperor during a pagan ceremony. The difficulty of explaining the following large-scale but sporadic persecution from such a stimulus doesn't detract from its severity.

Anyone reading the literature would be struck by the gruesomeness and imagination of the tortures and deaths and might be left with the impression Christians lived with this fear as an everyday threat. Probably not. One scholar estimates fewer than 1000 died.[29] So why the impression of mass deaths? For one thing, the church seems to have preserved the stories of many of the deaths for, shall we say, recruiting purposes. It might strike a Thoughtful that someone's awful end wouldn't be an inducement to convert. But look at it in another way. An individual who endured such pain and agony, while holding fast to the Christian faith, testifies powerfully to the nature of that faith. Tertullian, an early third-century Christian author, described the blood of martyrs as seed.[30] The Thoughtful, unprepared to die for many, if any, things, find such a death silly or useless. But doesn't the nagging thought occur maybe there is a Truth there if someone willingly undergoes such an ordeal? (Today, we give psychological explanations for such behavior, as the actions of some Muslim suicide bombers.) At any rate, that explanation helps account for the preservation and widespread notoriety of the stories of tortuous deaths of the persecuted.

## The Scholars Appear. Writings.

Writings about Jesus and aspects of Christianity continued unabated. The four Christian scripture/New Testament gospels didn't become the final

---

[29] Rodney Stark, *The Rise of Christianity* (Princeton University Press, 1996) 179.

[30] Tertullian, *Apologeticus,* trans.T.R. Gover, (Harvard University Press, 1960), L.

word for decades, centuries even, and, as a result, more lives of Jesus, more gospels, appeared. At last count more than 30 such writings are known, some in whole, some only in fragments. In the first century, letters (some falsely attributed to Paul) made the cut, finding their way into the Christian scripture/New Testament, and some didn't. Openly apocalyptic literature appeared, describing the end time including Revelation and Shepherd of Hammas, the former ultimately accepted as canon, the latter not.

In the second century, writings, not later included in the Christian scripture/New Testament, appear that became sources for the growing church. Bishop Ignatius (c.110) on his way to a martyr's death in Rome wrote letters about church governance (by strong bishops). Justin Martyr (c.160) further distinguished Christianity from Judaism. Irenaeus, in Lyons (modern France), wrote a five-volume refutation of Gnosticism, a version of Christianity that lost out in the long run. Origen wrote a lot as well, some of which would later be heretical; free will, universal salvation, allegorical interpretation of text, all suggest the integration of Greek philosophy and Jewish theology. Eusebius, writing at the time of the Emperor Constantine's conversion, produced, *inter alia*, *Ecclesiastical History* and *The Martyrs of Palestine*, sources from which we draw much Christian history. Once the scholars appeared, the general drift of their writing was to interpret scripture allegorically, something fundamentalists resist today. And, being scholars, they disputed among themselves.

The new faith emphasized its continuation with the past. Matthew's gospel, written when the Jesus people still consisted of lots of Jews, had pillaged the Hebrew Bible/Old Testament to show how Jesus fulfilled that scripture. Later Christians continued to make the connection to show Christianity was not a novelty, but part of an old tradition. This solution coincided with the general culture's preference for tradition and the Roman government's toleration of old religions. The final version of the Christian scripture/New Testament as we have it now came from a long, not well-recorded process. In the early second century, Marcion, a Christian leader in Rome, proposed a canon, an accepted set of writings to use, but his theology—the God of the Hebrew Bible/Old Testament differed from the

God of the Christian scripture/New Testament—was ultimately rejected by Christian leaders who, in their disputes with him, proposed their own canon. Other disputes over other issues similarly winnowed out writings until 367, when Athanasius listed the contents of Christian scripture/New Testament of today.

While disputes over theology account for some choices about acceptable writings, the final result lacked a theologically harmonious unity, as the writers used different titles for Jesus and adapted to the failure of the end time to occur. Various forces combined to produce the diversity in the canon. That the involvement of Jesus' original disciples, as authors or sources, came to be one test, but other than some vague traditions, we have no factual evidence they were; after all, they were illiterates from the bottom of Galilean society. Paul's letters were accepted because he came to the tradition early, therefore and some other letters, now included in the Christian scripture/New Testament, were attributed (falsely) to him. Church politics played a role (*Quelle* surprise!!) as church leaders, bishops, began claiming their authority came in direct descent from the original disciples. Hence writings extolling those disciples found willing supporters among the church leaders.

All was not easy sailing. The letter of James, attributed to Jesus' brother, was controversial because it emphasized the value of good works in the salvation story, a position at odds with the rest of the Christian scripture/New Testament. And Revelation, now the final book, raised eyebrows with its apocalypticism (read it and contrast it with other Christian scripture/New Testament works.) which has always been popular with millenarians and end time folk, if not with the Thoughtful. Its inclusion probably resulted from the belief John, a disciple, composed it.

An example of an academic dispute, not settled until well after the emperor became a Christian, was the doctrine of the Trinity, wherein God was Father, Son and Holy Spirit—one substance but three persons. In one of those Greek-based academic curiosities "*homoousion*" (same substance) was the word chosen while dissenters who thought the Son was a person merely of similar substance ("*homoiousion*") with the Father. What a difference an "i" makes! All of this complexity grew out of the need followers had to describe Jesus as more than a man who knew God intimately. That need and the failure of the end time to occur led Christian leaders to posit a future life, an eternal life, rather than being satisfied with a Kingdom of God here and now.

From a modern perspective, the thinkers ignored two topics that seem to be very relevant: slavery and wealth. Christianity wasn't alone in ignoring slavery as philosophers and other religions remained similarly silent. The potential had been there, however, as the early Jesus people, in their initial enthusiasm, had acted upon the belief all Christians, including slaves, are equal. Uproar resulted. Paul wrote a letter to the Colossians saying, *inter alia*, "Slaves, obey your earthly masters" (Colossians 3:22). His letter to Philemon similarly supports the status quo. The most positive spin scholars can put on this attitude is Paul thought the end time was near and therefore changing the existing social order was unnecessary. By the time the church concluded the end was not neigh, the conservative forces of society had taken control and slavery never became an issue. No other church writer revisited the issue and, when the church achieved political power in the fourth century, still nothing was said or done.

Inequalities of wealth also were passed over as Christians offered no criticisms. Like many Hebrew Bible/Old Testament prophets, Jesus has little good to say about the rich, though he must have been supported by someone, perhaps a woman, who had a fair amount of surplus wealth. It seems likely the early Jesus people in Jerusalem practiced sharing of property but how widespread that practice was among Christians or whether it died out or disappeared during one of the Roman purges of that city isn't known. Monasteries, of course, came to practice individual equality in poverty though the monastic institution itself could be wealthy. In the latter part of the Middle Ages, various groups practiced communal sharing (e.g., Beguines, Brothers of the Common Life) as did many small sects in Protestantism (e.g., Shakers, Hutterites). However, on the whole, the church has not acted upon Jesus' initiative and its doors have always been especially welcoming to the wealthy.

### Success! Internal Challenges.

Bishops' powers didn't go unchallenged. The ideal of perpetual virginity and hermits produced individuals with tremendous prestige, and hermits often had a vision of the ideal Christian life that lay beyond the reach of church organization. Virginity seems to have grown from a (mis)interpretation of some of Paul's writings. While the church remained comfortable with marriage (though the church didn't directly involve itself in weddings: that development came much later), it banned divorce and frowned upon remarriage following a partner's death. Hermits fled civilization into the desert, especially in Egypt, partly to separate themselves from what they saw as churches that fell short of the Christian ideal. Their denial of the body in pursuit of the soul reflected the strength of Plato's ideas and produced some curiosities, including the stylites (the flagpole sitters of their day, who lived, literally, above the world atop their columns).

The persecutions of the mid-third century produced many Christians who had denied their faith but, after the cessation of the troubles, wanted to rejoin the group. Many bishops felt such action was impossible, but some individuals who had been imprisoned for their faith, giving them more moral authority than a bishop, started certifying the fallen should be readmitted. This matter of what to do with the lapsed would resurface again after the Great Persecution. The bigger issue here is whether the church would be a select group of the most holy or a welcoming organization with many members who were less than the ideal.

## Beginning or End? Constantine.

After the Great Persecution in the early fourth century, things changed dramatically. The number of Christians grew, but we lack reliable numbers. Scholars' estimates run from 2 to 25 percent of the population of the Empire being Christian. Membership had spread widely through the Empire and even beyond in the East. The city, not the countryside, had the Christians, and Gentiles, not Jews, had come to dominate the movement.

The organization, the canon, the practices, the creeds—all were challenged when the Roman Emperor Constantine converted to Christianity. With that conversion the nature of Christianity took an unexpected, and not entirely wholesome, turn.

During these early centuries, Christianity became not the religion of Jesus but a religion about Jesus (his death and resurrection). The idea Jesus was divine was widely accepted, although it posed a problem for monotheists. From a Thoughtful point of view, this development seems a wrong turn.

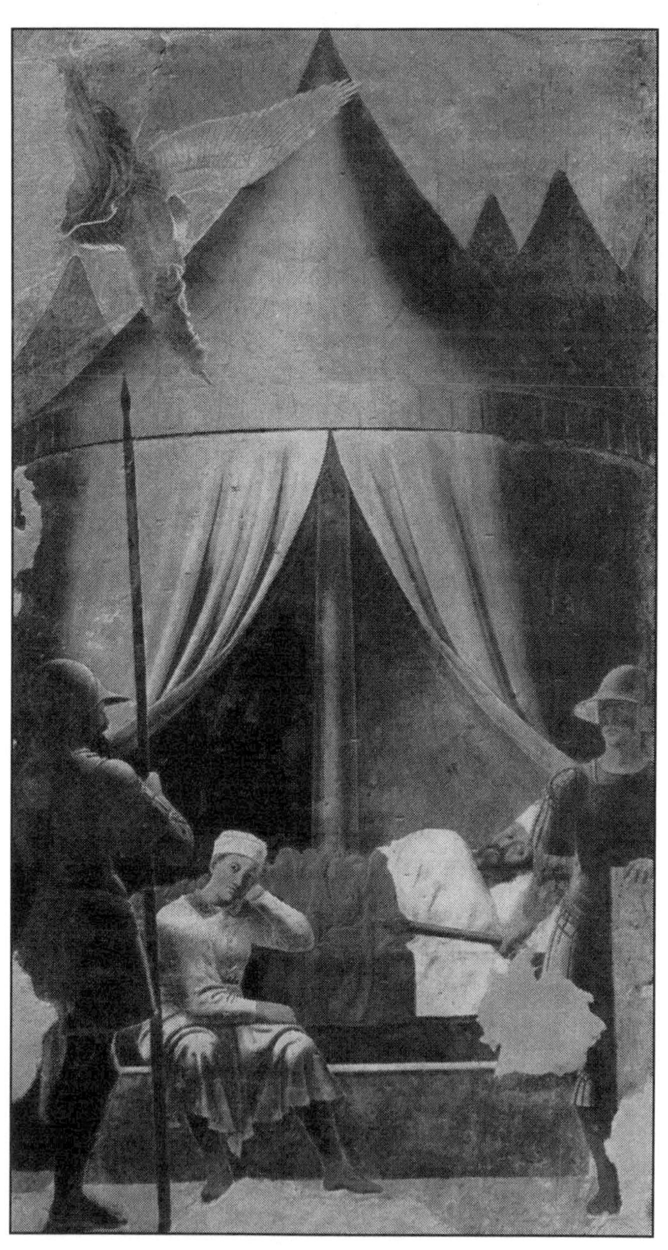

*The Dream of Constantine*

# SIX

# *Success, Fragmentation, Near Death, Success—The Middle Ages*

## Victory or Submission?

### Constantine Converts.

The Roman Empire, over which Diocletian had set two co-emperors, one in the East, one in the West, survived in this bifurcated form for almost two centuries. Although Diocletian intended to give two men imperial authority to control and direct armies against external enemies—Persians in the East, Germans in the West—in the end, when things got calm on the borders, the two emperors fought each other. When one emperor died, no clear rules existed for choosing a successor so several generals would jump up, battle it out with their armies, until, by a Darwinian process, only one still stood.

In 312, one of these generals, Constantine, the son of an earlier co-emperor, prepared his army for his final battle; win he becomes emperor, lose he dies. The night before, Constantine had a dream in which he saw a cross and heard the words "In this you will conquer." He knew about Christianity so when he awoke he ordered his solders to paint a cross on their shields and, lo and behold, he won the battle and became emperor. In those days when one succeeded militarily, one assumed one's god superior to the god of one's opponent. Constantine drew that conclusion and became a Christian. Make no mistake, this event didn't involve an altar call or a discovery of the wonders of forgiveness; Constantine made a business decision. All ancient cultures had an official, unifying religion; now Rome had Christianity. (Not baptized until his deathbed, some of his behavior might be considered unchristian, such as killing his son for allegedly sleeping with his wife.)

After Constantine became a Christian, several things in the Mediterranean world changed. He didn't make Christianity the official religion—that development came in 395—but Christians could openly practice their faith, buildings could be erected, and the power of the empire could be used (not for good, though). Soon after his conversion, bishops sought Constantine's intervention in a controversy; seeking a unifying religion for all in the Empire, he complied. Next, he had to call a council of church leaders to deal with a dispute about the nature of Jesus. While he permitted non-Christians to practice their rites, he showered money, power, and tax exemptions on bishops. Since all subsequent emperors (except one who only lasted two years) were Christians, the church quickly consolidated its power. And the Roman aristocracy, seeing a career move, converted. Hereafter Christians, not too concerned about the government or the pagans (only in the fifth and sixth centuries did the remnants of paganism disappear), could dispute among themselves. And they did.

Did the church capture the empire or did the emperor capture the church? The church, and Christianity, had morphed from a people with no power pursuing a life inspired by a poor peasant to an organization with the ultimate power. Maybe this change wasn't a positive development.

## The Church.

### One God? The Trinity.

The experience of Jesus' followers, which we call the Resurrection, almost immediately began to raise problems about Jesus' nature and his relationship with God. This problem—Jesus as Christ, both God and man—manifested itself in the developing doctrine of the Trinity. Not simply explained, the Trinity dogma asserts one God exists in three persons, Father, Son, and Holy Spirit, but only one substance. At least that idea became the official position.

The making of Jesus into part of God can be traced. Paul saw it happening at the Resurrection (Romans 1:4). Mark, the first gospel, put it at Jesus' baptism by John the Baptizer (Mark 1:10). Matthew and Luke moved it back to Jesus' conception, though they differed in the details (Matthew 1:18 – 21; Luke 1:35). John, the last gospel, portrayed Jesus as always a part of God. Within a century of his birth, Jesus had become God.

By the second century, Jesus had been joined by the Holy Spirit as a part of God. The Spirit of God, early Christians found, worked within them and their fellowship; as demonstrated in their feelings and their actions, the Holy Spirit had to be God. But Jews had always worshipped only one god, and Christians had no inclination to abandon such monotheism.

Tertullian (c. 200) made the first serious effort at working out the issue. A lawyer, he described God as having one substance (not the material concept but one of status— "he is a man of substance" doesn't necessarily imply wealth). God also has three parts, three ways of operating. The issue did not rest there. The nature of Jesus as Christ occupied minds for several centuries and giving the Holy Spirit equal time challenged those same minds.

For most, the result likely comes from a council in 381, a creed commonly, but mistakenly, called the "Nicene Creed." Rolling these views—God, Jesus as God, the Holy Spirit—into one deity didn't happen easily; the result many still find unsatisfactory, and few today can grasp. If, after reading the Nicene Creed, a Thoughtful finds this matter confusing or unsatisfactory, take solace in the fact it is confusing, and few, over two millennia, have ever figured it out. In terms of getting on with life, does it really matter?

### Losers. Heretics.

The church, being a political as well as religious organization, had leaders who engaged in political maneuvering, often for personal gain (though leaders usually claimed the reason was for Truth). While contending for offices and influence, church leaders often seized upon a belief as a means of defeating their opponents. In the resulting struggle, one side won, the other lost, and the winners declared their view "orthodox" and the losers' view "heresy." The winners often wrote a creed that they insisted all accept as a means of smoking out their enemies. Heresy, therefore, is nothing more than the belief of the losers and, in church history, what was orthodox in one year or century might be heresy in another. Attacks on dissidents and heresy became easy, and common, after the church became public with Constantine's conversion. Enforcement of uniformity—after all, Truth means we all subscribe to it—also became common, and disputes flourished in the fourth-century church. The following details at great length some of the disputes as a means of demonstrating the foibles of the educated, but not Thoughtful, believer.

After his death, Jesus was soon being described as divine, which led to the formulation of the Trinity: Father, Son, Holy Spirit. This interpretation in turn raised the issue of Jesus' humanity and most of the heresies revolved around the nature of Jesus. For simplicity of organization, we can divide the heresies into two groups. The first group were the heresies that were most quickly and easily settled and involved church organization and threats to the power of the bishops. The second group produced more intellectual arguments that went on for centuries (in some cases) and might be loosely described as worthy of debating societies in that the outcome probably didn't matter in the great scheme of Christian history and theology. The first group of beliefs disappeared as the lack of organization proved fatal, whereas the second group still survives around the world in various branches of Christianity.

In the first group we have already met Gnosticism in the second century and, resurfacing even after Constantine's conversion, it seems to have had a particular following in Egypt. Gnosticism, lacking organization, had lots of variety. Bishops had little difficulty uniting against Gnosticism because, with its belief in secret and special knowledge of God, it threatened church organization and episcopal control. After all, those who had such special insight couldn't be directed by bishops, and, indeed, had no need for the church at all. Hence, heresy.

Somewhat similar to Gnosticism, Montanism (also called Phrygians after a city in Asia Minor) appeared late in the second century. Anticipating an eminent second coming of Jesus, Montanists encouraged celibacy, fasting, and martyrdom. Their criticism of the laxity of Christians combined with a belief the Holy Spirit continued to speak through prophets, including women (horrors!!), made the belief unpopular with the bishops. Criticism of one's behavior and competition for leadership, especially by women prophets, was no way to run a church, at least for a male bishop. Montanism became a heresy though for doctrinally muddy reasons. The notion of continuing revelation, of God adding to scripture, was squashed.

During the Great Persecution of Diocletian, after 303, many church leaders, in response to an imperial order, gave their scriptures to the authorities to be destroyed. After Constantine's conversion and the safe public appearance of the church, leaders who had remained steadfast in their faith viewed those "traitors" (*traditores*) harshly. Donatus, a North African bishop, led a campaign to declare the traitors and their sacramental actions, baptisms, etc., ineffective and outside the church. In essence, the dispute became one of whether the efficacy of a sacrament depended upon the state of the officiating individual—valid if he were pure, invalid otherwise. Donatus lost, and his successful opponents declared sacraments by their very nature worked; the spiritual condition of the priest being irrelevant. The resolution, from a bishop's point of view, meant the laity wouldn't be in a position to criticize officialdom's behavior and disrupt a service. The winners won by appealing to Constantine, the new emperor.

In the Western part of the church, Pelagius, a British monk, proposed in the early fifth century sin came from a wrong choice and that, though good works, people could obtain salvation. Part of a continuous debate in Christianity over how the individual achieved salvation, the issue of good works has never completely disappeared. Some believe God grants salvation without any effort by the individual and others think one earns salvation through a lifetime of holy activity, with lots of nuanced positions in between. Pelagius struck at church organization because the official position was people, when born, had "original sin" (inherited from Adam's first sin of the apple), which required baptism to be eliminated. Original sin appeared as a church doctrine at least as the early third century, though the Pelagian dispute did much to solidify it as official doctrine. The problem put simply: no original sin, no baptism, works merit salvation. Q.E.D. no need for church sacraments and organization. Hence, Pelagianism had to be a heresy.

The second group of heresies involved people taking opposing sides on an issue that had little lasting importance. These issues didn't threaten church organization, but on at least some level, involved intellectual argument and episcopal pride and ambition. Many of these disputes involved the nature of Jesus, an issue on which the Christian scripture/New Testament provided little guidance and several possibilities. Might Christianity have traveled a different road had the various debates gone the other way? Unclear.

No sooner had Constantine dealt with Donatism than bishops confronted him with a church racked with a dispute over the nature of Jesus as Christ. Arian, an Egyptian priest, taught Jesus wasn't coequal with God the Father but had been created at some point. Arius' bishop condemned the view but it still spread throughout the East. Constantine became involved, calling a council of the church leaders at Nicaea in 325. This council, the first of the entire church leadership (at least in theory if not in attendance), included 300 bishops and many priests and laity. The resulting document sought to settle the matter in favor of Arius' opponents. Arianism didn't fade away because some bishops kept the issue alive, and a later emperor tolerated it.

Another doctrine—ultimately the heresy with the most legs, at least in the East—was Monophysitism, another argument about the nature of Jesus. Monophysitism held Jesus had one nature, partly divine, partly human, whereas the Western view gave Jesus two natures, one human, one divine. Proposed by Apollinaris, a Syrian bishop in the fourth century, the view addressed the problem of the human Jesus. If human, could Jesus have sinned? If so, how could he then bring about human salvation? The counter arguments said this view rejected the Jesus of the gospels and still he needed to be human for him to be the Savior. Condemned by a council in 451, Monophysitism continued to present problems for Christian leaders for years afterward.

While Arius made Jesus less than God's equal and Monophysitism made Jesus less than fully human, Nestorius, bishop of Constantinople, made Jesus wholly human and separate from the divine. This solution produced more arguments and another council at Chalcedon, near Constantinople. In the resulting creed Christ was entirely God and entirely man, but his humanity and divinity are not separate nor united. And Nestorianism declared a heresy.

These latter heresies, Monophysitism and Nestorianism, became the basis of branches of non-Western Christianity as, for example, today the Armenian and Ethiopian Coptic Churches are Monophysitist, and Nestorianism survives in India.

In the fifth century, a different kind of dispute, one about the Holy Spirit, broke out as the Western church added "and the Son" ("filioque") to the Nicene Creed. The issue, whether the Holy Spirit, the third part of the Trinity, proceeded solely from the Father or from the Father and the Son, provided another example where the substance of the dispute escapes the Thoughtful. The East demurred and the sides never agreed.

### The Major Solution. The Nicene Creed.

As the upshot of these disputes, church leaders drafted what now is known as the Nicene Creed (though this creed differs from the one drafted at the council of Nicaea in 325). In part, it defines what the Western church accepts as the resolution of these debates about Jesus and, ultimately, the Trinity:

> We believe in one God, the Father Almighty, Maker of heaven and earth, and of all things visible and invisible; and in one Lord Jesus Christ, the only-begotten Son of God, begotten of the Father before all world, God of God, Light of Light, very God of very God, begotten, not made, being of one substance with the Father, by whom all things were

> made, who for us men and for our salvation came down from heaven and was made incarnate by the Holy Spirit of the Virgin Mary, and was made man, and was crucified also for us under Pontius Pilate, he suffered and was buried, and on the third day he rose again according to the Scriptures and ascended into heaven, and sitteth on the right hand of the Father, and he shall come again, with glory, to judge both the quick and the dead, whose kingdom will have no end; and we believe in the Holy Spirit the Lord, and Giver of Life, who proceeded from the Father and the Son who with the Father and the Son together is worshipped and glorified, who spoke by the prophets. And we believe in one holy, catholic, and apostolic church. We acknowledge one baptism for the remission of sin. And we look for the resurrection of the dead and the life of the world to come. Amen.

Those who didn't accept this creed, faced expulsion, as it ended:

But as for those who say, There was a time when He was not, and before being born he was not, and that he came into existence out of nothing or who assert that the Son of God is of a different hypostasis or substance, or is subject to alternation or change, those the Catholic and apostolic church anathematizes.

These episcopal disputes sought, bishops said, to unite all Christians under one theological tent, Truth, but instead produced a multi-tented campground of many truths as most of the heresies survived somewhere. Arianism was the favorite of the Germanic tribes outside the Roman Empire. Monophysitism remained popular in Syria and Egypt. Nestorians left the Roman Empire for pastures further east.

How much of the theological content of the Nicene Creed is found in the Christian scripture/New Testament? Almost none. The Thoughtful might well ask exactly why the nature of Christ and the definition of the

Trinity mattered so much. If these matters all seem a bit too complex, and perhaps irrelevant, you are seeing the results of Greek education on the ancient mind. Whereas many cultures accept vagueness and inconsistency, the Greeks always asked "why" and "how," of Christianity, seeking answers in a very complex theology. And Greek capacity for argument about anything boggles the modern mind. The Emperor Constantine, a tough Roman soldier, not a Greek-educated intellectual, had little patience for this line of debate. During the Arian controversy, he wrote to the parties such doctrinal niceties were "of a truly insignificant character and quite unworthy of such fierce contention."[1] Historically, few Christians have had a clue about the issue of the nature of Christ, and today probably even fewer take note. Those in the pew take all sorts of positions, reviving many of these heresies, but now, as then, nothing much flows from such opinions. They can duly recite what is called the Nicene Creed and rarely focus on its content. A Thoughtful non-believer can be excused for thinking these things must be important, but they really aren't, except to theologians and nitpickers.

**Practices.**

By the second century, the Eucharist had become the central part of Christian worship. The Greek word "Eucharist" means "giving of thanks" and is also called the Lord's Supper, communion, and mass. The actual event, sharing bread and wine, resembles rites in other religions of the day, such as Mithraism. Early on, the thanks given focused on God sending Jesus to Earth and his resulting death and resurrection. The idea the bread and wine became Jesus' flesh and blood appeared in the second century but only in the ninth century did someone enunciate the doctrine known as transubstantiation, which the Lateran Council adopted as official doctrine in the thirteenth century. Only the baptized could receive the Eucharist; probably in the thirteenth century, the wine ceased being given to laity out of fear of spillage, wasting Christ's blood. By the end of the Middle Ages, the Eucharist had almost magical qualities as physical substances, bread and

---

[1] Eusebius, *The Life of the Blessed Emperor Constantine*, Book II, ch. LXVIII.

wine, transformed into body and blood of God, all administered in a language, Latin, which few understood. No wonder sixteenth-century reformers fought over the interpretation of the event so much.[2]

Baptism, the other major Christian practice, dates back to John the Baptizer. In the early church, baptism was preceded by a period of study and observation by others, which might last as long as three years. When the event finally occurred, it signaled entry into a new life and was considered so major subsequent back-sliding often meant readmission would never be possible in one's lifetime. Baptism was a one-shot act, no rebaptisms, and involved the notion of forgiveness of sins. As a subsequent serious sin might result in forfeiture of the benefits of baptism, some delayed the event as long as possible, which may account for Constantine only being baptized when on his death bed. Already disputes flared as to whether the proper method was sprinkling or immersion and whether infant baptism was appropriate; these issues are alive in today's denominational disputes.

By the fourth century, ideas and practices still associated with Christianity had taken root. Clergy had special status and wardrobe, separate from laity. Believers celebrated Lent, the period before Easter, often by fasting, and acknowledged other special days, Palm Sunday, Maundy Thursday, and Good Friday. Singing during worship already existed in the first century, and by the fourth century the usual practice was antiphonal. The giving of ten percent of one's income, tithing, found favor. The deadly sins had leveled off at seven: pride, greed, lust, envy, gluttony, wrath, sloth; however, controversy arose as to whether any sin could not be forgiven. Believers transferred their previous worship of pagan gods into honoring Christian martyrs as saints; in some cases, the pagan gods themselves became saints as well, easing the path into the new religion. The proliferation of saints, relics, and pilgrimages was well under way.

These myriad practices were governed, or attempted to be governed, by a church hierarchy of priests and bishops. Five bishops, Rome, Alexandria, Antioch, Constantinople, and Jerusalem, had emerged as preeminent; when

---

[2] Kenneth Scott Latourette, *A History of Christianity* (HarperSanFrancisco, 1975), vol. 1, 197-201, 530-32.

political Rome divided and then disappeared in the West in the fifth century, the bishop of Rome was left to his own devices; as a consequence, a Western church emerged.

What did those Greek-educated churchmen not do? Criticize slavery and the rich.

## Departures.

### Where'd Rome Go?

No big battle. No major disaster. Rather, the Roman Empire in the West just became less effective, shrunk, faded away ....

Things went downhill in the fourth and fifth centuries. The economy couldn't support the defense budget Diocletian established so the armies got smaller. As pressure from outside the Empire's border increased—Persians in the East, Germans in the North—many of the armies were pulled back to protect the Empire's economic, cultural, and intellectual core: the East. On Christmas Day, 406, Germans crossed the frozen Rhine and gradually walked all over the West during the next half century, even sacking the city of Rome in 410 and 455. In 407, the armies left Britain. So pervasive was Germanic influence and power in 476 a German leader had the symbols of the last western Roman Emperor sent to Constantinople. No more Roman emperors in the West. Germans rule.

The Germanic migrations constituted perhaps 5 percent of the population of the West and their regimes essentially established themselves as the new aristocracy. However, widespread slaughter or even displacement of the Roman nobility did not occur. We have the papers of a Roman aristocrat, a distant relative of a western emperor, who decided the future lay in the Christian episcopate. He was right. He became a bishop, and he wasn't the only one.[3]

[3] Sidonius, *The Letters of Sidonius*, trans. O.M. Dalton (Clarendon, 1915).

These were dark times. Government pretty much disappeared as German war bands ruled. Christian in that they respected churches and monasteries, they didn't practice "love thy neighbor" as their creed. Learning, confined to monasteries, became very rudimentary, little more than basic literacy. Heresies and episcopal rivalries disappeared as survival became the goal.

A new threat, Islam, then appeared. In Arabia, Mohammed (570 – 632) had visions which he later used to construct a new faith. Drawing on both Jewish and Christian traditions, the new religion soon lacked any central direction (no equivalent of the Western pope or the eastern emperor), but its relatively simple tenets and practices combined with the weakness of the inheritors of ancient Rome's lands propelled Islam into very successful growth, in numbers and territory. (Though tolerant of Christians and Jews, Islam imposed a tax on them; conversions rapidly followed.) Muslims, starting from their base in Arabia, rapidly conquered much of what had been classical Rome. Egypt, long a stronghold of Christianity, fell by 642. The rest of northern Africa and the holy land were under Muslim control by 709. Crossing the straits of Gibraltar, Islamic armies conquered most of Spain and, in 732, a century after Mohammed's death, fought a battle at Tours in central France. Their defeat there stopped the advance, but the resulting control of the Mediterranean effectively turned Western Christianity inward with concentrating its centers of influence in Rome, the Rhine valley, and monastic pockets scattered about. The elimination of Alexandria, Antioch, and Jerusalem as centers of Christian influence left only Rome and Constantinople, further cementing the West/East division that had been growing for centuries.

Occasional bursts of light appeared as in the reign of Charlemagne (768 – 814). Grandson of the man who defeated the Muslims in 732, he undertook a revival of, if not the glories, at least some semblance of ancient Roman grandeur. He reinvigorated monasteries, patronized some learning, conquered some pagans, and died with descendants who lacked the ability to continue his efforts. The appearance of Vikings and Magyars complicated matters, and violence and disorder reigned, again. In the West, the period from 600 to 950 was a near run for the church and Christianity.

Both survived only in the monasteries and in the token acceptance by the Germanic rulers.

## Fleeing the World. Monks.

Thoughtfuls often think they would welcome a life of solitude, but retreating for a lifetime at a monastery becomes very, very rarely the preferred solution. Not so for much of Christian history. But then they didn't have cell phones and air conditioning to give up when they took their vows.

Once Constantine converted and the church joined the world with all the attendant trappings of power, Christianity spread quickly. Not surprisingly, some of the new members lacked the sincerity and dedication existing earlier. Such laxness offended some, and they sought to avoid contact with such worldliness by isolating themselves. One solution, sitting atop a column, separated oneself from the masses while literally and symbolically rising above the *hoi polloi*. Simeon the Stylite became so famous for his loftiness, sitting atop a fifty-foot column that crowds flocked to him for advice for more than 30 years.

Already in the second century in Egypt, fleeing society by leaving the settled areas resulted in hermits scattered across the desert. If earthly thoughts still crossed a hermit's mind, he or she (some were women) would inflict some sort of discomfort, denial, or torture on the body to distract and as penance. Many ate strange diets, stood for hours while reciting prayers, or underwent sleep deprivation, but creativity produced such ingenuous practices as weighing oneself with chains, self-castration, and walling oneself in a cave. The competition—I can withstand more pain than my neighboring hermit—led to such extremes one can be forgiven thinking pride had become paramount.

By the early fourth century, under the leadership of Pachomius (d. 346) hermits organized themselves into communities, each self-sufficient. Rules developed to replace the ascetic competitions with disciplines of prayer and work. In the West, Benedict (480 – 543) established a monastery near Naples, requiring monks establish a daily regime of four hours of divine service, four hours of prayer, six hours of labor, and ten hours of eating and sleeping; the Benedictine Rule. Upon entering monkdom, one took vows of poverty (no individual possessions though some monasteries were wealthy and life was not spartan), chastity (you know), and obedience (to the abbot who ran the place).

Each monastery, a world unto itself with no external supervision, attracted supplicants. Benedictine Rule proved wildly popular and monasteries sprang up everywhere in the sixth and seventh centuries. Women had their own monasteries, but it is estimated men outnumbered them ten to one, as society worried about keeping women safe even in a separate institution. Besides providing a refuge from the violence and disorder of the day, monasteries preserved ancient learning, undertook charitable work, and converted the peasantry.

As with many institutions, change crept in. Soon monasteries used peasants for manual labor so monks, largely from the noble class, could engage in more "study." Political rulers sought monks as administrators and advisors because they were literate thus returning those monks to the very world they had fled. People financed monasteries by paying for prayers for their souls, and the efficient administration of property led some establishments to become very wealthy. With no external supervision, laxness and downright dissipation could occur. However, until the twelfth century, Benedictines were a monopoly of the Western monastic movement.

Monasteries, however, provided cells of Christianity in a very troubled world, and monks practiced Christian virtues while bringing the countryside to Christianity. On the downside, the purists retreated, leaving the church run by those less pure, only too often time servers. To give them their due, without monks, Christianity would have perished in the West.

## Catholic Isn't Catholic. The East.

Early in its history the church referred to itself as "catholic," meaning "universal." However, the slow metamorphosis of the Roman Empire in the West into several territories loosely ruled by various Germanic peoples paralleled a division of the church into Western and Eastern branches. The separation proceeded slowly with periodic attempts at reconciliation, but by the twelfth century, two traditions had emerged, called Catholic in the West and Orthodox in the East.

While this separation was occurring, the bishop of Rome, hereafter referred to as the pope, led the Western portion by prestige and influence but did not dominate. (For the era of the pope you thought always existed you must await the twelfth century.) This papal preeminence in the West arose from the convergence of several forces.

Matthew's gospel reports Jesus saying, "And I tell you, you are Peter and on this rock I will built my church, and the gates of Hades will not prevail against it. I will give you the keys of the kingdom of heaven, and whatever you will bind on earth will be bound in heaven, and whatever you loose on earth will be loosed in heaven" (Matthew 16:18 – 9). This, the Petrine doctrine, gave Peter preeminence and also accounts for the presence of keys in papal statues and paintings. By tradition, i.e., no concrete evidence, Peter, the chief disciple, went to Rome where he was martyred and where his tomb was later erected. The church later designated him the first bishop of Rome/pope. Additionally, as the emperors increasingly abandoned the city of Rome—Constantine building a New Rome (Constantinople) in the East—the bishop of Rome/pope was left as the most important person in the old capital. These individuals increasingly functioned as the chief civil official, the mayor. Leo I (440 – 61) negotiated with passing hordes of Germans and Huns in an attempt, sometimes successful, to spare the city. Gregory I (590 – 604) collected taxes, provided welfare, trained soldiers, and defended the city against the Lombards, all traditionally roles of the civil government.

Doctrinal disputes usually involved the pope as figures in the East, including the Emperor, sought papal opinion and approval. The pope did not rule the church but served only as one, and probably the most eminent, bishop; as first among equals, his position carried weight. In the heresy debates about Arians, Donatists, Nestorians, etc., popes participated, though they rarely had the final word. However, future disputes, such as the Filioque and Monothelite ones, tended to find Eastern bishops aligned against the pope.

After the great disputes over the nature of Jesus in the fourth and fifth centuries, iconoclasm, the presence of art in religious structures used for worship, dominated the years between 700 and 850. Those who favored use of such images (icons) argued they helped the worshiper understand difficult theological concepts by associating them with recognizable forms, often biblical individuals. Opponents feared—rightly in many cases—the simple would worship the images in the same ways pagans treated their images. In the West icons failed to become much of an issue, perhaps because bishops concluded their uneducated congregations of Germans required such images. Many other considerations—hopes for conversion of Muslims, influence of the Emperor in the church, ethnic rivalries, personal ambitions, the usual stuff—entered the calculation. The Emperor in Constantinople, guided by his bishops, banned such icons in 725, breaking statues and whitewashing walls. For more than a century, the contending sides alternated in power with icons being permitted again in 784, banned in 813, restored in 843.

In matters not so theologically charged, the East and West went their different ways. The East permitted divorce, let priests (but not bishops) marry, and used a liturgy in the local vernacular (the West stayed with Latin). The West reconciled sinners in the church's apse; the East didn't. Western monks had slaves; Eastern didn't. The East accepted widows as nuns; the West didn't. The East excommunicated those not receiving communion for three consecutive Sundays; the West didn't. Even the date of Easter differed.[4] However, increasingly the West became ignorant of the East and didn't care.

The popes desired independence from the Eastern Emperors, who had physically seized one pope in 545 (Vigilus) and another in 653 (Martin I) in efforts to coerce their agreement to Monophysitic and Monothelite issues, respectively. But to gain this independence, they needed military protection from a new Germanic group in Italy, the Lombards. As Spain had fallen to the Muslims, England was ruled by lots of kinglets, and Germany was still pagan, the pope turned to the rulers of the Franks. In 751 the pope injected himself into Frankish affairs to help Pepin seize the throne from an inept

---

[4] R.W. Southern, *Western Society and the Church in the Middle Ages* (Penguin, 1970), 57.

king. In 800, the pope crowned Pepin's son, Charles the Great (Charlemagne) as emperor. (Sources differ as to whether Charlemagne sought his title or the pope tricked him into it.) In return for these papal efforts, the Frankish rulers invaded Italy, defeated the Lombards, and gave a portion of central Italy to the pope to rule, the origin of the Papal States. As a result of all these activities the pope had some confidence of independence from the Eastern Emperor and a record of making Frankish kings. While the pope created the Holy Roman Emperor to show his strength, the long-term consequence became the dispute between the popes and the Holy Roman Emperors; could popes dispose of Holy Roman Emperors and what role did Holy Roman Emperors have in the church? These questions resemble today's church/state matters.

The final straw occurred in 1054 when a papal delegation went to Constantinople to negotiate various differences between East and West. Upon failure, a member of the delegation, Cardinal Humbert of Silva Candida, threw a papal bull of excommunication on the altar of Hagia Sophia, Constantinople's largest and central sanctuary. In retaliation the Eastern patriarch promptly excommunicated the pope. The East and West churches divided permanently into the Catholic and the Orthodox.

## Acme.

### The Pope You Thought Existed Always. The Papal Monarchy.

The ascent from the darkness of the early medieval period began about 950. The economy of Western Europe was quickly expanding and several rulers brought some of the violence under control with new political institutions. The church underwent an amazing revival, producing the recognizable medieval church.

It all began at the monastery Cluny in eastern France (to oversimplify a bit). The abbot there somehow reinvigorated the monks to become more monk-like. The idea spread, and soon monasteries everywhere filled with monks filled with a mission, a mission to make Christian society actually

Christian: eliminating pagan practices, reducing violence, caring for the poor, etc. After reforming their fellow monks, they turned their attention to the church hierarchy—the pope in particular. Popes had fallen on evil times, and some of the tenth-century occupants of the chair of St. Peter rate little better than common criminals. What little effectiveness the pope had derived from the myth of Peter; in some ways, St. Peter, or maybe even his purported tomb in Rome, had more power than the pope. With a high-mindedness and some help from a Holy Roman Emperor who shared the reforming zeal, the reformers got one of their own named pope in 1049.

A reformed papacy began a campaign to reform all of society. Bishops, more closely supervised, became more bishop-like. Any religious pretentions kings had were increasingly downplayed and eventually disappeared, leaving the clergy the sole authority to deal with God. Also those clergy, until the development of cities, had a monopoly of education and were usually exempt from secular matters, such as taxes and courts. The nobility were brutish thugs given to coveting one another's land, needed distraction. Conveniently, the Eastern emperor suffered a major military defeat at the hands of the Turks, and, lacking resources, asked the West for military aid. Pope Urban II seized the moment and preached a crusade, a war for Christ against Muslim control of Palestine, the Holy Land. Soon, many of the thugs started eastward, the First Crusade and the pope had an army.

The first crusade, begun in 1096, was followed by several others. Theoretically led by a papal representative, though controlling the ambitious and violent nobility was probably beyond the capability of any man, all crusades lacked unity. After the first crusade, the following ones, excluding ones going to the Holy Land, were launched against heretics in France, Greeks in Constantinople, peasants in Prussia, and even papal opponents in Italy.

If the crusades provided the military arm of the new papacy, popes also created the first bureaucracy since the end of Rome. With a monopoly of the educated men of the day, the pope began to develop the first early modern monarchy, with an establishment later copied by kings. Keeping copies of documents, a new idea, resulted in the papal chancery. Keeping tabs on the hierarchy of the church and meeting special needs produced papal legates, traveling agents of the pope. Keeping papal elections free of political interference resulted in the closed conclaves we still witness. A large body of canon law emerged that dealt with aspects of church and lay life. The only missing element in the papal monarchy was a regular and substantial income, which meant financial needs became the Achilles heel of the monarchy, as it would of kingly regimes later.

Codifying the reforms of the society and clergy occupied the Lateran council of 1215, which enunciated numerous rules. Priests could not marry, wear bright clothing, or hunt. Laity could only seek marriage partners outside seven degrees of kinship (a rule almost impossible to observe in a peasant village and difficult even among upper nobility). Divorce became impermissible. The sacraments were limited to seven in number: baptism, confirmation, Eucharist, penance, holy orders, matrimony, and extreme unction.

Innocent III, the most powerful pope in history, showed the power and purpose of the reformed papacy. Besides calling the Lateran Council and preaching a crusade against French heretics, he readily confronted royalty when he thought their actions threatened Christianity, declaring "No king can reign rightly unless he devoutly serve Christ's vicar" (i.e., the pope).[5] In England, the king, John, desperate for money, left bishoprics vacant in order to collect their income and rejected Innocent's choice as Archbishop of Canterbury. Innocent responded with an interdict, forbidding sacraments in England (only baptism and extreme unction could be performed), an interdict that lasted more than four years. John's overall financial stress caused his nobles to revolt; Magna Carta, the first chapter of which promised the church independence, resulted in 1215. In his surrender to the superior power of the church, John even gave England to the pope and took it back as a fief. (Such a bad job overall no English king has been named John since.) The rulers of France and the Holy Roman Empire had similar, unsuccessful, encounters with Innocent.

---

[5] This quote is from one of Innocent's letters. It is widely used in the literature but never with a citation.

While papal involvement was a prerequisite for any crusade, papal control was rarely effective; therefore, crusaders could never be truly termed a papal army. The papacy had succeeded in creating a state with laws and courts, an administration holding even the power of life and death. However, in the absence of an army, popes had to rely on excommunication and even that power relied on secular help.

The papal monarchy worked well for the church but exerting temporal authority eventually caused problems. Clergy status was elevated. Popes ceased being Peter's Vicar and became the Vicar of Christ, a much stronger basis for action. For a century and a half after 1159, most popes were lawyers because issues of litigation and organization dominated the church's life. The church, with the pope at its head, was a ship of salvation in an ocean of chaos and violence. For the elite who ran the church, it gave them a purpose and a place in the world, a meaningful life. And the organization was tiered, much like a wedding cake, with all authority eventually deriving from the pope, in theory at least.

## A Church for All. If You're Noble.

After around 1050 many monks began seeking a more personal, more spiritual experience than the one the increasing aristocratic, wealthy, idle Benedictines could provide; the Cluny reforming effort had stalled. The result was a profusion of new orders that, once in place, offered a wide variety of opportunities. The Cistercians retreated from the world and built their monasteries on the frontiers. Pursuing a stricter form of the Benedictine Rule, the Cistercians grew quickly after Bernard of Citeaux joined (he isn't the St. Bernard of dog fame). They worked the land themselves—not renting it like Benedictines—a practice soon given to laymen who lived under monastic discipline (a rare situation whereby illiterate peasants could feel assured of salvation). Two unexpected consequences of this arrangement developed: Cistercian monasteries, exploiting virgin land and living simply, became very rich, and the peasant monks periodically revolted in protest of their lesser status. Other orders following a similar path to contemplation included Carthusians (who couldn't talk among themselves) and the

Brigittines (an order largely aimed at women which was founded in Sweden around 1350). Even violence, the favorite pastime of medieval nobility, found a monastic outlet as the Templars and Hospitalers permitted monks to fight while remaining true to vows. Begun during the crusades, these monks often provided protection for pilgrims to the Holy Land, which soon led them into banking as the pilgrims could give the monks money in, say, Paris and receive it back in Jerusalem (early travelers' cheques).

For those interested in service, groups following the vague Rule of Augustine sprang up. Often urban, they provided education, care for the sick, help for the poor, etc. Usually priests, they lived together and shared property but did not have elaborate buildings. One group, the Trinitarians, worked solely to free captives seized in the Mediterranean by Muslims or pirates. Advantages of canons included the little cost required to establish a group of canons (no buildings or other structures); if their task was fulfilled, they passed out of existence without anyone worrying.

A final variation on the religious lives was the development of the mendicant orders, the friars. Partly a response to the Waldensians, a group in France sought to wander and preach in apostolic poverty, the friars—chiefly Franciscans and Dominicans—originally lived by begging. Well-educated and effective preachers, they brought religion to the masses in the cities and the countryside. Thus, more mendicants came from the poor than the other orders, an exception to the general practice of only recruiting from the nobility.

Most of these groups had a branch or division for women; as a result, some women, such as the abbess of Fontevrault, could be quite powerful. However, estimates put the ratio of woman to men across orders run at about 1 to10.

The papal monarchy had a big tent so all sorts of spiritual desires could be accommodated. The church provided outlets, within accepted bounds, for those who sought contemplation or action, administration or war, service or preaching. A very successful, and encompassing, organization by the year 1250, the church was an institution that any ambitious university graduate would join.

# Troubles.

## Heresies. Again.

In the latter Middle Ages, various movements appeared that appealed to the non-elite and challenged the organized church. The church challenged many and declared some heretical, the first heretical groups (rather than individuals) since the late Roman Empire. Anticlericalism was often the defining quality behind these movements, and the Thoughtful can quickly discern why the church would decide they were heretical. At the end of the twelfth century, many groups sprang up, usually outside the church structure.

In approximately 1170, Peter Waldo, a rich merchant in Lyons, had the Bible translated into the vernacular; after studying it, he concluded Christians should live like Jesus' apostles did—in poverty. He gave away his money and began preaching. He gathered a small following of similarly inspired men but eventually ran into trouble with the clergy, who disliked his preaching about poverty since they had no intention of practicing it. Condemned in 1184 by the church, the sect continued, spreading through France, Germany, and Spain and expanding its criticism to indulgences, purgatory, and clerical celibacy. While the Inquisition dealt with many of them, some Waldensians may have survived to the see the Reformation fulfill their hopes. Ironically, Francis of Assisi, a generation after Peter Waldo, got his group, the Franciscans, recognized by the pope despite holding similar views as the Waldensians. However, even there, some Franciscans later ran into trouble over the issue of apostolic, and clerical, poverty.

Less obviously Christian, another heresy appeared before 1200 in southern France and northern Spain. Called "Cathars" (Greek for "pure") or Albigensians (because of their numbers in the city of Albi), they were led by priests called *perfecti*, who had vowed to abandon family and become, in essence, vegans. Cathars divided the world into spirit (good) and material (bad) aspects. As all matter was evil, the sacraments, using bread and water, were useless, Jesus wasn't really a man, and reincarnation reoccurred until one's soul was pure enough to be saved. As the materialism of the clergy was such an easy target, the Cathars quickly encountered church opposition. To make things more complicated many local nobles adopted the faith as it sanctioned their seizure of church property. Pope Innocent III countered by preaching a crusade and sending members of the Inquisition to destroy both Cathars and Waldensians.

In the Low Countries, houses filled with women who wished to live together without monastic vows; a community called the "Beguines." (The corresponding male group, the Beghards, also lived together but attracted less attention as they were considered less scandalous.) Practicing poverty, the Beguines supported themselves by spinning, weaving, sewing, and other traditional feminine tasks. They sought to serve the poor and generally tried to help society's sufferers. Their implied criticism of church wealth eventually brought them condemnation in the early fourteenth century. Seen as gentle souls, helping the marginalized, the Beguines appeal to the Thoughtful.

To today's Thoughtful, the medieval heretics might appear more attractive than church officials.

**The Inquisition.**

If the Thoughtful have one negative image of the late medieval church, it is the painting by El Greco, *Portrait of a Cardinal.*[6] Richly dressed in red, with not a trace of Christian love, he embodies the power and corruption commonly thought to characterize the church of the day. The Inquisition's object was heretics because such might anger God, cloak political opposition, threaten church wealth, offer opportunity to seize heretical wealth, and perhaps all of the foregoing. Attacking heretics proved difficult because local church officials might be relatives, secular leaders disliked the turmoil persecution brought, and many heretics being poor by birth or choice were quite mobile.

---

[6] Portrait of a Cardinal, Probably Cardinal Don Fernando Nino de Guevara. The Thoughtful can ignore the fact that technically the cardinal doesn't belong to the Middle Ages as the painting captures so well the image of the Inquisition.

After several failures at dealing with heretics, Pope Gregory IX established a group in 1227 in Florence, which later became the Inquisition, and it slowly grew to encompass much of southern Europe. Staffed largely by Dominicans whose simple lives and obvious devotion did not contrast with the heretics, the Inquisition proved fairly successful, eliminating the Cathars and largely suppressing the Waldensians. The negative impression of the Inquisition arises from its dealings with beliefs and ideas, rather than actions, as well as procedures that included anonymous accusations and torture, all things open to abuse. Add the incentive that a heretic's property was forfeited, sometimes to the church, sometimes to the secular authority, and sometimes to the accuser, and things often got out of hand. Unrepentant heretics were handed over to secular authorities (the churchmen wouldn't bloody their own hands) for punishment, usually death by burning. The Thoughtful are correct in thinking the inquisition represented some of the worst excesses of medieval churchmen, men who knew they had Truth.

**The Secular Side. Kings and Emperors.**

Once safely ensconced under Constantine, church leaders began to realize they had a problem: their relationship with civil authority. Today, to oversimplify, we call this church/state matters. The leaders got no assistance from the Christian scripture/New Testament as about all it reports is Jesus' answer about taxes, "Render unto Caesar that which is Caesar's, unto God that which is God's" (Mark 12:17). No help there.

Constantine established the precedents when he intervened, at the request of church leaders, in the Donatist and Arian controversies. His successors built upon his actions and developed a theory, Caesaropapism, that supported the emperor as both a civil (Caesar) and religious (pope) leader. This idea took root in the East but lacked appeal in the West due to the Western emperors' weakness and the residence of the pope in the West. The papacy eventually established its primacy, at least in the West, and when the last emperor disappeared in 476, the pope had no intention of letting the Eastern emperor rule the church or him. The struggle was protracted, with some violence and shady dealings, and merged with the story of the separation of the Eastern and Western churches.

Once the pope decided he could find protection with the Frankish monarchs in the eighth century, he performed an act that proved ambiguous. He crowned Charlemagne Roman Emperor, a position historians and later medieval folk called Holy Roman Emperor. While crowning someone appears to give the pope the power, in fact Holy Roman Emperors quickly understood the benefits of Caesaropapism and the struggle of Emperor and pope began.

The major point of contention involved choosing bishops. While in theory the local community did the choosing, in fact political rulers—kings, dukes, earls, barons, etc.—tended to dominate the local community's choices. Rulers took an interest because they needed educated advisors and administrators and churchmen provided these. Besides filling the offices of chancellor, justices, etc., bishops administered wide acres, both their own and the ruler's. Under the the practices of feudalism, bishops had sizeable private armies at their, and their master's, disposal. No ruler could be indifferent about the quality or loyalty of the bishops in his domain.

The reformers, from Cluny onward, sought to break this control and establish a truly independent church. The resulting struggle, called the "Investiture Controversy" when it involved the Holy Roman Emperor, played out at different times all over Europe. Usually the struggle began with an empty bishopric and the ruler and the pope naming their choices. Local communities divided so all could claim their choice as the "true" one. The pope would then excommunicate the ruler whose followers, sensing an opportunity, promptly revolted, claiming they could not be loyal to so unchristian a leader. The ruler would attempt to reestablish his authority with military might. Fighting, bombastic communiqués, rival bishops, sometimes rival popes, and the like preceded a compromise. All these events slowly moved the pope/ruler disagreements from "organizational politics" to genuine struggles for dominance after 1200. One result was excommunication and interdicts became ineffective. The ultimate upshot was the local community could freely choose whomever they thought best for the role;

however, the ruler's representative could be in the room during the vote. Of course, when that representative expressed an opinion, only the unwise ignored it. So rulers kept control, but the church had the appearance of independence.

The reformers' desire to free the church of lay interference also led to disputes about "criminous clerks," clergy who broke the law. The church claimed exclusive jurisdiction over such individuals but rulers demurred. Again, various compromises appeared, and no clear winner emerged. In England, this dispute got Thomas Beckett killed at the altar of Canterbury Cathedral, thus providing T.S. Eliot a plot for *Murder in the Cathedral.*

Popes, chosen by the College of Cardinals, were not ignorant of international affairs and frequently took sides, which led kings and emperors to try to sway the choice for pope. In 1305, a series of complicated maneuvers, including an election stalemate that led to a hermit being selected pope, produced a crisis. To resolve the crisis, the man finally chosen as pope, Clement V (1305 – 14) served as the Archbishop of Bordeaux in southwestern France, never made it to Rome, stopping at Avignon, just outside France's border in Provence. He and a string of successors ran the church without ever appearing in Rome. To all intents and purposes, the French king had maneuvered control of the papacy, and people referred to the period 1305 to 1378 to as the Babylonian Captivity. (For the first Babylonian Captivity, see chapter 4.) The papacy never really recovered from this debacle although subsequent events contributed to the predicament. The church ultimately fell before the rising power of the late medieval monarchs.

## Further Disaster. Divisions and Culture.

Influential Christians, bishops, abbots, and theologians began to worry about a papacy resident in Avignon and pressure mounted for a return to Rome. At last, in 1378 the cardinals, preparing to choose a new pope, held the election in Rome. A city in turmoil with nobles and mobs looking to control the papacy led the cardinals to select Urban VI (1378 – 89) whose election promises included a return to Avignon. Once chosen, he had a change of heart (or he'd been lying—after all, it was an election) and declared he'd stay in Rome. The horrified cardinals fled and once back in Avignon selected Clement VII (1378 – 94) as pope. Two popes elected by the same cardinals. The Great Schism had begun and the church had two leaders, both elected by the same cardinals. And they didn't like each other. Also both popes had pressing needs for money so the use of indulgences grew, and corruption in litigation became rampant.

This state of affairs lasted until 1409, when under various pressures, the two camps met at Pisa, deposed both popes, and elected Alexander V (1409 – 10). Now, not one, not two, but three popes competed for Christian loyalties and revenues. Moving quickly this time, church leaders met again, at Constance, in 1414, deposed all three popes and elected Martin V (1417 – 31). This time it took; the church had only one pope and all professed loyalty to him.

The story gets worse. Once the Great Schism was ended, everyone noticed the Renaissance was in full swing, the era when history, art, architecture, and other good things—but not religion—were the foci. In fact, the period was indifferent to religion, perhaps even amoral as typified by Machiavelli's *The Prince*.

Popes, being educated men and aware of cultural trends joined the party. St. Peter's, the papal church, was rebuilt; Michelangelo painted the Sistine Chapel ceilings. Generally, the church availed itself of the best artists and architects had to offer. But the amoral thing became the problem. A series of popes behaved in less than popely ways. Pope Sixtus IV (1471 – 84) took care to get his 11 nephews and 2 nieces good positions in the church, lack of merit notwithstanding. Innocent VIII (1484 – 92) didn't follow in his predecessors' footsteps as he had his own children to get taken care of. (Remember, the rule about clerical celibacy dated at least back to 1215.) Next came Alexander VI (1492 – 1503), a Borgia, who took things to the next level as he clearly maneuvered to get his son Caesar to succeed him as pope, turning the papacy into a heritable monarchy. (He failed.) Julius II (1503 – 13), one of Sixtus IV's nephews (remember him?)—so the papacy did become a family business—receives a bit of fame for hiring Michelangelo. The last Renaissance pope, Leo X (1513 – 21), came from the Medici, the family that ruled Florence, the center of the Rennaisance. By the time church leaders selected a pope who was not in the Renaissance tradition, the Reformation was well under way and the church was no longer of one piece.

The late medieval church became less tolerant of diversity as popes condemned Spiritual Franciscans and the Franciscan doctrine of poverty. The church increasingly lost influence in the emerging cities of northern Italy and Flanders. Many of the religious orders failed to follow their founders' idealism. How far Chaucer's *Canterbury Tales* portrays reality is disputed, but the mere existence of that work speaks volumes about the church of the day.

Many practices developed in the heyday of the papal monarchy in the twelfth and thirteen centuries became abused, distorted, or corrupted. Crusading was reduced to taking a vow to go on crusade followed by a monetary payment to escape the vow but still retaining the benefit of the forgiveness of sins that accompanied the vow. Indulgences, forgiving specific or all sins, generally became available and, before 1500, were available to benefit those dead and in purgatory. Visiting churches in Rome or, later, local churches on special occasions gained the sinner a plenary indulgence. What had begun as honest efforts to reduce the fears of the faithful and address the problems of penance had become, in many cases, a scam.

Popes, desiring to maintain their independence from secular rulers and to avoid a repetition of the seizures that had occurred by Byzantine and Holy Roman Emperors, as well as Norman rulers of southern Italy, began developing the Papal States in central Italy into a genuine unit, a buffer. As a consequence, popes increasingly behaved like any other ruler, making alliances, scheming to overthrow opponents, and supporting wars against their enemies.

### Common Folk.

Scholars have written much about Christian organization and doctrine because those are what can be found in the available sources. Literacy was confined to the upper orders and, at times, almost exclusively to churchmen. As a result they wrote about things that interested them: bishops, heretics, monasteries, theological disputes, and the like. What the mass of society believed or did is largely unknown because the literate few lacked interest. Miracles and rituals seem to have dominated the attention of the lower orders. Early in Christian history relics became a focus of popular attention, and an occasional judicial ordeal apparently brought God into a reality for many. [7]

Early church history provides examples of popular piety in the stories of martyrs. While the numbers were not great, the details indicate a few early Christians were perfectly happy to confront death, often a gruesome death, for their faith.

One event illustrates popular religion occurred shortly after Urban II preached the first crusade. While churchmen and nobility took a year to get organized, the peasants of the Rhineland decided they could start on their own. The resulting Peasants' Crusade first attacked the Jews in the region as, after all, they, like Muslims, were not Christian. Then the unorganized crowds started for the Holy Land, helping themselves to (i.e., stealing) food along the way. When they arrived in Constantinople, the emperor aided their crossing into Asia Minor where Muslims promptly killed the lot. In 1212, a similar outburst of popular piety occurred among the poor, and the resulting "crusade" never left the shores of western Europe; few ever made their way home.[8]

In the late thirteenth century and continuing for a least a century, groups of men publicly scourged themselves in penance for sins. Moving from city to city and soon spreading beyond the origins in northern Italy into France, Germany, and the Low Countries, the flagellants seem to have been a response of the masses to famines, plagues, and like. Eventually, the church banned them, and they died out.

Pilgrimages to various locations, whether to the holy land or more nearby places, such as Canterbury for the English or Santiago de Compostela for the Spanish (though both also attracted international pilgrims), were

---

[7] Southern, *Western Society*, 29-30.

[8] This is the so-called "Children's Crusade." Scholars disagree as to whether language usage at the time meant "children" were the country poor or what today would be called teenagers.

undertaken, sometimes as penance and sometimes in hope of a miraculous cure for a disease or condition. In the fifteenth century, the biography of Margery Kempe details the life and travels of one illiterate but intrepid Englishwoman who visited the Holy Land and Spain in pursuit of her faith.

At the end of the Middle Ages, the practice of selling indulgences may have given the masses some hope of a salvation that had too frequently been limited to the elite but, as with so much, details are lacking, even as to how much money was raised, and from whom.

In the late fourteenth century, a movement (one now attractive to the Thoughtful) appeared in the Netherlands. Geert Groote led individuals to cluster in houses, much like the Beguines had centuries earlier. Holding property in common, they continued to work in the community while dedicating themselves to kindness and prayer. Known as the *devotio moderna*, the new devotion, they escaped censure as they continued worshipping in their local churches and resisted criticizing the church of their day. Their lives, collected into stories, show common people acting on Christian ideals in a way the Thoughtful can admire.

What common folk believed was most likely a mishmash of various Christian doctrines, religious myths, and perhaps some pre-Christian ideas. The Thoughtful have read surveys of American Christians today, when literacy is well neigh universal, that record beliefs about reincarnation, angels, the devil, pets in the afterlife, etc. These beliefs stray far afield from what most Christian denominations teach so there is no reason to believe medieval folk were all good believers of orthodoxy.

Whether the wealth and grandeur of the church—massive cathedrals and monasteries, expensive vestments, elaborate rituals, etc.—created awe and strengthened belief or engendered disrespect and even hatred cannot be known. The striking paucity of peasant revolts can suggest either acquiescence or hopelessness among a group close to subsistence level.

How much the masses knew of the squabbles and maneuvering of the elite is unclear. During the Arian disputes of the fourth century, it was reported everyone in Alexandria had an opinion on the matter. During John of England' problems with the pope, the absence of various sacraments during the interdict should have caused trouble but none is reported. The Great Schism, with competing claims to church offices, similarly had no reported effect on the masses. The masses are largely silent. The Christianity we know about in the Middle Ages was that of the nobility.

*Martin Luther*

SEVEN

# *Fragmentation (Again) and Irrelevance—Reformation and Enlightenment*

## Fragmentation. The Reformation.

### An Easy Target. State of the Church.

Indulgences, the sale of forgiveness of sins, the particular practice Martin Luther attacked, were symptomatic of a greater problem of the church: its need for money. By the end of the Middle Ages, the pope needed a lot of money to fund his huge operations of warfare, politics, church building, and the like. Also the events since the beginning of the Babylonian Captivity in 1309 had given kings and other rulers significant control over the church in their territories, and they often used that control for non-religious purposes, e.g., reward followers, pay officials, win support among the nobility. At the bottom of the church's pyramid, the priests were not well educated or supervised and saw their position not as a calling but as a decent living. And the fires of reforming enthusiasm had been banked in the monasteries, which provided a comfortable life for their inhabitants; when the English king gathered an inventory of the state of monasteries, as a preliminary to seizing them, the list, though probably exaggerated, contained enough examples of unmonkly behavior to justify closing down the whole operation.

Additionally, simony, the purchase of church positions, never completely eliminated by reformers in the twelfth century, flourished; therefore many church officials took their office owing money—they had borrowed to buy the office. All of these people needed money, and to the average parishioner or noble, they were not doing much to earn it. Chaucer had made sport of churchmen in *The Canterbury Tales* and things had not improved. One was required to tithe (give 10 percent of income to the church); they then had to pay extra for baptisms and funerals (which were often badly conducted, practiced nonchalantly, in return for the fee). Non-residency, the result of holding several offices, also offended those who wanted full-time clergy. Scandalous personal lives of some clergy affronted the sensibilities of many. Even before Luther, city governments, which would provide many a hotbed of reform, were on the move against the clergy's corrupt administration, concubines, and greed. Also the immunity from taxes and the separate judicial system rankled those who valued fairness, as did exemptions from civic responsibilities such as military service. Much of the fervor of the early Reformation came from widespread anticlericalism, hatred even, at all levels of society, a product of these practices.[1]

One example of the things that were coming to be seen as problematic is provided by Frederick the Wise (1463 – 1525), the ruler of the German territory of Saxony perhaps not coincidentally the place where Luther lived. Frederick's local church contained more than 17,000 relics (or maybe only 5,000, scholars differ), including 35 pieces of the True Cross, the Virgin Mary's milk in a vial, a piece of the burning bush by which Yahweh spoke to Moses, a part of Jesus' manger, remains of an infant killed in the Massacre of the Innocents, crumbs from the Last Supper, fabric from the clothing of various biblical characters, and much more. By honoring these relics properly, a worshipper could reduce time in purgatory by more than 100,000 years (or maybe 2 million years, again scholars differ). All these relics were

---

[1] Anticlericalism has resurfaced, especially in the Roman Catholic denomination in light of recent scandals. Gary Wills, *Why Priests? A Failed Tradition* (Viking, 2013).

owned by the man who would protect Luther, a reformer who came to criticize the veneration of relics. And Frederick had only one collection of the many, perhaps thousands, scattered around Europe.

The genius of Luther's solution, and that of other reformers, was to sweep away all intermediaries between the individual and God. Protestants were freed of the clergy, and Protestant ministers were of no higher status than other church members. While anticlericalism never disappeared—the Thoughtful have heard people complain the minister has a soft life, working one day a week, etc.—the reformers' positions greatly reduced the animus in the Protestant world. Also, the state of the church did not go unnoticed, as lots of folk thought the church of the day needed reforming. Although that reforming effort, the Reformation, broke up the unity of the Western church, it also cleansed it of most of the abuses.

### Keeping Groups Straight. Vocabulary Issues.

Before getting too far into the Reformation discussion, the Thoughtful need to grasp some labels various groups acquired. The outcome of the Reformation divided Western Christendom into many parts. Throughout the Middle Ages, that Western part of Christendom had been called "catholic" (universal) even though it clearly didn't encompass all Christians. During the early days of the Reformation, people divided into reformers and traditionalists, the beginnings of Protestants and Roman Catholics. During the early, confusing years, a meeting at the city of Speyer of the Holy Roman Empire's leaders produced a decree against religious innovation. One group, the reformers, "protested" that decree, the origin of "Protestantism." Their opponents, the traditionalists, remnants of the medieval catholic church who would stay loyal to the pope in Rome are called "Roman Catholics." At that time, Protestants were largely, in modern terms, Lutherans, but the term encompassed all who did not maintain allegiance to the pope in Rome and opposed the Roman Catholic Church. Hence it included Lutherans, Zwinglians, Anabaptists, and many more, already in existence or appearing later. Today, Lutherans, Methodists, Presbyterians, Baptists, Mennonites, and innumerable other denominations are labeled "Protestant" even though their practices, beliefs, and organizations differ widely, often more widely in some cases than their differences with Roman Catholicism.

All denominations claim descent from Jesus but then argue about various things, mostly organization. Almost all Protestant churches began with the belief the Middle Ages represented a corruption of the true church and so they disregarded developments during that period. Many histories portray Protestantism as an offshoot of an institution was always run from Rome; the branch of a tree whose trunk was Rome. As the flowchart in the Appendix suggests, a better metaphor is a river with its headwaters at Jesus and a delta its mouth represents today's plethora of denominations.

While the Roman Catholic Church looks like the late medieval church with popes, bishops, monks, etc., some of its doctrine differs. Today other denominations also lay claim to direct descent from the medieval church. Most notably, the Church of England sometimes refers to itself as Anglican Catholic. A Syrian Catholic Church is loosely connected to Rome. In the United States, a Polish National Catholic Church appeared in the late nineteenth century due to feelings among immigrant Poles the Roman Catholic Church paid them insufficient attention. Also using "Catholic" is the Old Catholic Church of America.

The portion of the medieval church that retained its loyalty to the pope did not sit idly by as reformers criticized it and snatched territories from its grasp. The pope's response was slow in coming as he was often more afraid of the Holy Roman Emperor and his ambitions than those of the reformers. Many Roman Catholics saw value in reforming ideas but traditionalists carried the day, despite numerous efforts at compromise. Finally, in 1545 a council of bishops met at Trent. Over the next 13 years they hammered out positions, some reformist but most conservative, that now constitute today's Roman Catholic Church. Most important to the popes, the council did not seek to control or lessen the power of the papacy. After Trent, the Roman Catholic Church and its leader had no interest in compromising with Protestants. Also, the Roman Catholic Church and its leader became increasingly irrelevant in the affairs of Europe.

Protestants, all various stripes, shared several beliefs. All accepted the Bible, not individuals or church tradition, as the ultimate authority. All considered the individual to have direct access to God, without the intervention of clergy or saints, the "priesthood of all believers." All rejected the medieval interpretation of the mass ("transubstantiation"), but they didn't agree on a new interpretation of that event. All accepted married clergy and denied the higher value given to a monastic calling. However, once Protestants opened the door by giving all access to the Bible, proliferation abounded. Anyone could read the Bible, find support for a doctrine or practice that varied from existing denominations and set up a new one. This cycle continues today.

The difference in governance among Protestants, perhaps their most notable characteristic, arose from decisions regarding how close to the time of Jesus the group sought to return. Those who retained bishops went back to the early second century. Those with boards of elders returned to the late first century. The more congregational Protestants returned to the middle of the first century of the Jesus movement. Some even postulated the only way they knew they had correct structure and doctrine was if they were, like the early Jesus people, persecuted. Go figure.

Before the Thoughtful get bogged down in doctrinal or organizational differences, however, crasser reasons can be offered for the diversity that came to characterize Western Christendom—power. Governance—how a denomination is organized—came to be a distinguishing characteristic. The Church of England kept the hierarchy but substituted the monarch for the pope; today, the leader of the Church of England is not the Archbishop of Canterbury, but the monarch. Lutherans kept hierarchy to the extent of bishops. Calvinists rejected bishops in favor of local congregations supervised by a local board of elders. Other Protestants rejected any formal governance structure in favor of congregational autonomy and democracy. And, of course, Roman Catholicism retained the medieval hierarchy, with pope atop, supporting bishops, with priests dealing with the people. And behind all that variety lies various social groups—nobles, merchants, lawyers—who benefit from the governance structure.

Doctrines and practices of rival groups were criticized, but greed probably also played a role in the religious variety. Reformers disliked the church's wealth and the apparent idleness of so many church officials. Whenever reformers obtained political power, they dissolved monasteries and stripped bishops of the wealth even if they didn't abolish the bishoprics outright. As a result, rulers acquired great wealth, which also permitted them to accept the abandonment of indulgences that had often provided them money. One estimate is Henry VIII acquired one-third of all England's land as a result of his break with the pope. Elsewhere, the simplicity of Protestant services threw lots of valuable metals on the market as church property—chalises, candlesticks, statues—was melted down. Ideas look more attractive when their consequences include material gain.

The variety of groups, their many names, their apparent very tiny differences, all can pose a challenge to the Thoughtful not raised in a church tradition. Hang in there as not everything is important, and some things may become clearer.

## The Egg. Christian Humanism.

The Renaissance is omitted from this story because it was a fundamentally secular event. Its praise of the amoral (think Machiavelli) removes it from the Christian tradition. However, one aspect, humanism, proved to be crucial to the event called the Reformation.

During the Renaissance (meaning "rebirth," which refers to the discovery of ancient, especially Roman, ideas and structures), people began exploring their histories, and as Italy was the scene of so much Roman activity, ancient Rome became a favorite topic. They closely studied Latin, and later Greek, seeking knowledge of past ideals and guidance to the good life, a generally secular search. In northern Europe, men, remaining within the church, tended to limit their studies to the early church and it ideals. The Englishman Thomas More, using such humanist knowledge, created a fictional world, *Utopia*, in which people actually lived the Christian ideals. In France, Jacques Lefevre d'Etaples's researches into religious history uncovered differing translations of the Old Testament book, the Psalms. He produced the *Psalterium Quincuplex*, a Psalter in which five versions were printed in adjoining columns, something unsettling to those accustomed to accepting the Bible without question. The Dutchman Erasmus wrote the satiric *In Praise of Folly* with its sharp attacks on many church practices and the clergy. The dominant European intellectual of his day, Erasmus sought to unite Christian love and piety with classical humanism and civil virtue. He also produced a Greek translation of the Bible that differed in part from what had been the standard Western Bible, the Vulgate. With his studies and writings, Erasmus "laid the egg that Luther hatched."[2]

### The Spark. Indulgences.

Since the early days of the church, indulgences had been given but they grew slowly and became more and more abused. They offended Martin Luther so much that his response started the Reformation. The theory behind indulgences was the death of Christ and the saints built a reservoir, a huge surplus, of redemption God had then given to the pope to use. Once this theory was in place, motives of compassion, charity, greed, and the like led popes to expand indulgences in many circumstances since there was no check on the pope's power or limit to the supply of indulgences. The real potential for abuse began in 1095, when Pope Urban II, in organizing the first crusade, declared that participation would replace all other penances for a crusader who died having repented and confessed his sins. In other words, a straight entry into heaven was the lure for a noble considering the crusade. And only popes could issue this free pass.

By 1200, popes had extended the indulgences to those who gave money for a crusade. By 1300, secular rulers received indulgences as part of the pope's political maneuverings. In 1300, a pope granted indulgences to all repentant and confessed sinners who visited Rome's churches, a boon to the

---

[2] An example of the consequences of such study of the ancients is found in the Latin and Greek versions of Romans 1:17, the verse from which Luther took his justification by faith, the key term of the Reformation. In the Latin the sentence is active so it means those who love God have faith. In Erasmus's Greek translation, the sentence is passive so God gives faith. Diane Butler Bass, *A People's History of Christianity* (HarperOne, 2009), 164.

local tourist industry—as many as 2 million people may have taken advantage of the offer. By 1350, one could buy an indulgence for use at the moment of death—it wiped your slate of sins clean.

Things grew apace. Popes wished to extend their power and enhance their wealth, localities wanted in on the thriving activity; everyone wanted salvation. Forgers appeared. The straw that broke the camel's back for Luther came in the late fifteenth century when indulgences became available for the deceased. One could get one's relatives out of purgatory with a gift to the church. These indulgences provoked Luther to action that ultimately led him to abandon loyalty to Rome. The pope needed money for the rebuilding of St. Peter's in Rome. In Germany, Archbishop Albrecht of Mainz borrowed money from the Fugger banking house to help him obtain the archbishopric of Magdeburg and the bishopric of Halberstadt. When Johann Tetzel sold the indulgences around Wittenberg, the pope and archbishop (and the banker Fuggers) divided the proceeds. Salvation for sale for everyone, and the price was not steep.

**The Impetus. Martin Luther.**

On October 31, 1517, Martin Luther (1483 – 1546) posted a list of complaints on a church door in Wittenberg, Germany. He sought to debate the church's practice of indulgences. To Luther, indulgences infuriated him because the pope was selling something (forgiveness) that God gives freely; not only were indulgences a swindle, they conflicted with scripture. Luther had no inkling this was the first step in a journey that would lead him and many others to split the medieval church into many parts. Luther and the many others hoped to reform the church, hence "Reform-ation," not sunder it.

Luther, son of a domineering father whose success as miner gave him ambitions for his bright son, gave up the possibility of becoming a lawyer to become an Augustinian monk. He never could reconcile his worthlessness, in his eyes, with pleasing God enough to earn salvation. In the course of his studies—he was on the faculty at the university at Wittenberg—he concluded God's justice was so great that a sinner could never expect anything but divine punishment. Instead the sinner must rely on God's mercy and trust one is saved— "justification by faith" it came to be known. This approach meant sin was less important, and correspondingly, the church's role in overcoming it less vital.[3]

Luther's challenge to indulgences brought forth justifications from the church that did not satisfy him. If the pope had all this power over the after-life, why didn't he use it out of Christian love rather than turning a profit? That question was never really answered. Instead, papal power was asserted, but Luther found no support for this papal power in the Bible. The church's tradition of use of indulgences and their approval by the early Church Fathers also failed Luther's test of a biblical basis. Finally, he was driven to say if the Bible didn't approve it, it was wrong. After lots of maneuvering, including his excommunication, Luther was driven to rely on the Bible alone (*sola scriptura*) at the Diet of Worms (Diet = meeting, Worms = city) in 1521. Speaking of the Bible and his own writings, he said "Here I stand." With that statement, Luther discarded 1,400 years of church activity, and the Reformation was on.

Luther went on to translate the Bible into German, which moved the dispute to the populace. His numerous books and hymns, including "A Mighty Fortress is our God," spread his ideas in a way any modern PR person can only envy. The churches that followed Luther emphasized preaching, removed images (often smashing them in the process), celebrated the Lord's Supper with bread and wine (not bread only as in the past), and generally abandoned many medieval practices.

### Where? Germany!!

Luther's successes and survival owed much to the political confusion of the Holy Roman Empire. "Germany" was a geographical area, like the Midwest, but fragmented politically into over 400 semi-sovereign entities. The Holy Roman Emperor, once so strong, had suzerainty over all but power over little. The Hapsburg family had provided emperors since 1438, but each one had to be elected by the leaders of the more powerful German states and

---

[3] For an interesting study of how Luther came to his decision about justification by faith, see the psychohistory by Erik Erikson, *Young Man Luther* (Norton, 1958).

each election provided opportunities to bargain away more of the emperor's powers. What power the emperor had came from territories he personally controlled such as Austria and Hungary. By a fluke of marriage and inheritance, the emperor, beginning in 1519, was Charles V who, besides ruling Austria and Hungary, had the areas of the Low Countries (which included today's Belgium and the Netherlands), Spain, southern Italy and Sicily, Milan, and other scattered units, including some in the Americas. While such a base appears powerful and rich, in reality it often proved a burden as Charles could be distracted from dealing with Luther by myriad other concerns of his holdings, including wars with France and the Turks. By contrast, the monarchs in England and France had more control of their territories and their churches and fewer outside distractions. Perhaps Italy was too secular due to the Renaissance to take an interest in reform.

The divisions in Germany gave Luther protection as his own prince, Frederick of Saxony, hid him after his condemnation in 1521, and Charles lacked the resources and attention to capture him. With no central authority in Germany, the various local rulers, including city-states, could permit the spread of Lutheranism with impunity. It was 1547 before war broke out, but Lutheranism was too entrenched—despite Roman Catholic victories, the Peace of Augsburg in 1555 preserved Lutheran successes. Luther died in 1546, unmolested by imperial authorities, and Lutheranism survived because of imperial weakness. Though the populace could be fervent, politics and war governed the Reformation's outcome.

### Luther's Siblings. Other Reformers.

Luther wasn't the father but the eldest brother of the Reformation in that once he was in the field, many other reformers joined him; by 1530, Europe was filled with criticisms of church practices and, increasingly, its doctrines. In reaction to the church's emphasis on sin and earning (or paying for) its removal by actions, "good works" in the language of Christianity, reformers searched the Bible and brought forth the doctrine of faith. For Luther, heaven was too great a reward ever to be earned; it was graciously given by God.

All one needed to get to heaven was faith, trust; one didn't need the priests to provide sacraments or saints to pray. To reduce further priestly power and control, reformers translated the Bible into various vernaculars so all could read it, a tremendous spur to literacy.

In Zurich, the preaching of Ulrich Zwingli (1484 – 1531) led to the sweeping away of all sacraments and the stripping churches of ornamentation. He was supported by the city council, which seized control of much of the government from the traditionalist bishop. Reforming ideas proved popular in cities with independent governments, of which there were many in Germany, as the councils greatly increased their power and wealth (confiscating church, especially monastic, property). With Zwingli, a stricter form of reforming took hold. Whereas Luther tolerated many traditional practices, such as wearing robes and singing hymns, Zwingli and others like him favored simple services in simple buildings. Doctrinally, Zwingli differed from Luther mainly on the issue of the Eucharist, believing it a reminder of Christ's death whereas Luther retained a more traditional view. Luther and Zwingli could never agree on a doctrine of communion and Zwingli's dislike of ritual furthered their differences. Though he also rejected the doctrine of good works, Zwingli thought people should nevertheless lead lives helping the poor, avoiding drunkenness, choosing peace over violence, etc. Rejecting any separation of church and state, he created a tribunal to enforce Christian living, including compulsory church attendance.

Other reformers, such as Conrad Grebel (1498 – 1526) who was initially a follower of Zwingli in Zurich, believed baptism should be reserved until the believer could make a conscious choice to join the church (e.g., no babies). Anyone baptized as an infant, the universal practice, had to be rebaptized as an adult. These rebaptizers, "Anabaptists," soon came to provide the radical wing of the Reformation, and the term was applied to many groups for whom infant baptism was not the crucial issue. Whereas the medieval church baptized everyone at birth, which bringing them into Christendom, the Anabaptists reserved that act for adulthood, so membership was optional. More important than the baptism difference was the Anabaptists' position on the relationship of church and state. As the medieval church and governments had cooperated, Anabaptists took themselves out of that connection, depriving them of the state's protection. When troubles broke out between Anabaptists and others, the most common form of death for the former was, ironically, drowning. It was said, during one struggle in the Netherlands, the canals were choked with dead Anabaptists.

After Luther, the most influential reformer was John Calvin (1509 – 64), a French lawyer who wrote *Institutes of the Christian Religion* in 1536, continuously updating it. Calvin settled in Geneva and, though he and Luther agreed on the worthlessness of good works and accepted baptism and communion as sacraments, he took Luther's teachings further. As God was all-powerful and all-knowing, God knows everyone's fate from the beginning; people were "predestined" to heaven or hell even before birth. And there was nothing they could do to change their destination. Predestination seems an unattractive idea to the Thoughtful, but it spread rapidly and widely in the sixteenth century. Not surprisingly, most who took predestination seriously decided they were among the saved, the elect. For the populace, salvation by faith and predestination permitted foregoing indulgences as the result was the same, and cheaper.

If one is predestined, no matter which direction, why behave, why attend church services, etc. as one's destination cannot be changed? Calvin's answer was the purpose of life was not to obtain salvation but to honor God, and people could honor God by godly behavior that followed Jesus' teachings. If one is damned, one should praise God's justice, and, if one is saved, one should praise God's mercy. In any case, a godly life was required by God. If the citizens of Geneva wouldn't behave correctly, the government would enforce rules about such things. Drinking, dancing, theatre and the like were limited or banned, and one version of Puritanism was born. Calvinism, much more than Lutheranism, became the aggressive face of Protestantism. Also the Thoughtful should reflect on the idea the purpose of life is not to seek one's individual salvation—predestination settles that matter—but to serve and honor God.

### *Via media*. England's Trek.

In seeking a divorce, Henry VIII of England created the Church of England, breaking with the pope. In the earlier years of the Reformation, Henry wrote a diatribe against Luther, for which the pope gave him the title "Defender of the Faith." However, Henry produced no legitimate male heir to his throne. He had married his deceased brother's widow, Catherine, and became convinced God was punishing him for violating a biblical rule.[4] There is no reason to be cynical here; Henry, like many today, saw God's hand acting in life, in his case, denying him a son. Life was made more complicated in that a woman, Anne Boleyn, was playing to become the new queen. Also the pope was afraid of Catherine's European family and unwilling to give Henry the divorce his predecessors had often given others. After prolonged negotiations and litigation, Henry broke with Rome, making himself the new head of the Church in England; the king became the pope, in England. Oh, and he also took all the monastic lands. However, in terms of doctrine and practice (except for services in English and the Bible translated into English), the English church didn't change a lot; that change was left to Henry's son, Edward VI, who reigned from 1547 to 1553.

A convinced Protestant with even more convinced advisors, Edward presided over doctrinal changes that brought England to the Protestant forefront with the destruction of statues and the end of some traditions, such as prayers for the dead in chantries. (Some chantry money went to provide grammar schools so, again, cynicism is not in order.) Edward's death brought Mary to the throne, a woman (a novel concept) and a traditionalist who tried to return the English church to its 1520s state. Mary reopened some monasteries and made a cardinal Archbishop of Canterbury but otherwise made little progress, and her death in 1558 enabled her sister, Elizabeth, to become queen. In her four and a half decades of rule Elizabeth produced a church that looked Roman Catholic (priests, though often married, in clerical garb, rituals such as incense and bell ringing) but talked Protestant (the basic statement of faith, the 39 Articles, was decidedly reformist). Whether

---

[4] Leviticus 20:21.

Elizabeth found this middle way, a *via media*, by conviction or because she just couldn't make up her mind is grist for the mills of today's scholars. Her compromise disappointed reformers who sought the abolition of bishops, clerical vestments, old rituals, saints' days, the sign of the cross, kneeling, and the like. Their desire to purify further the church gave them the name "Puritans," but their hopes were frustrated, and they died off.

Those born in England in 1515 and still living in 1570 experienced a very topsy-turvy world. Raised in a church that was as medieval as any in Europe, they, in the 1530s, saw their king declare himself head of the church, displacing the pope. In 1547, the king died and his son and advisors gave England a leading reformed church. The son's death in 1553 put his sister on the throne who returned the church to its 1520s state. Her death, in turn made another sister queen who permitted a very odd church, for the Reformation, to exist.

### Jesuits. Modern Roman Catholicism.

Ignatius of Loyola (1491 – 1556), a Spaniard, wanted reform in a church where the hierarchy was still lagging. To effect that change, in 1534 he founded the Society of Jesus, the Jesuits, which would become the core of the Roman Catholic response to Protestant challenges. His *Spiritual Exercises* emphasized obedience and the Jesuits were trained amid scenes of martyrs' deaths. Jesuits anticipated dying as martyrs and soon became the foot soldiers of the Roman Catholic Reformation. Recognizing the territorial nature of the struggle, they especially sought to convert or keep rulers. As teachers, confessors, and preachers to the powerful, their own power in Roman Catholic territories became substantial. Loyola, like Christian humanists, believed in education and Jesuits soon founded excellent schools and universities. By the 1540s, Francis Xavier was leading a mission to Japan, and all American Midwesterners know the stories of the Jesuits who explored the North American wilderness in the seventeenth century. Jesuits appealed to the emotions in their religious art, and the Baroque expressed Jesuit values well. However, being powerful, they also gained a reputation for slipperiness in argumentation with a willingness to use doubtful means to achieve what they considered glorious ends. Some believed their casuistry excused bad acts. Whether they were dedicated servants of the new Roman Catholic church or the *eminence grise* of many royal actions depends on where one looks.

The criticisms of the medieval church by reformers finally registered with the papacy. The resulting Council of Trent spent some time on abuses, but most of the attention was on clarifying and protecting doctrine. Almost all major Protestant views—predestination, primacy of the *Bible*, priesthood of all believers—were rejected. Salvation came from good works and faith. The veneration of saints, the cult of the Virgin Mary, the Latin mass, all criticized by Protestants, were affirmed. The emphasis on the beauty of holiness contrasted with Protestant simplicity in the services. All seven sacraments were retained. The modern Roman Catholic Church emerged from the Council's decisions, sometimes called the Counter Reformation.

## New Participants. The Masses.

The Reformation affected the entire spectrum of society, top to bottom. Kings, aristocrats, merchants, peasants, women, men, all got excited and involved. Luther's "A Mighty Fortress is Our God," the original top-of-the-charts song, was sung by soldiers marching into battle. Religious fervor made one's enemies evil, and atrocities resulted. The end of a battle could result in hangings for the defeated. Luther's emphasis on the individual's relationship with God, and his rejection of the tradition of clerical superiority quickly took root among German peasants. In the mid-1520s peasants revolted, looted church property, and generally challenged the established order. Luther's *Against the Robbing Murdering Hordes of Peasants* sanctioned killing the rebels; perhaps 10,000 peasants died as a result.

More positive, the Reformation instigated the spread of literacy among Protestants. With the Bible translated into the more languages and widely available because of the printing press, people seized the opportunity to read it. Long sermons, boring to the Thoughtful today, provided instruction and entertainment in the sixteenth century. Thousands of Anabaptists died because they were rebaptised, and in England John Foxe chronicled the execution of several hundred Protestants, mostly craftspeople, under Queen Mary (thereafter "Bloody Mary" to Protestants), which suggests reforming ideas had reached all ranks.

**Again? Doctrine.**

Not surprisingly, reformers revisited many of the doctrines the church had settled on over the centuries. As most doctrines had been hotly disputed before conclusions were reached, the opportunities to hotly dispute them again were laying close at hand.

Interestingly, several of the early controversies were not reopened. Reformers were content with traditional positions about the Trinity and the nature of Jesus, both things argued over in the first 500 years of Christianity. Perhaps reformers realized what the Thoughtful have concluded—these issues aren't very important in day-to-day thinking about religion.

Salvation, the right relationship of the individual with God, became the primary doctrinal issue of the Reformation. Sin is the rupture of that relationship, and how one goes about repairing it is the focus of the salvation arguments. This argument intertwines with interpretations of the life, death, and resurrection of Jesus so variations are nearly endless. (The Thoughtful should be aware salvation need not involve any view of an afterlife.)

If one views Jesus primarily as a teacher, his words about how to live and what a new life entailed are the important things. This view usually drifts in the direction of what theologically is called "works" (often contrasted with "beliefs"), living a morally responsible life. Many early church writers liked this approach.

Others focused on Jesus' death and often interpreted it as restoring humanity's relationship to God. One consequence was all had salvation—universalism—and therefore thinkers had to work out how such a situation applied to people with bad behavior. For some early writers the notion of penance, giving satisfaction to God for bad behavior, dominated, and logically, something like purgatory was necessary for those who hadn't done so at death. Penance, an idea attractive to the ancient Roman lawyer Tertullian, requires a God, often an angry God, who judges whether one's efforts at penance are sufficient to overcome the sin. The medieval church developed guidelines in this regard which turned the whole affair into legalistic channels and made the individual's life into a regime of following rules.

A few authors, largely in the Eastern tradition, saw Jesus' death and resurrection as a means by which the individual believer gradually united with God. A life of contemplation, often culminating in a mystic encounter with God, was one popular outcome of this view.

Augustine set the understanding that dominated the Western medieval church. To him God begins the process of salvation by giving people the freedom from sin (actually Augustine thought Jesus accomplished this). Moreover, God, in the Holy Spirit, gives people the knowledge and will to live a righteous life. This idea connects loosely with the concept of predestination, God knows or chooses which individuals will get salvation. Unfortunately for the average believer, predestination often leads to the conclusion one can do nothing to affect the ultimate result. This idea was downplayed in the Middle Ages but resurfaced with a vengeance with the sixteenth-century reformers.

The Roman Catholic response to Luther, formulated at the Council of Trent in the 1540s, begins with much the same ideas: God originates salvation but the individual must respond by good works while retaining notions of sin and penance. In essence Protestants and Roman Catholics don't differ all that much in the theology of salvation in that the former see it as a one-time event and the latter as a process; also the role of the church as an institution involved in salvation is viewed differently by the two groups.

While Protestants and Roman Catholics differed on lots of things, for the average Christian those differences were most apparent in the various attitudes and doctrines about the Lord's Supper, the mass, the Eucharist, communion. Based upon Jesus' last meal with his disciples, this sacrament grew out of gatherings early followers of Jesus had, including meals, all of which was sort of codified in the gospels. With the passage of time, the church declared the bread and wine could only be dispersed by a priest if they were to be truly effective as "an outward and visible sign of an inward and spiritual grace." The medieval church settled on the dogma of transubstantiation which meant the bread and wine really changed into Christ's body and blood. Roman Catholics still believe in this physical transformation. The Thoughtful should ignore the gruesomeness of all this discussion and the possibility a stomach pump might resolve the matter.

Luther, while keeping the event as a sacrament, rejected transubstantiation in favor of consubstantiation. To Luther, the bread and wine were not altered materially, and he used the analogy of putting an iron bar in a fire; it changed—got red hot—but still remained iron. Other reformers, such as Zwingli and Calvin, declared Jesus was indeed present in a spiritual, not a physical one. For them, the sacrament is a memorial that helps the participant remember Jesus' life, death, and resurrection. Depending on the theologian and the denomination, it is also a thanksgiving, a communion, a supper, a show of faith.

The issue of exactly what this sacrament was became one of the easiest distinguishing tests in the Reformation. As everyone took part in it and its theology could be made fairly simple and understandable to the illiterate peasantry, the questions about it could become, literally, a matter of life or death. Things have calmed down by today.

If one gets serious about religion, the nature of the denomination's definition of church becomes relevant, and this was the subject of many a disagreement. The medieval Western church baptized all at birth so membership was not an issue. After the Reformation, things changed. Some denominations have a version of "You all come"; others demand public adherence to certain beliefs, and a few require tithing—all things that date back to the Reformation. And some, such as some Anabaptists, monitor behavior enough they will shun the company of the wayward or even ban them from services.

Sixteenth-century Christians also differed on other things, such as the end time (eschatology), which involved views on the Kingdom of God, the resurrection of the dead, the nature of the resurrected body, the final judgment, hell, and the like. All were things the peasants could approach in concrete terms and understand, and misunderstand. As a result the theologians soon returned to the medieval church's practice of cloaking such concepts in ambiguity. That act has not stopped modern believers, especially Protestants and more so, fundamentalist Protestants, from reading the Bible and developing firm opinions about such arcana. The Thoughtful should approach such matters at their own risk, recognizing two millennia of thought by Europe's best minds have not produced consensus.

## Consequences. Wars, Politics, and Capitalism.

### Killing for Christ. Religion and Politics.

As lots of folk now had Truth, though it varied from that of their neighbors, warfare resulted. Various denominations attempted to bring others to their Truth. Killing for Christ sparked a lot of violence until a stalemate led to the agreement all people in a political territory—kingdom, duchy, city-state—would have to accept the religion of the ruling authority, or move: *cuius regio, eius religio*—whose region, his religion. Truth therefore depended on where you lived, but it took lots of deaths for this idea to be accepted. Toleration would come later.

Wars and civil wars about religion broke out almost as soon as Luther finished his 95 theses. In Germany, in 1524 some peasants took his message to mean their oppression was unchristian, their landlord oppressors being no different than the clergy Luther attacked. The resulting Peasants' Revolt saw perhaps 300,000 in arms. Luther was appalled and raised no objection to the nasty reprisals of the nobility.

Anabaptist leaders emerged everywhere, often in ways that threatened the world of many others. Jacob Hutter led a group that banned private property and held everything in common, this group became today's Hutterites. In Munster, in 1534 Anabaptists captured the city from its Roman Catholic bishop. The bishop, with an army, laid siege, and as things became more desperate in the city, things became more radical. Community of property was followed by community of love; things all other Europeans, Roman Catholic or Protestant, abhorred. When the Anabaptists lost, their ideas were permanently tainted by this radicalism. The word "Anabaptist" became a bogeyman in the Reformation. Thereafter Anabaptists turned to avoidance of society and its temptations. Menno Simon led groups who shunned involvement in government, sought to worship in peace, and were pacifists; the Mennonites were the outcome. .

After 1540 Germany was the scene of fighting between Protestant princes and the Holy Roman Emperor, Charles V. After Roman Catholic France entered the fray in 1551 against the Holy Roman Emperor (such was the nature of politics), the tide turned against Charles, and in 1555 the Treaty of Augsburg gave the ruler (prince or city council) of each territory the power to determine the religion of the inhabitants. Things remained quiescent until 1618 when the future Holy Roman Emperor provoked the Protestant Bohemians into revolt. The resultant fighting, the Thirty Years' War (1618 – 48), decimated Germany with the Holy Roman Emperor dominant until the 1630s when Lutheran Sweden in the person of Gustavus Adolphus intervened. The Lutherans, helped by the Roman Catholic France (again opposing the Roman Catholic Emperor), turned the tide and the Treaty of Westphalia in 1648 left Germany fragmented politically and religiously. All very confusing. Thereafter, wars in central Europe, though common, involved dynastic and power issues more than religious ones.

France fell apart after 1560 when Catherine de Medici, of the Florentine Medicis, came to dominate public life as the queen mother. Thirty years of chaos followed with aristocrats scrambling for power, and fervent masses massacring one another. Catherine orchestrated the slaughter of 20,000 Huguenots (Protestants) on and after St. Bartholomew's Day in 1572. In 1594 Henri IV, a Protestant, ended the violence by converting to Roman Catholicism when his siege of Paris failed. After his switch, Paris opened its gates, and Henri, who apparently cared little for denominational niceties, declared "Paris is worth a mass." Religiously, France remained peaceful until 1685 when Louis XIV revoked the toleration of the Huguenots, forcing their flight to points abroad, including the American South.

The hot box of religious fighting occurred in the Low Countries where Calvinists, Lutherans, Anabaptists, and Roman Catholics could, and did, appeal to foreign powers for support. England and France intervened to thwart Spain, the area's overlord. Spanish mercenaries killed 7,000 in

Antwerp in 1576, and a long, drawn out war resulted in an independent Protestant north (today's Netherlands) and a Roman Catholic south under Spanish rule (today's Belgium). The northern portion, not religiously homogeneous, developed a *de facto* toleration.

In the British Isles, John Knox, leading an armed uprising in 1559, brought reformed Protestantism to Scotland. Unfortunately, the ruler was Mary, Queen of Scots, a Roman Catholic, but she was thrown out in 1567. Thereafter Scotland remained calm until the late 1630s when the King Charles (also the king of England) undertook some religious changes, which provoked a revolt during which the Scots ejected all of Charles' agents. Thereafter Scotland remained reformed with a presbyterian form of church governance, though politically governed by England's king.

In England, the same Charles I, son of Elizabeth's successor, James I, started a movement to emphasize "the beauties of holiness" and make other changes which some thought smacked of Roman Catholicism. Charles's wife and queen was a French Roman Catholic who didn't convert which only fueled suspicions. Doctrinally, the ideas of the Dutchman Jacob Arminius (1560 - 1609) crept in—he reinterpreted Calvinist predestination to predestination with a small whiff of free will, too radical for strict Calvinists. Believing their church under attack, a new batch of Puritans sprang up and, as they met with as little success as the first batch under Elizabeth, more than 100,000 of them left the country, largely for New England. Those who remained eventually provoked a war, which Charles lost, and introduced a reformed church. In the 1640s and 1650s, the breakdown of governmental control led to a proliferation of groups, some secular, some religious, with names such as Levelers, Seekers, Ranters, Diggers (land in common), and Quakers. Despite their military success, the reformers never established a regime that satisfied all, or even most, of the English. In a very strange turn of events, Charles's son was invited to be king and reigned for 25 years as Charles II. Himself personally tolerant (though he was baptized a Roman Catholic on his deathbed), Charles II permitted a legal toleration of sorts for extreme Protestants (called "Dissenters" as they dissented from official doctrine and practice). Charles II died without a legitimate child (though several of the other kind), and his brother James II became king. An open Roman Catholic James II lasted only three years before the nobility rebelled, drove him from the country, and invited his Protestant daughter and her husband from the Netherlands to reign as William and Mary. All very confusing. Thereafter England continued to have an established church that was a compromise of Roman Catholicism and radical Protestantism, with a small section of the populace having their own, more reformed, churches, and enjoying a limited toleration.

Eastern Europe, with less population and wealth, saw less fighting. In southern Europe, Italy had some persecutions but no major wars. The Inquisition continued working in Spain, whose rulers were involved in wars elsewhere.

While the masses occasionally took Reformation ideas to extremes, the ruling orders increasingly exploited those ideas for dynastic, national or imperial gain. Roman Catholicism found support among the Hapsburgs of Germany and Spain and the rulers of France, although eight civil wars in the sixteenth century threatened the integrity of that nation. Protestants produced Gustavuus Adolphus of Sweden who nearly created a Swedish empire in northern Europe, and Dutch rebels carved out a bourgeois republic in the unpromising delta of the Rhine. Germany endured the Thirty Years' War and France the St. Bartholomew Day's Massacre. Everywhere the deaths of martyrs created continual struggles with the authorities. Assassinations, something more or less new, claimed several leaders including William of Orange in the Netherlands in 1584 and Henri IV in France in 1610. It was not a period characterized by love and forgiveness.

By 1560, the religious map of Europe had taken the shape it still retains, by and large, despite the wars of the succeeding century. From 1560 to 1600 the wars involved the possible survival of Calvinism in France and the Netherlands. The wars throughout Europe continued until 1660, but the map of 1560 changed little. Lutherans occupied Scandinavia, and parts of Germany; Calvinists were in the Netherlands and Scotland, parts of Switzerland and Germany; and Roman Catholics controlled southern Europe. Bohemia being the major exception where a Protestant country was completely turned Roman Catholic during the wars. The exhaustion resulting from the wars led to a *de facto* toleration in many areas. The real consequence of the "Wars of Religion" was the strengthening of the state, whether monarchial or otherwise. However today the vast majority of Europeans are not religious, and the church buildings are largely deserted. And after all that thunder and fire.

### The Winner. The State.

In the early years of the Reformation, monarchs, aristocrats, and city-state bourgeoisie fought for political power to further their particular views on religion. By the end of the sixteenth century, however, a new view joined fervent religiosity. In England, Elizabeth I, and in France, Henri IV can be described as *politiques*, more interested in ruling than having the right religion. Elizabeth avoided "windows into men's souls" and created a national church that looked almost Roman Catholic—bishops, genuflecting—but was doctrinally Calvinist. Henry IV, he of "Paris is worth a mass," converted to Roman Catholicism and ruled all of France peacefully.

The seventeenth century included the Thirty Years' War, begun as a fight over religion but ended as a struggle among political giants, the Hapsburgs of Austria and Spain, Gustavus Adolphus of Sweden, and Richelieu of France, and numerous other smaller regimes. Roman Catholic France and Lutheran Sweden had no difficult allying against the Roman Catholic Hapsburgs. In England, a civil war among king, nobles, gentry and London merchants became heavily influenced by religion, finally ending with limited religious toleration. Religion intensified and enflamed armies, resulting in many atrocities, but did not dictate the result. Thereafter, religion sometimes offered an opportunity, sometimes an excuse, for actions such as when the aristocracy drove the Roman Catholic James II from the English throne or and when Louis XIV, in 1685, revoked privileges of Calvinists, many of whom were merchants and artisans. In neither case was religion the dominant motive.

By the middle of the eighteenth century, Europe had a complete range of political regimes, from strong monarchs, through aristocracies, both landed and mercantile, to hints of democracy. However, religious affiliation didn't correlate with government structure.

France, Prussia, and Russia, the three most centralized countries with fairly strong monarchs, favored Roman Catholicism, Calvinism, and Orthodoxy, respectively. Powerful landowning aristocracies ruled England and Poland, but the former was Anglican and the latter Roman Catholic. The Dutch republic and Venice were both in the hands of merchants but separated by Calvinism and Roman Catholicism. Religion had, *in fine*, been a tool in the struggles among kings, nobles, and merchants, but it had not determined the outcome.

Almost everywhere the government controlled the religious organization, which meant involvement in personnel decisions and a general toning down of religious intensity. Any vitality found in the eighteenth century occurred in the sects, not the national churches. As governments came to control the church of their area, they used it as a means of social control. Nobles and later the bourgeoisie dominated government; no important politician was a cleric after 1660. So complete was rulers' domination in 1773 the pope was persuaded to suppress the Jesuits, the group that had done most for Roman Catholicism's success after the Reformation. Rulers worried Jesuit power and connections across borders were inconsistent with the growing state.

### Christianity Discovers the World. Expansion.

The beginnings of the spread of European power around the planet occurred as reformers argued religion. Generally these expeditions were driven by Horstman's three g's: God, gold, and glory, not necessarily in that order. The latter two, the quests for wealth and fame, often took precedence over the first but the word of God always had a part. Whether Jesuits in New France and Japan, Spanish priests in Mexico, or English Puritans in Massachusetts, gathering the locals accompanied the gathering of gold and glory. The success of the missions was erratic. Japan had a flourishing Christian community for a while, and in other places missionaries adapted to local traditions in ways that sometimes made the Christianity almost unrecognizable. And, of course, if the locals refused the offer of the new faith, killing them and taking their land was justified more easily.

Spain's conquest of what today is Latin America dwarfed the efforts of other European expansionists. Besides bringing Christianity, the Spanish also brought diseases to which the locals had no immunity, smallpox and malaria especially; within a hundred years of Columbus's contact with the Americas, it is estimated the population dwindled from twenty million to two million. Black slaves from Africa were imported to remedy the resulting shortage of labor. The Spanish saw the Americas, particularly Peru and Mexico, as opportunities for economic exploitation and were ruthless in doing it. Jesuits and Dominicans sought to convert the Indians and, sometimes, to protect them from the worst excesses of the conquest. Soon the Roman Catholic Church had many new members, although what those members knew or thought about Christianity is not well recorded.

### Something New. Capitalism.

While the Reformation produced diverse churches and many wars, the economy of Europe changed, growing in wealth and diversity, and scholars have puzzled over any possible connection. After all, if things happen at the same time, they might be connected in some way. Marx, in the nineteenth century, thought Protestantism succeeded because it captured the capitalistic values of thrift and self-reliance. Max Weber's *Protestantism and the Rise of Capitalism* appeared in 1904 and turned Marx's idea upside down, arguing Protestantism encouraged capitalism. After deciding the strongest economies appeared in Protestant areas, Weber set off a scholarly debate that well exemplifies that genre. His arguments and his data were questioned, reworked, and added to until the Thoughtful would give up puzzling it out. The thrust of the argument was Protestant ideas about salvation, in particular predestination, led believers to work harder, be thrifty, spend wisely, save much, etc. in an effort to learn if they were among the saved. While the theory of predestination originally precluded such knowledge, believers couldn't live with the uncertainty so they began to connect worldly success with divine approval. If one prospered, it was a sign one was predestined for heaven.

A very unfortunate corollary meant lack of success pointed to damnation so the poor deserved to be poor as they were headed down anyway. Today Weber's argument has more currency among non-scholars and is trotted out to explain way certain groups in the United States (read blacks) haven't prospered as well as others, or why certain areas of the world have economies that lag—their values (i.e., their non-Protestant work ethic) hold them back. Scholars, on the other hand, are skeptical of such a monocausal explanation applied in so many differing situations. The Thoughtful can choose—Marx or Weber—knowing scholars think the issue can't be resolved. Basically, it boils down to whether ideas have effect, a philosophical issue.

## Who Cares? The Enlightenment.

### Christianity's Challenge. A New View of Nature.

As the Reformation era reformers created new churches while questioning the medieval church's doctrine and practices, other men questioned the medieval view of the natural world. That view, a composite of Greek and Christian ideas, relied heavily on Aristotle, an ancient Greek, and Aquinas, a medieval scholar. A search for causes rather than descriptions—why objects fall, not how—characterized the Middle Ages, and, of course, all causes led back to God. The details of this activity need not occupy the Thoughtful who understand the close observation of the world was not then the rule as it has since become.

The development of science, as it is understood today, began in the sixteenth century and included studies of planetary motion and gravitation. A Pole and a contemporary of Luther, Nicholas Copernicus (1473 – 1543), found the Ptolemaic system that had described the heavens since Roman times too complex. That system put the earth at the center of things and, in describing the orbits of the heavens about the earth, had myriad epicycles. As a man of the Renaissance he knew the ancients had thought about a heliocentric system, and like many of the time, he reintroduced the old theory. Unfortunately for him, the observations didn't confirm the theory. His circular orbits for the planets required Copernicus to reintroduce epicycles, which had made the Ptolemaic system so complex and confusing.

Several men put mathematics into play, and the view of the world never looked the same. Though he didn't accept Copernicus's new theory, the Dane Tycho Brahe (1546 – 1601) built Europe's best observatory with which he made detailed observations of the heavenly bodies. Johannes Kepler (1571 – 1630), a former Brahe assistant, using his master's numbers, fit them into a new sun-centered system by giving the planets elliptical orbits, the law of planetary motion. With the addition of two more laws, Kepler set what we call science on its modern path—theories fit data and results can be replicated, e.g., laws. A contemporary of Kepler, the Italian Galileo Galilei (1564 – 1642) posited the uniformity of nature and, like Kepler, sought mathematical certainties in it. He also accepted the Bible as true but thought, as to nature, the holy book had words quite different from their "true" meaning. With the addition of the theory of gravity, Isaac Newton (1642 – 1727) unified the work of Copernicus, Galileo, and others to explain how planets moved and apples fell. The presence of mathematics—Newton was the co-discoverer of the calculus with Gottfried Leibniz (1646 – 1716)—in Newton's work gave precision to the natural world. However, these men weren't all "moderns," as Copernicus was a biblical literalist, and Kepler was mystical and took astrology seriously, as did Newton; beginning with Galileo, the Thoughtful can recognize people who think like the Thoughtful.

No longer did the universe revolve around humanity; rather, humans began to appear as very small specks of dust in a very, very large arena. God retreated from being the chessmaster in the sky, moving pawns around on earth and making crops grow and disasters to occur. While many had always had a more abstract view of God, the new view became nearly universal among the educated classes, distancing them from many other believers, a separation that remains today.

The efforts of the astronomers, Galileo's infusion of mathematics into the explanation of the world, the calculus created by Newton and Leibniz, all together constructed a world view that has caused many a Thoughtful, fearing the mathematics, to avoid science, though accepting of the view.

## New Examinations of the Bible.

The attitudes of questioning accepted wisdom and using empiricism even appeared in traditionalists. In Ireland the Archbishop of Armagh James Ussher (1581 – 1656), calculated the creation of the world as occurring on October 23, 4004 B.C.E. Using the Bible, he strung together events and lives that permitted him to accomplish what had been rarely attempted in the years since the Bible had been settled upon over a millennium earlier. His wasn't the only effort but has remained the most popular.

Since the early days of Christianity, the idea floated around there were people prior to Adam and Eve, based upon the actions of Cain after his slaying of Abel.[5] In 1655 Isaac de La Peyrere (1596-1676) published arguments that made Preadamite ideas widely available. One understanding was the Bible, being a book about Adam's descendents, only discussed the Jews whereas the Preadamites were the ancestors of the Gentiles. Later renditions of the Preadamite theory led to them being the ancestors of the various races, and later still, to a hierarchy of the races. The relevance of all this information to the Thoughtful is the Preadamite idea provided a way to accept the Bible while reducing it to just one story of humanity's history.

Another stream of this new approach came to be called the "higher criticism." While Erasmus (1466 – 1536) and Spinoza (1631 – 77) looked at the Bible differently than their medieval predecessors, higher criticism really got under way in the eighteenth century. A close examination of scripture began to produce suggestions any biblical book may have had multiple authors and editors. Largely a German activity, this flowered in the nineteenth and continues today.

## The Church Denied. The Intellectuals.

While the astronomers regularized the heavens, others collected worldly data that, in toto, offered serious challenges to Christianity as then constituted, and not all easily accepted that result. The explorations taking Christianity outside its largely European setting brought knowledge of the

[5] Genesis 4:17.

world back. The wide variety of customs among peoples who led civilized lives challenged European notions of Truth, religion, and morality. The king of Siam, showing a tolerance and understanding that could only bother the religious, questioned the Europeans' view of one religion when he opined if God had wanted one faith, He could have so ordered it. When Europeans discovered Egyptians and Chinese who had histories going back beyond 4004 B.C.E., the contradictions became historical as well.

Many events, such as the English civil wars, combined with this knowledge of the world led political thinkers into new worlds. In *Leviathan* Thomas Hobbes (1588 – 1679) described a state of nature—before government—where the life was one "solitary, poor, nasty, brutish, and short." The Englishman John Locke (1631 – 1704) proposed a human mind that, at birth, was a *tabula rosa*, a blank tablet, which meant education was all. Locke also described a state of nature that led to less harsh results than Hobbes suggested and gave government the job of protector of life, liberty, and property, a view Thomas Jefferson echoes when he wrote the Declaration of Independence. Religion, including Christianity, played little part in this kind of thinking.

The scientist Blaise Pascal (1623 – 62) tried to reconcile the new scientific understandings with religion. Recognizing the failure of his efforts, he proposed "Pascal's wager," which argued it is better to believe God exists and be wrong than to believe God does not exist and be wrong. In the former, the believer loses only a little time and effort, but in the latter, eternal bliss is forgone.

Pierre Bayle (1647 – 1706) serves as a capstone of the new edifice with his creation of the *Dictionnaire historique et critique*. He catalogued kings who brought misery, popes who were unpopely, and the like. Skepticism about the past and, indeed, of all knowledge became common. Only close observation of the world and its constituent parts could provide truth, an attitude still common today.

### Women's World? Witchcraft.

Commonly perceived as a fact of life in the dark Middle Ages, witchcraft actually appeared largely in the Reformation era. Today scholars tend to approach the subject sociologically and put it in the context of the poor peasant society, where begging widows were common because of inheritance rules. To begin the discussion, the Thoughtful should know witches did exist in the sense a few people worshipped the devil, but they were too few to account for all the attention lavished on the subject. As in many areas, evil and its explanation are the gist of the matter. A major impetus to the later crazes came in 1484 when a papal bull sanctioned the idea of witches and, in 1486, when the book *Malleus Maleficarum* (The Hammer of Witches) described witchcraft. The book gave cues to those questioning suspected witches as to what to look for and ask about—e.g., people died suddenly, farm animals got sick, storms destroyed crops. If someone, usually a poor woman, had muttered a curse in response to a rejected plea for charity, the explanation became clear: she was a witch. More than 70 percent of the accused were women, which reflected Christianity's long-held suspicion about the daughters of Eve. Once an accusation occurred, the attitude of the authorities became crucial as any support of the allegation could often create a group hysteria which today would be studied by psychologists. The Thoughtful are most familiar with the trials in Salem, Massachusetts, in 1692, but those came towards the end of the witchcraft era. Witchcraft persecutions died out when Enlightenment ideas about how nature worked found residence among the authorities, but not before an estimated 50,000 had been executed.

## Exhaustion. Toleration.

No, religious toleration did not happen much. Early on, reformers began disagreeing about all sorts of things, e.g., vestments, the wedding band, general hair-splitting worthy of medieval scholasticism occurred. In efforts to keep Protestants in one tent, some, such as Martin Bucer (1491 – 1555) in Strasbourg, preached *adiaphora*, things indifferent, believing Christians could differ over small things without setting up new churches. Thus, clergy vestments, certain rites, wedding rings became symbols of idolatry for some, which Bucer hoped to ignore. More often than not, such moderation failed. Whenever toleration occurred, it was more often the result of political calculations about the feasibility of suppression than the intellectual conclusion that it was a good thing.

The civil wars in France ended when Henri IV issued the Edict of Nantes in 1598, granting limited toleration to the Calvinist Huguenots. In 1685 Louis XIV felt strong enough to revoke the Edict, making France uniformly Roman Catholic. In England, various groups sprang up in the 1640s and 1650s as a result of the breakdown of governmental authority during the civil wars. After the wars ended and the monarchy was restored in 1660, limited toleration to those groups—Dissenters—was granted. In Russia, the Old Believers opposed tsarist reforms involving the numbers of Alleluias in the liturgy and the number of fingers used to cross oneself. After perhaps 20,000 of them burned themselves to death, a limited toleration was granted. Eventually European intellectuals, such as Voltaire, the pen name of Francois Arouet (1694 – 1778) and Gotthold Lessing (1729 – 81), and the ruling elites decided on toleration as a position in the eighteenth century because they thought religion would die anyway, so why worry?

## God Still Exists. Deism.

After the white-hot intensity of the Reformation, religion eventually lost its emotion, at least in the upper reaches of society. By the eighteenth century, enthusiasm was frowned upon as rationality became more important. Gradually the Enlightenment accepted the view of a world operating by understandable rules. The Scientific Revolution, as scholars name this period, created a mechanical view of the world, where rules, laws, mathematics controlled. This use of logic and reason removed God from the day-to-day running of nature and instead assigned the deity a role as creator and first cause, and even those roles were challenged. In a commonly used metaphor, God became a watchmaker who designed and built a watch, wound it up, and then watched it tick away. The world, once created, runs by the same natural laws as a watch. The methodology of science, in theory at least, was begun by close observation of nature and proceeded to the formulation of universal laws, not from philosophical concepts guiding a search for confirming details. The Roman Catholic Church became hostile to science, fearing it would destroy important doctrines (such as transubstantiation), but Protestant churches were less concerned, perhaps because scientists' close observation of nature paralleled Protestants' close examination of the Bible. Freemasonry flourished among deists as it well represented their view.

For deists, God created the world but that event ended divine participation. They rejected such things as the resurrection of Jesus, his miracles, prayer, etc. They believed clergy were participating in a fraud designed to enrich themselves and control the peasantry. Religion, if it meant anything, involved how one treated one's fellow human beings, and Jesus' moral teachings could still be a part.

### Religion Responds. Pietism.

The growth of religious rationalism and deism produced a reaction that emphasized the religion of the heart and emotionalism. Beginning among German Lutherans in the late seventeenth century, pietism promoted personal faith, not doctrine. Count Nicholas von Zinzindorf (1700 – 60) accepted this new approach and converted some exiled Moravians on his estate. Soon Moravians (aka Moravian Brethren) moved beyond their homeland and during one of their services in London the Anglican clergyman John Wesley (1703 – 91) felt his heart "strangely warmed." Together with his brother Charles (1708 – 88), he began preaching sermons filled with fervor and in new environs, the out-of-doors. Called "Methodists," a term of derision, for their systematic and serious approach to religion, they soon found their listeners numbering in the thousands, largely among the working classes. This pietism found its way to America, and in the nineteenth-century it had worked its way up the social scale where it accounted for a change in personal behavior as well as attention to such things as slavery.

## Conclusion.

The scientific questioning of received wisdom and quest for universal laws soon spilled over into attitudes to religion. The age of exploration revealed many peoples around the planet who lived moral lives without the structure and strictures of Christianity. The history of the Reformation era wars demonstrated Christianity's claim to love one's neighbor and forgive one's enemy was too often ignored in favor of killing for Christ. When religious leaders accepted the territorial basis of religion, a certain cynicism religion was the tool of the powerful could not be suppressed.

The Enlightenment, the response to this period, and other factors, brought a major challenge to Christians, of all stripes, and many of the attitudes formulated in the seventeenth and eighteenth centuries exist today. The leading minds of the Enlightenment became increasing hostile to organized religion, especially Christianity, which they saw as superstitious and controlled by selfish churchmen. Already by 1700, miracles, the Resurrection, Jesus as a God, anything that violated the new understanding of nature had been rejected by John Toland (1670 – 1722) in his *Christianity Not Mysterious*. The structure of the churches and the practices were criticized as elaborate undertakings to control the populace and milk them of their money so churchmen could lead lives of indulgence, power, and, often, immorality. By the end of the eighteenth century, atheism appeared more than occasionally and found numerous followers among French revolutionaries. And, the educated laity had replaced the clergy as the leaders of society.

The culmination of these developments occurred during the French Revolution when Maximilien Robespierre (1758 – 94) created a Temple to Reason in the cathedral of Notre Dame, but Voltaire established the tone even earlier, when he, in writing about religion, exclaimed *escrase l'infame* ("crush the infamous thing")

*The Statue of Liberty*

## EIGHT

# *Variety and Vitality— The United States*

The Thoughtful can more easily observe some of the poles around which believers cluster by examining the history of the United States rather than early Christianity. Governance, doctrine, practice, experience, all have a wonderful diversity in America. Organization by top control or democratic messiness often defines the denominations. Community or individual focus, whether for eternal salvation or personal behavior, pops up in various places. Is the group only for a select few—the elect, the pure—or open to all? The answer repeatedly produces new, purer, groups, especially among Baptists.[1] The relationship to government, whether passive like Paul's in ancient times and the Amish's today or active in its desire to control, like medieval Catholicism and many fundamentalists today or something in between those two extremes has provided much grist for religious mills. Emphasis on sacraments and organized worship services usually offends those seeking spiritual rewards, which creates another division between liturgicals and pietists. For the people in the pews perhaps the biggest division

[1] This duality is sometimes labeled "exclusivists" and "inclusivists." Others label denominations as Evangelical/Conservative, Traditional, Ecstatic, and Mainline, or Liturgical Protestants, Pietistic Protestants, and traditional. Or in other ways.

is whether their religion is rational or emotional. And finally, many worshipers and some scholars adopt American exceptionalism, the idea that the interpretation of the past of the United States is unlike any other country, a view that is relatively common in the disciplines of economics and political science; this idea results in seeing the people, or at least the Christians, of the United States as a "chosen people," a term ancient Israelites and the seventeenth-century English applied to themselves. If organized American Christianity has a primary theme, it is schism and division in the earlier period were replaced in the twentieth century by mergers. Whether those thinking about religion become more or less diverse or intense remains an open question.

With all this diversity, it is difficult to document the experiences and perspectives of those in the pews. In all probability, most churches have attendees and even members who believe doctrine and stories that would appall church leaders, and the pewsitters may not even know how out of line they are. And certainly those leaders believe things they dare not share with the pew occupiers. For example, surveys suggest a majority of Americans think all religious folk, and even atheists, get eternal life—universalism—something that would scandalize many fundamentalist pastors. Moreover, one gets eternal life by being a good person, a view rejected by those who think "proper belief" crucial.[2]

The faith of our fathers is no longer our faith as a quarter of Americans have left the denomination of their childhood. Whether the denomination seeks to evangelize and increase membership is not universal; for instance, some, such as the Amish and Hutterites sustain themselves and even grow internally. Accommodation to the modern world led to successions and divisions in the nineteenth century and, often, still defines fundamentalism today. Hatred even has its role as anti-Catholicism was rife until at least the election of John F. Kennedy in 1960, and no love is lost today when fundamentalists describe many liberals. And race is the red thread running through the fabric of all American history, including religious history.

---

[2] A good source to see this diversity is www.religions.pewforum.org/pdf/report2-religious-landscape-study-full.pdf, accessed August 20, 2013.

The United States is perhaps the most religiously diverse country on the planet. Virtually every sect of Christianity exists here, and most varieties of non-Christianity have a foothold. Moreover, in surveys Americans indicate considerable interest in their faith and in participating in their faith's institutions. Why this U.S. distinctiveness?

First the numbers:[3]

| Group | Number | % |
|---|---|---|
| Roman Catholic | 57,199,000 | 25.1 |
| Baptist | 36,148,000 | 15.8 |
| Methodist | 11,366,000 | 5.0 |
| Lutheran | 8,674,000 | 3.8 |
| Presbyterian | 4,723,000 | 2.1 |
| Mormon | 3,158,000 | 1.4 |
| Episcopalian | 2,405,000 | 1.1 |
| Churches of Christ | 1,921,000 | 0.8 |
| Jehovah's Witness | 1,914,000 | 0.8 |
| Assemblies of God | 810,000 | 0.4 |
| United Church of Christ | 736,000 | 0.3 |
| Christian Generic | 32,441,000 | 14.2 |
| None/No Religion | 34,169,000 | 15.0 |
| Total | 228,182,000 | 100.0 |

These figures reveal how adults describe themselves and probably inflate the total believers as many are skeptics but don't want to acknowledge it publicly. Many call themselves "Protestant" or "Christian" but specify no denomination. Roman Catholicism, while containing a quarter of the population, has

[3] Source: Barry A. Kosmin and Ariela Keysar, "American Religious Identification Survey," (Program on Public Values, 2009). www.americanreligionsurvey-aris.org, accessed August 23, 2013. Many smaller denominations are omitted from the above list. The survey was taken in 2008. William M. Newman and Peter L. Halverson in *Atlas of American Religion* (AltaMira, 20002) give a history and membership patterns in geographical terms of most American Christian organizations. The work is marred, from this book's perspective, by a distinction between denomination and sect, a distinction this book does not make.

many "Cafeteria Catholics" who pick and choose the doctrines and practices they accept; others are rare attendees and rarer participants, so that number is inflated in terms of its importance. Mormons count everyone who was baptized even if they are not involved. Many denominations, both Roman Catholic and Protestant, contain a significant number of nearly lapsed members who attend only at Christmas and Easter—"Chreasters"—but continue to identify themselves with a particular denomination. Baptists, of course, are such a diverse and weakly structured denomination their influence is less than their numbers. Lumping Methodists and Wesleyans together combines groups that practice dramatically different approaches. Lutherans also covers groups that range, theologically and behaviorally, from the extraordinarily conservative to the quite progressive. All that said, the numbers still reveal the unique variety that makes up American Christianity.

## The Spice of Life. Immigration.

Christian Europe, whence most American immigrants have come, had national churches, meaning a particular denomination received government support and often, at least in the immediate post-Reformation centuries, banned dissent (open dissent at least) from that denomination. As a result, those arriving on American shores from Italy were Roman Catholics, from Scandinavia Lutherans, from Ireland Roman Catholics or Presbyterians. As today many retain the faith of the ancestors, the Thoughtful might reflect, if a denomination has Truth, it can be inherited.

### The Early Birds. The Protestant Nation.

While smaller groups were often on the ships crossing the Atlantic, the first settlers were predominately English Protestants. The people who populated New England were dissenters from the official church in England, something that occurred in the early seventeenth century as that national church moved, in the eyes of many, away from Calvinism. Called "Puritans" because they wished to purify the Church of England of any trace of its pre-Reformation character, particularly bishops, these folk, especially in the 1630s, decided new lands offered the best prospect for their faith.

In that same period, traditional Anglicans were founding and expanding Virginia and the Carolinas. They attempted to recreate of the world of England with large estates (worked by slaves, not agricultural laborers as in England) and Anglican priests presiding in the churches. In the eighteenth century, Methodism began appearing among Anglicans. Also in the Chesapeake Bay area, Lord Baltimore founded a colony for English Roman Catholics, but few ever appeared and those were soon outnumbered by their Protestant, largely Anglican, neighbors.

Later in the same century, William Penn established in Pennsylvania a refuge for Quakers, another group dissenting from the Church of England. Besides Quakers, Anabaptists, in the form of Mennonites and their offspring, the Amish, were attracted to Penn's colony. Mennonites, who had often moved to the fringes of Europe to escape persecution and governmental involvement, came in droves between 1663 and 1760. The Amish, a stricter version of the Mennonites, arrived largely in the 1740s. Other Protestant groups, very diverse from one another, came from Germany in such numbers Pennsylvania became known as the home of the Dutch, a corruption of Deutsch. Some Dutch Protestants also settled in New Amsterdam, but their numbers were never large and they stopped immigrating when the colony came under English control and was renamed New York.

The European Protestant propensity for division appeared almost immediately in America when the inhabitants of Massachusetts fell to squabbling and banished those who disagreed with the dominant Puritan establishment. Led by Roger Williams, these people trekked south and established Rhode Island with a predominantly Baptist complexion. Baptists were soon found in all the colonies.

After 1685, a few Huguenot (Calvinists) fled France to the Carolinas. In the eighteenth century, immigration continued, largely from Britain, augmented by people from Ulster (descendants of Scots who had colonized the northeastern corner of that island in the late sixteenth and early seventeenth centuries. These folk brought their Presbyterianism with them and settled in the backcountry of Virginia, especially the Shenandoah Valley, and the Carolinas. Like the Baptists, Presbyterians soon appeared throughout the colonies. Also the colony of Georgia was established under Anglican auspices.

By 1776, approximately 2.5 million people inhabited the 13 American colonies though only 10 to 20 percent were members of a denomination.[4] While most were "unchurched," the governing orders, from north to south, were Puritans in New England, a Baptist enclave in Rhode Island, a mixed bag in New York and New Jersey, though largely Anglican, a Quaker and German Protestant mix in Pennsylvania, and the Anglican South of Maryland, Virginia, the Carolinas, and Georgia. Very, very heavily Protestant, mostly of English ancestry, with a large streak of dissent from the established English church, the colonists had created their own Establishment with the New England Congregational and the southern Anglican churches receiving financial support from the colonial legislatures. The American Revolution affected Anglicans and Methodists, the two groups with the closest ties to England, as virtually all Anglican and many Methodist clergy left for the mother country. Finally, outside the 13 colonies, a small Roman Catholic presence existed in New Orleans, Detroit, and Quebec. While numerically Congregationalists, Presbyterians and Anglicans were the largest, the diversity of the colonies and the lack of effective governance above the local level meant uniformity in any denomination was only a hope.

## Methodists, Baptists, and Pentecostals. The Great American Religions.

The three most successful of American Protestant denominations, as measured by number of members, appealed to those lower on the economic scale by providing intense emotional satisfaction as well as hope for salvation. Though not original to the United States, Methodism and Baptism were the great religious success stories of the nineteenth century and Pentecostalism

[4] Roger Finke and Rodney Stark, *The Churching of America, 1776-1990* (Rutgers University Press, 1992), 25. One problem of measuring religious attitudes is that membership has tended to be an elite phenomenon.

of the late twentieth and twenty-first centuries. In all three denominations, the period of growth relied on lots of enthusiasm and emotion. While today most Methodists and many Baptists are fairly sedate, such was not the case in the early days in the nineteenth century and still isn't in Pentecostal and some Baptist churches. Perhaps the major reason for the astounding growth was the large amount of local control exercised by the individual congregation.

The Thoughtful are not too excited about theology though they recognize it has accounted for a lot of debate, and killing, in Christian history. In the U.S. the success or failure of several denominations depended in part on how they expounded Protestant theology, especially Calvinism. The Reformation era of the sixteenth century produced predestination as a dominant idea, one many immigrants brought with them to America. The problem some had with predestination was it is cold and sterile with a deity that is a stern judge; the individual can do nothing to affect the outcome, the hoped-for salvation. One solution to the problem was the work of Jacobus Arminius (1560 – 1609) a Dutchman who argued divine sovereignty was compatible with human free will. Arminius accepted the sovereignty, the omnipotence, of God, but then injected free will and human responsibility into the action. Logically, this approach may not be very convincing, but it was wildly successful in getting converts. The general scheme of those who wanted to maintain the power of God was that God offered grace and the would-be believer has to accept it, something person is free to do or to reject. (If God is all-powerful, then God is also all-knowing. So God knows who will accept grace, which closes the circle to predestination again. Except we think we made the choice even though God knew what choice we'd make, which doesn't seem to be free will. But, anyway....) Today some Baptists and all Methodists and Pentecostals accept this understanding of grace.

In the early nineteenth century, much of the preaching and conversions occurred in what the Thoughtful would call a revival atmosphere. One observer of a meeting in early nineteenth-century Kentucky listed some of the various responses of the repentant sinner:

> "The bodily agitations (were) called by various names... The falling...would, generally, with a piercing scream, fall like a log on the floor, earth, or mud, and appear as dead... The jerks...affect in some one member of the body, and sometimes the whole system... When the whole system was affected, I have seen the person stand in one place, and jerk backward and forward in quick succession, their head nearly touching the floor behind and before....The laughing...was a loud, hearty laughter, but one *sui generis*; it excited laughter in none else.... It is truly indescribable.... [T]he...subject in a very happy state of mind would sing most melodiously, not from the mouth or nose, but entirely in the breast, the sounds issuing from thence.... It was most heavenly. None could ever be tired of hearing it.[5]

Ever since this form of public repentance was popularized, camp meetings and revivals have often been scenes of such actions. Most groups cannot maintain such a level of excitement and eventually settle down and look like other, more sedate denominations. Those seeking more emotion and feeling the group has become too accommodating to the world will break away and the process is repeated all over.

The first half of the nineteenth century witnessed the phenomenal growth of Methodism. John Wesley, the founder of Methodism, had essentially an Arminian take on Calvinism. God gives the sinner a nudge and the sinner responds. The new believer later has confidence things are changed, and therefore does change, an event called "sanctification," a significant feature of Methodism. Later the believer moves to "Christian perfection," a uniquely Wesleyan contribution, in which sin, defined as a voluntary transgression of a known rule, doesn't happen any longer. To keep the converts

---

[5] Barton W. Stone, "A Short History of the Life of Barton W. Stone Written by Himself," in Sydney E. Ahlstrom, *A Religious History of the American People* (Yale University Press, 1972), 434-435, originally published in *Voices from Cane Ridge*, ed. Rhodes Thompson, (Bethany Press, 1954), 68.

moving along, Methodists set up small groups—classes—to monitor one another's behavior and reinforce the new life. "Methodism" refers to those following Wesley's ideas; the major group in the early nineteenth century was the Methodist Episcopal Church and today it is the United Methodist Church, though many others exist.

Wesley was English and while his movement prospered there, it thrived in the United States, growing from insignificant numbers in 1800 to 6 million, or more than over 6 percent of the population, by 1900. With itinerant preachers serving several congregations and a hierarchical structure of circuits, districts and conferences which was the result of the work of Francis Asbury (1745 – 1816), Methodism was especially popular in the frontier areas of the Midwest, and by the end of the century, had become the denomination of the middle class. While Methodism had a hierarchical governance structure with preachers as congregational leaders, the reality resulting from the circuit riding of the preacher was the congregations were left with much local independence. The organization of classes—small groups that involved testimony, admonition, prayer, and study—furthered that local control. All in all, Methodism fostered a sense of community on the frontier. A schism over slavery divided the movement into Northern and Southern wings in 1844, which did not reunite until 1939; however, that North/South division is still visible today whenever Methodists meet to vote on social issues. More than Baptists, Methodists are spread fairly evenly across the country, with the heaviest concentrations in the South and middle Plains States. The Thoughtful should reflect, while much of today's Methodism is middle class, and consequently sedate, the denomination's growth in the early nineteenth century occurred under circumstances similar to the camp meeting revival described above; today, it is certainly not "your father's Methodism."

Baptists also had stunning growth throughout the nineteenth century. However, as Baptists are not a single or unified denomination, this growth is deceptive. In America, Baptists, though rooted in the Calvinism of the Reformation, sprung from New England Puritanism, but they quickly fragmented into numerous sub-parts, so much so that the label covers an extraordinary range of beliefs and practices. Baptists only accept those who make a voluntary confession of faith and are baptized by total immersion (no sprinkling for them). This attitude means the baptism of babies is useless as the rite can only come when one makes a conscious choice about Christ. However, after that, agreement among various Baptist sects ends; in doctrine, Baptists are all over the board. Some reject Calvinism and believe individuals choose whether to be saved, hence Free Will Baptists. Some think Jesus died for the sins of all, and some, adhering to their Calvinism, think Jesus' death was only for the elect, those predestined for salvation; hence General and Particular Baptists. Even the issue of missionary activity—seeking new converts to Christianity—is controversial. Those opposed to such work are labeled Primitive Baptists and believe God alone will somehow get the elect into the church. As most Baptists have at some point a personal experience of their worthlessness and God's love for them, labeled the "conversion experience," they expect those "born again" members to behave in ways consistent with that experience, which often means restrictions on behavior such as drinking, dancing, gambling, etc.

Baptists form congregations with little connection to one another. As a result, congregations split, often over issues other Christians might find inconsequential. Baptists have sayings: "Whenever two Baptists meet, there are three opinions." and "Baptists multiply by dividing." However, they do form loose groups, such as the largest, the Southern Baptist Convention, with their own colleges and seminaries but with strong local independence.[6] Today the major Baptist associations divide along regions (American Baptist is northern, Southern Baptist is southern), races (National Baptists are black), and issues (Regular Baptists reject many aspects of modern life). Other Baptist groups include Six-Principles Baptists, Seventh Day Baptists, Free Will Baptists, General Baptists, Liberty Baptists, Separate Baptists, United Baptists, The Old Two-Seed-in-the-Spirit Predestinarian Baptists, and Baptist Church of Christ. All in all, Baptists are so diverse and so local that generalizations break down quickly. However, such diversity made Baptist churches easy to set up in the nineteenth century and very popular

[6] For a survey, including listing of the many variations, of Baptists, see Bill J. Leonard, *Baptists in America* (Columbia University Press, 2005).

as well. Today, Baptists are found throughout the nation, numbering about 1 out of 6 Americans, and comprise nearly 50 percent of all church members in the old Confederacy.

Evangelical excitement in a group is difficult to maintain over a period of time. The early converts may remain enthusiastic but tire of hearing about sin and damnation. Moreover, that message usually has less appeal to their children, raised in the church. Consequently, preachers shift the message and the fervor goes cold. This development describes Methodism and some branches of Baptism after 1850, when they settled down as their early converts found stability and, often, some financial success. Respectability set in and church-going sometimes took on an air of something that was expected, but the excitement was gone. And, often, so were the children who found their parents dull and their theology uninteresting. With the increasing prosperity of its members and middle class appeal, the revivalist elements ebbed and worldliness crept in. Methodists continued their camp meetings though they eventually "calmed down," and became settled communities with permanent cottages, essentially summer resorts. Progressive ministers, organs, tolerance of Darwinism, and the Social Gospel were seen by some as signs the denomination had lost its way. Schism occurred over the issue of accommodation with society especially in the 1890s. The Holiness movement resulted as the Church of the Nazarene, Free Methodists, Church of God and others sought to maintain a simpler, "purer" form of Methodism. Baptists, with their congregational organization, simply kept splitting.

Pentecostalism, growing largely out the Holiness movement and yet another brand of Methodism, appeared in 1906 and has become the third larget American religious group. Pentecostalism, now the fastest growing group in world Christianity, appeared in a church on Azusa Street in Los Angeles (it had existed elsewhere but never caught on). Methodism's early growth through revivalism meant doctrine was less important than experience, a situation that appeared repeatedly in new groups that were founded with excitement at their core. Interpretations of Wesley's theology produced a group that moved beyond the conversion experience and sanctification to an event, called "the baptism of fire," which often included actions like shouting and seemingly involuntary spasms, reminiscent of the camp meetings of the frontier Midwest. The distinctive quality of Pentecostalism is speaking in tongues ("glossolalia"), which occurs when believers become so possessed they break out into indecipherable sounds, unknown languages. (In Christian history, Pentecost was the day Jesus' disciples were given the capacity to speak other languages so they could undertake missions beyond Palestinian Jews (Acts 2:3 – 4).) Not a unified group, Pentecostals, like Baptists, pop up in small congregations quickly and easily. With little connection among congregations and few U.S. seminaries, uniformity is not enforced by any authority. Some Pentecostals accept restrictions on life (no smoking, gambling, short skirts, etc.) and sometimes go further and ban television and movies. An extreme example includes the handling of poisonous snakes as a sign of being among the religiously saved (obviously not a fast growing sect). Unlike most of American Christianity, Pentecostalism often features interracial congregations though many have, over time, taken on predominately black or white membership. While a Statement of Fundamental Truths was produced in 1916 to guide Pentecostals, and the Assemblies of God denomination unites many, Pentecostalism, by its nature so personal, fragments easily. Pentecostalism is strongest in the lower Mississippi valley.

**More Groups.**

The U.S. religious scene became more complicated after 1800. In the absence of governmental sanction, support, or enforcement, American Protestant denominations continued to fragment in the nineteenth century with new groups constantly appearing and immigrants bringing additional faiths to the United States from their European homelands. Germans, and later Scandinavians, brought Lutheranism, largely to the Midwest, and soon had more than 60 denominations, most ethnically based. Disgruntled Dutch found new homes in Michigan and Iowa; once settled, they almost immediately fragmented with the more conservative forming the Christian Reformed Church. Roman Catholicism appeared in growing numbers first with the Irish, then Italians, Poles, and others. The Orthodox version of

Christianity appeared with Greek immigrants at the end of the century, and the only significant non-Christian immigration was that of Eastern European Jews. Already by 1850, the religious map had been greatly altered as the denominations most prominent in 1800—the Congregationalists, Presbyterians, and Anglicans, who had 50 percent of active Christians then—had been surpassed by Methodists, Baptists, and Roman Catholics who had 34 percent, 21 percent, and 14 percent, respectively.[7]

Protestantism had always been prone to division as all are encouraged to read the Bible, and few guidelines are widely accepted. European governments kept some control; in the eighteenth century a *de facto* tolerance existed in most places, at least if the dissenters caused little political trouble. In the United States, especially in the nineteenth century, religious groups blossomed, quarreled, divided, died, and generally made the patchwork of American religion even more variegated.

Utopian communities popped up as visionaries sought to gather their members separate from the profane world. In the first half of the nineteenth century, these utopian groups appeared everywhere. Shakers, originating in England, grew to perhaps 6000 members by 1850, and the excitement generated by their meetings produced the nickname. The Rappites, first in Harmony, Pennsylvania, and later in New Harmony, Indiana, awaited the millennium while opposing procreation. A group at Oneida, New York, on the other hand, practiced "complex marriage," (not monogamy) while prospering in the metal trades; today they have become a corporation without its former religious urgency. The Amana Colony in Iowa, another separatist group, also continues today though as a cooperative. And the Mormons had their beginnings with this same communitarian urge. While more than 100 such separatist communities were founded, most depended on the charismatic leadership of a man or, more rarely, a woman; when that person died, the community withered. Today the Hutterites, who practice communal ownership of property, came to the United States in the 1880s, and can traces their beginnings to Reformation days, constitute one of the few surviving

---

[7] Finke and Stark, *The Churching of America*, 55.

groups, with perhaps 100 communities in the Dakotas and nearby Canadian provinces.

Millennialism, the idea the world will end (and usually soon) resurfaced, most notably with William Miller (1782 – 1849) in the burned-over area of upstate New York ("burned-over" in the sense of a religious hotbed). Using the book of Daniel in the Hebrew Bible/Old Testament, Miller calculated the Second Coming of Christ would occur in 1843; when it did not, he recalculated it to 1844; these predictions garnered Miller a sizeable following. The designated dates passed uneventfully. The failure of Miller's predictions about the end of the world did not end such millennialism, and some of his followers went on to found the Seventh-Day Adventist denomination (1863). Jehovah's Witnesses, also in this tradition, set the new end time in 1914. Today both these denominations have revised things so a date certain is not certain any more.

Alexander Campbell (1788 – 1866) took another tack—called Restorationism—and hoped to reunite all the denominations into one. These "Campbellites" emerged in the 1830s as part of that movement but failed in their goal and soon became the Disciples of Christ, just another denomination among many. Growing out of the frontier revivals, the Disciples were strongest in the Midwest and grew rapidly, becoming one of the half dozen largest Protestant groups by 1900. Feuding over accommodation with the world ended in a split with the conservatives forming the Churches of Christ, concentrated largely in the South.

In New England, especially Boston, many descendants of the Puritans, now called Congregationalists, began questioning traditional doctrines, especially the Trinity. Soon they moved away from Christianity, eventually denying the divinity of Jesus and began worshipping a single God. The movement, labeled Unitarianism, included many of New England's intellectuals in the early and mid-nineteenth century; the Thoughtful have encountered them as Transcendentals. And, at about the same time as Unitarianism was beginning, other Christians interpreted their early history and theology to mean everyone, all humans, had been saved by Jesus' death. These

Universalists, many of whom were from the lower orders, eventually merged with Unitarians in 1961.

As the nation slowly divided over slavery in the run-up to the Civil war, so did the denominations. In 1844 the Methodists split, the Baptists (operating as a loose association) divided in 1845, and Presbyterians suffered the same fate in 1857. The smaller denominations, often more regionally based, sometimes had similar tensions and, often, divisions.

Still another version of Christianity grew out of the late nineteenth-century interest in the problems science was raising with a non-material version of the world. The creation of Christian Science by Mary Baker Eddy (1821 – 1910), with its rejection of medical intervention in favor of spiritual healing, occurred in an age when hypnosis, séances, and theosophy were popular.

The latter half of the twentieth century witnessed contradictory movements. In the 1960s, many Protestant denominations buried the hatchet and started combining, thus the ecumenical movement began. At the same time, many rejected all denominations and began establishing independent, non-denominational congregations, some of which became huge—now called megachurches. This rejection in turn created a reaction in which believers sought less structure, less bureaucracy, no statement of belief or creed, and a more spiritual approach. Often very small, a group of such folk might meet in a house, the label "emergent" has been applied to them.

And the process of new groups forming is not at an end, and probably never will be.

### The Mormons.

A smaller, though rapidly growing, group is originally American though now also found elsewhere in the world. The Church of Jesus Christ of Latter-Day Saints has its headquarters in Salt Lake City and is strongly centralized under a First President and Council of Twelve, with a hierarchical structure of bishops down (though they use terms like "regions," "stakes," and "wards"). Numerous other Mormon groups—perhaps as many as 100—have split away, mainly over issues of governance, but none is very large.

Formed in the 1830s in upstate New York by Joseph Smith, Jr. (1805 – 44), Mormons base their faith on the Bible and *The Book of Mormon*. The latter book, which Smith claimed to have found on golden tablets and translated himself (no one else ever saw the tablets), contains a story, an epic of Israelites who made it to North America about 600 years before Jesus lived. Jesus appeared to them, after his resurrection, but internal feuding eventually led to their extinction in war, the last survivor creating the golden tablets.

Mormonism varies significantly from most of mainstream Christianity, in both belief and practice. Most famously, polygamy was practiced early but dropped officially in 1890, in response to pressure from the U.S. government. Other beliefs also diverge from Christianity in general. God (not Jesus) was once a man but somehow progressed, a process the individual Mormon can duplicate (called "exaltation") so the hereafter has multiple gods, hardly traditional monotheism. Thus the Trinity is rejected and Jesus is often described as an "elder brother," helping others in their journey. This process of exaltation can continue after death and can, by baptism of the deceased, even be begun after death.

Practices include avoidance of tobacco, alcohol, and caffeinated beverages (hence the popularity of root beer in Utah). Instead of marriage, Mormons practice "sealing" (same thing) except the family continues after death and the sealing ceremony involves special undergarments which are worn the rest of one's life (except, for example, in athletic events). Since sealing and many other Mormon ceremonies are closed to outsiders, rumors and speculations have dogged the group since its beginning and led to violent persecutions. The move to Utah followed moves from New York to Ohio (in 1831), to Missouri (in 1838) and to Illinois (in 1839)—all moves resulting from religious persecution. Finally, they left the United States. Ironically, the Salt Lake area, though part of Mexico when the Mormons arrived in 1845, soon became part of the United States as a result of the Mexican War (1846 – 8).

Many have their only contact with Mormons when two young men, in white shirts and ties, appear on the doorstep. This action is the result of the Mormon expectation males, during early adulthood, will spend two years doing such missionary work. No wonder apostates are rare; who wants to "fall away" and admit two years of one's life were wasted?

Some of these beliefs and practices have raised the question of whether Mormons are Christians. They obviously think so, but Roman Catholics, Methodists and Presbyterians, among others require Mormons who convert to their faith to undergo baptism, which implies a rejection of Mormonism as a branch of Christianity.

## The Roman Catholic "Flood."

While American Roman Catholicism had been around since early colonial days, the numbers had never been large. Maryland was founded in 1634 as a refuge for Roman Catholics from the British Isles, but Anglican settlers quickly outnumbered the Roman Catholics and dominated the colony by 1692. Other pockets of Roman Catholicism in far flung places, such as New Orleans and Detroit, were the result of early colonial efforts by European Roman Catholic powers. That distribution changed in the nineteenth century as Irish and German Roman Catholics immigrated. The Germans immigrated throughout the century but Irish numbers surged in the 1840s due to Ireland's potato famine. More nationalities appeared after 1880 as Poles, Italians, Serbs, Portuguese, and others joined the wave of immigrants coming to join the burgeoning U.S. economy. During the twentieth century, Roman Catholicism was further augmented by immigrants from Latin America. Today, Roman Catholics account for about one-quarter of all Americans.

While Protestants might see Roman Catholicism as monolithic, in reality it had internal divisions. Various ethnic groups brought different practices, honored different saints, and generally wanted nothing to do with other groups (a marriage with a co-religionist of another ethnic group was viewed as a form of apostasy by many). The nineteenth-century church was dominated by Irish prelates who, concerned with the effects of drink on their Irish congregations, supported the temperance crusade, whereas the German and Italian congregations wanted to keep their beer and wine, and said so, loudly.

Protestants reacted strongly to these immigrants and the newly established public schools became, in essence, locales for trying to convert Roman Catholics. In response, the Roman Catholic hierarchy established their own parochial schools to preserve their faith. But all was not peace in the denomination as, in the 1880s, Germans complained about Irish domination of the priesthood, complaints other groups echoed in the twentieth century. A major problem for American Roman Catholicism was the papacy's inability to grasp notions of the separation of church and state and the nature of American pluralism. Protestant fears were further fueled in 1870 when the doctrine of papal infallibility was adopted by the Vatican. Moreover, Pope Pius IX, reacting to developments in Europe became increasingly conservative, issuing a Syllabus of Errors in 1864 that, among other things, rejected democracy; in 1895 Pope Leo XIII called for government support of Roman Catholicism, something that fuelled anti-Catholicism nation-wide. The Vatican continued placing books on its Index of Prohibited Books and in 1907 issued an encyclical calling for all historical research into Jesus and the origins of Christianity to cease, effectively killing Roman Catholic intellectual life for half a century. Seeing Roman Catholicism as a self-serving organization dedicated to authoritarianism and keeping the masses in hapless, superstitious ignorance, Protestants were strongly anti-Catholic, a position that abated among intellectuals only after the reforms of Vatican II in the 1960s and among many conservatives when abortion appeared as a public issue in the 1970s.

Many of the immigrants, who had left countries with state churches, were only too happy to become unchurched while others were open to the preaching of faiths other than that of their birth. Nonetheless the Roman Catholic Church long had, and still has, a distinctly ethnic cast to its membership. Today the denomination is bedeviled by a decline of the parishioners who still accept and practice the religion of the 1950s, when believers were told, in the words of those who have rejected that world, to "pray, pay, and obey." Scholars have produced various categories to describe such members: Culture Catholics (baptized but know little of the faith and care less), Cafeteria Catholics (pick and choose among doctrines and practices), Lapsed (may even be in a different denomination). Perhaps more worrisome to the hierarchy is the dramatic drop in vocations; few men want to be priests, and Americans may not see many nuns in the future. Additionally, the decline in traditional Catholics and the rise of the Latino population will soon result in a church where whites are in the minority, though still run by (Irish) whites.

## Evangelicalism.

### Interesting Word. Evangelicals.

American religion has been distinctively marked by the trend within Christianity labeled "evangelicalism."[8] The term covers a variety of believers but its root in Christian history meant someone interested in spreading the faith—a missionary. In American religious life, it also now includes someone who has had a personal conversion experience—who is "born again." With its emphasis on conversion and repentance of the individual, evangelicalism often focuses on sin and the sinner, which is combined with the faith Jesus' death brought salvation to all. Evangelical preachers often assumed the style of revivalists; in the twentieth century, Billy Graham called his preaching "crusades." Traveling revivalists exploited the technology of the day to advertise and organize from city to city. Dwight Moody (1837 – 99) in the nineteenth century and Billy Sunday (1862 – 1935), a former major league baseball player, in the early twentieth century became famous as evangelists. At the heyday of the traveling revivalists in the years before World War I, it is estimated that were nearly 2000 were on the road, a tradition Billy Graham (1928 – ) continued to the end of the twentieth century. The style of the sermon was often emotional with constant reference to scripture, citing

[8] Definition is everything. While most surveys find evangelicals comprise 30-40 percent of Protestants, surveys done by the Barna group put them at 8 percent. However, Barna's definition of evangelical includes belief in the existence of Satan, the sinlessness of Jesus and some ideas that are considered evangelical by scholars but which self-defining evangelicals never even think about.

it much like lawyers cite case law. The atmosphere surrounding the sermons, whether in tent revivals, arena crusades, or church sermon, was loaded with expectation of sinners repenting.

This repentance, often called a "conversion experience" or being "born again," occurs frequently; about 40 percent of Americans today (almost all of them Protestants) claim it has happened to them. Generally, the born again event occurs in the late teens or early twenties, the age psychologists say people are seeking their identity. It is preceded by a period that may verge on religious depression ("I'm worthless." "I'm so sinful there is no hope." "I try to be good but always fail." etc.) that can be encouraged by hearing sermons about evil human nature. Suddenly, an insight, a "warming of the heart" (John Wesley's expression), a feeling occurs God loves you and forgives all your sins. Then a calm, a peace "that suprasseth all human understanding," descends on the individual, ending the depression and bringing a new outlook on life.

While the new life is expected to include personal behavior "better" than it was before, in reality things often stay about the same, and the born again look like much of the rest of America. Their sexual activity is about the same though, surprisingly, their divorce rate is a bit higher. Not surprisingly, given the disproportion number of born again in the South, they are more racist than the average American. (Promise Keepers, a huge organization of evangelical husbands who undertook to honor their marriage vows, has nearly died because the leadership took a stand again racism.[9])

The general approach of evangelical preachers produces what some call "cheap grace," which brings forgiveness of sins with salvation thrown in. Beyond that, little is expected so today, unlike in the nineteenth century, the convert's life may not change significantly. Even sin is not much emphasized, unlike the old days, so some see the entire result of evangelical effort as little more than "feel better about yourself." This development often leads to an attitude of "I'm better than you because I'm a Christian," an unfortunate

---

[9] Ronald J. Sides, *The Scandal of the Evangelical Conscience* (Baker, 2005)

side effect. While Evangelicalism has an impulse to share the message and do mission work, it often turns off the Thoughtful.

Moving from frontier camp meetings in the early nineteenth century, evangelicalism continued, even in the cities, and found in preachers, such as Moody in the last quarter of the century, spellbinders who knew how to draw crowds. With the simple message "God loves you," Moody and numerous others, less well known, organized revivals with the sophistication of modern business. Advance men, publicity, and organized rallies could produce legions of the saved, who, after Moody moved on, became the concern of local ministers, often a difficult task as the revival excitement passed.

In the nineteenth century, Evangelicalism produced the great reforming movements, such as anti-slavery, temperance, and suffrage for women. Late in the nineteenth century, a few great preachers, called "Pulpit Princes," emerged in the large cities. They didn't preach doctrine but emphasized the essential goodness of people rather than the traditional Calvinist view of depravity. This "Christianity lite" appealed to middle class congregations, self-satisfied with their financial success, which should not surprise the Thoughtful. Some emphasized current events and the conditions of the poor; their preaching led to the Social Gospel. Others made accommodations for Darwinism and biblical criticism, and the reaction to them produced Fundamentalism. In the twentieth century, Evangelicalism often has limited itself to the personal aspects of religion. In fact, in much of society where Evangelicalism's appeal is strongest, opposition to social action is also prominent. Indeed, many evangelicals believe society's ills are merely the result of individual sin. Poverty, for instance, is not a social problem calling for governmental action but the result of individual bad choices and can be remedied only at the level of the individual—a gospel of wealth for the rich and a gospel of work for the rest. While today's Evangelicals are less interested in social or political reform than their nineteenth-century predecessors were, they are often very interested in matters sexual, such as abortion and gay marriage. (They oppose these things.) As a result, they vote very heavily Republican. To the extent they are literalists—and not all evangelicals are—they tend to be anti-intellectual.

Today it is argued evangelicals look just like the rest of us in terms of demographics such as divorce, education, recreational activities, etc. [10] However, they have a perfect Bible that guides their lives and a personal Jesus, not things the Thoughtful value. Thoughtfuls probably think of evangelicals as folk who are determined to witness to others for their faith, often too much and too often. They tend to make Thoughtfuls uncomfortable.

**Shake It Up. Great Awakenings.**

The Great Awakening, the first of several outbursts of fervor in American Protestantism, occurred in the 1730s and 1740s, largely in New England. Spurred by effective preaching, especially by the Englishman George Whitefield (1714 – 70) and Edwards, the event emphasized the immediate, personal religious experience of audience members. An associate of John Wesley's, Whitefield was the most spectacular preacher of his day, speaking to open air crowds numbering in the thousands (even getting money from the deist and skeptic Benjamin Franklin). The Thoughtful are familiar with one of Edwards's sermons "Sinners in the hands of an angry God" with its image of God holding the sinner over the pit of hell much like an individual might hold a spider over a fire. Predestination still dominated the preaching.

As the nineteenth century began, the Second Great Awakening was underway. A defining characteristic of the Second Great Awakening was revivalism. The Midwestern frontier and eastern cities both were the sites of enthusiasm and camp meetings; the combination camping and religious experience became common. Daylong preaching and praying combined with the mentality of peer pressure produced professions of faith and hopes for changed lives. In 1801, Cane Ridge, Kentucky, was perhaps the largest of its day, drawing thousands. The theology of the Second Great Awakening was a mix of Calvinism and Arminianism; given the prevalence of uneducated preachers at this gathering it may not have been all that well thought out. The rigors of predestination, the lack of a role for

---

[10] Sides, *Scandal, passim.* This book's thesis is not universally accepted.

human will, almost always led to a shift towards Arminianism in which people have a bit of choice. Thus Wesley's views were attractive, and Baptists kept dividing over the matter.

New organizations, such as the American Bible Society (1816), which made cheap scripture widely available and American Sunday School Union (1824), a non-denominational effort to bring reading and writing to the frontier, were joined by a wealth of colleges; each denomination founded several, but Congregationalists, Presbyterians, Methodists and Baptists led the way. By the mid-century, Roman Catholicism had also joined the college-founding action.

Awakenings, both local and national, have continued. Some describe the 1980s and 1990s as one such period although the Thoughful lived through those years and barely noticed.

### Drink. Temperance, Then Prohibition.

Christianity had never had any trouble with alcohol until the nineteenth century. For much of world history, water, especially near cities, has been polluted by sewage, butchers' offal, chemicals from cloth and leather working, etc., so drinking beer or wine was healthier. Moreover, in the past beer, not the transparent liquid of today, was nearly a soup and has been called "liquid bread." Beer might average 3 – 5 percent alcohol and wine 8 – 12 percent, but the discovery of distillation produced beverages that could reach 50 percent alcohol, creating a new world of drink. Though known in the late Middle Ages, distilled drinks did not become widely available until the seventeenth and eighteenth centuries. Whiskey, gin, vodka, and rum could be produced from easily available agricultural products, such as grain or potatoes, and eighteenth-century London's "Gin Craze" resulted in people getting "get drunk for a ha'penny, dead drunk for a penny." When Scots, hidden in the Highlands, drank whisky to inebriation, no one worried much. But when gin became popular in urban London, with results painted by Hogarth, concern arose. The Methodists took an early stand against drink, an early connection of religion and temperance. Wesley's theological ideas about the redeemed sinner seeking perfection, while of little interest to the Thoughtful today, motivated many of his followers to live with fewer vices.

In America, the local drinking establishment had long been the locale of socializing and business for colonials. What made alcohol, particularly distilled alcohol, a problem was the spread of population away from the seacoast and the waterways running to that coast. Farmers in the back country and beyond the Appalachians found the cost of getting their produce, corn, wheat, barley to the population centers prohibitive. Converting that produce to whiskey made financial sense as the liquid product was cheaper to move to the coast than its solid predecessors. And what didn't make it to market was consumed at home. So important was whiskey, in 1794 the nascent republic faced its first internal challenge under the new Constitution when Pennsylvanian back country farmers protested a federal tax on whiskey, the Whiskey Rebellion. In New England, production of rum, "demon rum," was important for the export (and slave) trade. By 1800, reformers appeared who were concerned about the level of consumption of distilled beverages. And perhaps they should have been. Estimates by historians vary, but the annual consumption for every white adult in the United States averaged somewhere between 5 and 15 gallons.[11] However, in an agricultural community, working while influenced by, if not being under the influence of, alcohol presented fewer risks than in the modern world. With fewer mechanical devices that pounded metal or hurled down a highway, the early nineteenth-century American could survive the day while slightly buzzed. Anyway, drinking water was often foul.

Appeals for temperance by the medical community may have had some effect, but the major thrust came from the preachers. With Methodists and Baptists thundering about the consequences of sin and the need to repent before Jesus' Second Coming, attacks on alcohol proliferated. The problem, however, was the Bible doesn't forbid drinking alcohol, and Jesus even turned water into wine. Without biblical prohibitions, those preachers thumping their Bibles had to turn to verses that criticized drunkenness or interpret "wine" to mean grape juice. The early critics tended to preach against the

---

[11] Norman Clark, *Deliver Us From Evil* (W.W. Norton, New York, 1976), 15. W.J. Rorabaugh, *The Alcoholic Republic: An American Tradition* (New York, Oxford University Press, 1979), 8.

abuse of drink while later reformers decided one drink could lead to abuse (the gateway argument so common in anti-drug literature today) so total prohibition was the only solution.

The American Temperance society, founded in 1826, grew rapidly and by the 1830s may have claimed membership by 10 percent of the population, not just the adult population. Taking the pledge ("I won't drink.") became a feature of many revivals. And consumption did drop by the 1840s.

Though beginning as a movement to limit drinking to "temperate" amounts, total prohibition became a goal. Often, an initial discussion occurred over whether to include wine, an indication of the class bias of the issue. If alcohol wasn't inherently evil, violence, neglect, and poverty were the consequences to the individual of excessive drinking and became the duty of Christian society to control. In 1851 Maine banned the production and sale of alcoholic beverages and thereafter enacting a "Maine law" became a goal of reformers. While various states passed such a law, becoming "dry," enforcement was sporadic and repeal common.

There things lingered as slavery took up the public's attention. The Women's Christian Temperance Union (WCTU), founded in the 1870s, became a vehicle for middle class women ("ladies") to act in society by seeking the closure of those businesses selling drink. Later ably led by Frances Willard (1839 – 98), a stout Methodist, WCTU women invaded saloons, knelt and prayed, and quickly became a standard weapon in the battle against drink. Women, especially middle class women, still voiceless in the politics of the day, had found power, and the WCTU became one of the first single issue pressure groups in American politics. While issues of crime and poverty loomed large in the arguments, the emphasis was often on the loss of self-control accompanying drinking alcohol, and self-control was identified with being middle class.

In most of the nineteenth century, the reformers came from the pietistic denominations, especially Methodists and Baptists, while they were opposed, weakly, by the Episcopalians, Germans Lutherans and Roman Catholics. With the influx of beer-drinking Germans in the first half of the century and poor Irish in the 1840s, an ethnic quality to the division became apparent. Indeed some reformers saw the labels "drunken Irishman" and "beer-drinking German" as redundant. By 1900, the Roman Catholic hierarchy had divided along ethnic lines as the Irish leadership believed temperance was necessary for the improvement of their flocks whereas the German bishops clung to their beer.

The waves of immigrants from eastern and southern Europe reinforced and reinvigorated the notion something needed doing. Settling in urban enclaves and with traditions of beer and wine drinking, these new Americans found cramped living conditions and long hard working hours could be ameliorated by repair to a neighborhood drinking establishment. Such saloons were also the headquarters of political parties, which perceived as corrupt by many of the middle class, and even occasionally served as brothels and haunts of criminals increased pressure for prohibition. Industrialization meant work became more dangerous and employers less tolerant of the hung over and absent workers. German opposition was marginalized by World War I. By the 1910s, the battle lines were drawn as much along ethnic and social class lines as denominational ones; opposition to drink became a feature of the "respectable middle class," a status issue in the vocabulary of the sociologists. The stage was set for Prohibition.

In 1895 a major force for prohibition, not just temperance, the Anti-Saloon League, was founded, a distinctly male organization, and one dominated by Methodists. Prohibition's appeal was strongest in rural American and among "native" Americans (read non-foreign born). In some ways it was rural Protestantism's cry against the new world of the twentieth century. The drive for prohibition coincided with the rise of Fundamentalism which is not accidental; they were intimately connected. With this group's support and intense political lobbying, the League won dry laws in many states and helped pass the Eighteenth Amendment in 1919.

The movement against alcohol flowed and ebbed as temperance, accompanying the excitement of the Second Great Awakening, helped women find a new role in society, and morphed into prohibition. However, in the 1920s many concluded Prohibition actually increased drinking in urban areas and the widespread disrespect for the law was unhealthy for society. Shifts in the political landscape helped President Franklin Delano Roosevelt achieve repeal of Prohibition in 1933. However, though legal, the sale of alcohol is still regulated by the various states. Most commonly, drink can't be purchased on Sunday morning, church time, and, in the South, various communities remain dry. Some denominations, particularly in the Baptist and Holiness traditions, still expect their members to forego alcohol. Though not overtly religious, Alcoholics Anonymous, and other programs dealing with problem drinkers, look and function much like a religion (a "higher power" is needed to overcome drink). While the moral arguments still float around, the debate has shifted to the health issues of drink. Concern over alcohol has shifted to concern about alcoholism.

### The Great Divider. Slavery.

Early followers of Jesus didn't have any quarrel with slavery. The Bible had no verse condemning the practice and early writings admonished slaves to obey their masters (1 Peter 2:18, Ephesians 6:5). Common in the Roman Empire, slavery survived into the Middle Ages, but the details are obscure as to numbers and prevalence. The medieval church, with its many institutions—monasteries, bishoprics, parish churches—owned slaves, and numerous church councils dealt with how they should be treated. Very generally, the church permitted slavery but sought to give Christian slaves some protections. Serfdom, which appeared around the year 1000 as a result of economic changes, meant slavery was less important and led to the change of status of many slaves into serfs.

As European slavery died out—it was nearly nonexistent in 1400—the lands of the Americas produced another chapter in the Christian story. In the Americas, Christian Europeans had no hesitation in enslaving Indians and, when the numbers became inadequate, bringing black slaves from Africa. Christians from all the trading areas of Europe engaged in the slave trade, and the various denominations, Roman Catholic and Protestant, said nothing.

In American history slavery dates almost to the beginning of the first European settlement; the first black slaves appeared in the Chesapeake area in 1619, one year before the Pilgrims touched Plymouth Rock. Slavery was soon found in all the colonies though increasingly the southern area predominated; Jesuits even owned land farmed by slaves. Eli Whitney's invention of the cotton gin in 1794 opened a new chapter in the history of slavery as cotton could now be produced in sufficient volume to compete as a fabric. Tobacco and rice cultivation was increasingly concentrated on lands where slaves did the labor.

Quakers, early in their history, disliked slavery, a position arising from their strong belief in the equality of all people. In the late eighteenth century they became the leaders in rejecting slavery, even expelling slaveowning members and organizing an antislavery group. Methodists and Baptists composed strong statements against slavery—Methodists decided preachers couldn't hold slaves and members should free theirs while Baptists, being congregational went many directions—but both denominations slowly backslid in the face of strong opposition from the South. The new federal Constitution, in apportioning representation for the House of Representatives, counted free persons and three-fifths of all "other persons" and also permitted the ban of slave trade after 1808. (In most slaveholding areas of the New World, a constant stream of slaves from Africa was necessary to maintain slave numbers; the United States was the exception in that slaves reproduced in sufficient numbers to maintain and later increase their total population.) By 1800 most northern states had abolished slavery or provided for a gradual elimination over time.

Blacks, slave or free, were attracted to Christianity, especially its preaching of God's concern for every soul. In the South, Methodists and Baptists had significant success among slaves; it is estimated a quarter of a million slaves worshipped as Methodists, but firm numbers are hard to come by. In the North, blacks worshiped both among whites and separately in all-black congregations, but again numbers are scarce.

The antislavery issue slumbered from about 1800 to the 1830s when, with Quakers in the forefront, a movement seeking abolition spread quickly in the North. Christians fought for abolition more than any other group; the historian Page Smith, in *The Rise of Industrial America* could discover "no prominent abolitionist, black or white, who was an avowed freethinker, atheist, or agnostic."[12] Christians supported abolition because of their belief all souls are equal (an idea only later applied to gender and still rarely to social class). The South reacted by banning anti-slavery writings and speeches and producing Christian reasons supporting slavery. Southern Christians produced arguments about black inferiority. ("[T]he curse of Ham": Ham, a son of Noah, saw his drunk father naked and told his brothers who covered Noah but Noah was so outraged by his son's actions, he cursed the descendants of Ham to be servants. Ham later moved to Africa (Genesis 9:20 – 5).) This story, Paul's call for obedience to masters, and general notions of patriarchy provided a support for slavery. Also, bringing heathen Africans to Christ justified the institution of slavery. The two areas, North and South, moved apart as northern Christians began to see society as well as the individual in need of change whereas the southern branch focused only on the individual, a situation that continues to exist today.

Political events, largely in Washington, made the running in the years up to the Civil War as statehood issues, slavery in the territories, and the Dred Scot decision exacerbated the divisions. In *Uncle Tom's Cabin*, Harriet Beecher Stowe, a fervent Congregationalist, greatly stirred northern passions, while the equally fervent John Brown aroused southern fears with his attempted raid at Harper's Ferry.[13]

For the large denominations, abolition and slavery became entangled with issues of governance, just as slavery and federalism did in the political arena; inconsistently, the South usually sought a strong church hierarchy and strong states. Knowing the potential for divisiveness of the matter, leaders tried to avoid it. However, whenever slavery did arise as a debate in the years after 1840, the large denominations divided into northern and southern parts. The Methodists, with a clear governing structure, battled it out in 1844 at their General Conference in New York City and the sides

---

[12] Page Smith, *The Rise of Industrial America* (McGraw-Hill, New York, 1984), 554-5.

[13] Christianity was not the only force operating here. Abraham Lincoln, according to John T. Stuart, his law partner, "went further against Christian beliefs ... than any man I ever heard." Lincoln never joined a church or made a profession of faith. His reference to "providence" could mean a divinity or personal works of the natural order. Allen Guelzo, *Abraham Lincoln: Redeemer President* (Erdmans, 1998), 81.

became irreconcilable. Baptists, organized along congregational lines, also split into northern and southern wings in the 1840s. Ironically, the Southern Baptist Convention, founded in 1845 to help unify southern Baptists in face of the antislavery onslaught, was a break with the tradition of local independence of the very congregational Baptists. Presbyterians managed to avoid schism until 1861, when the fighting had begun, only by largely suppressing discussion, though maneuvering within the denomination was intense. Episcopalians, Lutherans, and Roman Catholics avoided division until war made them a *de facto* reality, because these denominations lacked a national organization, authority or platform where the issue could be fought out, and divided upon. Congregationalists, concentrated largely in New England, avoided division. (Internationally, most Christian groups opposed slavery, though the Vatican only condemned it completely in 1888.) When war came, both armies, North and South, were certain God was on their side.

The war produced another of Christianity's great musical works, Julia Ward Howe's "Battle Hymn of the Republic." During the war, clergy held revivals that converted many, in addition to ministering to the sick, wounded, and dying. The end of the war brought forth various views on its causes and consequences, and, while reconciliation between the North and South proceeded in many areas, the issue of racism kept the South an essentially separate country, often with separate denominations.

The black churches in the South, especially Baptists and Methodists, saw great growth and soon encompassed over one-quarter of the black population. As the only institution where blacks ran things free of white domination, the churches, besides having an active social and cultural role, became the focus of political efforts, a situation that continues today in both the North and the South.

### Smoothing the Coarse? Manners.

Historians often skate over the changes of personal behavior during the nineteenth century. Perhaps coarseness, rough behavior, and violence dissipated; if so, who or what contributed to it seems difficult to determine or measure. Certainly the appearance of a middle class concerned with respectability, culture, or taste did produce individuals given to less public excess of the kind so often labeled "sinful." Methodism was a movement of and for women, and as more women sought to become "ladies," they pulled their husbands and children along. Such ladies often found themselves on pedestals which annoyed twentieth-century feminists, but the pedestal was an advance at the time over the subjection and barbaric treatment too common in the early nineteenth century. Whether, in fact, the world experienced less "sin" may hinge of matters of definition—e.g., is adultery worse than owning a dangerous coal mine? And what part did Christianity, or the denominations, play in this story? Did strictures to "love thy neighbor" have an effect? Does it matter where one looks: urban or rural, upper or working class, men or women? Whatever went on, the United States in 1900 looked significantly different than it did in 1830, and the denominations certainly tried to produce that difference.[14]

Self-control became a mantra in the years after the Civil War—the middle class feared the effects of alcohol, sex, or many other vices which might precipitate their fall into the ranks of the masses below them. Respectability tended to seek fences to control behavior. While temperance continued to be a major part of Protestantism, other controls of individual behavior also occupied attention. Prostitution, pornography, birth control—in other words, sex—generated numerous crusades. Anthony Comstock (1844 - 1915) pushed for many changes, resulting in the Comstock Act of 1873, which banned using the mail to send obscene materials. As a result of such actions and a shift in sentiment, public discussion of anything sexual virtually disappeared.

With the excesses of distilled alcohol controlled, at least somewhat, and slavery abolished, many denominations moved sin from a matter of individual concern to one of society. If America was to be God's "chosen people," the nation needed attention. Thus began what has come to be called the

---

[14] Norbert Elias, *The Civilizing Process* (Blackwell, 2000), originally published in 1939, opened the issue but little work has since been done on this development. Steven Pinker, *The Better Angels of our Nature: Why Violence has Declined (Viking, 2011)* has lots of numbers, particularly for Western Europe, but religion is not a theme.

"Social Gospel," the movement by denominations to alleviate some of the sufferings of the people, especially workers.

## The Great Divide Today. The Culture War.

Americans divide themselves in many ways, political, religious, ethnic, racial, but for many scholars, the culture war exists between traditionalists, those seeking "conformity with the ordering principles inherited from the past," and progressives, those wanting "emancipation of the human spirit and the creation of an inclusive and tolerant world." [15]

### The Believer Looks Outward. Social Gospel.

"The poor will always be with us..." (Matthew 26:1), a statement that has long justified Christians in taking few steps to alleviate poverty. And yet a clear theme of the Hebrew Bible/Old Testament is the prophets' outrage about the treatment of the poor. And Jesus, besides being a poor Galilean himself, talked and worked with the poor and the marginalized. To take a quote from Matthew and ignore the rest of the tradition is very selective reading. Another interpretation says a good Christian doesn't hobnob with the rich but works among the poor. Hence, "the poor will always be with us...."

Christians probably contrasted with Roman world by the charity they extended, particularly to their members. Sources suggest care for the poor, widows, and orphans was a feature of Jesus' people. This activity became a fixed policy; in the Middle Ages, one-quarter of church receipts was to be reserved for the poor. The Reformation upset this system and increasingly the

---

[15] Whether a culture war exists or ever did is controversial. Most disputants agree there is a culture war among the elite of the nation but whether it extends further into society is the argument. For a summary of this matter, see James Davison Hunter and Alan Wolfe, *Is There a Culture War?* (Brookings Institute Press, 2005). Most Thoughtful have little doubt that these issues are pronounced in American life, especially religious life. (The quotes are from page 2.) A sociological survey of American religion is Robert D. Putnam and David E. Campbell, *American Grace* (Simon and Schuster, 2010).

burden of caring for the poor fell on the government, usually the local unit, parish or county. Industrialization, with its periodic swings of unemployment, and population growth soon swamped some localities. In addition to these factors, in the United States the flood of immigrants after 1880 helped create urban slums that further overwhelmed local resources.

Responding to the effects of urbanization and immigration, many Protestants, especially the clergy, shifted away from the evangelical emphasis on individual salvation, good works, and piety, and began efforts to attack poverty, crime, slums, child labor and the like in the cities. Labeled "the Social Gospel," this movement started in the late nineteenth century and crested early in the twentieth, about the same time as the Progressive movement in politics. Examples include a Congregational minister, Washington Gladden (1836 - 1918) in Columbus, Ohio, who combined religion and politics as he served on the city council, supported unions, and attacked racial problems. In *Christianity and the Social Crisis* Walter Rauschenbusch (1861 - 1918), a professor teaching at Rochester seminary, deemphasized the individual's moral and spiritual responsibility in favor of reforming society.

However, the Christian response to poverty has not always been, well, Christian. Natural cheapness may be one cause of minimal intervention, but Calvinism reinforced this attitude as some decided those who were predestined to be saved would receive a sign on this earth which at least hinted at their ultimate destination. That sign often turned out to be material prosperity. After all, why shouldn't God take care of the good folks? The unfortunate corollary was many decided the poor were that way because they were damned. In essence they "deserved" to be poor. This approach has been further buttressed by the belief the poor are poor because of bad choices they make, such as gambling, drinking too much, doing drugs, getting pregnant young, dropping out of school. In fact, the bad choice many poor people made was choosing parents who were poor; poverty is an inherited condition. (Think about that.) Moreover, this idea also meshes with social Darwinism, which led some to the conclusion those with wealth were better adapted to the world than those without money.

On the other hand, the supporters of the Social Gospel, with a faith in "Progress," using the new social sciences, developed the belief society's economic and social conditions affect the outcome of many lives. They then sought governmental and denominational help in attacking the problems of the city. The Social Gospel movement attracted the same folks who were moving to accommodate religion to the world of the twentieth century, which helps account for the lack of interest in social questions by fundamentalists, who were rejecting such accommodation. The push for social and economic reform led Protestants to form the Federal Council of Churches in 1908, the forerunner of the National Council of Churches. Though not directly involved in the Social Gospel movement, Roman Catholic leaders, whose denomination's members made up a large part of the factory population in many regions, often found themselves entangled in the issues of unions, working conditions, hours of labor, child labor, etc. Other facets of the movement included books and articles attacking the problems, reform-oriented politicians, and settlement houses (Jane Addams's Hull House most notably). And, to a considerable extent, the issues that interested the Social Gospel movement still interest many progressive Protestants and their denominations.

To some extent the nineteenth century saw Christians dividing with rural, conservative churches less likely to engage poverty than their urban, progressive cousins, a situation that still exists. Today denominations that focus on individual salvation tend to see individual decisions as the root of poverty; consequently, these churches focus on individuals. And pastors of many churches will, if they espouse a position on social justice, hear mumblings "pastor should stick to preaching and stay out of politics."

### The Believer Looks Inward. Fundamentalism.

Growing out of a squabble in the Presbyterian Church, the term "Fundamentalism" came from a series of twelve books published between 1910 and 1915 entitled the *Fundamentalist* which laid out the core doctrines which defined, and still define, Fundamentalism: (1) inerrancy of the Bible, (2) the Virgin Birth, (3) Jesus' death for our sins (atonement),

(4) Jesus' miracles literally happened, and (5) Jesus' bodily resurrection. The books went on to attack Roman Catholicism, Socialism, Mary Baker Eddy, German Biblical (historical) criticism, and many other aspects of the world of knowledge of the day. They were a general outburst of anti-intellectualism.

Many Christians grew concerned as science seemed to be replacing religion as the explanation for the world's workings, particularly among the educated. And clergy were being replaced by scientists as the leaders of society. With the growth of knowledge about geology and evolution, the conclusions of the higher criticism of the Bible and lessening concern with individual salvation by denominational leaders, many denominations began wrestling with these issues in a struggle between fundamentalists and modernists, who accepted the new ideas. While the bigger issue was attitudes to the modern world, the focus of the fight was often on the Bible. Was it "inerrant," free of error? Denominations struggled with the issues after 1890 and still do.

When a Christian claims the Bible is "inerrant," the Thoughtful should ask "In what sense?" After all, the term has lots of nuance. The most basic definition of inerrant requires God to dictate the Bible to writers. A shade less strict is a definition insisting the Bible is always accurate and factually true. Even less strict, some see inerrant only as to matters of ethics and salvation, so Genesis can be metaphorical. Often, Evangelicals say the Bible is "inspired" by God, leaving the door open to lots of variation as the Thoughtful could argue they have read a book or attended a concert where one could genuinely say it was inspired by God.

The pattern usually was for the conservative, those most wedded to the older views, to leave the denomination. The Christian Reformed left the Dutch Reformed, the Church of Christ departed from the Disciples of Christ, the Holiness folk seceded from the Methodists. Many in the pews migrated to denominations or congregations more to their liking as the issue, even in denominations that didn't split, had internal separations.

Today, those labeled "fundamentalist" often are in the Holiness and Pentecostal traditions and many Baptist churches. In mainline denominations and Roman Catholicism the clergy and many members reject fundamentalism but, in the absence of sermons and homilies on the topic, many in the pews accept the fundamentals, never suspecting that others reject them. Thus the Thoughtful will meet people from many denominations who are fundamentalists, but may not realize the "official" denomination has long rejected those positions.

While evangelicalism need not be fundamentalist, the overlap in the United States today is quite significant numerically. Perhaps this situation isn't surprising as the emphasis on individual conversions leaves the converts to their own devices, which may include Bible study. Sermons, seeking not to offend with theological niceties, emphasize "love," without too much content, while many congregational activities are designed to build community, not change behavior. Believe in "religion" and don't worry about "doctrine" aptly describes many members. Without guidance about the complexities of scripture, converts often become inerrancy believers. Hence the dominance of fundamentalism among evangelicals.

In the twentieth century evangelicalism took to the airwaves, first radio, then television. Radio brought the voices of Billy Sunday (1862 – 1935), Aimee Semple McPherson (1890 - 1944) and others to the masses while Oral Roberts (1928 – 2009), Pat Robertson (1930 – ), and numerous other evangelists are frequently on television throughout America. The radio and television preachers, not only competing with other forms of entertainment, also have had to spend significant energy and time on appeals for money, without a captive congregation passing the collection plate. Again, the viewer, the individual sitting at home, finds little guidance in interpretation of scripture and gravitates to fundamentalism.

Many twentieth-century evangelical preachers, such as Billy Graham, never had to invest much time in pastoral care or helping the converts continue to grow. As a result the evangelical message often was stuck at the entry-level of knowledge of Christianity. Depth was not encouraged.

Henry Emerson Fosdick (1878 – 1969), in 1922, preached a sermon entitled "Shall the Fundamentalists Win?" at First Presbyterian Church in

New York City in which he denied scriptural inerrancy, the virgin birth, the Second Coming and other cherished beliefs of the conservatives. Fosdick, whose sermon captured the attention of the educated, went on to a long pastorate at New York City's The Riverside Church which he turned into a bastion of progressive Protestantism.

In 1925 John Scopes (1900 -70) was tried in Dayton, Tennessee, for violating a Tennessee law that prohibited the teaching of evolution in the public schools. The trial turned into a circus. Clarence Darrow (1857-1938), a famous Chicago lawyer defended Scopes while William Jennings Bryan (1860-1925), three-time candidate for President as a Democrat, aided the prosecution. Bryan, a wonderful orator described the trial as a struggle between science and Christian faith and an attempt to degrade all Christian beliefs. Scopes was found guilty but the media exposure, mainly newspapers, as radio was still in its infancy, painted fundamentalism as a belief solely for the uneducated backwaters in rural America.

A subset of fundamentalism today is referred to as dispensationalism. This idea involves reading the Bible and finding God had a plan that included seven ages through which people must live. Not surprisingly, we're near the end, which makes this approach a form of millennialism; indeed 20 percent of Americans believe the world will end in their lifetimes. While such a view has been around since at least the first century, its modern genesis dates to John Nelson Darby (1800 – 82), an Englishman, who formulated the seven ages. His ideas were picked up by C.I. Schofield (1843 – 1921) who produced the *Schofield Reference Bible*, which, with its extensive annotations showing how all the connections, hints, and clues confirm the dispensational scheme, is still very popular in some fundamentalist circles. The tremendously successful *Left Behind* series of fictional books is based upon this view and shows tha big money can be made exploiting it.

Today, fundamentalism continues to flourish with school boards frequently confronting the problem of evolution. Thoughtfuls have little truck with this but about 40 percent of Americans still believe the Bible to be inerrant, whatever meaning they give to the term.

**The Thoughtful Look Elsewhere. Science.**

Why is evolution such a problem for many? Biblical inerrancy is the issue. When people read the Bible as a literal account of the past, they begin with the creation stories (there are two, but they skip of over this matter) and quickly conclude these are inconsistent with the process and timeline laid out by evolution's supporters. In their world, where only one thing can be true, when two ideas are inconsistent, both cannot be right. Moreover, to reject even one little part of the Bible as untrue then calls the entire work into question. Such folk have no willingness, or maybe capacity, to conclude parts of the Bible are history, parts are metaphor, parts are theology, parts are fiction, etc. Things are all or nothing.

But biology isn't the only discipline that causes problems. Much learning of the past two centuries has conclusions and understandings that make for restless nights. Geology, with it strata, reaching back millions and billions of years, clashes with the date 4004 B.C.E., which is calculated from the Bible for the creation of the earth. Anthropology and world travel have produced knowledge of many societies that function well, with justice even, but without the knowledge of the Christian God. Space exploration raises the prospect of finding another planet inhabited by beings; did Jesus appear there too? Psychology with its probing of the unconscious mind, raises the possibility humans are not in complete control of their actions, making punishment for sin an unfair consequence.

One distraction in the evolution debate is its description as a "theory." That statement means it isn't a "law," like gravity, which works every time (so far as we know). Nor is it a fact, Richard Dawkins notwithstanding,[16] which is a verifiable event, e.g., a camera could catch the happening. Theories do change; the Ptolemaic explanation was replaced by Copernicus's; Einstein's gravitation subsumed Newton's as a special case. Thus, while evolution might be someday superseded or subsumed by another theory, at present it explains everything very, very well. It is indeed robust.

---

[16] *The Greatest Show on Earth* (Free Press, 2009).

In Europe, Pope Pius X (1903 – 14) weighed in for Roman Catholicism. Throughout the nineteenth century, popes had fought a holding action against democratic ideas, Biblical criticism, and the march of science. In 1864 Pius IX (1846 – 37) published a "Syllabus of Errors" in which he aligned Roman Catholicism not just with the conservatives but also with the reactionaries. In 1907, in the culmination of this resistance, Pius X issued an encyclical attacking all signs of "modernism" and ordered the hierarchy to eliminate it from all organs of the denomination, especially educational institutions. While Pius X stunted Roman Catholicism's growth, especially in theology, the tradition and hierarchical nature of the Roman Catholic denomination enabled it to avoid schism. Also, those in the pews often focused more on tradition and ritual than belief and did not even seem especially concerned.

Today, creationism is the favorite idea for many. The world was created 6,000 years ago, fossils were the result of Noah's flood, and so on. All modern science conflicts with this view which is not a problem as many adherents are scientifically illiterate. Oh, an occasional scientist can be found who supports creationism. The Thoughtful will recognize all of this approach as part and parcel of the either/or stage discussed in Chapter 2.

Perhaps as few as one out of seven Americans accepts evolution without any mention of God, which is no surprise as people calling themselves atheists are scarce on the ground. Another third accept evolution but believe God created the world, triggered the Big Bang. Which leaves nearly half of the citizens of twenty-first century United States accepting creationism. Scary, huh?

A Thoughtful believer's approach might include the idea science describes accurately creation, the Big Bang, evolution, etc., but all has no meaning without God. When one accepts the idea of a deity, though not a supernatural one, then life comes into focus.

### The Red Thread. Race.

The great American problem, race, also divided, and still divides, Christians. In the pre-Civil War era where the vast majority of blacks being slaves in the South, slave involvement in religion is difficult to assess. They were often forbidden to assemble due to fear of revolt so they attended church with whites, though seated separately. However, there were some black preachers, but what effect Christianity had on slaves will probably remain one of history's unknowns. In the North, bad treatment in some congregations led to the formation by the 1820s of separate black denominations, most notably African Methodist Episcopal Church and African Methodist Episcopal Zion Church, which, by the time of the Civil War, had perhaps 30,000 members. In the world of the whites, before the Civil War the major denominations split among North/South lines with clergy from each side being prominent in the slavery debate.

After the Civil War, black Christianity came out in the open. By 1900 black Baptists, like white Baptists, were intensely congregational and had coalesced into the National Baptist Convention; four different Methodist groups, included the two older northern ones, had perhaps a combined membership over 2.5 million out of a total black population exceeding 8 million. Late nineteenth-century emphasis on missions, imperialism, and temperance dominated white denominations, and racial fairness suffered as two of those three ideas often reinforced racist attitudes.

From 1920 to 1960, over 2.5 million blacks moved north in the Great Migration and after 1950 about 50 percent of the total U.S. black population resided in the North, mainly in large cities. The Baptist and Methodist traditions continued to predominate although the presence of storefront churches of indeterminate denomination was significant. Pentecostalism originated in 1906 in a predominately black congregation in Los Angeles and had has tremendous appeal in the black community; the Church of God in Christ is the major denomination though Pentecostalism lends itself to small independent congregations. Over time, black denominations follow the same pattern as white; the second generation is less "enthusiastic" than the founders and the greater the wealth of the congregation, the more sedate the services, though whatever the changes, blacks seem to tithe at much greater rates than whites.

Black churches, the rare American institution where whites did not run things, quickly became, after the Civil War, the core of black identity and source of black leadership, both religious and political. Martin Luther King, Jr., and many other black leaders in the civil rights struggle emerged from church settings, a situation that continues into the twenty-first century. The Baptist denominations were, and are, attractive to many because the absence of hierarchy leaves no place for white domination. Today about 80 percent of black Christians are Protestants, with maybe two-thirds being Baptist, about 10 percent Methodist, and less than 10 percent Roman Catholic. Moreover, blacks claim to be church members at a higher rate than whites (80 percent vs. 63 percent) with heavily female congregations.[17] Generally, pastors are not well educated (two-thirds have no college coursework) partly because so many are Baptists where anyone can begin a congregation.

Black churches, in the North and South, and northern white churches were among the motors that kept the civil rights movement moving in the 1950s and 1960s. Clergy preached, prayed, marched, lobbied and were found in most areas of that major American event. However, while almost all denominations and churches welcome people of color today, the great American problem of race is still evident Sunday morning, which has been described as having "the most segregated hour" of the week. Pentecostal churches are the lonely exception to this generalization.

### Ethnicity.

While Roman Catholics had been present from early colonial days, and German Roman Catholics steadily immigrated in the nineteenth century, the flood of Irish peasants fleeing the potato famine in the 1840s quickly gave the American church a Hibernian character. So much so that by the 1880s, German parishes were upset enough to seek separation within the denomination, wishing not to be governed by the Irish-dominated hierarchy. Later arrivals—Italians, Poles, et al.—had similar desires. This problem

---

[17] Barry A. Kosmin and Seymour P. Lachman, *One Nation Under God: Religion in Contemporary American Society* (Harmony Books, 1993) 133. This is a valuable study, with many figures, of American denominational religion. These numbers date from the early 1990s but there is no reason to expect things to be much different today.

continued into the twentieth century when Roman Catholics from Latin America protested their inferior status within the denomination.

Ethnic communities often retained their native language and a clergyman from outside the group was handicapped in dealing with his parish. Further, the Irish, long described in Great Britain as "priest ridden," may have deferred more to the clergy than many other ethnic groups. And, despite a strongly hierarchical administration in Europe, the various Roman Catholic nationalities had developed local practices which they brought to America. Different saints and festivals were celebrated.

Other denominations also reflect the survival of national origins. Lutherans from northern Europe, settling largely in the Midwest, retained their separate identities, with Swedes having their denomination, Finns another, Germans several, and so forth, until about two dozen Lutheran denominations existed. Eastern Orthodoxy, arriving with the post-1880 immigration tide, has divided along ethnic lines, as Greeks, Russians, Serbs, Bulgarians, and others clustered into their own parishes.

**Death Penalty.**

Contradictions within contemporary Christianity surface in death penalty discussions. The commandment "Thou shalt not kill" gets variously translated, often as "Thou shall not murder." Besides permitting military service, this translation sanctions the death penalty. At the denominational level, the Roman Catholic and most mainline Protestant denominations oppose the death penalty while fundamentalist and conservative Protestants support it. (Some Thoughtful might find ironic these denominations are also strongest in the pro-life movement.)

## Gender Matters.

Several, apparently unrelated topics are much debated, though usually generating heat, not light, and revolve around sex and the issue of gender roles. For many, though not the Thoughtful, the jobs of the sexes are those tradition has given us. To oversimplify, women should stay at home, do house-like things, and be the primary caregiver for the children. (Women in the "traditional" mold work outside the home in about the same percentages as others, though they are less likely to see themselves as feminist.[18] ) Men are to earn the family's income and be generally involved in more public activities. Some denominations—Mormons, Amish, certain Baptists—keep women out of most church responsibilities. The debate, however, often uses moral categories and the Thoughtful can wonder why homosexuality, for instance, attracts so much attention while adultery doesn't—the latter is actually mentioned in the Ten Commandments which should make it more important. Society and economics help shed light on these matters as the divisions in society somewhat coincide with rankings provided by those two disciplines; those higher on the socio-economic ladder tend to be more tolerant and open to new developments in matters of gender.

**Sex and Kids.**

For several decades schools have been the scene of battles over what to teach children about sex. Many, usually not the Thoughtful, do not want schools saying anything about matters sexual as (1) this is a parent's job, and (2) knowledge will lead to action. Many parents shirk this responsibility, and children learn from many sources, situations which don't sway those opposed to sex ed.

A related issue is the effort to get teens to take vows to be sexually abstinent until marriage, which is what some want the schools to teach in lieu of sex ed. Recent studies suggest such vows are ineffective and may even be counterproductive as the promise makers, when they do engage in premarital sex, are less prepared to avoid pregnancy. Also, some evidence suggests all the attention to sex may encourage earlier marriage, which correlates with higher divorce rates.

In both these situations, some social science, often badly done, has been trotted out to support a moral decision already made—premarital sex is

---

[18] Putnam and Campbell, *American Grace,* ch. 8.

wrong, period. Also both examples involved what some see as fundamental parental rights and gender distinctions—dads teach sons, moms teach daughters.

**Divorce.**

A prominent issue doctrinally, for some churches though probably not for those in the pews, divorce was relatively easy in the period of the Hebrew Bible/Old Testament though not much is heard about it. In the Christian scripture/New Testament Jesus clearly spoke against divorce (right before he criticized wealth) (Mark 10:2 – 12, 21). He said this in the context where the Pharisees were baiting him, but writings subsequent to Mark's gospel don't water down his statement even though the clarity of the rule he pronounced was at odds with his general practice of not prescribing behavior. (One can speculate the absence of Joseph, Jesus' father, from events after the nativity might account of Jesus' harsh attitude to this practice.) Whether divorce was common in Jesus' day is difficult to know though Herod Antipas, ruler of Galilee and son of Herod of the nativity story, had a highly publicized divorce (the criticism of which is traditionally thought to be the reason he executed John the Baptizer).

As far as can be discovered, the early church followed a no-divorce policy, which continued through the Middle Ages. In the late medieval period, the Western church began granting annulments to the rich and powerful who wanted to shed their spouses. (An annulment recognizes the marriage wasn't valid in the first place. A common ground was consanguinity, nearness of a kin relationship, which was relatively easy to allege as European nobility intermarried and records weren't always complete.) This practice was, in the eyes of some, an abuse. England's Henry VIII didn't care if it was an abuse, he just wanted in on it. The pope's refusal precipitated England's break with Rome. At the Reformation, most Protestant reformers rejected marriage as a sacrament and permitted divorce, usually for adultery. The incidence of divorce, however, was not high.

When divorce was permitted in America's colonial era, numbers were kept down by social pressures. This practice began to change about the middle of the twentieth century, and the altering of the grounds from fault (e.g., adultery) to no fault (couple wants a divorce, no reasons needed). Late in the twentieth century the numbers peaked at nearly one divorce for every two marriages. Protestant denominations accept the divorced as members and generally make little of it; the Roman Catholic Church still forbids remarriage after divorce, though annulments are beginning to grow again. Many Roman Catholic priests just don't ask questions, and congregational life goes on.

### Women Clergy.

Christian institutions, like the rest of Western society, have been dominated by men historically. Oh, a few rich widows had power and influence early in the Roman period, and an occasional abbess made her presence felt in the Middle Ages. Certainly many a Protestant pastor's wife labored long and hard in the service to her husband's congregation, but it was he to whom all looked for leadership and inspiration. It was only in the twentieth century women obtained leadership roles in many denominations. Today, virtually all Protestant denominations have women clergy, though not in the numbers as the men. The historical situation is ironic in that it appears the majority of church attendees from Roman days to today have been female, and in many congregations much of the work has been done by women.

The Roman Catholic Church still maintains a male-only clergy, and, while Orthodox Church priests can marry, their bishops cannot. The rationales for this position are varied. For some, clergy should follow the example of Jesus who was apparently single (which partially helps explain why *The DaVinci Code* idea of a married Jesus was controversial). Roman Catholics have to overlook the fact Peter, Jesus' chief disciple and the first bishop of Rome by their lights, was married. Another reason for the unmarried state is it frees men from the concerns and distractions of family. However, some men rose to be pope during the Renaissance despite illegitimate children, whom they busily placed in church offices. And Protestants have prospered despite married leaders. In many cases, Protestant dynasties were established whereby son followed father and grandfather into the pastorate.

A scriptural basis for this treatment of woman is found in Paul's first letter to the Corinthians in which he wrote "women should be silent in the churches. For they are not permitted to speak...." (1 Corinthians 14:34). (This passage, even in English, reads like an addition to the original letter, which is the consensus of scholars today.) Those seeking a passage permitting women to lead the church often point to Deborah, a judge in the period of the Hebrew Bible/Old Testament.

**Abortion.**

Dividing American along several lines, abortion had, before the late twentieth century, a limited religious dimension. Until recently, many of the historical creeds included words to the effect Jesus would someday return to judge "the quick and the dead." Presumably this word choice was meant to encompass all present and past humanity, or maybe souls. The choice of "quick" reflected the historical understanding of pregnancy. The only way a woman had of knowing she was pregnant was the fetus moved, "quickening," something that occurs towards the end of the third month of pregnancy. While men might believe the cessation of a woman's periods means pregnancy, in fact that event could also be caused by malnutrition, exercise, stress, or disease. If a woman thought her problem was one of these, she might resort to any number of things to restart her periods, some of which might be abortifacients. There is evidence a plant grew along the Mediterranean Sea in northern Africa was used during Roman times for such a purpose; it is now extinct. (Wonder why?) So historically life began at quickening.

In the United States, the attack on abortions in the late nineteenth century came from a couple of directions. The major players were physicians who used such bans to drive out "quacks" and midwives from the business of women's care; women's health was not really the issue. A second front involved a fear middle class women were having abortions, and those heavily breeding workers were not; therefore the middle class would soon find itself "swamped" by the masses. (This attitude resulted in the banning of birth control at the same time.) Abortion was termed illegal although doctors continued to perform it, and perhaps the total numbers didn't fall much.

The issue resurfaced in the mid-twentieth century as doctors, who were performing abortions as part of their general practice, became worried they might be subjecting themselves to legal sanctions. In the 1960s, feminism took an interest in the matter as women began seeking educational opportunities at the college level beyond teaching and nursing; abortion became part of ideas about women controlling their own lives. Also, women were moving into the workplace and an unplanned pregnancy began to have greater "costs" in terms of career, or even money.[19] A Supreme Court case, *Roe v. Wade* in 1973, struck down state laws totally banning abortions in favor of a graduated approach by trimesters of the pregnancy; for the first three months, abortions had to be legal, and after that period, certain state controls could be made. Since, the opponents of abortion, pro-life, have sought both to overturn *Roe v. Wade* and hem in abortion's availability with lots of minor restrictions.

For those who wonder what the Bible has to say about this matter, relief is not at hand. The Thoughtful may have noticed the Bible is not quoted much, except to say "Thou shalt not kill." Some versus in Exodus (21:22 – 5) can be interpreted to be relevant; those suggest an action which causes a miscarriage is less serious than one causing a death. However, interpretations of those verses vary (*quelle* surprise) so help cannot be found there.[20] While the pro-life movement concentrates on life defined as beginning at conception, the pro-choice movement looks to a more nuanced definition of what it means to be "alive" and a "person," vaguer terms and ones make the commandment irrelevant. (Again, as so often in American debates, the sides are yes/no versus more/less.)

The sociology of the abortion issue is reflected, to a considerable extent, in the various denominations. As a general rule, college-educated women

---

[19] In Japan and India abortion became popular at the same time it was debated in the U.S. In neither country did it become entangled in the gender roles debate and, as a result, it is much less controversial.

[20] James L. Kugel, *How to Read the Bible* (Free Press, 2007), 265-8.

tend to be pro-choice and other women pro-life. Men are a little harder to pin down though they are more visible in the pro-life movement. There is also a perception, partly true, the non-rich get abortions at a higher rate (just the opposite of the nineteenth century), and this in turn often gets connected to that great American prejudice, race. The sociology suggests one way to view the debate is those who see women as careerists and those who see them as mothers. A corollary is pro-choice are the "strivers," seeking to improve themselves. Denominations, therefore, that appeal to a college-educated clientele tend to be pro-choice and the others pro-life. Mainline Protestants are usually pro-choice, while Roman Catholicism and fundamentalists are pro-life. Studies suggest, however, the women in the pews get abortions at about the same rate, regardless of their denomination's position. None of this issue is clear cut as people can be found on both sides who don't fit the sociological generalizations.

**Homosexuality.**

An issue the Thoughtful associate with conservative Christianity, homosexuality, doesn't play a large role in the Bible. It is condemned in a couple of places, especially Leviticus 18:22 and Paul's letter to the Romans, 1:17. At the root of today's debate is the issue of whether one chooses to be homosexual or whether it is innate; little research is being done on this matter, however.[21]

The Thoughtful have all seen the emails discussing the many prohibitions found in the Hebrew Bible/Old Testament—kill disobedient children, don't mix materials in clothing fabric, don't cut your beard—and wonder why homosexuality gets such special attention. Partially, the hostility was cultural as non-Jews, especially Greeks, had long practiced what we call homosexuality. In its classic form, however, such behavior involved an older

---

[21] Some work is showing that inheritance of acquired characteristics does happen, at least in some animals, as a gene can be silenced by the environment and that gene, still silenced, will be passed along to progeny. If it is possible a gene exists for homosexuality that can be activated or silenced, then perhaps the incidence of homosexuality can be increased or decreased. But then homosexuals don't breed in quite the same numbers as heterosexuals. And the Thoughtful may not care about any of this.

man and a pubescent boy with a purpose more than sexual; it resembled what we would call mentoring—a man was educating a boy in various areas of Greek life. The Greeks may not even have had a term for the relationship we call homosexual. In the West, historians think the issue was not especially alive in the church until the twelfth century when ideas about changed behavior of cloistered monks became prominent.

Today, the vehemence of some Christians against homosexuality stands in stark contrast with their silence about other activities banned or criticized somewhere in the Bible. The Thoughtful can understand this, and the anti-abortion stances, as related to the role of women. Homosexuality, for such folk, confuses the roles, who stays as homemaker, who raises children, etc.? Also psychological fears some men have they will be mistaken as homosexuals, beyond the scope of this work, contribute to the intensity of the hostility. Conservative Christians are fairly united against the tolerance of homosexuality whereas mainline and progressive Christians are more conflicted. More than any other issue, homosexuality threatens to split denominations.

**Sex.**

Among conservative Christians opposition to premarital sex outranks all other issues which helps explain the desire for education to include abstinence rather than the proper use of birth control. Abortion and homosexuality (especially same-sex marriages) come next on the list of important issues for such folk which comes as no surprise. And much, probably most, of this approach to sex issues dates from the sea change in sexual attitudes and practices in the later 1960s and early 1970s.[22]

All of these matters are extensively discussed, with even an occasional study to support the arguments, but increasingly the debate is shrill with absolutists— "thou shalt not"—seeking to ban or punish certain kinds of behavior. At root, things seem to come down to differing attitudes to matters sexual—can sex be only fun or must it also be something else? While the anti-abortion is framed in terms about "saving life," it often is also about

---

[22] Putnam and Campbell, *American Grace*, 117.

punishing those who engage in reckless or inappropriate sexual activity. "You play, you pay," a saying among some pro-lifers, catches the position well. Abortion is perceived to be a practice among the poor and the black which easily plays into other American prejudices. It also relates to the roles of women. The line-up of the denominations is approximately evangelicals, fundamentalists, and Pentecostals against the rest with nonbelievers siding with the rest. Roman Catholicism, more than most denominations, is divided as the hierarchy is staunchly anti-abortion and anti-birth control, while those in the pews go their own individual ways; in 2000, 71 percent of Roman Catholics ignore the denomination's position on birth control and 64 percent think remarriage after divorce is okay even though the official doctrine is crystal clear.[23]

The Thoughtful might well conclude for many types of Christians pleasure equals sin.

## Class.

Christianity has other aspects besides self identification or membership, beliefs and practices. While the Thoughtful are vaguely aware of it, they are often surprised to learn of the economic disparities among the faith traditions.[24]

---

[23] William V. D'Antionio et al., *American Catholics: Gender, Generation, and Commitment* (AltaMira, 2001), 43. The birth control number was up to 82 percent in 2012. www.gallup.com/poll/154799/americans-including-catholics-say-birth-control-morally.asp, accessed August 20, 2013.

[24] Kosmin and Lachman, *One Nation Under God: Religion in Contemporary American Society*, 260. I have omitted from the original table numerous denominations as well as those calling themselves "Protestant" or "Evangelical" but not specifying denomination. These numbers date to the 1990s. More recently, the Pew Foundation has surveyed for income levels among and within denominations. That data cannot be compared directly to what is shown here but the overall outline appears to be very similar. www.pewforum.org/2009/01/30/income-distribution-within--us. accessed August 28, 2013.

| Group | Median Annual Household Income |
|---|---|
| Jewish | $36.7 K |
| Unitarian | 34.8 K |
| Episcopalian | 33.0 K |
| Eastern Orthodox | 31.5 K |
| Congregationalist | 30.4 K |
| Presbyterian | 29.0 K |
| Hindu | 27.8 K |
| Catholic | 27.7 K |
| Churches of Christ | 26.6 K |
| Lutheran | 25.9 K |
| Mormon | 25.7 K |
| Methodist | 25.1 K |
| Assemblies of God | 22.2 K |
| Nazarene | 21.6 K |
| Jehovah's Witnesses | 20.9 K |
| Baptist | 20.6 K |
| Pentecostal | 19.4 K |

While there are rich Pentecostals and poor Episcopalians, someone looking for a rich marriage partner would be well advised to haunt the halls of the latter denomination.

This disparity has led to many an academic fracas about why certain groups prosper more or less. While Marx thought religion was the "opiate of the masses," a drug fed the poor that promised a nice afterlife in exchange for not making trouble in a present less-than-ideal life, the issue was best formulated by Max Weber (18641864 – 1920) in his work *Protestantism and the Rise of Capitalism.* The ensuing debate sought to find causation between certain doctrines (read predestination) and economic success. In Europe, why did the English prosper and the Irish and Poles didn't? Roman Catholicism was the easy answer; some saw that faith tradition as anti-intellectual and others its doctrines supported acquiescence, not acquisition. The argument eventually petered out but still pops up when the "culture" of a group (read American blacks) is believed to hold that group back economically.

Probably the best explanation for the American income numbers lies in who emigrated and when. Hindus do well because there aren't many of them and many of them are doctors and engineers. Jews have prospered because, unlike most groups, they brought skills, urban-related skills, and settled almost exclusively in the prospering cities, where incomes are typically higher. Unitarians, Episcopalians, Congregationalists, and Presbyterians have all been here a long time and have had the opportunity to grow with America's growth during the Industrial Revolution. Irish, Poles, Portuguese, Italians and many other Roman Catholics came later and from close to the economic bottom of the societies they left; with few skills and little capital, they were destined for manual labor. Methodists and Baptists pay the price for their mass appeal in the nineteenth century to the unchurched who were often from the lower orders; Baptists are further held back by their numbers in the South where incomes are lower. The emotional approach, combined with the strong community, have great appeal to the poor by the Pentecostal denominations. Thus, history, not theology, explains much of the disparity among the groups. As an aside, the status rankings of these groups ("Would you want your child to marry a _____?") tracks reasonably closely the income numbers, with Unitarians at the top and Jehovah's Witnesses at the bottom; we're all egalitarian but we'd rather our children marry rich than not. And religious denomination is a good guide to rich.

However, one aspect of the culture war has been an increasing willingness to judge most, maybe all, public issues by a standard of morality. A legacy of the vitality of American Christianity which often infused non-religious aspects of life with moral seriousness, this attitude makes compromises difficult. And it may encourage violence, whether against abortion providers or foreign nations (who are always "the bad guys").[25]

Many fundamentalists have little contact with folk having other views. Summer camps, charter schools, colleges, publishing houses, internet sites,

---

[25] Steven Pinker, *The Better Angels of Our Natures: Why Violence has Declined*, (Viking, 2011), "The world has too much morality." 622.

radio and television, and the like have created a world which reinforces the narrowness of the fundamentalist view. Increasingly, whether the issue be evolution, global warming, biblical scholarship, or the like, the fundamentalist response has been one of denial. No conversation, much less dialogue, occurs. Some pushback against the anti-intellectualism of many fundamentalist has occurred with, unsurprisingly, charges of heresy soon being hurled.[26]

## Church and State.

### Little Toleration Here. Colonial Activities.

Few things excite the populace like a good dispute over the relationship of religion and the government. Ever since Christianity captured the Roman Emperor Constantine (or was it the other way round?), the issue has bedeviled religious and political leaders. While theorists often proposed a "two oxen" view of the situation with both institutions, state and church, pulling society towards a better place, the reality more often witnessed a struggle for supremacy, such as the Middle Ages between Holy Roman Emperors and popes. The Reformation brought some change as cuius regio, eius religio (whose region, his religion) came to define each political territory's religion, though the English turned the phrase on its head, insisting the monarch share the national religion. Establishment, when government money helps support a religious institution, was the rule, though minority groups always kicked at it. Generally, the established church in a country wanted a religious monopoly in its political world but history went a different way. After much bloodshed, a de facto religious tolerance set in. In England, the Anglican established church was forced to abide the presence of other Protestants ("Dissenters") though that minority had political disabilities, i.e., they could not hold office.

---

[26] Karl Giberson and Randall J. Stephens, *The Anointed: Evangelical Truth in a Secular Age* (Harvard University Press, 2011).

The American colonies continued the practice of establishment and political disabilities. Although the Pilgrims and Puritans objected to the established church in England, they quickly set up the practice in New England, as taxes were used to pay salaries of ministers and build and maintain buildings. Maryland, though settled as a refuge for Roman Catholics, became both Protestant and lacked toleration. Even when toleration appeared to be the norm, as it did in Pennsylvania, belief in aspects of Christianity was required, at least of officialdom. Anglicans, as they arrived in other colonies, replicated the English world and established their church and sought to create monopolies; by the time of the American Revolution began, Anglicanism was established in New York, Virginia, Maryland, North and South Carolina, and Georgia. Rhode Island, on the other hand, under the Baptist leadership of Roger Williams (1603 – 83), managed to avoid the snares of establishment and create a religiously tolerant colony.

The American Revolution brought some change to the Establishment issue. With the adoption of the First Amendment to the Constitution— "Congress shall make no law respecting an establishment of religion, or prohibiting the free exercise thereof"—establishment at the federal level was forbidden and toleration granted. However, religious establishments remained in the states of Massachusetts, Connecticut, and New Hampshire, as did political disabilities (an office holder or voter had to be a member) there and elsewhere. Massachusetts only abolished establishment in 1833. Whether most Americans were members of any denomination at the time of the Revolution is debated, though most probably would have called themselves "Christian" if asked.

The First Amendment only limits the federal Congress; it does not affect the individual states. With the adoption of the fourteenth Amendment after the Civil War, the federal relationship to states was very significantly altered; today, the First Amendment is deemed to restrict also the states' actions in areas of religion.

**Deists All. The Founders.**

Today a great deal of debate rages around whether the United States is or ever was a Christian nation, and energy is spent on what the Founders, those who were present at the creation of the Constitution, believed. Well, they weren't Christians.

The eighteenth-century founders George Washington (1732 - 99), Benjamin Franklin (1706 – 90), Thomas Jefferson (1743 – 1826), John Adams (1735 - 1826), and James Madison (1751 - 1835) played important roles in the formation of the United States and all were deists (they accepted a God, but not the divinity of Jesus, an idea Adams called an "absurdity"). They weren't radicals in this position; most educated people of the eighteenth century were deists. In their public pronouncements, the founders used words to describe God some can interpret as being Christian but were entirely consistent with their deism, such as "Governor of the Universe," "Nature's God," "Divine Providence," "Creator," and "Almighty Being." Most thought religion had a role in getting the common herd to behave, morality, but with education, religion would fade away. Moreover, their fear about religion was it created zealots who would seek to dominate those of different faiths and religion often gave clergy too much power.

Washington studiously avoided communion at his local parish church in Virginia, and no ministers or prayers were used at his death. Franklin, in his *Autobiography*, explicitly laid out his faith and it wasn't Christian. Jefferson, though attending his local parish church, went through the gospels, cutting out the parts he thought reflected the real Jesus which meant he ignored the miracles, birth, and resurrection; his result, *The Life and Morals of Jesus of Nazareth*, was published by order the Congress in 1904. Adams, being a good Bostonian, ended life as a Unitarian and wrote in *A Defense of the United States of America,* "It will never be pretended that any persons employed in that service (drafting the Constitution) had any interviews with the gods, or was in any degree under the inspiration of heaven."[27] James Madison had a burst of religious enthusiasm early in his life but thereafter guarded his public statements and even his private conversations so closely many were left with the impression he was not a Christian.[28] He also worked

[27] John Adams, *History of the Principal Republic of the World: A Defense of the Constitutions of Government of the United States of America* (1794).

[28] David L. Holmes, *The Faiths of the Founding Fathers* (Oxford University Press, 2006).

to defeat a bill in the Virginia legislature that would have provided support to teachers of Christianity.

The U.S. Constitution, which all participated in drafting, combines English practices and institutions and a knowledge of history, especially of Roman history. The "Senate" came from Rome, and the idea of division of powers comes from Monesquieu, a Frenchman writing about England. However, today some insist it is all biblical, citing Isaiah 33:22. "For the Lord in our judge, the Lord is our lawgiver, and the Lord is our king...."

Finally, in 1799, when all but Franklin were still alive and active in politics, the United States entered into a treaty with Tripoli, an Islamic country, that stated the United States "is not in any sense founded on the Christian religion." Case closed.

### The First Amendment. Free Exercise.

The free exercise portion of the First Amendment has led, for the Thoughtful, to some curious issues. Who would have thought unemployment compensation might produce a large number of lawsuits about religion? However, once the Thoughtful reflect on the matter, it becomes apparent denying someone government benefits because that individual wouldn't work on certain days of the week does seem an issue worth considering, even litigating.

Sunday closing laws have been upheld even though they meant Orthodox Jews couldn't sell two days a week—Saturday and Sunday—not the one day—Sunday—of other retailers. On the other hand the Supreme Court has let the Amish exempt themselves from compulsory school attendance laws, but employers of the Amish have to pay social security taxes despite the Amish belief in providing for their own old age. Tax exemptions were denied to Bob Jones University because it practiced racial discrimination on religious grounds. (That decision, not the *Roe vs. Wade* abortion case, started the culture war.)

The Mormon practice of polygamy aroused strong hostility in the nineteenth century. While their attempts to leave the United States and settle in Mexican territory were thwarted when the United States annexed much of the West after the war of 1846, Mormons continued the practice. However, when Utah sought admission as a state in the 1890s, Congress refused the request until the proposed state constitution was amended to forbid polygamy. Earlier, the Supreme Court had upheld a federal law that banned polygamy in the territories, something aimed specifically at Mormons. The federal onslaught against polygamy in the late nineteenth century—denying voting to polygamists, planning to seize Mormon church property—prompted the leader of the Mormons to declare in 1890 the policy was no longer sanctioned by the denomination.

The modern concern with free exercise was kicked off by the Jehovah's Witnesses in 1938. They attacked, successfully, municipal restrictions on distribution of pamphlets without prior permission, prohibitions on solicitation of money without state approval, and, most famously, the requirement of flag salutes in schools (they considered that practice idolatry). The Witnesses didn't win all their cases but enough to give the free exercise of religion a substantial basis upon which judges, politicians, and scholars could draw. Other free exercise issues have involved the legality of using peyote in religious rites, ordinances keeping the Santeria denomination (which practices animal sacrifice) out of a city, and limitations on charitable solicitations by churches from nonmembers.

A footnote to the Thoughtful. While all sorts of unusual, indeed odd, religious practices may have themselves protected by the First Amendment, the Thoughtful should not consider establishing a new religion that includes some of their own unusual activities. Generally, the Supreme Court has granted free exercise protection only to older, better known, or sizeable groups. Just like ancient Rome.

### The First Amendment. Establishment.

Since the end of religious establishment early in U.S. history, the issue has lingered. Most often, the matter involves governments involved in some sort of favoritism to denominations, trying to give money in some form. Schools are usually the nexus of the dispute.

School prayer has a half century of disputes and litigation as the dominant group, usually Christian, often fundamentalist, wants prayer, but a minority is offended. These disputes generate a lot of heat, not much light, and seem to incite some unchristian feelings on all sides. Other school issues have involved teaching something about religion, again usually Christianity, such as the Ten Commandments. Creationism also falls into this category. More subtle, less offensive, issues involve money. Schools run by denominations have long sought subsides from governments, for all sorts of things—books, buses, teacher salaries, buildings, computers—and judges have labored mightily to decide what's proper and what isn't.

Christmas brings the annual dispute somewhere over the display of a nativity scene on public property with public funds. Other establishment issues involve employment discrimination, tax exemptions, grants to church-related colleges, money for counseling services, and so on. Though much of this matter is symbolic— "the government supports us because we're Right and True"—the upshot has been to make religion, and especially Christianity, a divisive issue. And the Thoughtful can reflect whether the sum total of hate in the world is increased by these activities. The lawyers, on the other hand, know where they stand.

Religious history in the United States has shown aspects of everything Christianity has evinced in its history. Today's Christianity is, by and large, less dogmatic, less exciting, than it has been in the past, but even that generalization doesn't apply to all denominations all across the country. And what any discussion can't capture is the emotion that so often characterizes the lives of believers. American religion has moved from sticks to carrots, hell to heaven, sin to grace, and Good Friday to Easter, as it simmered down.[29]

Truly, American Christianity has been, and is, varied, and vital.

---

[29] Stephen Prothero, *American Jesus* (Farrar, Straus and Giroux, 2003).

# MISCELLANIES

*The Grand Inquisitor*
*Cardinal Don Fernando Nino De Guerera*

# NINE

# *Tidbits: Interesting, Odd, Little Understood, or all of The Foregoing*

For more than two millennia Christians have acted in ways and accepted ideas that the Thoughtful find curious, odd, little understood, or, not to put too fine a point on it, weird. What follows is a sampling of those things from Israel to Christianity, which is divided roughly at the time of the Reformation, with a few things at the end that don't fit anywhere else in this book. The Thoughtful remember from their education, especially if they were raised in a Protestant denomination, the Middle Ages had some practices rational people would have trouble accepting, but it turns out, those didn't cease when reformers broke up the medieval church.

## Israel.

### Creation.

Christians have long used the Bible to calculate the beginnings of the world. As the authors of the Hebrew Bible/Old Testament used genealogies and the ages of people as an organizing theme, it is possible to make a timeline back to the creation of the world. The most successful, or at least most popular, was done by James Ussher, Archbishop of Armagh in Ireland, in 1650. His efforts resulted in setting creation as occurring the night of October 23, 4004 B.C.E. This year was long included as an annotation to the King James version of the Bible and still is popular with some Christians today. Millenarians, who predict the end of the world, often located the final day as October 23.

**Abraham.**

One of the patriarchs and the (legendary?) ancestor of the Jewish people, Abraham was chosen by God and promised his descendants would inherit the world, Genesis has stories of his trust in God and his willingness to undergo trials, the most famous is the near sacrifice of his son Isaac. He observed the law even though God hadn't given it yet (that action comes with the Moses story). As a mark of the covenant with God, Abraham and his (male) family underwent circumcision, thereafter one of the marks of his descendants. By one tradition, his sons, Isaac and Ishmael, became the source of Jews and Arabs and their enmity explains that hostility today.

Paul, in the Christian scripture/New Testament, reinterprets this story of Abraham to make him an exemplar of trust in God, similar to how Gentiles trust in God through Christ.

Only in modern times has the historicity of Abraham been studied, creating many more problems with the inconsistencies. If Abraham existed at all, it was about 1700 B.C.E., and he would have been a nomad with a family god, a man and a god around which stories accumulated.

**Moses.**

Moses represents the figure who led the Israelites (only they wouldn't have been called that yet) out of bondage in Egypt in what is called the Exodus. This event is foundational in later Jewish religion and is remembered in Judaism with the Passover rites. Traditionally, Moses was the author of the first five books, the Torah, of the Hebrew Bible/Old Testament.

During the wanderings in the desert east of Egypt and before arriving in Palestine, Moses received the Ten Commandments from Yahweh atop Mt. Sinai. In Jewish religion, he, along with Elijah, was treated as one of the greatest prophets (hence their joint appearance at the Transfiguration of Jesus (Mark 9:2 – 13)).

Scholars today have doubts Moses existed. If the Exodus occurred, the time was c.1300 B.C.E., but the dessert has no archaeological evidence to support the passage of Moses and his followers, and Egyptian records make no mention of the departure of such a people. He name itself may mean "son of" or "child" or perhaps "drawn out of water" in Egyptian. The story of the pharaoh's daughter finding him in a basket in the Nile parallels stories in Mesopotamia about Sargon and Italy about Romulus and Remus; scholars tend to see such stories as covers for obscure origins of a successful usurper. (Would you accept your teenage daughter's story about finding her baby in the river?) Perhaps the strongest argument against his existence is the absence of any mention of Moses by the prophets before 500 B.C.E., which suggest he was created by the Deuteronomist to flesh out the storyline author was developing.

The overall message of the Exodus is God leads you out of your bondage, to whatever you are bound, and sustains you during hard times, which has been a consistent theme of Judaism and Christianity.

### Elijah.

A ninth-century B.C.E. prophet, Elijah promoted the Yahweh cult at a time when many were worshipping other gods of the Palestinian area. Also in common with many prophets, he argued for righteousness and social justice. Ultimately, he was transported into heaven on a fiery chariot without tasting death. Many more miracles are associated with Elijah than with other prophets. John the Baptizer seems to be modeled on him. Also, he, along with Moses, is reported by the Synoptic gospels to be with Jesus during the Transfiguration, when atop a mountain Jesus' "face shone like the sun, and his clothes became dazzling white" (Matthew 17:2). Elijah's return was commonly believed to be a harbinger of the Messiah. In reality, his story legitimates an usurpation of the kingship of Israel, and much of the story echoes the later life of Elisha and strongly also smacks of folkloric themes.

**Ahab.**

A ninth-century B.C.E. ruler of the northern kingdom of Israel (874 – 53 B.C.E.) after the separation into two kingdoms, Ahab has a negative press in the Hebrew Bible/Old Testament; indeed, he is described as Israel's worst king. He is pictured as supporting Canaanite gods and not following the commandments of Yahweh (1 Kings 18:18). He married Jezebel, a daughter of the king of Tyre and Sidon and one of the nastiest characters in scripture; she is portrayed as having too much power and promoting foreign gods. They clashed with the prophet Elijah and met bad ends (1 Kings 16:29 – 40; 2 Kings 9:30 – 7). In sources outside the Hebrew Bible/Old Testament, however, Ahab is portrayed as a successful monarch, victorious in important battles, and financially solvent. It appears, therefore, either the Deuteronomist had access to materials not available to us or he needed to have Ahab fit his theme of unrighteousness leading to disaster.

Of late, archaeology has produced evidence palaces attributed to Solomon might better belong to Ahab. In other words, did the Deuteronomist downplay and criticize Ahab, a ruler of the northern kingdom of Israel, in favor of David and Solomon, rulers of a united kingdom that included what became Israel and Judah? Certainly, the treatment of Ahab fits the Deuteronomist's theme a little too tidily.

**Samaritans.**

When the Assyrians in 722 B.C.E. deported the 10 tribes of Israelites of the defeated northern kingdom of Israel, resettlement of the area occurred, maybe at the instigation of the Assyrians. The settlers may have intermarried with the remaining survivors of Israel and at some point, built their own temple on Mount Gerizim, perhaps because the people of the area were rejected by the Jews returning from the exile in Babylon. Later, when the Jews achieved independence from the Seleucids, that temple was destroyed and a diaspora occurred. By Jesus' time, Samaritans were seen as an inferior culture by Jews (hence the power of the good Samaritan parable) while they, along with the Essenes and Christians, rejected the Temple leadership in Jerusalem.

### Ark of the Covenant.

In ancient Jewish religion, the Ark of the Covenant was a wooden box, covered inside and out with gold, and had various external decorations (Exodus 25). Containing the Ten Commandments and miscellaneous other things, it was carried by the Israelites everywhere, including into battle, which once resulted in it being captured by the Philistines who returned it after being afflicted with various problems (perhaps including hemorrhoids).[1] When Solomon built the Temple, it was placed in the innermost room, the Holy of Holies, which the chief priest entered only once a year. The Temple was destroyed by the Babylonians in 586 B.C.E., and presumably the ark was destroyed also. At any rate, no further mention is made of it to the satisfaction of scholars. However, stories have keep popping up that the ark is in various places: the priests buried it on Temple Mount, various folk spirited it away to Egypt or Ethiopia, Indiana Jones in the film *Raiders of the Lost Ark* dealt with it.

### The Temple.

The center of worship for the Israelites of the Hebrew Bible/Old Testament was the first Temple, built by the king Solomon in the middle of the tenth century B.C.E. in Jerusalem. By consolidating several shrines and centralizing worship in one location, Solomon hoped to control the priesthood better. That Temple was destroyed in 586 B.C.E. by the Babylonians in the reprisals against the rebellious Jews. The Jewish leadership was then sent into exile in Mesopotamia. When allowed to return to Jerusalem in the 530s B.C.E., these leaders, or their descendants, soon undertook to build the second Temple. Herod, yes, Herod of the nativity story, renovated the second

---

[1] 1 Samuel 5.

Temple about 20 B.C.E., turning it into perhaps the most elaborate temple in the Roman world, the total complex covering an area larger than 30 football fields. During a Jewish revolt, the Romans destroyed the second Temple in 70 C.E. The Dome of the Rock, a Muslim shrine, has occupied the site since the seventh century.

Jews, throughout the Roman empire paid an annual tax to support the Temple (Matthew 17:24) and sought to make an annual pilgrimage there. Priests made daily sacrifices, and pilgrims could purchase animals for sacrifice and exchange money for the Tyrian shekels, which were the official currency of the Temple. A complex covering acres, the Temple had areas of increasing restriction beginning with the court of the Gentiles, through the court of the women, then the men (surprise!), and finally to the holy of holies entered only by the high priest once a year. The priests made their living from the Temple and had powerful political influence under the Romans. With a staff of 700 priests who rotated monthly and numerous others workers—gatekeepers, guards, and so forth—a total of perhaps 20,000 people were financially dependent on the Temple.

The Christian scripture/New Testament suggests the troubles, and deaths of John the Baptizer, Jesus, and Paul—resulted from conflicts with the Temple authorities. John, with his practice of baptizing for remission of sins, offered an inexpensive alternative to Temple sacrifices, something the priests could not abide. (The traditional explanation, from Josepheus, was Herod feared John's ability to generate large crowds which presaged revolt.) Jesus clearly ran afoul of the Temple authorities. Upsetting the tables of the money changers and animal sellers, he also preached a message that probably obviated any need to sacrifice at the Temple so the authorities quickly pressured Pilate to execute him. Paul continued what by then was a tradition of hostility to the Temple organization. By rejecting "the Law," Paul interpreted Jesus' death and resurrection as a one-time sacrifice. Additionally, Paul included Gentiles in his mission, further distancing the nascent Jesus movement from the Temple. In 57 C.E. Paul took money he had gathered from his groups to Jerusalem to help support the Jesus' followers there. (Led by Jesus' brother, James, that group probably practiced community of property and maybe was impoverished.) Exactly what happened is unclear. Paul probably had a dispute with James about the Gentiles; he may have taken a Gentile into a forbidden area of the Temple; or he may have been attacked in the street by some Jews offended by his work among Gentiles; or maybe all three of these possibilities occurred. The Jewish authorities were unsympathetic, and that was the beginning of the end of Paul. John the Baptizer, Jesus, and Paul all died because of threats they posed to the Temple and those who ran it.

**Dead Sea Scrolls.**

In 1946 some shepherds discovered manuscripts in a cave near an ancient site called Qumran on the Dead Sea. Over the next decade more manuscripts were recovered from nearby cases until the total exceeded 900. Then followed three decades when a small group of scholars monopolized access to the manuscripts, a monopoly finally broken in the 1990s.

The various scrolls were written from 200 B.C.E. to about 100 C.E., most in the first century B.C.E. They presumably were hidden in the caves during the Jewish revolt of 66 – 70 C.E. Any connection with a group of Jews called Essenes is still a bit controversial as is their exact connection with the nearby site of Qumran; little evidence exists to explain either the Essenes or Qumran..

The writing is Aramaic and Hebrew. All the books in the Hebrew Bible/Old Testament are represented in the scrolls except for Esther, but there are no Christian scripture/New Testament books among the scrolls. The scrolls show the Masoretic text, one of the earliest Hebrew texts we have to provide a basis for translations, is fairly accurate, though produced nearly a thousand years later. On the other hand, enough variation from other texts appears so the scrolls have destroyed the idea than an "original" text of any scripture can ever be decided upon as the texts were frequently rewritten with a freedom in the retelling of stories.

Initially, it was hoped the scrolls might include mention of Jesus. They don't. They do, however, contain material about the messianic hopes of the day, hopes that included two Messiahs—one a priest, the other a king. For the Thoughtful, the scrolls provide the earliest available copies of many texts and help illustrate the Jewish world in which Jesus operated.[2]

## Ancient and Medieval Christianity.

### Palm Sunday.

The Christian holy week begins with Palm Sunday and ends with Easter, a sequence based on the Synoptic gospels (Mark 11:1 – 1; Matthew 21:1 – 11; Luke 19:28 – 44). Scholarly attention to those events has, however, produced some problems as external facts often don't line up well, and many of the stories lack witnesses/reporters.

The week opens with Palm Sunday when Jesus rides into Jerusalem astride a donkey (well, a donkey and a foal in Matthew's gospel but that's his problem with reading Greek).[3] The crowds wave palms and lay their garments on the pavement while shouting "Hosanna." Jesus then proceeds to the Temple where he causes a scene involving money changers and dove sellers.

The laying of garments on the pavement echoes 2 Kings 9:13 when Jehu was crowned king of the northern kingdom in the ninth century B.C.E. The palm waving looks more like what Jews did in the autumn during the festival of Tabernacles (Sukkot) as does the shouting of "Hosanna." John, in his gospel, doesn't mention the procession as an antecedent to the Temple fracas (12:12-9).

The event in the Temple occurred, in Mark, the day after Palm Sunday; in Matthew the day of Palm Sunday; and in John near the date of Passover. The Synoptics put this event in the last week of Jesus' life; John put it early in Jesus' public career. The Temple was the center of Jewish religion and devout Jews paid a tax to it and maybe donated money. Money changers were there

---

[2] See Geza Vermes, *The Complete Dead Sea Scrolls in English* (Penguin, 2004).

[3] The donkey ride comes from Zechariah 9:0 although Matthew misreads his Greek sources and has Jesus arrive astride two animals.

to enable the devout to obtain the correct coins. The problem: they left two weeks before Passover so they would not have been present on Palm Sunday, which was less than a week before Passover. The dove sellers were also a convenience to the devout as making animal sacrifices was an important part of the Jewish religion. Jesus was protesting abuses, probably by Temple authorities who charged the money changers and dove sellers so much that they, in turn had to raise their prices. Or maybe he was challenging the entire sacrifice edifice.

**Virgin Mary.**

For the Thoughtful, the stories about Mary, Jesus' mother, combined with the plentiful art still seen in museums and churches often constitute a major aspect of medieval Christianity and the modern Roman Catholic Church. The Thoughtful should learn this view of Mary grew gradually with some aspects only becoming official dogma in the last two centuries and there is little scriptural basis for it.

The gospels contain a handful of references to Mary, the bulk of which are in the nativity stories of Luke and Matthew, stories that bear no relation to historical reality. As portrayed in the gospels, Jesus' relation to Mary was odd because she is given no role and barely is mentioned. When, early in his ministry, he visited his hometown, Nazareth, the reception was hostile. Later in his ministry he was told his mother and brothers were nearby, but he, in essence, distanced himself from them (Mark 3:31, Matthew 12:45, Luke 8:19). At his death Mary is said to be present (John 19:25). But that is it.

In the nativity story, Matthew, in his gospel, wrote for a Jewish audience, probably Jesus people, and attempted to show how Jesus fulfilled many passages of the Hebrew Bible/Old Testament and therefore the Jesus movement was a legitimate part of Jewish religion. One of the passages he used was from the book of Isaiah where mention was made of a future child to be named "Immanuel" ("God is with us") (Isaiah 7:14). In Hebrew this child was to be born of a young woman ("*almah*"), but when the passage was translated into Greek in the third and second centuries B.C.E., the word chosen was "virgin" ("*parthenas*").[4] In drawing upon Isaiah, Matthew, who was using the Greek version of the Hebrew Bible/Old Testament, made Mary a virgin, despite the fact he had started his gospel with Joseph's genealogy back to Abraham and David which implied he saw Joseph as Jesus' father. And anyway, the Isaiah passage was speaking to an immediate future, not a distant one.

Another possibility here is Jesus' conception might have been scandalous. A second-century critic of Christianity, Celus, had a story Jesus' father was a Roman solder, Pantera.[5] Several gospel verses suggest Jesus was illegitimate and the early followers of Jesus had to deal with that rumor; virginity of Mary was a solution (e.g., John, ch. 8).

Matthew and Luke portrayed Jesus as a son of God and by the end of the first century had made Jesus divine. Undoubtedly this development merged with the general cultural notion of important men being born of human women with divine fathers. Apollo, Perseus, and Dionysus among the gods had divine and human parents in Greek myth, Buddha, Horus, Mithras, Zoroaster in other traditions, while similar parentage was given to men such as Pythagoras, Plato, and Alexander the Great. As a result of the divinity of Jesus, Mary's story moved from the virgin birth, to perpetual virgin, to immaculate conception (hers, not Jesus'), to Mother of God, and finally to a bodily assumption into heaven. By the fifth century, at the latest, the church thinkers had blown this development up into the Virgin Mary, Mother of God, with which we are familiar.

In the twelfth century, Bernard of Clarvaux (1090 – 1153), perhaps the most influential man of that century, preached a series of sermons about the Song of Solomon. The thrust of his message was to make the Song of Solomon, a series of human love stories, into an allegory of God's love for humanity, and Mary played a role in this story. She brought "softer," "feminine" qualities into a religion where the deity was often portrayed as a stern

---

[4] Howard Clark Kee, "The Gospel According to Matthew" in *The Interpreter's One-Volume Commentary on the Bible*, ed. Charles M. Laymon, (Abingdon, 1971), 611.

[5] In the nineteenth century a tombstone of a Roman solder named Pantera was discovered in Germany. That is the only historical support for Celsus's story.

judge. She was approachable, stood by humanity like a mother, and could intercede with God for us because a son can deny his mother nothing. The popularity of Mary quickly spread. Cistercians, one of the new monastic orders, were dedicated to Mary, and the new cathedrals built at this time, especially in France at Laon, Paris, Amien, and Coutance, were dedicated to Mary, our lady ("Notre Dame").

Early in the fifth century, Augustine formalized a doctrine known as "original sin." In his view, when Adam and Eve sinned (i.e., had sexual intercourse) in the Garden of Eden, they contaminated the species, and all subsequent people were born with the sin of their conception. Thus one purpose of baptism was to remove that sin. Now, once Jesus was seen as divine, he couldn't have any sin, original or otherwise, so obviously he wasn't born as a result of human sexual intercourse. Then, someone decided Mary also should be free of original sin so her conception was "immaculate," though there is no scriptural basis for this idea. Moreover, as she remained sinless and tombless, the assumption was her body was taken into heaven at her death (the "Assumption"). Again, no scriptural basis for this interpretation. These two ideas, the Immaculate Conception and the Assumption, became official dogma of the Roman Catholic Church in 1854 and 1950, respectively, though they had been around for over a millennium.

For the Thoughtful, this tale is a marvelous example of the ironic course of history. One decision—Jesus is divine—then led to a cascade of other problems which led to the edifice of doctrine which strains credulity. Little of the edifice is relevant to the core of Christianity which suggests it can be ignored by a believer and life will go on. And it is and it does.

Mary is found in several places in popular culture. "Hail, Mary" is a very popular Roman Catholic prayer and also a last ditch effort in football to throw a touchdown pass into the end zone at the end of a half or game.

**Supersessionism.**

The Thoughtful understand the Hebrew Bible/Old Testament was written and used as a basis for Jewish religion. However, very early the Jesus people began seeing it as background to Jesus. Thus Matthew ransacked it for material to use in his gospel in order to show how the Hebrew Bible/Old Testament was fulfilled by Jesus. As a result, supersessionism was introduced to explain how Jesus superseded the Hebrew Bible; this view has been dominant in Christian history and is still alive in many denominations. In some way it also has contributed to anti-Semitism by portraying Judaism as an outdated faith.

**Son of Man.**

Sometimes translated "Son of Adam," the troublesome term "Son of Man" changes meaning over time. In the pre-400 B.C.E. portions of the Hebrew Bible/Old Testament, it means "man," "humanity," "people," a generic term. Later writings, beginning with the book of Daniel, were interpreted to mean "Messiah" (non-scriptural materials such as 4 Ezra and 1 Enoch similarly use it). How, if at all, Jesus used it is argued by scholars, as some think it was added by later followers. His early followers increasingly used it to mean Messiah for the time he was living and, after his death, to mean end time judge or advocate. Or, it described his humanity, when alive, and his divinity later. All very confusing.

**Jesus' Second Coming.**

Enshrined in the Nicene Creed, Jesus' Second Coming will occur someday, but the details are fuzzy. In general, Jesus will raise the dead, hold the last judgment on people ("judge the living and the dead"), and inaugurate the Kingdom of God.

The idea Jesus would return took root among his earliest followers despite the absence of any such idea in the Jewish religion of the day. Paul, by the 50s, describes this Coming (e.g., 1 Thessalonians 4), and the gospel writers followed (e.g., Matthew 24). Certain events were thought to presage the Second Coming; one of them, the destruction of the Temple in 70 C.E., gave great hope to Jesus' followers. However, that hope for an immediate return slowly died and the church began projecting it into the indefinite future.

Christians in the United States began focusing on the Second Coming in the 1840s, resulting in a couple of new denominations; the Seventh Day

Adventists and Jehovah's Witnesses, both of whom set dates for the Second Coming which did not pan out. Another twist came from Dispensationalism, which involved dividing history into periods, dispensations, which would end with Jesus' second appearance. A variation involved Jesus taking believers in what was called the Rapture, and leaving the remaining to wage a millennium-long war after which he would come again and establish the Kingdom of God.

The Second Coming called the "parousia" (Greek for arrival) has become a metaphor for the Thoughtful. The Thoughtful can read John 17:3 to say eternal life is available in the present to the believer ("And this is eternal life, that they may know you, the only true God, and Jesus Christ whom you have sent."); therefore John 14:23 is not about a literal Second Coming but rather about spiritual presence here and now (And Jesus answered him, "Those who love me will keep my word, and my Father will love them, and we will come to them and make or home with them"). Thus it can be envisioned as a description of the individual "seeing" Jesus, his arrival, in a way that ends that individual's world. Alternatively, the idea of Jesus' return is the expression of a hope for peace and justice on Earth. Or, like many Christians, the Thoughtful can ignore the idea entirely.

**Tongues.**

Something most Thoughtful have not encountered is someone speaking in tongues (glossolalia). In the Christian scripture/New Testament, speaking in tongues is described in two ways. In Paul's writing, an individual, probably in a state of ecstasy, utters incomprehensible babble (which Paul says someone else can interpret). Paul doesn't encourage speaking in tongues as he thought it was too selfish an act (1 Corinthians 14) even though Paul himself spoke in tongues during his private prayers (1 Corinthians 1:18). Luke, on the other hand, describes events at the Pentecost, 50 days after Jesus' death, during which followers miraculously received the ability to speak languages other than Aramaic, their native language.

Incomprehensible speaking, also occurred at Delphi in ancient Greece where priests interpreted the utterances (and, in responses, gave the famously ambiguous answers). Similar language may have occurred at the festival of Demeter at Eleusis.

Today's Pentecostalism originated in 1906 in Los Angeles, where speaking in tongues is part of worship. The major denominations of Pentecostals are the Assemblies of God and Church of God in Christ, although many Pentecostals belong to a group with only one congregation. Around the world, Pentecostalism is one of the fastest growing branches of Christianity.

**Saints.**

Early on, saints were Jesus' followers, especially those whose lives imitated Jesus, a usage still practiced today. However, also very early on in Christianity the idea certain individuals, especially martyrs, outperformed the mass of believers (getting killed in the process) and such folk got the designation of "saint." As no one person or body controlled the awarding of the title, saints proliferated. Indeed, to facilitate the conversion to Christianity, many pagan gods became saints and their altars became holy locations for the Christian faithful.

By the time of the Reformation, saints numbered in the thousands, and most reformers repudiated the idea of saints; the Roman Catholic Church began winnowing the saints who were former pagan gods and folkloric figures only in 1969, a process the Orthodox tradition has not adopted.

Saints are not worshipped (in theory at least) but are asked to intercede for the living, hence specific saints are identified with specific illnesses. Moreover, various objects associated with saints were deemed to have special qualities. (see the Relics section below)

Today canonization in Roman Catholicism is a long process of investigation of the would-be saint's life. Two miracles, which occurred after the individual's death (all saints are dead), must be attested to. At some point a trial occurs in which a canon lawyer is assigned to argue against canonization or argue on behalf of the devil, a devil's advocate. Canonization is neither dead nor dying in Roman Catholicism; Pope John Paul II (1978 – 2005) canonized nearly 500 people, a number which exceeds the total of all other popes since 1600.

## Relics.

The Thoughtful, especially when touring in Europe, have encountered displays of relics and behavior implied relics were worshipped. What's going on here?

The special role of relics appeared in at least the second century. Most were connected with Jesus, his mother Mary, or martyred saints, and were efforts to gain intersession of those folk before God for the believer. (God appears to be a king-like figure in the sky, making judgments on human souls.) By the eighth century relics were included in altars, and legal oaths were sworn upon them. The crusades, with the opening of trade to the Holy Land, also opened a floodgate of relics as crusaders and pilgrims brought back almost anything not tied down. For example, someone calculated the number of splinters of the True Cross, the cross upon which Jesus was executed, would, if assembled, constitute a forest. The Shroud of Turin, the cloth in which Jesus allegedly buried, with its negative photographic image of a man, has been discredited often by scientific tests, but believers claim the tests were flawed, biased, wrong.

During the Reformation, Protestants generally disregarded relics whereas the Council of Trent, which formed modern Roman Catholicism, generally confirmed them. The chief criticism of relics has been believers' tendency to worship them, which constitutes idolatry. The Thoughtful might approach them as relics of the past when they linked the supernatural and natural worlds in an age when many concepts had to be visually represented. Today they are merely curiosities of that past.

## Angels.

Please!! To the Thoughtful it is bad enough some Christians think God is the great chess player in the sky, moving us poor mortals around like game pieces, but to add angels to the mix is just too much. And, of late, angels are a growth industry.

In the Hebrew Bible/Old Testament, angels appear occasionally as messengers and members of the heavenly court, like courtiers around a king. They were located somewhere between humans and God, most famously in the Great Chain of Being where gradations of angels are as numerous as are the species between humans and pond scum. Scholars think angels originated when the many gods of the early Israelites were downgraded and Yahweh elevated; the old gods became subservient to Yahweh as angels. Revelation (12:7-9) describes a war between angels before humans existed as an explanation for the origins for the devil. The medieval church speculated about this matter, but in modern times, especially for Protestants, the concept has nearly disappeared.

The Thoughtful can meditate perhaps angels become popular when God seems to be too distant, abstract, or judgmental. Angels also reflect a human tendency toward polytheism as life just seems too complicated for one being to tend to it all.

**Apostolic Succession.**

Some denominations, especially Roman Catholics and Episcopalians, claim their bishops were created by bishops who, in turn, were created by bishops, and so forth, all the way back to the first twelve disciples—the apostles. This idea originated early as Paul was aware of it in the 50s. Such a chain—the Apostolic Succession seems unlikely given the sketchiness of the early Jesus congregations and the collapse of society in the Dark Ages, the period from c.600 C.E. to 800 C.E. This connection guaranteed "correct" teaching—i.e., teaching handed down directly from Jesus. The chief consequence is it can be a roadblock to efforts to unite denominations. The Thoughtful can puzzle over why such pride and importance are placed in this alleged tradition.

**Creeds.**

Christianity is unusual, perhaps unique, in its formulation and use of creeds. The Christian scriptures/New Testament books have some short affirmations of certain beliefs (1 Corinthians 153 – 9; 1 Timothy 3:16), which might have been used liturgically or as part of baptismal proceedings. By the third and fourth centuries creeds were getting more elaborate, representing a struggle within the church for political dominance. After the emperor

Constantine's conversion, creeds could be enforced by state authority and dissenters, most often bishops, could be driven from their positions and perhaps even expelled from the organization if they could not agree with an official creed.

During the sixteenth-century Reformation, creeds were again used to define groups. As the reformers began to debate over the use of works in salvation, the age of baptism, and other doctrinal and ritualistic matters, creeds were drawn up, first to effect a compromise of disputing groups and later to stake out a claim to Truth. Creeds, therefore, have usually been more divisive than unifying; and have easily become tools to remove one's opponents from positions of power and influence.

Confession of faith is the more modern term for a creed, but many confessions are far more detailed than were the early creeds. For instance, whereas the Nicene Creed used today runs 225 words, the Belgic confession of 1561, a basic confession used in Reformed churches, approaches 10,000 words.

**Monasticism.**

Early on in Christian history, as more Romans converted, inevitably not all were as pure or holy as others thought appropriate. One response was to avoid such sinners in order to avoid temptation and contamination. Some, namely stylites, erected pillars and took up solitary residence atop them; food from their admirers was hoisted up to them. Others retreated from society into the desert and became solitary hermits. In some places hermits clustered together and a community emerged, a development associated with Pachomius in Egypt in the fourth century. He promulgated a set of rules which regulated the lives of the men in the community, the monks.

Monasticism came West in the sixth century when Benedict founded a monastery at Monte Cassino in Italy. His set of rules regulated the monks there and eventually elsewhere, and Benedictines dominated religious culture until the twelfth century. With the political and economic revivals that began in the tenth century, many men sought outlets for their religiosity beyond retreat to a monastery, which was often heavily involved in secular affairs. The result was canons regular, who often worked in cities in a variety of charitable tasks, and mendicant friars, who wandered about with preaching as their focus. Various other foundations occurred, some even for women; until the late Middle Ages, the church had a wide variety of options for those seeking outlets for their religious urges. At the Reformation, Protestants rejected monasticism, and today one can hear "There's no such thing as a solitary Christian," so complete has been the rejection of the isolated, secluded life.

**Filioque.**

Translated from the Latin, "filique" means "and the Son." Another of those political struggles within the early church, the dispute reflects the hairsplitting that emphasis on dogma produces. The Nicene Creed is involved, and by the sixth century, the idea surfaced that the Holy Spirit, the third part of the Trinity, proceeded from the Father and the Son, not just the Father. As a consequence of this dispute, the church further divided into Eastern and Western parts in the years before 1000.

**Augustine.**

Along with Martin Luther, Augustine is one of the most important thinkers in the traditions of the Western church, and along with Paul, some see him as Christianity's second founder. He engaged in disputes with various Christians (Donatists, Pelagius, for example) during which he developed a theology that long dominated and remains very important.

His doctrine of grace developed during his debate with Pelagius who argued humans can take the initiative for their own salvation, whereas Augustine insisted only God could overcome humanity's sinfulness. Augustine argued people are "fallen" in that they have rejected God's original created order. This "original sin" cannot be surmounted by humans but rather needs God's intervention with "grace," something totally unmerited by sinful being. (Baptism was posited by some as removing original sin. Thus, to many, baptism of infants, common by the third century, cheapens the grace of God and smacks of "going through the motions.") The Thoughtful are likely to side with Pelagius's theory. They prefer, generally, to believe people have the ability to be saved through good works over Augustine's view of humanity, with its weakness and powerlessness in the face of sin. Ultimately, Augustine's thinking supported the notion of predestination, an idea not much developed in the Middle Ages but which had a great future in the Reformation.

Augustine also wrote extensively about the Trinity and proved very influential in the Western church. His views contributed to the separation of the Eastern and Western versions of Christianity. In discussing the Holy Spirit, part of the Trinity, Augustine argued it proceeded from the Father and the Son, a view rejected by the Eastern branch. (see the Filioque section *supra*)

**Blood.**

The Thoughtful have feelings ranging from discomfort to disgust when they hear Christians singing hymns with such words as "nothing but the blood of Jesus" and "there is a fountain filled with blood" or discussing how Jesus' blood and his crucifixion saved us all.

In the Hebrew Bible/Old Testament, when a Jew or the Jewish people as a whole committed or omitted certain acts, an estrangement (sin) from God resulted. A sacrifice was necessary to heal that division, to restore a right relationship with God. Often the sacrifice involved the blood of an animal because blood was synonymous with life. (There is some evidence very early on in Israelite history human sacrifice was practiced.) An important Jewish ceremony, the Day of Atonement, included killing a bull and a goat and setting a second goat free in the wilderness, presumably carrying sin away (hence "scapegoat").

Jesus did not seem to worry much about such acts, and Paul actively rejected them. However, the early followers of Jesus had to explain his death and the older notions of sacrifice quickly suggested themselves. His death, therefore, was not senseless or a result of Roman perceptions of a rebel but was rather a means of reconciling all humans with God, once and forever.

To the modern mind, this is all a bit, or a lot, strange but it was how the early followers wrapped up Jesus' life and death into a theology that fit their traditions.

**Stigmata.**

The appearance of the wounds of Jesus, especially in the hands, feet and side, began, it seems, with Francis of Assisi (1181 – 1226), whose wounds were reportedly evident two years before his death. Since then, more than 300 cases have been recorded; interestingly about 280 of those cases involved women. They vary—with some bleeding, others having swollen flesh. Non-religious interpretations have been largely psychoanalytical (considered a form of hysteria) with the officials of Roman Catholicism, where the vast majority occur, tending to ignore it. One curiosity: the side of the body on which the torso wound appears correlates with whatever painting the recipient had seen.

**Inquisition.**

Established by the medieval church in 1233 to deal with the Cathar heresy in southern France, the inquisition spread to other countries later. Its bad reputation stemmed from proceedings generally associated with accusations of heresy; beliefs were questioned, trials were secret (to keep the heretical ideas from being publicized), witnesses might not be identified, and torture was sometimes used. If the accused repented, penances were imposed; if the accused did not repent, the accused was handed over to the lay authorities (the church wouldn't kill anyone) for punishment, which was usually burning at the stake.

Ferdinand and Isabella used the inquisition in Spain after 1480 to examine people who had converted to Catholicism from Islam and Judaism to determine if any backsliding had occurred. El Greco's portrait of the Spanish Grand Inquisitor (Cardinal Nino de Guevara) also contributes to the bad image, as he certainly looks sinister. The total number executed was, at most, a few thousand, probably less, but the Spanish Inquisition functioned into the nineteenth century.

## Indulgences.

When a sinner felt penitent about a sin and confessed it to a priest, forgiveness and absolution followed. However, a smudge still darkened the soul of the sinner so penance must be undertaken, while alive or in purgatory, to erase that blemish. Originally penance was fairly arduous—prayer, fasting, charity, pilgrimages—and limited to once in a lifetime, but it got watered down and could often be undertaken by a payment of money.

By Chaucer's time in the fourteenth century, the practice of buying forgiveness of penances was far enough developed he created a character, who carried forms with blank spaces for the name of sinner, the sin, and the amount paid. And somewhere along the line, this practice was expanded by the idea the lives of the church's saints had been so good they had accumulated a lot of extra bits of good behavior, a Treasury of Merit, which popes claimed to control and dole out in indulgences. Around 1480, indulgences were further expanded to include forgiveness for a deceased sinner. Thus by payment of money, a soul could be released from purgatory

In 1517 indulgences were being sold in Germany to help build St. Peter's in Rome and to repay a local archbishop for the money he had spent to obtain his office. Martin Luther found the church's practices about indulgences, in theory and in practice, to be wrong—so wrong they he invited a public debate on the matter. From this debate, the Reformation grew and soon the medieval church had been shattered into many parts, all from a squabble over penances for sin.

## Pilgrimages.

A journey to a holy place, a pilgrimage, was often to seek divine help (e.g., Lourdes and healing) or as an act of penance, often in lieu of a public penance. By the Middle Ages pilgrimages were big business, and one consequence was the discovery Palestine, with its many holy sites, was not in the political hands of Christians. Ergo, the Crusades.

While Palestine was a favorite destination, locations closer to home developed. French cathedrals were built on the knowledge the pilgrims on the road to Spain's Santiago de Compostelo would spend time resting in the cathedrals along the way. In England, Canterbury, holding the tomb of the martyred Thomas Beckett, was the premier site, but many lesser-known places existed. Today, pilgrimages still occur but their relation to sin and its forgiveness is less marked.

**Limbo.**

An idea developed in the medieval church about the eternal fate of those never baptized but otherwise almost sinless, e.g., newborns. These babies were not admitted to heaven because they were tainted with original sin but were still able to reside eternally in a place with no punishment. While newborns were at this "limbo," other subtleties existed such as the status of the Hebrew Bible/Old Testament figures who were devout but obviously never encountered Jesus.

Never made an official doctrine and without scriptural basis, this limbo was an easy mark for reformers, and its kinks remain to puzzle the Thoughtful. Neither Protestants nor Orthodox groups accept the notion of limbo; since 1992 the Roman Catholic Church also has been slowly backing away from the idea—Pope Benedict XVI seemed to endorse a 2007 report that limbo isn't doctrine—but he never officially rejected it. Like Purgatory, limbo became irrelevant when the idea of an afterlife vanished, something the Thoughtful consider likely, indeed acceptable.

**Missions.**

From the beginning, the followers of Jesus, unlike adherents of most world religions, wanted to spread their understanding of him, his message, and his significance. Matthew's gospel reports Jesus as saying "make disciples of all nations" (Matthew 28:19). The traditional story has each of his early disciples going to a separate nation, but there is little evidence to support this story. Paul is by far the best-known early missionary, and his letters to his converts make up a substantial portion of the Christian scripture/New Testament. His squabbles with other followers of Jesus over Jewish religious practices are well documented in the Book of Acts. Other missionaries clearly existed; the early manual (*The Didache,*

c. 100 C.E.) contains instructions to early communities about how to receive such folk. Later, Patrick (5th century) preached and converted people in Ireland, Columbanus (d. 1615) in Gaul (France), and Boniface (c.675 – 754) in Germany. Other missionaries converted peoples more on the fringe of medieval civilization (Scandinavians, Slavs, et. al.). After the Reformation, Roman Catholics, mostly through the efforts of Franciscans, tried to spread the word worldwide while Protestants concentrated on native peoples they encountered and conquered, largely in North America. By the twentieth century, much missionary activity concentrated on alleviating illness and helping disaster victims more than conversions, though a vague division exists between denominations doing charitable work (mainline Protestants and Roman Catholics) and those seeking converts (more fundamentalist Protestants). These trends continue in the twenty first century.

**Excommunication.**

Excommunication emerged early in Christian history as the nascent church excluded people who behaved in a way (think sin) considered inconsistent with Christian beliefs. The rest of the congregation was to shun the person, but more importantly the individual was denied church rites, especially the sacraments. After Christianity became the religion of the Roman Empire and then of medieval Europe, the consequences of excommunication became more than just spiritual; society on the whole encouraged its members to avoid the outcast. For kings and nobles in those feudal days, excommunication meant one's vassals were freed of their oaths to one, i.e., rebellion was legitimate.

However, the line between sin and political opposition to the church organization could often be thin or movable. The Investiture Contest of the eleventh century produced papal excommunication of a German Holy Roman Emperor over the issue of who was top dog in those days. Once that boundary had been crossed, popes blatantly used excommunication in attempts to gain more political power; such actions caused the power to fall into disrepute, and political leaders ceased to fear excommunication.

Excommunication is still available in many denominations, not just Roman Catholicism, but rarely used. Some denominations in the United States such as the Amish, sometimes practice shunning which, in a close knit group, can be devastating to the individual.

**Santa Claus.**

Saint Nicholas, a bishop of Myro in modern Turkey about 300 C.E., had stories told about his generosity to the poor, and he became the patron saint of Russian children, giving them presents on his feast day, December 6. Over the years and with movement westward, the bishop's robe became the red suit and the various other trappings the Thoughtful associate with Christmas were added to his name and the tradition. While the nineteenth century was crucial in American developments, the entire tradition seems very malleable and has numerous international variations. He is not an important figure in the history of Christianity.

**Babylonian Captivity.**

The term "Babylonian Captivity" covers two separate historical events. The first, and the more literal, occurred in the sixth century B.C.E. when the population (or at least the leaders) of the southern kingdom of Judah, the area in and around Jerusalem, were deported by their conquerors to live in Babylon, 600 miles to the east. They or their descendants were allowed to return to Jerusalem later in the sixth century. This event is also called the "Exile."

From 1309 to 1377 C.E., the popes, long-time residents in Rome, found the city too tumultuous and the power of the king of France too great to be opposed, so the papacy took up residence at Avignon, just outside the kingdom of France. The need for money led to the development of new procedures to raise same as well as some personal corruption. Add in behavioral improprieties, and the result was activities that led the poet Petrarch to describe Avignon as the "sewer of Babylon" because Babylon had long been described in the Hebrew Bible/Old Testament as an ungodly city. The pope seemed to be held captive by the king of France and the behavior at Avignon was often ungodly. Hence Babylonian Captivity.

### Scholasticism

Angels on the heads of a pin, how many are there? Such is the popular image of scholasticism, a term that goes back to ancient times but which is used most often to describe the scholarship of the Middle Ages. Scholastics taught at schools—places, in the West, where teaching little beyond reading and writing by a select few. By the twelfth century, these scholars had evolved into more specialized fields such as philosophy and theology. With the appearance of the university in the thirteenth century, scholasticism became confined to that institution.

The usual means of a scholastic argument was the dialectic, the purpose of which was to use opposites to rule out error, resolve contradictions, and reach a Truth. The image of arguing about how many angels could stand on the head of a pin was actually an argument about infinity. As angels had no substance, a very large number could be crowded onto a small platform. If you added one more, what would the new number be? The Thoughtful may recall the difficulties of understanding infinity from their days of mathematical study. In Christianity, scholasticism was a logical development from the role of Greek-educated leaders in the early church. In fact, many of the categories and concepts of ancient Greek thought popped up again in scholastic arguments. As they do today.

### Lent.

A period of 40 days, not including Sundays, before Easter, Lent was first mentioned in the fourth century. It was a period of fasting (one meal per day), with no meat or fish; this tradition led to the celebrations immediately before its commencement: Carnival, *Carne vale*, farewell meat. It was, in medieval times, a period of penance for those in trouble with the church; they were welcomed back into good graces towards the end of Lent.

### Donation of Constantine.

A forgery of the eighth century purporting to record the Emperor Constantine's conversion and cure from leprosy, all done by Pope Sylvester I. In gratitude, the emperor gave the pope secular rule of Rome and central Italy (the Papal States). In reality, the Carolingian kings gave that area's control to the pope in the eighth century, but the pope didn't want to be beholden to them; hence the forgery. The document was exposed as a forgery by Lorenzo Valla in 1440 and is one of the first signs of the awakening of historical consciousness in the Renaissance.

## Modern Christianity.

### Witchcraft.

Most world cultures have practices that can be labeled as "witchcraft" which is one response to the problems of bad, evil even, things that happen to people. In the Western tradition, most associate it, incorrectly, with the Middle Ages while, in fact, the major outbursts occurred in the sixteenth and seventeenth centuries, after the Middle Ages.

The search for someone to blame, a scapegoat, often focused on those on society's margins, the poor, the old, often women. In an age when clergy could, and did, pray for divine intervention to affect warfare, bring rain or cure disease, it was an easy step to think those things were the result of the devil's actions. Just as God had angels to help, so the devil must have had witches. Scholars explain the spate, in which perhaps 100,000 people were executed, as connected to the economic and social upheavals of the day. Torture led to confessions, and witch hunters profited from the mania that resulted. The issue died out about 1700 as skepticism more heavily influenced the intellectuals. Also the cultural leaders of the eighteenth century distrusted passion and promoted reasonableness, which helped bank the fires of the craze.

## Pilgrim's Progress.

In *Pilgrim's Progress*, one of the most popular books in English language literature (which the Thoughtful have never read), John Bunyon (1628 – 88) follows the travels and travails of the character Christian as he moves to the Heavenly City. Several names and places, such as "Slough of Despond" and "Mr. Worldly Wiseman," have become common in everyday language of the Thoughtful.

## Masons.

Masonry, or freemasonry, developed in Britain in the seventeenth century and spread to the Continent in the eighteenth century. The lodges practiced a kind of religion in that they sought to improve their members' behavior. Belief in a Supreme Being is the credo, basically a deism, which led to hostility by organized religions, especially Roman Catholicism. Secrecy, including handshakes, passwords, ceremonies, and lodges not open to the public, has led to many charges of undetectable, maybe sinister, influence on public affairs. In the eighteenth century perhaps 50,000 members discussed Enlightenment ideas, and many of society's leaders were members, including George Washington and Benjamin Franklin

In the nineteenth century, schisms occurred and today Masons around the planet belong to several separate groups. Women are not admitted as members but often have separate, similar organizations such as the Order of the Eastern Star. In the United States, Scottish Rite, a subpart of Freemasonry, is popular and encompasses a system whereby a Mason progresses through 33 degrees, with such titles as Brother of the Forest and Elu of the Twelve. Masonry may be declining in popularity as the Thoughtful probably do not know many Masons today.

## Millenarianism.

The belief the end of the world is coming, soon, has a long history in Christianity. Jesus' early followers, including Paul, thought it would happen in their lifetimes, and when it didn't, some of their writings had to be reinterpreted. The last book of the Christian scripture/New Testament, Revelation, while written to explain problems and persecutions to Christians of the late first century, has been the source of ideas about the end, the second coming of Christ, etc., throughout history.

The idea of an end time being near was alive in the Middle Ages, but the church didn't encourage it. Not surprisingly, during the Reformation things heated up among some Protestants, especially many Anabaptists. Things started to get precise when James Ussher, Archbishop of Armagh in Ireland, working during the tumultuous years of the English Civil War, calculated the creation of the world to be October 23, 4004 B.C.E. From that date people decided the second coming would be 6000 years after the creation and would inaugurate the 1000 year millennium. (All this 7000-year stuff comes from 2 Peter 3:8 where the writer equates one day for God as 1000 years; and since creation took seven days, that period will be the earth's age span also.)

Nineteenth-century America produced several millenarians and some of their followers still exist, though with dampened certainty about date of the end time. Whether the last era precedes or follows the second coming of Christ has been open to debate. The American fervor began when a Vermont Baptist farmer, William Miller decided, from his study of the Bible, the end would come in 1843. Thousands accepted the idea; as 1843 closed, Miller recalculated and came up with October 22, 1844 (October 22 comes from Ussher's calculations). After another disappointment, the Millerites stayed convinced of an imminent end but quit setting dates. (Twice bitten, they got wiser.) They morphed into the Seventh-Day Adventists and became sabbatarians (worship on Saturday, the Jewish Sabbath). (Today, they also have a penchant for health food; John Kellogg of cereal fame was a member.)

The next appearance of this type of thing occurred in the 1870s when Charles Taze Russell (1852 – 1916) discerned the end-date was 1914, and his followers organized as Jehovah's Witnesses. After 1914 passed, 1915, 1918, 1920, 1925, 1941, 1975, and 1994 were all tried. Settling down as a denomination, Jehovah's Witnesses believe heaven is limited to 144,000 admittees, a number they find in Revelation. In U.S. history, Jehovah's Witnesses, who are also sabbatarians, have been especially prominent in Supreme Court cases involve church/state issues.

Today, a common approach to the end times is called "Dispensationalism." Dispensationalists read the Bible and decide world history is divided into seven dispensations—eras—which turned out to be 1000 years each. Not surprisingly, they also concluded they lived in the sixth dispensation, and the crossover to the seventh will be exciting, to say the least. Perhaps the most popular dispensationalism is associated with the Rapture, the beginning of the last era. Today's Rapture comes from the mind of John Nelson Darby, an Englishman, who believed in a single moment the true believers will be whisked away to heaven where they will have front row seats to watch a seven-year carnage of struggle between evil and those left behind who were shocked into Christian belief by events. Then Jesus will return, defeat the forces of evil at Armageddon and rule for 1000 years, the seventh and last dispensation.

In 1909 Cyrus Schofield produced a very popular Bible that supported this malarkey; his Bible is still in print. This basic outline provided grist for the mill of several authors, most notably those of the "Left Behind" books which have sold in the millions. However, there is not just one scenario as Hal Lindsey in *The Late Great Planet Earth* had the Soviets as the bad guys, something events have overtaken. The Thoughtful might read one of these books or at least a summary and be scared about what some people will accept. The appeal of the Rapture is almost entirely to Protestants and the more fundamental among them. No scholar takes any of this gibberish seriously, but some powerful people, most famously James Watt, Secretary of the Interior under Ronald Reagan, have accepted it. Rapture enthusiasts—like millenarians historically always—think the end will come during their lifetimes. From the Thoughtfuls' point of view, one of the nasty consequences of believing in the Rapture is the world, ending soon, need not be tended to. When a Secretary of the Interior of the United States thinks fire will soon consume things, he is not very interested in conservation. Also, millenarians tend to see themselves as superior, knowing, as they do, they'll get to watch the rest of us struggle for seven years.[6]

Now, fast forward to 1999 C.E. and recall all the hoopla about Y2K, the year 2000. Some of the fear and anticipation was computer programs could not handle the conversion to year 2000, but most was pure millennialism. (Recall if the world was created in 4004 B.C.E., time had run out in 1996, but apparently math and details are not strong suits with millenarians.)

In addition to these events, many of which look silly with the benefit of hindsight, some tragedies have unfolded as a result of millennial thinking. More than 900 members, including children, of the People's Temple, an organization founded by Jim Jones in the 1950s, committed suicide in 1978 in Jonestown, Guyana. Terming their religion "apostolic socialism," they drew on parts of Christianity as well as other thought systems. In 1997 nearly 40 members of Heaven's Gate committed suicide in San Diego. Founded by Marshall Applewhite, Heaven's Gate combined some Christianity with a mishmash of ideas about other worlds and other dimensions. The Branch Davidians, a splinter group of Seventh-Day Adventists, located themselves in Waco, Texas, under the leadership of David Koresh. In 1993 nearly 80 people died during a standoff with agents of the U.S. government. And these kinds of groups aren't limited to the United States as the Order of the Solar Temple, Colonia Diguidad, and other similar cults flourish around the world. They all seem to share some of the apocalyptic thinking that many Christians find in Revelation in the Christian scripture/New Testament and are led, dominated, by a charismatic individual.

The Thoughtful can reflect virtually all millenarians think the end will come in their lifetimes. The ego, the arrogance, of believing the deity organized the world around oneself!! Hmm.....

### Papal Infallibility.

Since at least the twelfth century, maybe as early as the fifth century, the bishops of Rome (popes) have claimed a position within the church that is

---

[6] See Barbara Rossing, *The Rapture Exposed* (Westview, 2004) for a fuller critique of this notion.

superior to all others, be they bishops, emperors, mystics, or councils. The notion, in certain circumstances, the pope cannot speak error has lingered in the shadows for a long time. However, it was only in 1870 Pius IX got the First Vatican Council to agree to the idea of infallibility meaning in certain select and special situations, the pope can utter Truth. No list of these utterances exists and they haven't been common. Nonetheless, they constitute an obstacle to Roman Catholic dealings with other denominations and cause the Thoughtful to wonder at the logic of this part of Christianity. To Protestants the doctrine reinforces all their beliefs and prejudices about the nature of the person in the Roman Catholic pew.

**Syllabus of Errors.**

Two sets of propositions condemned by the popes in 1864 and 1907 rejected much modern thought, including the following:

-prophesies and miracles in the Bible are not literally true

-Protestantism is another form of Christianity (versus being error)

-moral laws do not need divine sanction

-public schools are to be secular

-the pope "ought to reconcile himself to, and agree with, progress, liberalism, and civilization as lately introduced"

-and more than140 similar statements.

The general thrust was traditional religion, as defined by the pope, was correct and modern study of the same was forbidden. The documents had the anti-intellectual effect of crippling Roman Catholic abilities to pursue science or biblical studies.

**Christian Science.**

In the nineteenth century, the conflict of science and religion began that endures today. Various efforts to reconcile the two or escape any contradiction include Christian Science. Mary Baker Eddy (1821 – 1910) developed views of Christianity and Jesus that argued evil and sickness can be conquered by God's love, especially in prayer. Hence, medical treatment, which wasn't much help at the time anyway as germ theory wasn't accepted, is foolish. These ideas fit well with the late nineteenth-century efforts to bridge the material/spiritual divide, but the Thoughtful are more likely to seek treatment for medical matters elsewhere.

**Scopes Monkey Trial.**

In 1926 John Scopes, a Tennessee science teacher, intentionally violated a law prohibiting the teaching of evolution. In the subsequent trial William Jennings Bryan and Clarence Darrow, two famous lawyers of the day, squared off, and, after eight days, Scopes was found guilty and fined $100 by the judge. On appeal, the conviction was voided on the technicality the jury, not the judge, should have set the fine. There was no retrial.

The case was further publicized in 1955 with the play *Inherit the Wind* and its subsequent film. The U.S. Supreme Court, in another case, subsequently voided such anti-evolutionary laws such as Tennessee's. The overall result of the trial and its subsequent treatment has been to identify the anti-evolutionist movement as uneducated.

**Snake Handling.**

One of the more bizarre practices found in Christianity is the handling of poisonous snakes by believers as a sign of their faith. The scriptural basis is Mark 16:17 – 20. The Markian verses were not part of the original version of that gospel but were later added, probably in the second century. In the United States, the practice itself is limited to some small (no wonder!) pentecostal sects, largely in the Appalachian region. The practice is illegal in many states, but law enforcement usually ignores it.

**Faith Healing.**

Whenever folks think the world can be changed at God's will or whim, efforts will seek to bring changes about through appeals to God; hence, certain kinds of prayer. Faith healing is a type of prayer used when a condition, perhaps a disease or a birth defect, is changed, cured, by prayer and the laying on of hands in a public setting, usually a church, by clergy. The practice is not limited to Christianity, the reported actions of Jesus in the Christian scripture/New Testament form a basis for it. The Roman Catholic Church even has a ritual for driving demons out of an affected person: exorcism. And Christian Science as a denomination is premised upon a belief in the efficacy of the practice. The pentecostal tradition has its share of faith healers from Aimee Semple McPherson in the 1920s and 1930s to Oral Roberts after the mid-century. Studies of the results of faith healing consistently fail to find evidence of success of the practice and, in fact, occasionally turn up outright fraud. Of course, believers who see an attempt at faith healing fail can fall back on the explanation the sufferer's faith wasn't strong enough, a nasty slap. The idea that positive thinking and belief can bring about improvement in some people is not doubted but the Thoughtful don't see God operating in any way that supports faith healing.

### *The DaVinci Code.*

Why was *The DaVinci Code* controversial in some religious circles? (If you haven't read it or seen the movie and want to maintain the suspense, don't read this section.)

The book's theme—Jesus and Mary Magdalene were married and had children whose descendants are alive today—is fictional in that absolutely no evidence exists to support it. However, no evidence explicitly denies it either. Moreover, enough good history is scattered throughout the book to lend credibility to the conspiracy theory, which, like all conspiracies can't be proved. So there you are.

Why does it matter if Jesus was married? Married or single, the gospels are silent so no problem of literalism is involved. It seems that, at some level, many believers, who see Jesus as God, have trouble thinking of him as a sexual being (they ignore the problem of how the Holy Spirit, another aspect of God, got Mary pregnant). That the church in the Middle Ages and the Roman Catholic Church today advocates celibacy for the clergy probably contributes to the rejection of this possibility, since the clergy are supposedly living in imitation of Jesus. But some Protestants, usually the more fundamentalist sort, also had great difficulty with the idea of Jesus' marriage and their clergy are not celibate. Probably this problem is the power of tradition operating. As few had ever thought of Jesus in the married state, they had trouble accepting another hypothesis. Certainly, his life, as reported in the gospels, wasn't consistent with the responsibilities of a husband and father; wandering about with no apparent means of support isn't what a good man, much less God, should do. To the Thoughtful, this controversy seems all out of proportion. Why was it important?

**Psychohistory.**

One fad swept through parts of the scholarly communities in the twentieth century was the application of the ideas of Sigmund Freud to aspects of society beyond the individual on the couch. One practitioner of this approach was Eric Ericson, now known for his idea about stages of adult life, particularly the "mid-life crisis." Ericson used his theories in writing about Martin Luther, the great sixteenth-century reformer. Though Ericson couldn't talk to Luther, something many Freudians think essential, he did benefit from the large number of writings by Luther and about him by his contemporaries. The result, *Young Man Luther*, sought to interpret Luther's life in terms of his relationship with his father. To Ericson, Luther believed he could never earn his father's love and respect—the old man does appear to have been foreboding and probably controlling—which led Luther to reject the medieval church's notions earning God's favor by good behavior and performing the sacraments. Hence, Luther came to believe God's love couldn't be earned but had to be taken on trust, a belief reformers summarized as "justification by faith." Ericson believed Luther came to this insight while in the closet (toilet), and it was so liberating, so freeing, his lifetime problem of constipation ended simultaneously. An entertaining, unprovable theory.

A sixteenth-century mystic, Teresa of Avila, attempted to convey a mystical experience she had:

> An angel in body form, such as I am not in the habit of seeing except very rarely … not tall, but short, and very beautiful.... In his hands I saw a great golden spear, and at the iron tip there appeared to be a point of fire. This he plunged into my heart several times that it penetrated to my entrails. When he pulled it out, I felt that he took them with it, and left me utterly consumed by the great love of God. The pain was so severe that it made me utter several moans. The sweetness caused by this intense pain is so extreme that one cannot possibly wish it to cease, nor is one's soul content then with anything but God....[7]

Psychohistory can add some spice to Christian history, especially if one remembers a lot of Freudianism is about sex. For instance, reread that passage with Freudian glasses on. Fun, huh?

### Church of Scientology.

Founded by L. Ron Hubbard (1911 – 86), a science fiction author, in the 1950s, Scientology has religious ideas, such as reincarnation, mixed with science and social science. It appears not to have any elements of Christianity in it despite the use of "church."

### Spirituality.

Many folk today claim to be spiritual but not religious. What this may mean is they think there is something beyond, outside, whatever, this material life. They also probably mean "religion" denotes organizations, usually churches, the denominations. Some consider themselves Christians while others pursue their understandings of world religions, and many practice activities they consider "spiritual," such as meditation, prayer, yoga. As a generalization, spirituality is an individual, not a group, pursuit.

---

[7] J.M. Cohen, trans., *The Life of Saint Teresa of Avila by Herself* (London, 1957) 210.

# Miscellany.

## Soul.

"Body and soul"—an expression so common the Thoughtful have rarely concerned themselves with it. For many Christians, the soul, with its hoped-for destination in heaven, is the be-all and end-all of life's earthly purpose. However, the soul is a curiosity as scientists can find no place for it in their explanations and examinations of human beings, even though a Massachusetts doctor weighed six dying patients and concluded the soul tipped the scales at 21 grams

Ancient Jews did not divide the human into body and soul or body, soul, and spirit—these notions come from other places. The Jews of the Hebrew Bible/Old Testament, which probably included Jesus, had no account of human division. Thus when the post-Exilic literature spoke of a resurrection, it envisioned folks reappearing much like they had existed before death. The Greeks, on the other hand, had a rich variety of views of the human which included a body-soul duality. Most famously, Plato's myth of the cave in *The Republic* separated our world from the "real," "true" world of Forms. Similarly, the human soul, considered separate from the body had the task of seeking God—not the God of the Jews or Christian but the ultimate center of being, perfection, goodness, whatever. When Greek-educated folk started joining Christianity, they brought this baggage of a body-soul dichotomy with them.

Some Jews, starting about the time of the Maccabean revolt, began to envision a resurrection, and notions of soul fit this view easily, as it was clear bodies disintegrated after death. Hellenistic thought provided the soul, so for some Jews of the Jesus era, a soul that had eternal qualities was imaginable. Once Christians accepted these notions of a body-soul dualism, they fit nicely with an afterlife; all part of the developments of the first few centuries of the Christian era.

Today, many Christians consider the soul their true essence. That soul will rise ("fly") to heaven and so resemble the body it will be recognizable to and by others. Some folk have "out of body" experiences, often during surgery when they view events from high in the operating room. (One surgeon placed objects atop cabinets such that they would be visible only from the ceiling; no one reported seeing them.)

**Tradition.**

A major difference between Protestants and Roman Catholics today arises from attitudes to the past. Protestants, ever since Luther, have denied the validity of events and interpretations since, and other than, the Bible. "*Sola scriptura*," ("only scripture") is their motto. Roman Catholics, on the other hand, accept traditions that have developed since the early days of the Jesus people. For instance, Paul wrote in Ephesians 5:31 – 2 marriage was a sacrament, and so it developed even though Jesus had said nothing on the matter. (The medieval church's development of the sacrament of marriage was based on a bad translation, which is another issue.) Today Protestants do not treat marriage as a sacrament though the Roman Catholic Church still does.

Similarly, the words attributed to Jesus that Peter was the rock upon which the church was to be built, combined with the (unprovable) tradition Peter was the first bishop of Rome (bishops didn't exist yet) were developed into support for the leadership of the pope in the Roman Catholic Church.

**Unitarians.**

Rejecting the doctrine of the Trinity and the divinity of Jesus, Unitarians prefer worshipping a God without those complications. Unitarianism has been around throughout Christian history but received a boost at the Reformation when Michael Servetus (1511 – 53) and Bernardino Ochino (1487 – 1584) espoused the view, which was soon followed by Socinus (Fausto Paolo Sozzini) (1539 – 1604).

In the United States, shortly after the American Revolution, Congregationalist preachers in Boston often adopted the idea and, as they had no superior supervising them, many simply stopped worshipping as Christians. In 1961 a loose group called the American Unitarian Association merged with the Universalist Church of America, which believed salvation is for all, to form the Unitarian Universalist Association.

**Symbols and Numbers.**

Probably all religions have symbols, though some such as Islam don't use them in art. Ancients had an elaborate use of numbers of mystical or symbolic purposes. Even a casual reader of scripture spots 3, 7, 12, and 40. Today the number 3 pops up in lots of situations (repetitions in jokes; family size: dad, mom, kid; folk tales, even some anthropological interpretative structures). Its use in the Resurrection story and the Trinity should not, therefore, be a surprise. Umberto Eco's *The Name of the Rose* captures, in fiction, this attitude well. Several books and websites go into much more detail and with more examples. Christianity, especially in the Middle Ages, became rife with the symbolic numbers, colors, and words, and what follows is a minimal listing.

Numbers:

1 unity, God
3 Trinity
4 world (directions, winds), gospel writers
7 totality, perfection (source might be phases of the moon)
12 tribes of Israel, Christians worldwide (source is lunar calendar)
40 testing (Flood duration, Jesus in wilderness) (source is length of a generation)
666 a mark signifying evil in Revelation 13:18
1000 large number, infinity

Colors:

| | |
|---|---|
| Green | triumph over death |
| Red | blood, fire, violence |
| Black | death |
| White | victory |
| Blue | heaven |
| Gray | repentance |
| Purple | penitence |

Words:

| | |
|---|---|
| Apple | sin |
| Chalice | communion |
| Cross | Christianity, Jesus' death (comes in lots of styles) |
| Dove | Holy Spirit, peace |
| Eagle | Resurrection |
| Fish | Jesus Christ, God's Son, Savior (Greek first letters of those words spell "fish" in Greek), also disciples as fishers of men |
| lamb | Jesus |
| ox | strength, service |
| pomegranate | its many seeds are the universal Church |
| shamrock | Trinity |
| triangle | Trinity |

Just as today certain numbers, especially 13, connote bad things, the book of Revelation (13:18) gave the number 666 as the number of "the beast," all part of the apocalyptic vision of the scripture. In the Hebrew Bible/Old Testament, the apocalyptic book of Daniel also has lots of numbers about the end time. Today the Rapture folk think this is the seventh, and last, age of people. And the Thoughtful remember too well the hullabaloo over Y2K which was connected to this fetish with numbers.

## Evangelism.

In Christianity, the word means spreading the message about Jesus and dates from the very first days of the Jesus people. The authors of the four gospels are called Evangelists, because they are seeking to explain Jesus to the Mediterranean world. At the Reformation the term was sometimes applied to denominations focused heavily on the gospels rather than other parts of the Bible. In the United States today it is often used to refer to conservative Christians who are more open about their religion and their efforts to convert others than the typical mainline Protestant denomination member. To a considerable extent, the groups favoring evangelicalism and those interpreting scripture in a fundamental, literal manner overlap in membership (See chapter 8).

### Images of God.

The Thoughtful, depending on their background, may have images of the deity that are difficult to discard and may preclude an understanding of God in today's progressive Christianity. Voltaire's cynical remark we make God in our own image seems to hold true throughout history, even today.

In the Hebrew Bible/Old Testament, God appears in many ways. He is heard walking in the Garden of Eden. Meeting him in a burning bush and atop a mountain later, Moses later is led across the desert by a pillar of fire. Only in the very late book of Daniel does the grandfather image appear where he is described as "the ancient of days" (Daniel 7:9). More often, God's characteristics are described: loves like a forgiving husband (Hosea 2, 3), had tenderness of a mother (Isaiah 49:15), and so forth.

Michelangelo's Sistine chapel ceiling portrayal capped medieval art's attempts and provides the prototype today of a bearded grandfather floating in, or standing on, the clouds. (Athletes frequently point up after a successful performance.) Since then popular culture, such as movies and novels, has also had images including a cigar-smoking George Burns (Oh, God!) and a black woman (*The Shack*). In the West, God has often been a judge, white, and male. (Avoiding the use of the masculine helps the Thoughtful avoid an image of a supernatural being.)

Today's religious folk often end up with "God is a mystery" or the best image we have is Jesus (which some then visualize as a young man, *a la* Werner Salman's famous painting).

### Satan

Devil, Beelzebub, Metistopheles, Prince of Darkness, Lucifer, and lots of other names and titles are given to the supreme embodiment of evil. Often he is described as a fallen angel, a story told in Revelation 12:7 – 9. In the

Hebrew Bible/Old Testament "Satan" is used in the sense of "adversary" or "accuser," not the source of evil the term later came to mean. Thus Satan is a being around God who eggs the deity into mistreating Job. By the second century B.C.E., the word was used as a proper noun. However, the strict monotheism of Jewish religion did not permit Satan to be a rival of God or a source of evil. Christian scripture/New Testament writings very quickly started moving the word to identify a being who is the source of evil. Paul's letters, the earliest surviving Christian writings, contain hints of such a usage. In the gospels, Satan is often still the adversary, a tempter, but also appears in ways similar to today's usage. Jesus' exorcisms are described in the context of Satan being the master of the demons afflicting people (exorcisms appear less often in the later gospels as it opened Jesus to the criticism of being in league with the chief of evil). Also Satan tempts Jesus with visions of control and power, although at the end time, Satan and his followers will all be cast into eternal fire (Matthew 25:41). By 100 C.E., Satan has become a being, who is the embodiment of evil and who can rule in opposition to God.

Satan is a response to the problem of evil. If there is no force or person making evil things happen, God must be doing it, an unpleasant thought. On the other hand, if Satan is causing evil, an all-powerful God must be tolerating it, also an unpleasant thought. The Middle Ages saw a great deal of creativity as ideas about hell often dominated thinking. The modern view of Satan is largely a post-scriptural development. Christian art is filled with imaginative representations of the concept of Satan, and about one-third of Americans believe Satan is a living being.

*The Scriptorium*

TEN

# *Don't We Have Only One? The Bible*

For many, especially Protestant believers of a conservative stripe, leaving a discussion of the Bible to the last chapter reflects bad priorities. For them, the holy book is honored—indeed almost worshipped—and should be given pride of place next to Jesus. By now, however, the Thoughtful realize the story of Christianity is more complex than they, or many believers, had thought. A reason for the location of the chapter could be that understanding the Bible requires much prior knowledge, knowledge the Thoughtful now possess. Enjoy.

This chapter deals with subjects to which the Thoughtful have not given much attention: the Bible: its composition, copying, translation and themes. After all, the Bible is the Bible, is it not? No and yes. Few believers question the Bible is the Word of God, but there is much dispute about what are the actual words of God. Another way of phrasing is to say while the general messages of the Bible are agreed upon—though different groups place emphasis on different messages—the translations available are myriad. Moreover, life is more complex than that sentence suggests. Scripture has good stories, sources of hope, inspiration of personal understanding, discussions of how the world works, ideas about salvation, a covenant, personal holiness rules, examples of love and mercy, etc.; various groups latch onto certain aspects and as a result can have vastly different religious experiences. Often, groups believe and act so differently the Thoughtful might wonder if all variety is part of the same faith tradition.

The Thoughtful, having thought little about it, may be surprised to learn there is no "original" Bible or even any one book of the Bible. We have no work in the author's hand. None. Rather, what we have today are copies and translations of copies and translations. Moreover, each copy or translation has within it an interpretation, often not explicitly acknowledged, but an interpretation nonetheless.

Unlike scholars, readers, especially students, usually do not worry about the origin of a reading; they're too focused on mastering the text. However, in matters religious, especially Christian, arguments break out easily about the text, its accuracy and validity, because many believers seek to guide their lives by the words of the Bible. The purpose of the study of Christianity differs from other subjects, at least for some, as salvation (which means many things) is the object, not just enjoyment or deepening personal understanding. Most Christians read translations, often translations of translations; because they cannot settle on exactly what to include in the Bible, the disputes are endless.

Coming from a Greek word meaning "books," the Bible is a collection of books not necessarily intended to be gathered together. Today "Bible" is a singular noun and refers to those writings collectively. The Hebrew Bible, called the Old Testament by Christians, is the basis of Judaism. The Bible, for Christians, is divided into the Hebrew Bible/Old Testament and Christian scripture/New Testament. This division arose from theologians who decided the older books, the Hebrew Bible/Old Testament, contain the evidence of God's agreement with the Israelites which for many Christians predicted the coming of Jesus. The Christian scripture/New Testament contains the stories that make up Christianity and show the new agreement God has with Christians. Moreover, the contemporary Bible used by Christians is the result of a lot of pushing and pulling by individuals and groups; it only emerged after the second century. Judaism and some aspects of Christianity include different books and in different order in the Hebrew Bible/Old Testament; various branches of Christianity differ on which books they include. Many early writings were omitted from the Christian scripture/New Testament, but Christians do not disagree much, or at least heatedly, about its present content.

In this chapter the Thoughtful will discover that behind the Bible they read many issues are unresolved or are complex. It was not always so understood as close examination of scripture and the resulting discussion of the problems created thereby only got serious in the seventeenth century. Earlier thinkers knew of inconsistencies, but their general attitude to scripture did not lead to serious study of the issue. It was the increasing importance of skepticism during the period that goes under the general term "Enlightenment" that produced studies called "biblical criticism" or "historical criticism" or "higher criticism."

For some, however, such criticism is irrelevant because the present text—whatever its antecedents—is perfectly acceptable. In other words, the truth of the text can evolve when different people and cultures look at it. How we understand something today can differ from how an ancient Israelite or medieval peasant viewed it, because, after all, Truth is eternal; perhaps we all appreciate it a bit differently, making the exact accuracy, meaning, or background of any particular text less important. The story of the blind men in India touching an elephant illustrates one aspect of this as one man, touching the side, thinks an elephant is like a wall, another, handling the tail, likens it to a whip, a third, feeling the leg, suggests a tree. All are right, albeit partially. So it is with the Bible, according to some: it contains Truth illustrated in myriad ways. Of course, we all "see" that Truth only partially. This approach is most congenial to those in the Roman Catholic and Orthodox traditions.

Protestants, especially conservative Protestants, take a different view. Truth is eternal and unchanging, and our job is to grasp it. In theory, it should mean the same thing to us as to the ancients or those of the Middle Ages. For Protestants, therefore, the text of the Bible becomes important and "getting it right" can occupy minds. One consequence of this attitude is most critical scholarship about the Bible has been in Protestant circles, especially German Protestant ones. Whether the game has been worth the candle—whether all the energy spent finding the "best" version of scripture—has been a good use of human resources is a question the Thoughtful should confront by the end of this chapter. For many scholars, after the day is done and the scholarship has been published, what remains is not a certainty but a mystery; some things just cannot be grasped intellectually.

## Hard? The Best Text.

Is the text trustworthy? The Thoughtful have little concern about the Bible they might read. However, as the stories were written long ago, copied often, and finally translated, often through several languages, the text went through many changes before it appears today.

Almost all scripture, except the obviously fictional bits such as Esther and Job in the Hebrew Bible/Old Testament or the letters of the Christian scripture/New Testament, began orally and was transmitted orally for at least some time. Even after the oral stories were committed to writing, copyists may have altered them. Thus the stories of the kings of Israel or the events of Jesus' life were not immediately written; rather they passed from mouth to mouth for a while. As oral transmission preceded many of the writings, special problems are presented for scholars. Milman Parry, whose work in the Balkans in the 1930s initiated the study of this topic, found each recitation, each performance as it were, was unique as the speaker changed things. On the other hand, a more recent study of recitations of sacred works in India indicates they varied but little.[1] The Thoughtful's experience in this area was a game called "telephone" where a person starts a story and then it is retold privately, one at a time, to others in the room until the final person gives the rendition, which usually varied significantly from the beginning version. The Thoughtful can appreciate oral transmission makes

[1] William Dalrymple, "Homer in India," *The New Yorker* Nov. 20, 2006, 52

for troubles if faithfulness to the original event is the goal, and because oral transmission preceded many of the writings, special problems are presented for scholars.

Even after the text was written, there is no Hebrew "first edition" of the Hebrew Bible/Old Testament; the Masoretic text from the 900s C.E. is the version used today. While a Greek translation, the Septuagint, has been around since Roman times, its trustworthiness as being true to the "original" is open to doubt. A group of scholars have been working since the 1950s in the Hebrew University Bible Project to gather all known variations to produce the definitive Hebrew Bible; to date they have published three books. (One estimate is it will take 200 years to finish the project.) Similarly, the earliest surviving manuscripts of the Christian scripture/New Testament, from the early second century, are scraps, and none is an original. Only in the fourth century do more complete versions turn up. Moreover, when we get to the Christian scripture/New Testament, the huge number of copies—over 5000 in Greek—makes settling on a text even more challenging. Today the Nestle-Aland version of Christian scripture/New Testament is considered the best by scholars, and it is continually updated; so far over two dozen editions have been produced.

### Easy? Copies.

A major problem in the transmission of scripture across the generations has been the copyists, who have been sloppy, ideological, or ignorant. The practice of copying scripture introduced a great deal of variation, and in many cases, no way exists to find the "original" text. Getting to an early version of the Hebrew Bible/Old Testament is difficult as the sources are limited: Masoretic version, Dead Sea Scrolls, occasional Christian materials. Before Constantine's conversion brought educated Romans into the church, the copyists of the Christian scripture/New Testament would probably not have been of top quality so changes and mistakes crept in. And no way exists to determine the oldest as a twelfth-century text might be a copy of a fourth-century one while a fifth-century version only copied another fifth-century version.

The earliest mostly complete copies of the entire Bible—Codices Alexandrinus, Vaticanus, and Sinaiticus—do not always agree though they seem to date to the same time—they might be three of the 50 copies ordered by the emperor Constantine in the fourth century C.E. And it is beginning to appear passages were altered to fit local circumstances; after all, this was not canon yet. For instance, as Jesus became divine, the statement in Matthew's gospel that even he (Jesus) did not know when the end time would come became a problem; the troubling words "nor the Son" were therefore omitted. (Matthew 24:36) Certain Christian centers were more reliable copyists, with Alexandria probably the best. However, all these copyists produced variety and one estimate finds 400,000 variations.[2]

Clearly, material was added but when or where cannot always be determined. For instance, the Dead Sea Scrolls have several versions of the book of Exodus, each longer than the one before. The Christian scripture/New Testament contains the story of the woman taken in adultery which today resides in John's gospel (8:3 – 11). It is also found in some manuscripts after John 7:36 and 21:25 and after 21:38 of Luke; it is a good story but copyists could not settle on where it belonged so they put it where they saw fit. Whether copyists altered the Hebrew Bible/Old Testament is difficult to determine because little material exists before 900 C.E. The texts of the Septuagint, the Dead Sea Scrolls, and the Masoretic version, while not in perfect harmony, do not contain major differences. With Christian scripture/New Testament, however, for at least the first 100, maybe 200 years after Jesus' death, copyists sometimes altered, by a change or an addition, a manuscript to make it reflect what it "really meant" or "should mean." Comments written in the margins might be incorporated in later versions. And no one knows how many changes were made to harmonize, or at least remove the inconsistencies between, the four gospels. The letter writer Paul, as we have his work in the Christian scripture/New Testament, made some very harsh statements about the role of women in the new movement. However, a close reader of one text (1 Corinthians 14:34 – 5) notices the

---

[2] Bart D. Ehrman, *Misquoting Jesus* (Harper/San Francisco, 2005), 72, 89.

two verses about women seem to be additions as they interrupt the flow of the letter; someone inserted a personal view. Moreover, in some early texts, these same two verses are found after 14:40, which hints strongly they were not in the original. Another example comes with the only Christian scripture/New Testament reference in 1 John 5:7 – 8 to the Trinity, a doctrine church leaders fought over for years several centuries after Jesus' death; no manuscript made before the fourteenth century had those two verses so it is a copyist's addition.[3] In 1 Timothy 3:16, today's scripture usually calls Jesus "God" but the earliest texts use "he," a significant, and theological, change. An example of outright alteration to make something "mean what it should" comes from a manuscript of the letter to the Hebrews in the Vatican library. Long ago, someone erased a word and wrote in another, but a later reader, realizing the alteration, erased the new word put back the original, and, for good measure, wrote a note in the margin to leave it alone.[4]

Who knows how many errors have unintentionally slipped in? For instance, the Septuagint lacks the verses of 1 Kings 6:11 – 13. Were they dropped or later added? Internal problems show up as the copyist (or original author), working on the book of Ezra, when making a list of priestly ancestors of Ezra, apparently skipped a line of his source (Ezra 7:1 – 5 and 1 Chronicles 6:7 – 13). In Ezekiel 4:4 – 6, someone added or miscopied numbers which makes nonsense of the passage. Getting the story straight is clearly a challenge. The book of 1 Samuel contains many stories of the interactions of Samuel, a prophet and, literally, kingmaker, and Saul, the first king of the Israelites. The translator must work with a text in Hebrew, and the consonants for "Samuel" and "Saul" are the same, though in different order. A copyist's mistake any time over the many centuries the text has been copied could alter a sentence from its original meaning.

Copies of Christian scripture/New Testament have so many differences it is often impossible to determine whether the variation was intentional or not. However, some changes are apparent. A clear instance is the odd ending of Mark. It stops in mid-sentence, perhaps as a literary device or because

---

[3] Bart Ehrmann, *The New Testament* (Oxford University Press, 2000), 447.

[4] Ehrman, *Misquoting*, 81. Ehrman, *New Testament*, 445.

the author died or maybe part of the manuscript was lost. Later two versions of an ending were added, one including the dangerous practice of handling poisonous snakes as a sign of salvation (16:17 – 8). Also the gospel of Matthew was not written and never changed as, for instance, 24:36 (mentioned above) was altered so Jesus could remain omniscient. As with many early writings, numerous variations appear, as copyists altered details to fit their view of how the story should be told. Also a few "corrections" or changes crept in from other gospels; for example, 9:34, 16:2 – 3, 18:11, 19:29 (wife), 23:14, of Matthew and perhaps other verses probably come from Luke's gospel. And 11:25 – 30 stands out as unusual in Matthew's view of Jesus but does sound much more like the Jesus in John's gospel. In John's gospel itself, probably more sources were found or perhaps someone decided some creative writing was necessary as three chapters (15 – 17) appear "dropped into" a previous manuscript; Jesus says "Arise, let us go" at the end of chapter 14 but doesn't get moving until chapter 18. Chapters 1 and 2 of Luke's gospel look like later additions. And these examples just touch the surface of the changes to the original writings.

The gospels, written between 65 and 100, were based upon oral traditions, and additions expanded those traditions. One can imagine audience interruptions of a speaker with questions about Jesus' ancestry, his relationship with the deity etc. With research, the speaker could find some information, e.g., Jesus' brother James lived into the 60s in Jerusalem. Other additions were made to fit popular conceptions about holy men. Being the child of a god was well known in Greek, and probably in every other people's mythology; stories about Alexander the Great and Augustus included the notion their fathers were deities. Being a god even though a child of a human also occurred elsewhere; Apollo, the son of Zeus, was born of a Greek woman, and in Mesopotamia Gilgamesh had a goddess mother. Similarly, Jesus was portrayed as son of God. Descent from royalty was a common claim in families, especially noble ones, and can still be found in some of your neighbors' (fanciful?) genealogies; similarly, Jesus' descent from King David. Some additions were to serve a theological purpose such as the flight to Egypt of Jesus' family to escape Herod's slaughter of young boys, which has echoes of the story of Moses—which is a theme of Matthew's gospel—or the visit of the wise men/magi, making connections to non-Jews as well as the Near Eastern intellectual center of Mesopotamia. In Jesus' day miracles and resurrections were not unknown. Stories about Jesus are, therefore, often similar to those about Buddha, Horus, Mithras, and other figures from the religious history of other cultures. Virgin births, miracles, disciples, death and resurrection—the list can be lengthened considerably—all appear in connection with these other figures. So what is going on? One possibility is early followers of Jesus simply borrowed stories from other traditions and applied them to Jesus. Or, perhaps coincidences occurred. The Thoughtful can accept those possibilities, but the most attractive one is ancients had certain ways to explain things. A person of outsized influence in life had to be the child of a god. Miracles, especially nature miracles, demonstrated a god's favor or god-like powers themselves. Without disciples, the stories would disappear so of course there were disciples. Death and resurrection illustrate the unpopularity of the individual and the later discovery of that person's ideas or importance. And so it goes.

The gospels contain blatantly creative writing; whether the original author wrote them or a copyist added them to help with the narrative cannot be determined. Several episodes based on gospels themselves, have no possible source. For instance, Jesus, on the day before his troubles with the authorities in Jerusalem turned deadly, went to the garden of Gethsemane to pray. The gospels are very clear he was alone as he left three disciples behind who then fell asleep.[5] Yet the contents of his prayer are reported, and those contents do not sound like something he would have told the disciples later. Anyway, he was promptly arrested and ceased having contact with his disciples. Another example: during Jesus' troubles with the authorities, especially his trial by Pilate, Jesus and Pilate appear to be alone but their conversations are reported. In these instances one can ask how and from whom did the gospel writers learn the content? The stories of the garden of Gethsemane and Pilate's trial fit well the themes the authors are developing, and scholars

[5] Mark's gospel has a naked boy running away from the scene at Gethsemane, which may be taken from Amos 2:16 or it may be simply odd. Or something else.

therefore believe they are the creations of the authors (or maybe one author and then used by the others), not factual events. A clear example of a created story can be found in John's telling of the Nicodemus story (3:1 – 5). Nicodemus, a Pharisee came to Jesus at night to ask questions—scholars refer to this story as "Nick at Nite"—and engaged in a discussion in which Jesus says one must be "born again." Nicodemus asks how one gets back into the womb of one's mother. The source of the confusion is the Greek word "from above" (Jesus' meaning) can also mean "again" (Nicodemus's understanding). Unfortunately for the historical accuracy of the story, the same confusion does not arise in Aramaic, the language both spoke, because different words are used for the two ideas; the story does not go back to Jesus, but whether created by John or a copyist cannot be determined.

These issues do not invalidate the entire story in the gospels but they make one humble in being certain about any one detail. On the other hand, Mark, the first gospel author, writing in the 60s, probably had an audience, some of whom had experienced the living Jesus, so the amount of his invention may have had some limits, but later authors had more freedom. Matthew and Luke both get Jesus' great sermon from Q; in Matthew it is called "The Sermon on the Mount," and in Luke "The Sermon on the Plain." Moreever, Matthew's version is longer which suggests Luke's version is closer to the original. (Scholars have an understanding when two texts differ, the shorter is older; it is more likely someone expanded than abridged the text—such is the nature of writers, except those at *Reader's Digest.*)

Despite the efforts of at least a few copyists to harmonize the gospels, inconsistencies and problems remain. Many things the listener/reader accepts as part of the Jesus story are not in John's gospel. No birth story, virgin or otherwise, appears. Nor does any temptation in the wilderness and explicit baptism by John the Baptizer occur. Indeed John the Baptizer never is given the descriptor "the Baptizer." Jesus does not tell parables—some argue the shepherd and vine discourses are parables, chs 10 and 15—and performs no exorcisms; the latter maybe dropped because they were open to the argument Jesus was in league with Satan even though many scholars think the exorcisms are the most likely parts of the Jesus story to be factually true. The

Last Supper is not a Passover meal and lacks the Eucharistic language about bread and wine. Jesus' death is part of the story of the glorification of God and has no significance for humans i.e., no atonement. Apocalyptic talk and mentions of the Second Coming are absent, as are the Transfiguration and Gethsemane scenes. The fracas in the Temple, which the Synoptics portray as the start of the hatred by the authorities, is moved to a point early in John's gospel.

The overlap of the Synoptics and John include the stories of feeding the 5000, walking on water, and thrice denial by Peter of being a follower of Jesus. Jesus performs miracles (called signs in John) but far fewer of them in John. In the Synoptics, miracles are used as evidence the Kingdom of God is beginning, in John they are part of the glory of God theme. Indeed, the Kingdom of God language is used rarely (3:3, 3:5). Jesus is active in Galilee and around Jerusalem although more of the action occurs around Jerusalem in John than in the Synoptics.

The gospels we have today have some issues the centuries of changes have not eliminated: did Jesus send out 70 or 72 disciples, how many cups were used at the Last Supper, did Jesus on the cross pray for his enemies, which ascension story to use, did Jesus spend the bulk of his time in Galilee or Judea?[6] None of these is a deal-breaker but all point to the variation in the manuscripts.

After the best text has been settled upon, the printer can add problems. For English speakers, the King James Bible, translated at the time of Shakespeare (1611), long dominated religious services and study. However, that version has no original because the printer had two presses and mixed the pages from the two to produce his final copy.[7] Some amusing

---

[6] Number of disciples: Luke 10:1. The story, which does not seem to go back to Jesus but is an early follower's addition, might be based on the number of nations of the world (70 in Genesis 10, which was mistakenly translated in the Septuagint as 72) or upon the number of elders Moses chose (Numbers 11:16 where the number is 70 but two others shared the gift, 11:26). In Luke's gospel Jesus ascended to heaven on Easter night, but in Acts the ascension occurs 40 days later at Pentecost. Same author, different days; do themes override facts?

[7] Adam Nicolson, *God's Secretaries: The Making of the King James Bible* (Harper Collins, 2003), 225.

typesetting (the modern equivalent of copying) mistakes have occurred over the years.

- The Barker and Lucas version of the seventh commandment dropped "not" so adultery became compulsory in 1631.
- A 1717 Clarendon Press Bible (this is Oxford University) had a heading in Luke "The parable of the vinegar" (vineyard) Luke 20:9 – 19.
- In 1801 a Bible included "Let the children be killed" (filled) Mark 7:27.
- The 1966 Jerusalem Bible proffered "Pay for Peace" (Pray) Psalm 122:6.

F.H.A. Scrivener, in the late nineteenth century, located over 20,000 variations in the King James Version alone, most due to printers' mistakes.

**Oops! Translations.**

When it comes to translating whatever text is settled upon, an early writer already knew the problems. About 180 B.C.E. the translator of the apocryphal book Ecclesiasticus (also known as the Wisdom of Jesus son of Sirach) wrote "For what was originally expressed in Hebrew does not have exactly the same sense when translated into another language" (Prologue). Modern readers, familiar with any foreign language, appreciate this comment. Objects (e.g., chairs, pens) translate easily and well but concepts (e.g., Schaudenfreude, ennui) may not. Moreover, some words only appear once in scripture so no way exists to compare them with other usages.

The Hebrew Bible/Old Testament was written in Hebrew but the Septuagint, a Greek translation made in the three centuries before Jesus, was probably the text the writers of the Christian scripture/New Testament used. Most of the Christian scripture/New Testament was composed in Greek although the spoken language of Jesus and his disciples was Aramaic. The Bibles the Thoughtful read today are usually based on the Masoretic version of the Hebrew Bible/Old Testament and on various Greek versions of Christian scripture/New Testament. It was not always so; the sixteenth-century English versions and the King James Version often used Latin translations, particularly the Vulgate; those versions, in English, were translations from Latin which were translated from Greek which might have been translated from Hebrew!!

Grammar usages vary from language to language. Hebrew connects clauses with "and" whereas Greek and English prefer to subordinate one clause to the other. Idioms are notoriously difficult for non-native speakers to grasp. And to tell an English speaker a tense in Greek is "aorist" produces a blank look. Good translators clearly earn their pay.

Sources in Hebrew and Greek pose lots of challenges to translators. There was no upper case, no word separation, no punctuation, and no vowels (only consonants in Hebrew). An example of the problem facing a reader—in English for the benefit of the Thoughtful—would be an encounter with the letter "f." It could mean "if," "of," "oaf," "foe," "fee," or "fie." If "f" and the adjoining letter "r" are decided to be a word "fr," then the possibilities include "fra," "fri," "fro," "far," "fer," "fir," "for,""fur," "frau," "free," "fria," "fare," "faro," "fire," "fore," "fair," "fear," "four," "afar," and "afro." (And this choice assumes "fr" was not part of the letters of a word to the left or right in the line.) Vowels were added to the Hebrew only about 700 C.E. That effort did not entirely solve the problem as, for example, the translation of "GODISNOWHERE"—read carefully, two possibilities emerge.

Adding vowels to the Hebrew consonants had consequences, perhaps unforeseen. For instance, the origin of the Jewish dietary practices about not mixing meat and dairy is not simple. Deuteronomy (14:21), long translated as "You shall not boil a kid in its mother's milk," provided the basis for the kosher prohibition on mixing milk and meat. The translation issue is the Hebrew word "*hlv*," which has been expanded to "*halav*" as "milk." However, another possible expansion is "*helev*," meaning "fat." If that expansion is correct, then it really has the effect of prohibiting the killing of the lamb's mother, which would help preserve the flock.[8] Anyway, boiling meat in milk is not a very satisfactory cooking practice because the food

---

[8] Jack Sasson, "Should Cheeseburgers be Kosher?" *Bible Review* December, 19, No. 6 (2003), 40-3, 50-1.

often tastes sour. The Thoughtful should be getting the idea the words we read might not be those written.

Greek as a language was more complex than Latin—something early church leaders in the East never failed to mention when dealing with Western leaders—and English. As a result, what the Thoughtful read in the English language Bible is not as subtle as when it was written in Greek. For instance, John's gospel opens with "In the beginning was the word…." Even in English the meaning of this term is not immediately obvious, but in Greek, the word translated "word" (sorry) is "logos"; this gets very complex as "logos" can mean "message," "reason," "discourse," "a speech," "saying," "idea," and "teaching." Such linguistic subtleties help the Thoughtful understand when the early church came to work on its theology, the Greek-educated leaders had an arsenal of nuances available for their use. And use them they did as is evidenced when the discussions of Jesus, his divinity, relation to God, and the like are studied. It was easy to be a heretic, especially when a word is open to so much variation in meaning.

Because the old text lacked punctuation, other challenges arose. The placement of a comma could alter meaning. For example, Isaiah 40:3 is misused by all four gospels (Mark 1:2 – 3, Matthew 3:3, Luke 3:4 – 6, John 1:23) when putting words in the mouth of John the Baptizer. In Isaiah a way, a road, is to be prepared in the wilderness; in the gospels the proclamation of the way is made by an individual (John the Baptizer) in the wilderness. The present structure of chapters and verses was the work of an Archbishop of Canterbury, Stephen Langton, in 1225 (chapters) and a French printer, Robert Estienne, in 1551 (verses), but these changes very rarely create a problem or result in a strained reading. However, in many translations, Paul's letter to the Romans begins with a sentence that stretches over 7 verses.

A well known passage involving Jesus' birth, from Luke's Gospel, has theological significance. We are all familiar with the nativity story when the angels appear to the shepherds, saying "Glory to God in the highest, and on earth peace…" What follows "peace" is a linguistic and theological issue. Protestants have traditionally said "goodwill toward men," (King James Version) while Roman Catholics use "to men of good will" (Douay-Rheims

Bible) (Luke 2:14). A recent translation (Common English Bible) reads "among those whom he favors." The grammar problem is whether "good will" ("*eudokia*" in Greek) is a genitive or a nominative case—early manuscripts differ. The theological issue is whether God is sending that peace to all or only those who have earned it or some other favored group. Other translations have other words and phrases, and results.

Maybe the original author was intentionally ambiguous? The first words of the Hebrew Bible/Old Testament, "*b'reshit bara*", do not translate well. A literal translation is "At the beginning of "but no noun follows, so it would continue "At the beginning of he created...." The King James Version reads "In the beginning...." While the Common English Bible begins "When God began to create...." A subtle theological issue lies hidden here; the latter translation can imply our story (the Earth's) is only one chapter in a full story of God.

Today, many translation issues involve theological differences among Christian denominations. For instance, the people of the Hebrew Bible/Old Testament had the usual view of the afterlife of the people of the time and region: an afterlife existed, with no rewards or punishments; all fairly dreary. The notion an afterlife might entail rewards or punishments appears after the Jews return from their exile in Babylon where Persian religion influenced them. The first scriptural mention is in the book of Daniel probably written in the second century B.C.E. When it comes to translating the Hebrew "*Sheol*" (the word for the afterlife) in Psalm 55:15, some use "*Sheol*" (NRSV), some "hell" (KJV), and some "grave" (NIV).

Similar theological issues appear in the translation of Job 42:6. Most indicate Job confesses he should not have challenged God's ways; but a possible reading is he is resigned to the fact God will not apologize for the abuse Job has endured. And making Jews appear unpleasant shows up in, for instance, Ezra 7:3, when Ezra has convinced the men to disavow their non-Jewish wives. Do they also abandon their children? New Revised Standard Version and New International Version differ.

Some lesser problems occur, some relating to modern language usage or understandings. Words change meaning. The term "strong drink" for today's reader probably means distilled alcohol, which were created only in the Middle Ages. In scripture, it probably means pure wine versus a drink of 2/3 wine, 1/3 water, which was the ancient Jewish tradition. In Psalm 50:9 God is instructing the reader about sacrifices and, in earlier translations says "I will accept no bull from you." (Revised Standard Version) More recently the translator produces "I will not accept a bull from your house." (New Revised Standard Version) Also, metaphors of the past might make no sense. In the Book of Amos, God, speaking to the Israelites, says "I gave you cleanness of teeth" (Amos 4:6). So God is a dental hygienist!! Actually, the metaphor means "you went hungry" i.e., your teeth were clean because you had no food to eat. As a result of such problems more than 500 English translations exist. An early eighteenth-century hymn is entitled "Before Jehovah's Awful Throne," which jars the modern ear; how can God's throne be awful? Well, two-plus centuries ago, "awful" meant "full of awe." And in the King James Version "flesh" meant "food," not "meat" (Genesis 1:29). Meanings shift.

Rendering ancient practices into English makes the double entendres of the erotic love poem, Song of Solomon, a challenge. How does one reproduce (sorry) such entendres? And several psalms are acrostics with each line starting with a letter of the Hebrew alphabet, in order, something English translations rarely attempt. Finally, an occasional word has so many potential meanings the translator is at sea. Thus, in Proverbs 8:30 a word can be translated "master worker," "nursing child," or "confident," an interesting array of choices. Ambiguity in the text being translated leaves options available; at one time the Revised Standard Version and New International Version had opposite meanings of Job 13:15.

Finally, the modern translator also faces the choice of the best technique: formal or functional translation. Choosing between "formal equivalence," which maintains the structure, phrasing, and idioms of the Hebrew and Greek or "function equivalence," which captures the meaning of the original text for the modern reader produces significantly different results.

Motives to undertake a new translation range all over the board. The King James Version in the early seventeenth century resulted from a king unhappy with an earlier translation that typically used the word "tyrant" rather than "king." The Revised Version of 1885 tried to take account of scholarship that, inter alia, had decided certain verses in the King James Version were later additions. More scholarly work brought forth the Revised Standard Version in 1952, but Evangelical Protestants disliked the lessening of the links of the Old and New Testaments. In particular, the change from "virgin" to "young woman" in Isaiah 7:14 incensed them as they interpreted that verse as a prophecy about Jesus.[9]

A final example that illustrates the difficulties facing a copyist or a translator or both arises when some texts contain words allegedly recorded as someone spoke them. This is particularly true of Jesus' sayings. As it is unlikely anyone followed Jesus with a notepad, issues of oral transmission arise. Once that problem is solved, the possibility of miswriting must be confronted. One of Jesus' pithy statements is "[I]t is easier for a camel to go through the eye of a needle than for someone who is rich to enter the kingdom of Heaven" (Matthew 19:24). What an odd remark! Some have tried to locate a narrow passage on a road where camels had difficulty getting through or a Jerusalem gate that was so low camels had to be unloaded and made to crouch to get through, but the results are either unsatisfactory or contested. However, another explanation exists. In Aramaic, the language Jesus spoke, the word for "camel" is the same as the word for "rope" ("*gemal*"). One explanation is ropes were made of camel hair. It all becomes clear therefore the scribe wrote the word "rope" and when the gospel writer Matthew translated it into Greek, he made the wrong choice. To complicate the translation issue even more, the Greek words for "camel" and "rope" differ only by an "i" and "e", "*kamelos*: camel; *kamilos*: rope." So the saying could be a copyist's mistake. The saying has better symmetry and actually makes more sense with "rope." Hence, maybe Jesus said "[I]t is easier for a rope to go through the eye of a needle than someone who is rich to enter the kingdom of Heaven." Sound better? Or at least less nonsensical?[10]

---

[9] Nicolson, *God's Secretaries*. Peter J. Thuesen, *In Discordance with the Scripture: American Protestant Battles over Translating the Bible* (Oxford University Press, 1999).

[10] However, maybe the saying is accurately reported. Both the Talmud and Qur'an have similar sayings.

**My Copy. Today's Bibles.**

Today, printing the Bible is big business and the Thoughtful can be forgiven if they become overwhelmed by the number of versions of the Bible available. In 2005 alone Americans bought at least 25 million copies, mostly as gifts. Printings are aimed at niche audiences (moms, teens) with different cover colors (even camouflage for soldiers). Recordings of the Bible include sound effects. Commercialism is rampant and tends to reinforce the reader's comfort zone rather than challenge it. Many editions of the Bible have the theological slant of a particular group; the New International Version forewent accuracy in favor of doctrinal correctness. The King James Version (1611) is still very popular and its language sets the standard of religious discourse even today—it has been "updated" twice in the last fifty years. College students typically use the Revised Standard Version (1952) or the New Revised Standard Version (1989) as both were prepared by a committee involving Protestant, Roman Catholic, Orthodox and Jewish scholars so they are "neutral" on many big issues. The New American Bible is for Roman Catholics while the New American Standard Bible is for conservative Protestants, though Today's New International Version is more popular with that group. Non-literal translations often use colloquial language, almost slang, to convey what the translator thinks is the message of a text, and the vocabulary is often more limited.

The Thoughtful now understand no version of the Bible can be the true one because scholars have no way of finding the originals and the problems of getting from ancient sources to the modern world are myriad. Yet again, certitude is elusive. Is this a theme of this book?

## Putting it together. Composition.

Scripture, both Hebrew Bible/Old Testament and Christian scripture/ New Testament, has many genres: history, law, poetry, advice, fiction, music, etc. Much of it looks like history, but isn't; some is clearly fiction; a bit is theology; the rest is a mishmash.

**Miscellany. Hebrew Bible/New Testament.**

The Hebrew Bible, what most Christians call the Old Testament, is a collection of at least 39 books; to keep things confusing, some Christians include more books—the Apocrypha—than are found in the Hebrew Bible. Our earliest full copy in Hebrew, the Masoretic, dates from around 1000 C.E. Scholars use the term Hebrew Bible because it was written (mostly) in Hebrew for Jews who spoke Hebrew.[11] Christians call it the Old Testament as discussed above. Many Christians think God's agreement found in the Old Testament was superseded by a new agreement after the life and death of Jesus. (This "supersession" is not the position of this discussion which will be divided into the Torah, Political Stories, and Other Writings; traditionally, Jews divide their scripture into Law, Prophets, and Writings.)

Jews had not settled on a canon, a group of books to be "official," at the time of Jesus or for years after; Christians, therefore, could not, and do not, agree (surprise!) on which writings to include. The shortest Old Testament, with the fewest (39) books, is the Protestant one, which has the same books Judaism uses today, though the books are in different order. The Roman Catholic tradition includes several writings not in the Hebrew Bible or the Protestant Old Testament. Orthodoxy includes those used by Roman Catholicism and few more. Still other traditions—Syrian, Ethiopian—have other contents. The writings not in the Hebrew Bible and Protestant Old Testament but used by other Christian groups are commonly called the Apocrypha and date from about 300 B.C.E. to 100 C.E. Little of doctrinal importance is contained but some interesting historical activities are recorded. How and why these works came to be included or omitted is another one of those stories that brings little edification to the Thoughtful and is hereby ignored. To summarize, there is no "standard Bible" for all Christians.

When the content of the Hebrew Bible/Old Testament is settled, further problems arise because more than one version of some books exist. The

---

[11] The Hebrew Bible is divided into three parts, Torah, Niviim, Ketuvim in Hebrew, (Law, Prophets, Writings). The first letters of each are combined into Tanak, another name for the same collection. The Masoretic text, in Hebrew, dates to the latter centuries of the first millennium.

book of Esther comes with three choices, short, medium, or long. Which to use? The three additions to the book of Daniel include "Bel and the Dragon" (the easy winner of the best title among ancient writings). An extra psalm, the 151$^{st}$, pops up in some Greek versions. The Dead Sea Scrolls, dating to the intertestamentary period (last few centuries of B.C.E.), contain copies of most of the Hebrew Bible; four versions of Exodus are available with differing lengths and clear additions by the copyists.

Many Christians do not, or cannot, accept the idea the Hebrew Bible/Old Testament was not written to serve as a backdrop to Jesus and Christianity; these Christians ransack the work for antecedents and foreshadowing of Jesus. When the Christians came to assemble their canon, they rearranged the books of the Hebrew Bible/Old Testament so they ended that portion of scripture with Malachi, which they think points to the coming of Jesus. On the other hand, for scholars and many Christians, the Hebrew Bible/Old Testament is the story of the relationship of the Jewish people with and understanding of the deity as well as, inter alia, a collection of proverbs, some love poetry, and laws and rules of behavior. One author suggests the Hebrew Bible is simply a collection of everything that existed when it was compiled; it was a sweeping of the library's shelves, as it were. Certainly the inclusion of the Song of Solomon with its love and sexual themes seems odd to us.[12]

The Hebrew Bible/Old Testament was not written front to back; it was written in bits and snatches which were later compiled, edited, and supplemented into books with a continuous text. By analogy, the Thoughtful have written research papers by identifying a topic, gathering five books from the library, and composing an opus by selecting from those five books. Then a friend might proof it and make suggestions. Sometimes a unified paper resulted or sometimes the instructor's comments included "Lack of transition" and "Aren't pages 2 and 6 inconsistent?" One Thoughtful concern, plagiarism, did not bother ancient authors and editors as they were free in their use of others' work; no one cared, and it was not illegal. Biblical authors, however, had problems, at least as we see it, with consistency. For instance,

---

[12] Robert Conn, *All That's Left Unsaid/What You Didn't Learn in Sunday School* (unpublished manuscript).

the opening pages, the creation story, contain actually two stories—Genesis, chapters 1 and 2—and they cannot be made to jibe. The authors/editors found two sources, used them both, and apparently were not bothered enough to harmonize things; neither were subsequent editors and copyists. Or perhaps they realized that multiple views enhanced understanding.

Some portions, possibly predating 1000 B.C.E., were transmitted orally for a while, with the attendant problems that poses, and some texts, extant at one time, were not included and subsequently disappeared e.g., Book of the Wars of the Lord (Numbers 21:14); Book of Yashar (2 Sam 1:18); the story of the prophet Iddo (2 Chronicles 13:22). Portions were used in various ways: literacy instruction, songs in rituals, moral education. Consequently, they might get altered to fit changed circumstances by either addition (something did not make sense and needed elaborating) or subtraction (something did not make sense to a later user and was cut). Later works reinterpret earlier ones, e.g., Chronicles, Daniel, and Jeremiah. The toponyms (place names) reflect nothing earlier than the seventh and sixth centuries B.C.E., even when they appear in stories that would have taken place much earlier.

When the history of the Jews is learned, it becomes easier to understand the process of the compilation. Lots of manuscripts floated around—histories of David, codes of behavior—but no unified story was needed. Following some unsuccessful military adventures, a few thousand people, including all the elite, were transported in 586 B.C.E. out of Palestine into Mesopotamia, a period called the "Exile" (also called the "Babylonian Captivity"). Maintaining their culture, including their religion, suddenly became problematical, and priests began collecting the manuscripts and stories. Once their conqueror permitted these people to go back to Palestine, the process accelerated; by perhaps 450 B.C.E., the compilation of older material had progressed to the point that most of today's Hebrew Bible/Old Testament existed.

The first five books of the Hebrew Bible/Old Testament—called the "Torah" or "Pentateuch"—illustrate the forgoing discussion about how the final version emerges. Genesis, Exodus, Leviticus, Numbers, and Deuteronomy are viewed by scholars as a compilation of many early traditions. These first five books seem historical, but are not.[13] Rather they are a story constructed out of disparate material to give a background for the Israelites as a people (though that feeling as a group did not occur at the early date the Pentateuch implies). They begin (Genesis) with the creation of the world and some early material scholars identify as myth and folklore. The second book (Exodus) tells the story of how the Israelites escaped oppression in Egypt and wandered around for 40 years under the leadership of Moses. The ending of the book of Exodus and Leviticus describe the cult and lay out rules and practices for the Israelite religion and people, which became the core of Judaism. The fourth book (Numbers), so called because of its two census lists, also tells the story of the Israelites wandering in the desert for 40 years. The fifth and final book, Deuteronomy, has some more rules and brings the Israelites to the edge of Palestine, the Promised Land, where Moses dies.

Seventeenth-century scholars, such as Baruch Spinoza and Thomas Hobbes, had raised doubts about the traditional view Moses wrote the Torah. And even before scholars worried much about the creation stories in Genesis wherein Eve, Adam, and their boys are seen as the first people on the planet, it had been noticed other people are also clearly mentioned without any explanation of their origins. One solution, the Preadamites, proposed the Hebrew Bible/Old Testament was the story of the origins and history of the Jews, while other peoples might have their own origin and history stories.

Historical criticism really got underway in German universities in the eighteenth century. By the nineteenth-century, this criticism resulted in a proposal in 1883 by Julius Wellhausen (1844 – 1918), known as the "Documentary hypothesis," which sought to explain the differing wording and the repeated (and sometimes inconsistent) stories in the first five biblical books. From there, scholars moved on to examine the rest of the Hebrew Bible/Old Testament and the resulting conclusions—constantly

---

[13] The extent to which any of the Hebrew Bible/Old Testament is history, in the modern sense, see Robin Lane Fox, *The Unauthorized Version: Truth and Fiction in the Bible* (Knopf, 1992).

being revised—have demystified scripture and made it more approachable for the Thoughtful.

Basing his view upon different writing styles, inconsistencies in the texts, choice of words (e.g., name of God), general topics of interest, and other matters, Wellhausen suggested four authors: J (because God was referred to as Yahweh—Jahve in German), E (because God was called Elohim), D (or the Deuteronomist sections), and P (for priestly, the one who brought things together). Some conservative Christians do not accept this argument; Roman Catholic scholars only signed on in the mid-twentieth century.

Providing the basic narrative structure of the first three biblical books, J was composed sometime after 922 B.C.E., the traditional date of Solomon's death, and before 722 B.C.E. probably by someone living near Jerusalem in the southern kingdom of Judah. It contains the stories of the Garden of Eden, Cain and Abel, the Flood, the Exodus, and the patriarchs; God is shown anthropomorphically. The source of many of the patriarch stories, E, was also composed sometime after 922 B.C.E., probably in the northern kingdom of Israel. E also has stories of the Exodus and the patriarchs; some parallel J, some differ. Dreams and angels also appear. The third source, D, the "Deuteronomist", is largely found in Deuteronomy and dates to the years before and after 600 B.C.E.—before and after as it appears it was first written c. 625 B.C.E. and extended sometime after 587 B.C.E.. Dominated by law codes, D is concerned to centralize worship in Jerusalem and shutter the other shrines to Yahweh that were scattered around the countryside. (D, or a follower, also wrote a longer work, a sort of history, one that includes the books of Joshua, Judges, 1 and 2 Samuel, and 1 and 2 Kings.) A final source, P, derives its title because the author seems to be a priest, or at least is interested largely in priestly matters. It emphasizes ritual, genealogy, and the perks, privileges, and responsibilities of the priesthood. Composed after 600 B.C.E in Jerusalem, or more likely later during or after the Exile, it has stories that parallel those of J and E. The book of Leviticus appears after the Exile, and its many rules and regulations, food, etc. established the core of Judaism as we know it. Ironically these practices were decreed to be enforced by the non-Jewish king of the Persians, who ruled Palestine at the time.

Under this interpretation, the story was one of a progressive, developmental view of movement from polytheism to monotheism. Later scholars added a fifth author, H, to account for the uniqueness of the Holiness Code of Leviticus (chs. 7 – 26). Like a Thoughtful's composite research paper, some inconsistencies, such as two creation stories and two explanations for the origins of woman, were left in place; consistency was the hobgoblin of small minds to the ancient editors. This compilation was all done, it is thought, during or shortly after the sixth-century Exile to give Jews a sense of the corporate identity and help their culture survive.

Today, most scholars still accept the multiple author hypothesis but things have gotten more complicated. Much of the argument is over how much material is pre-Exile or based on pre-Exile writings. P, D, and H all seem to date to about the same time, and their varying views of God and life suggest Israelites were a very mixed bag when it came to beliefs and practices; certainly an evolutionarily progressive view of the idea of God is not possible. P's God is cold, distant, unmoved by prayer while D's is connected to the international Wisdom movement of the day. H is interested in social justice; D's focus on keeping the laws was an effort to bring people together when sacrifices, previously a community activity everywhere, had been moved to Jerusalem. Maybe there was continual creation, not just cutting and pasting, as time passes so the earlier authors were steadily modified. Some scholars, particularly in Europe, have jettisoned E and are about to dispose of J, leaving P to assemble many small blocks of earlier writing. Moreover, various authors have been presented herein as individuals (e.g., J, E, D, P) when it is likely, probable even, a group with similar interpretations—called "schools" by scholars—composed the works associated with the names. In the scholarly world today, the interpretations are not as neat and tidy as the foregoing suggests, but the basic themes are mostly agreed upon. The Thoughtful can appreciate this complexity and, because little of this matter is especially relevant today, not worry. This explanation does help the reader cope with inconsistencies and confusions these first five books contain and why so many themes can be located in them. The point, for the Thoughtful, is these scriptures—the Pentateuch or Torah—are a composite, a product of the era of the Exile and after; usually they are not contemporary with the events they describe.

The remaining books of the narrative portion of the Hebrew Bible/Old Testament fall into groups, the largest being the stories of kings. Though written earlier than the final version of the Pentateuch, the author(s) of those stories was aware of some of the material used in those later five books. These book resemble modern histories—well, older modern histories as they are all "swords and trumpets," not about societies—in that they tell the stories of the kings of the Israelites, starting from the end of the Pentateuch, when the Israelites were poised on the edge of the Promised Land, proceeding with its conquest—assuming it happened, something scholars doubt—a period of tribal struggle, the emergence of a monarchy, and that monarchy's division into two kingdoms.

Scholarly debate rages over whether the work is the result of a single writer during the Exile or has gone though several reworkings from the late eighth century though the sixth. A single writer—called "Deuteronomist"—was suggested by Martin Noth in the 1940s. Noth found an underlying continuity in language and culture in all those books, though the earlier sources are visible when the seams joining blocks of material sometimes appear. Josiah, king of the southern kingdom in the seventh century, gets a good press, which would suggest at least part of it dates from then (sycophants have always existed). In any case, the final product dates to about 550 B.C.E.

Whoever the author(s), the story is a collection of legends, folklore, chronicles, royal histories, memories, and other material; though having some inconsistencies, it projects a coherent account. All scholars recognize certain clear themes: worship should only be of Yahweh, monarchy ever since David has been a failure (though Josiah was good), hope for the future includes the restoration of the Temple, and Yahweh is active in history.

As king, Josiah had pursued many religious changes—purging the Temple of images of gods other than Yahweh, centralizing worship in Jerusalem, proclaiming the stories of the Torah (after a "sudden" discovery of a copy in the dusty corners of the Temple)—which were identical to the goals of the Deuteronomist. The overall theme is the righteous prosper and the wicked suffer; when kings were true to Yahweh and the poor were not badly treated, things went well, when they strayed, things did not. (Job and Ecclesiastes will later dispute this theme.) As can be seen from a modern perspective, theology, politics, and historical interpretation are bound together, and a history, by today's standards, is difficult to construct. The Deuteronomist was often fast and loose with the sources so that the final product does not jibe with material from other cultures. Little of all this material passes the modern scholar's test of validity: the last part of 2 Samuel, the two books of Kings, and probably some of Nehemiah—not much given how scripture is usually viewed.[14]

The foregoing writings look like histories though they often have a weak claim to that description; the remaining books of the Bible contain criticism, praise, and questions—a medley. In the Hebrew Bible/Old Testament a large segment consists of books by or about prophets: Isaiah through Malachi. Speaking for God about the present but not predicting the future,[15] these individuals, almost all men, appear as soon as kingship is established; prophets pretty much disappear when the Israelites cease to have political independence. Other books are quite varied: some are fiction (Esther—literary ironic reversal; Job—why evil happens; Ruth—theme of redemption), sexual language (Song of Solomon), songs (Psalms) and whatnot. This literature might contain truths but the Thoughtful would not confuse it with factual reporting. These books are not significantly different from the rest of world's literature and not used a great deal by mainline denominations. Such a large manuscript does not always hang together and has inconsistencies internally and with external sources is not a discovery which should surprise or alarm the Thoughtful; it was not written to be read as one book. It is only a problem if you seek to take it all literally and as divine truth handed down from on high.

---

[14] Fox, *Unauthorized Version,* spends 400 pages on this topic.

[15] When they did talk of the future, things didn't always pan out. King Jeroboam died peacefully (2 Kings 14:23) despite a prediction by Amos he would die by the sword (Amos 7:11); a sloppy editor failed to remove one of those texts.

A group of books, I and II Chronicles, Ezra and Nehemiah, seem to form a single work from an author called by scholars the "Chronicler." The story repeated much of that of the Deuteronomist and then came down to the Chronicler's present, about 400 B.C.E. King David got a big role and the kingdom of Israel (the northern kingdom) a small one. The Chronicler knew the Deuteronomist's work as well as the Pentateuch, and he also refers to perhaps two dozen other writings that never made the canon and are today lost. Still other interpretations, written after 300 B.C.E., did not get included but are still available and help the Thoughtful understand how the Jews of that era saw their earlier writings.[16]

**Followers' Views. Christian Scripture/New Testament.**

The composition issues of the Christian scripture/New Testament center largely around the gospels. While Paul's letters provide some grist for the scholarly mills—some letters look like they are combinations of separate letters—by and large those letters well convey Paul's ideas. On the whole, other writings are short, single-purpose and non-controversial. The gospels, on the other hand, have lots of variety of outlook, content, and construction.

In 1834, D.F. Strauss (1808 – 74) produced *Leben Jesu* (*The Life of Jesus*) in which he argued the gospels were not histories but efforts to convey the "truth" about Jesus in story form. Translated into English by George Eliot in 1846, the books led English churchmen to publish *Essays and Reviews* in 1860 which expanded historical criticism beyond the German-speaking world. The Germans, however, continued to make the running until late in the twentieth century; Americans have now joined the fray; Roman Catholics scholars, long held back by papal conservatism, became involved in the last half of the twentieth century.

After Strauss, scholars developed understandings of the compositional history of the gospels that included a missing source ("Q") and the reliance of Matthew and Luke on Mark, views that still hold the field. Since Rudolph Bultmann (1884 – 1976), who dominated the field for much of the twentieth

---

[16] James L. Kugel, *The Bible as it was* (Harvard UP, 1997), 3. James L. Kugel, *How to Read the Bible* (Free Press, 2007).

century and saw little reason to seek the historic Jesus, the study of Jesus has alternated between trying to uncover the "historic" (real) Jesus and the belief very little can be said with certainty about him, and therefore we should turn to how his message speaks to the present.

Because scholars have created several possibilities of how the Hebrew Bible/Old Testament was created, the Thoughtful might expect the same of the gospels. After all, the four canonical works are all telling the same story, the story of Jesus. However, no one explanation dominates gospel composition like the Documentary Hypothesis does for the Pentateuch. As with much of scripture, we have no eyewitness accounts, in this case of Jesus. Neither his contemporaneous followers nor the greater Roman world recorded anything that survives today. While over 30 gospels, stories of Jesus, have surfaced, several exist only in very fragmentary form, and many are, by today's standards, so fantastic that the Thoughtful would pay them no heed. The four gospels that made it into the canon are among the oldest, all probably dating to the first century C.E.; to repeat: they are not eyewitness accounts, though many literalists think they are. While all 4 gospels have names—Matthew, Mark, Luke, John—the names are traditional; no one knows who actually wrote them or how much change they underwent from initial writing to first surviving manuscript.

What we have then are traditions, stories and sayings handed down, often through several tellers, before they were written, and so their reliability is uncertain. (The old "telephone" game issue.) Arguing for great reliability, some scholars believe the gospels were written at a time close enough to the events eyewitnesses, though elderly, would have heard them and corrected any major errors of fact. Thus, the oral transmission, the "telephone" analogy, carries less weight.[17] Tradition has it Mark was close to the disciple Peter, Matthew was a disciple, and Luke was a companion of the letterwriter Paul. Also, some think John, the purported author of the fourth gospel was, in fact, one of Jesus' disciples. No factual support is available for any of this and the variations among the gospels argue against the tradition. In reality,

---

[17] See, e.g., Richard Bauckham, *Jesus and the Eyewitnesses: The Gospels as Eyewitness Testimony* (Eerdmans, 2006).

the gospels, to the extent they record events of Jesus' life, depend on oral traditions, though those traditions were not nearly so long as some that make up the materials in the Pentateuch.

The gospels were written to confirm, not create, faith; they explained things to people who were already followers of Jesus. They are not biographies. Why four gospels in the canon? One might be enough, but just as the first biography of Lincoln hasn't stopped scholars from churning out more, gospels kept being written. The inclusion of 4 was settled by probably 200 C.E. , and one early Christian, Irenaeus, justified four because four was the number of points of the compass and also is mentioned in Revelation as the number of living things around God's throne.[18] More weren't included, partly because they weren't consistent with what was becoming accepted as orthodox. One writer, Tatian, in the second century did combine all four into one, the Diatessaron, but it never found favor. While this effort was made to harmonize the four into one gospel, eventually all four were kept, apparently on the theory they promote belief by coming at things from different directions.

The environment in which the gospels were created, and which influenced their content, can be somewhat described today. Mark's audience, possibly in the city of Rome, had just endured the emperor Nero's persecution, so he presents Jesus as a suffering Messiah whose disciples will also suffer. Matthew's gospel rummages through the Hebrew Bible/Old Testament to find prophecies which he then has Jesus fulfill. Hence Jesus is the Messiah and is true to Jewish religion; indeed, Jesus is the fulfillment of that religion, so Matthew's listeners/readers are probably Jewish followers of Jesus. Luke, writing after the failed Jewish revolt of 66 – 70 C.E., had to deal with the failure of Jesus to return to Earth following the Roman destruction of the Temple, something many thought would occur. Also Luke sought to distance the followers of Jesus from the revolting Jews so as to win Roman tolerance. John's gospel has much less about Jesus' life and teaching and instead focuses on who Jesus "really" was; it is largely theology, thoughts about God.

---

[18] Roy W. Hoover, "How the Books of the New Testament Were Chosen," *Bible Review* 9 (1993), 47.

John's audience had clear Gnostic leanings so his gospel attempts to deal with that approach.

As to sources, we do not know what Mark had to work with when he set out to write his gospel. There was oral material available as someone had to be preaching about Jesus. It seems likely Mark lived in an area (Rome or Syria) where Paul had worked, and Mark, like Paul, emphasized the Resurrection; surprisingly, that event is not found in Mark's gospel. Scholars think they see evidence of earlier material in a couple of places where Jesus' nature or status is the topic (8:27 – 30, parts of 9:33 – 10:45). The two stories of feeding big crowds look similar enough some scholars think Mark had two sources that differed slightly and used both (6:30 – 44, 8:1 – 10). Whether generally Mark was merely repeating what was being preached or created something new (i.e., the theme of necessary suffering by a Jesus follower) is not something likely to be determined.

Other sources which were used by Matthew and Luke include Q. It was a collection of Jesus' sayings and teachings.[19] Scholars think these were gathered in Palestine, around 50 C.E. All four gospels also seemed to know an account of Jesus' final week, the Passion story, though all make their own, different, use of it. Finally, Matthew and Luke each includes some material not found in Mark or Q, which suggests they individually had other sources, perhaps oral, or they created some of the story themselves (called "special Matthew" and "special Luke").

Scholars are pretty much in agreement the writer of John's gospel did not know about the Synoptics (the other three gospels), and as his gospel was the last written, it had no influence on the earlier ones other than maybe an occasional copyist's editing for more consistency. Some small agreements between Mark and John are explained in that they had access to parts of the same traditional stories.

The version of the Hebrew Bible/Old Testament used by the gospel writers was the Greek translation of about 200 B.C.E., the Septuagint, and it had

---

[19] James M. Robinson, Paul Hoffman, John S. Kloppenborg, and Milton C. Moreland, *The CriticalEedition of Q* (Fortress, 2000). Perhaps Q can be dispensed with if Luke wrote after Matthew and with that manuscript in front of him, a view some scholars take.

problems; there is no single Septuagint but many variations. For instance the Hebrew version of Isaiah 7:14 reads a "young woman" will bear a son and the context clearly points to events in the eighth century B.C.E. It was originally a prophecy for its own day to convince a king not to make a particular foreign alliance. However, Matthew had a Greek translation which used "virgin" instead, which permitted development of the Virgin Birth stories. Thus the mistake in translation means Matthew is doubly wrong in his virgin birth story's scriptural antecedents. All the Virgin Mary material of Christianity is based upon a mistake, but a rather large industry has grown from it. (This verse is the easiest litmus test for the Thoughtful. If a translation uses "virgin" in Isaiah 7:14, it has been made to fit a denominational, not a scholarly, agenda.) This is an extreme example but Matthew's extensive use of the Septuagint and his occasional misreading of it make for some other interesting mistakes.

That interpretation leaves us with at least seven sources—Mark, Q, Passion week, special Matthew, special Luke, John, the Septuagint—which were used as building blocks by the evangelists. Mark used his own sources, the Passion week material and the Septuagint. Matthew's gospel, written fifteen years later, accepted the earlier evangelist's general outline of the Jesus story—teaching and healing in Galilee with a final journey to Jerusalem and execution. In fact, about 80 percent of Mark's work appears in Matthew's but it seems the copy of Mark that Matthew used was not quite the version we have today. Q and special Matthew were also used by Matthew. Luke, like Matthew, used Mark's gospel and Q as well as special Luke. And he may even create some material. He used about one-half of Mark, which makes up about one-third of his text, but he has odd omissions (Mark 6:45 – 8:26, 9:41 – 10:12) or perhaps his version of Mark is not the one we have. Q makes up about one-quarter of the gospel. Beginning with his "author's message" and continuing with structure of a journey, his rearrangement of the time sequence of Mark's events—seven times—shows he is clearly manipulating things to fit his theme. The source of some of the stories is unknown, but without Luke we would not have the Good Samaritan, the prodigal son, Zacchaeus in the tree, among others—all good stories that seem consistent with our understanding of Jesus. He omits details of the fracas in the Temple, the crowning of Jesus with thorns, the story of John the Baptizer and Herodias, and the three great hymns, Magnificat, Benedictus, and Nunc Dimittis. He also omits two miracles from Mark's gospel in which Jesus uses spittle to cure blindness; perhaps, this smacked too much of magic. How much he is moving the teachings and life of Jesus into new channels, channels that are those of the church is debated. Just to muddle things, it looks like Luke wrote one version and later lengthened it as two versions floated around in the early years.

John's gospel contrasts with the other three gospels, the Synoptics, in that he does not follow the same story line. The novelties in John include the Cana wedding water into wine miracle (which announces John's theme) and the raising of Lazarus from the dead, which becomes the reason the authorities decide Jesus needs to die. Jesus' final week, the Passion, differs in many details such as what occurs on which days. While the Synoptics are largely silent as to the length of time of Jesus' public activities, John's gospel mentions three Passovers which is the source for the popular notion Jesus' public life covered for three years. Jesus, popularly portrayed as in his early thirties, might have been nearly 50 (8:57). The most striking novelty of John's gospel to the listener/reader is the long speeches by Jesus detailing who or what he is. When told the "I am" usage echoes strongly God's self-titling in Exodus, the listener/reader realizes John's portrait of Jesus is a lot different from the one found in the Synoptics.

In the remainder of the Christian scripture/New Testament only the Acts of the Apostles has any aspirations to be a historical narrative, and scholars debate that. Written by the same hand as Luke's gospel, Acts gives some early history of the nascent movement of the followers of Jesus. It features Jesus' chief disciple, Peter, and the missionary, Paul, and the story traces the spread of the movement from Palestine to the describing what finally happened to the two chief characters, Peter and Paul; that outcome we only have from tradition, nothing in Acts.

The problem with its historical accuracy arises from the failure of the story to match with Paul's letters, which also describe some of his missionary wanderings. The writer of Acts seemingly did not know of Paul's letters and relied on other materials. Moreover, the clear theme of the two writings—Luke's gospel and Acts of the Apostles—gives the reader pause; maybe things were not quite as neat and tidy as the story suggests.

In the Christian scripture/New Testament the writings other than the gospels and Acts can be separated into Paul's letters, lots of other letters, and Revelation. Paul's letters make up a substantial portion of the Christian scripture/New Testament; written in the 40s and 50s, they focus largely on the resurrected Jesus and how that affects his followers. Paul, a missionary working in Asia Minor and Greece, succeeded in establishing several small congregations of Jesus' followers. After he moved on to form another group, his converts had questions, maybe disputes, and sought his advice on what to do. His letters, therefore, are not systematic treatises on Jesus but responses to his congregations. Nevertheless, a view of the Jesus movement among Paul's people can be pieced together. Mostly they appear to be "God Fearers," Gentiles who had been attracted to Jewish religion and attended Jewish meetings. Paul did not need to explain God or the nature of Jewish religion, except to deny the new followers needed to follow Jewish practices about, inter alia, food and circumcision. Paul, who was or had been an observant Jew, maybe a Pharisee even, believed in the resurrection of the dead, and that was how he interpreted Jesus. His letters contain very little about Jesus' life or teachings. Rather they discuss the resurrected Christ and what that might mean for his followers. Paul thought the general resurrection of everyone was about to start and Jesus had been the first, the frontrunner as it were.

The letters of Paul and others have little to say about Jesus' life or teachings; it is not clear if they were aware of the gospels. To the uninitiated, it looks like 13 of Paul's letters are included, but even a casual reader can detect differences because some of the letters were written by someone else and attributed to Paul. Why? To call Paul the author gives the letter more weight with the reader/listener. Academic dishonesty was not even an issue. The non-Paul letters give some insight into the early church and its structure as well as providing guidance about Christian living.

The final book of the Christian scripture/New Testament is Revelation. It is an apocalypse, similar to Daniel in the Hebrew Bible/Old Testament and many writings not included in the Bible. A phase in Jewish and Christian writings—from around 200 B.C.E. to 100 C.E.—apocryphal works are very symbolic and are a response to the current situation of the listener/reader. Revelation, in most scholars' view, was written in the years after the persecutions of the emperor Nero, in the 70s, or after the harassment of the emperor Domitian in the 90s. Tradition made the author John, one of the twelve disciples of Jesus; composition is located on Patmos, an island off Asia Minor, and the book is directed to churches on the mainland. While scholars can find no systematic persecutions in that area, local churches did face difficult times, and the thrust of Revelation is to describe symbolically what believers might expect. Today, Dispensationalism lifts many of its images from the book; many believers take Revelation as a prediction of the future. It isn't.

**Self-serving? Jewish Priests and Christian Leaders.**

When the Thoughtful consider the Hebrew Bible/Old Testament, as a collection of written documents, was probably produced by members of the priesthood—who were most likely to have been the literate class—it might not surprise that such a group was not all of one mind. Early on, the story goes, one of the twelve tribes, the Levites, was assigned the role of priest. They were not given any land, the story continues, as they were concentrated in cities and other worship locations, living off the sacrifices brought to those places. The Levites in the northern kingdom of Israel appear to have written the story of that entity with a bias against the kings; that bias shows up when their work is incorporated into that of the Levites of the southern kingdom of Judah. Josiah's activities in 622, concentrating all worship in the Jerusalem Temple—and under the control of the king—put most of the priests out of work as they had been serving local shrines.

During the Exile some of the priests in Babylon began claiming to be descendents of Zadok, the High Priest of Solomon. The Moses saga may have been elevated in order to support Zadokite claims because they claimed descent from Aaron, the brother of Moses and the (alleged) ancestor of all priests. Some Levites had stayed in Jerusalem, and when the exiles returned, disputes broke out as to who would staff the rebuilt Temple. The settlement with the Zadokites being the priests and the Levites doing singing, teaching, maintenance, standing guard and the like, apparently lasted to the Maccabean revolt. It was probably at this time the Chronicler rewrote the story that the Deuteronomist has composed. Why rewrite it? Perhaps to show the legitimacy of the Temple and priesthood in Jerusalem after the Exile seem to have been the goals. With their status marginalized in the rebuilt Temple, these Levites are candidates for the authorship of the proto-apocalyptic work of Isaiah 24:7 and Zechariah 9:14. The Dead Sea Scrolls community also appears to be a group hostile to the Temple priesthood of the day. Once we get to Jesus, the Zadokites had split, with the Sadducees running the Temple and the Pharisees seeking separation from Gentiles and observance of the Law.

With such rivalries, the Thoughtful would expect the various writings of the Hebrew Bible/Old Testament to favor or criticize the priesthood's opponents. That such bias cannot always be detected should also not surprise. The overall theme seems to be a progression from the Deuteronomist's desire to centralize worship in the Jerusalem Temple under supportive kings, through the Chronicler's attempt to justify certain priests' monopoly of the rites of that Temple, to the disgruntlement of some sections of the priesthood.

Another argument that supports the notion scripture was created to help the priesthood or maybe the aristocracy generally has arisen since 1990. A small group of scholars has posited a theory that the entire Hebrew Bible/Old Testament is the work of scribes writing in Jerusalem after the Exile.[20] Those scribes' purpose was to supply a story and an ideology for people whom the Persians had settled in the old southern kingdom, now called Yehud. These

---

[20] See, e.g., Philip R. Davies, *Scribes and Schools: The Canonization of the Hebrew Scriptures* (Westminster John Knox Press, 1996) and T.L. Thompson, *The Bible in History: How Writers Create a Past* (Jonathon Cape, 1998). See James Barr, *History and Ideology in the Old Testament: Biblical Studies at the End of a Millennium* (Oxford University Press, 2000). An archaeologist, Israel Finkelstein, has been in the forefront for this argument. See also Yairah Amit, *In Praise of Editing the Hebrew Bible Collected Essays in Retrospect* (Sheffield Phoenix, 2012).

immigrants, from somewhere in the Persian empire, were not descendants of the folk who were moved away by Nebuchadressar. David and Solomon, according to these authors, were at most tribal chieftains as there is no archaeological support for Jerusalem being a capital. The post-Exilic scribes, using some local memories and archives constructed a story featuring a golden past (David) and an Exile and return, all to support the rulers and the Temple of their day. For some scholars the creation is even later as David and Josiah look like John Hyrcanas, leader of the Maccabean revolt in the second century, and Solomon resembles the conqueror Alexander the Great. The immigrants went so far as to adopt a new language, Hebrew, and a chief god, Yahweh. As Jews had spread around much of the Mediterranean and Mesopotamian world during and after the Exile, some suggest the entire Exodus story is a metaphor for the Diaspora, and especially for the Jews in Egypt who might long to return to Jerusalem. Then, to add to the mix, a dispute over dating moves things maybe 100 years later than the usual dating. In summary, these scholars reject the results of the last two centuries of biblical scholarship to produce a new interpretation for which, the Thoughtful should know, little factual support has been found and perhaps never will. As a kind of conspiracy theory the absence of evidence only confirms a conspiracy existed.

In some ways, however, the disagreements between this new view and traditional views are not as large as the ballyhoo would suggest. Since the mid-nineteenth century, scholars have moved the compilation and composition of the Hebrew Bible/Old Testament from the years 1100 to 800 B.C.E. to the more recent period after 500 B.C.E. Most scholars now see the final production of the Hebrew Bible/Old Testament occurring after the Exile. And all realize the final compilers had to rely on at least some earlier materials; the argument is how much. The David and Solomon materials will eventually get sorted out if archaeology can get to the relevant sites; archaeological evidence suggests probably no one in Israel at the time of David and Solomon could write so their stories had to come later or be transmitted orally for a period. At a minimum over a dozen kings of the two kingdoms are mentioned in other sources so there is some factual basis for the Hebrew

Bible/Old Testament histories. As archaeology may never find evidence of all the people and events mentioned in scripture, the issue for the Thoughtful will come down to the one that divided scholars: is scripture taken as history if not contradicted by archaeology or only as history when it is confirmed by archaeology?

All this work and interpretation gets mixed up with contemporary life, namely the State of Israel and religious beliefs today. If developments are all this recent, some Christians and Jews get jumpy as antiquity is important to them. If Israelites only date from the sixth century B.C.E., does that affect a claim to the area now? Once the debates head in these directions, passion quickly overrules reason, and history and archaeology get twisted by all sides. It was always thus; the Hebrew Bible/Old Testament served more than just a religious function. And the Thoughtful considered the historical past a safe area for study!

As to the Christian scripture/New Testament, the texts do not so obviously support a group, but some details and the overall construction of that scripture do suggest the disciples and the movement's later leaders benefited. For example, the Christian scripture/New Testament tells of Jesus performing many miracles, some of them nature miracles such as walking on water and calming a storm. Some scholars argue the nature miracles were created to elevate the status of Jesus' disciples; they were present when Jesus controlled nature, and, by inference, they inherited such power after Jesus' death. The development of the idea of apostolic succession whereby church leaders were part of a direct line back to the disciples mean some of this aura passed to those leaders.

The clearest instance of scripture benefiting a group comes from the assembly of the canon, the writings ultimately included in the Christian scripture/New Testament. The earliest surviving bits, scraps really, come from the second century, and the first complete text is from the fourth century. Over 30 gospels—writings about Jesus' life—survive, many only as fragments. Many other writings were produced but only 27 were ultimately included in the canon; what came to be included in this canon were works written from 15 to 125 years after Jesus' death. The development of the canon—the books finally chosen—began around 140 when Marcion, a wealthy Christian, proposed the church reject all Jewish scripture i.e., the Hebrew Bible/Old Testament, and use only Luke's gospel and Paul's letters. To Marcion the Hebrew God, being nasty occasionally, was inconsistent with the God of the Christians. While Marcion's canon did not carry the day, the resulting squabble led others to a consideration of what was proper to include. After Marcion, the oldest, relatively complete list—the Muratorian Canon—seems to date to the late second century. It includes some writings that were later dropped—e.g., the Apocalypse of Peter—and does not mention some later included—Philemon and Hebrews. Still later lists also have omissions and inclusions until 367 when the first list of today's canon appears; that list came from Athanasius, bishop of Alexandria. The final list may have occurred earlier in the fourth century because the Roman emperor Constantine had ordered the creation of 50 Bibles, which would have probably established the canon. At heart, the Christian scripture/New Testament books were chosen because they helped the early believers in their faith journeys, i.e., the community created the Christian scripture/New Testament, not vice versa.

The criteria for inclusion included mention by early church writers, style, doctrinal orthodoxy, and apostolic composition. For example, the Gnostics lost out in early struggles, and their writings were ignored although John's gospel has Gnostic elements. In studying the historical Jesus, scholars find an early gospel, the gospel of Thomas, to be a useful source but its Gnostic leanings probably led to its exclusion. Until the discoveries in 1945 – 6 at Nag Hammadi in the sands of Egypt, much of this Gnostic material was unknown. Those sands have yielded lots of such Gnostic writings, so it is believed Gnosticism was popular in Egypt (or the dry sands were especially congenial to the survival of Gnostic writings).

This development of the canon benefited church leaders—bishops and priests—in that Gnosticism in particular would have endangered the church as an institution; every believer had access to and possession of divine "Truth," which would make controlling a congregation an exercise in herding cats.

A second event that redounded to the benefit of church leadership was the development of baptism as a requirement for membership. Something mentioned more or less in passing in scripture (was it an addition?), baptism developed in importance in the early church. Not the simple sprinkling of water on a newborn, baptism was preceded by a period—maybe 2 years—of study and examination of personal behavior. The individual in charge of that process held the ultimate weapon—access to salvation. Moreover, once members the congregants had their behavior monitored and could be excluded from the group—something later called "excommunication"—something Paul's letters seem to support.

## Agreement? Archaeology.

Archaeology, the other source for the era, has long been a boom industry in Palestine. It is possible more digging has occurred there than in the rest of the world combined. Long of interest to Europeans, archaeology became a tool to prove or disprove the Bible. For example, portions of the tablets containing the epic of Gilgamesh were first published in the 1870s; though not relating to Israelites, the flood story in that epic was celebrated as confirming the Noah story. Today, a bimonthly magazine, *Biblical Archaeology Review*, is devoted to reporting about discoveries and interpretations that relate to the Bible.

The mesh between the Bible and archaeological results is not always perfect. Archaeologists have found nothing that touches large portions of the Bible. As a result scholars of the era have divided into minimalists and maximalists. The former, the minimalists, accept stories from the Bible only when archaeology supports them, whereas the maximalists accept Biblical stories unless contradicted by the digs. The Thoughtful can find scholarly articles that disagree completely about some biblical event.[21] Most scholars today locate themselves somewhere between the two extremes.

---

[21] Yosef Garfinkel, "The Birth and Death of Biblical Minimalism," *Biblical Archaeological Review*, 77, no. 3 (2011), 48-53, 78, gives a good summary of this issue.

An example of this matter is the biblical report of the plight and flight of the Israelites under Moses: the Exodus. While the Bible is quite detailed about these events, archaeology has turned up nothing—no mention of the Israelites in Egypt or their departure or their 40 years of wandering. Because this story is the Exodus, and it is both a major event and a theme of Jewish and Christian history, scholarly battles were inevitable. One defense of the historicity of the Exodus story points out the biblical details mesh with known aspects of Egyptian life, e.g., brickmaking techniques and identifies biblical cities and fortresses with Egyptian counterparts. On the other hand, the article confirms nothing explicitly connects the biblical story with Egyptian archaeology or writings.[22] Maybe all it shows is the author of the Exodus story was familiar with Egypt, not that the Exodus occurred—or not in the way it is biblically portrayed. (On a literary level, it is the story of the release, escape, from bondage, a major theme for both Jews and Christians.)

Writings from other cultures of the day make little mention of the Jews. Assyria and Egypt were world powers but their interest in the inhabitants of Palestine was equal to the Thoughtfuls' interest in Belize today. Not much. No writing survives, if it ever existed, that is specific about the years before 1200 B.C.E. and very little before 900 B.C.E. David and Solomon ruled, according to the Bible, the greatest territory of any Israelite kings, but they get no mention by their bigger neighbors. Perhaps the Bible exaggerates their power, but they did live in a period, 1200 – 900 B.C.E., when writing was scarcer than before and after (a "Dark Age").

## Just History. Post-Biblical Writings.

Once we leave the Christian scripture/New Testament era, the sources for Christian history become like all other history; they are not often argued about for doctrinal correctness and the like. These sources are evaluated, lacunae are explored, biases sought—surviving writing is usually created

---

[22] James Hoffmeier, "Out of Egypt" *Biblical Archaeological Review* 33 (2007), 30-41. A convenient summary of the episode is chapter 5 of Michael Coogen, ed., *The Old Testament* (Oxford University Press, 2008).

by history's winners—themes created; then scholars debate. An illustration about historical interpretation: a children's puzzle involves a collection of numbered dots. By connecting the dots in the numerical sequence, a picture emerges. (An adult can often spot the picture before the connections begin: "it's a horse.") However, a few dots offer more possible pictures while lots of dots make things obvious. Similarly with sources. A few sources give lots of options for interpretation but with increasing numbers, the explanation almost forces itself on the reader. Until about 1600, the bulk of the sources, even dealing with secular matters, are internal to Christianity as the literate tended to be churchmen; sources also are a bit thin on the ground. After 1600 and especially after 1900 the data multiply and more and more are of non-church origins as governments expanded and more individuals became literate. And paper got cheaper..

However, problems remain. For instance, on Christmas day, 800, a king of the Franks, now known as Charlemagne, prayed at the tomb of St. Peter in Rome. With Charlemagne kneeling in prayer, the pope put a crown atop his head; the pope and some monks chanted "To Charles Augustus, crowned by God, great and peace-giving emperor, life and victory." So began the Holy Roman Empire, an important institution of the Middle Ages and for the church. Two sources survive that deal with this event: one tells of the pope surprising the kneeling king and it made him angry, the other that this event had all been planned in advance. Surrounding actions do not help as they too point in both directions: Charlemagne and a council had just saved the pope from some nasty criminal charges, and so the council that cleared the pope also persuaded Charlemagne to become emperor; but Charlemagne rarely used his new title after 800.[23] No real debate about the event, but the motivations of the actors are obscure. Thus it is with much history; nothing is ever easy but folk don't get excited about Charlemagne or the Holy Roman Empire like they do Jesus or Moses.

---

[23] S.C. Easton and H. Wieruszowski, *The Era of Charlemagne* (Van Nostrand, 1961), pp. 126-9.

# Themes.

**Covenant. Hebrew Bible/Old Testament.**

When the Thoughtful read the Hebrew Bible/Old Testament, they may only see it as a story of the Israelites and their God, but a moment's reflection brings the awareness such a big book (really books) probably has other possibilities of interpretation, some large, some small. Today, the Hebrew Bible/Old Testament is approached as a religious text, but its composition involved various groups putting forth their ideas, religious and political. Once scholars and politicians got into the act, the Thoughtful might despair of getting a good grasp of the material. The overall theme is God has a covenant with the Israelites as a nation; when they honor that covenant, things go well, but when they do not, troubles ensue. The essentials of the covenant are to love God and do the right thing, the two important injunctions run throughout the work, but the detailed meaning of those commands is not always clear. The Thoughtful can be forgiven for some cynical thoughts about how all this writing might serve some other agenda beyond the purely religious ones.

Israel's writings are not unique in the time and place of the Near East, but they are a bit unusual. Knowing and reciting scripture as part of worship does seem to be different as other peoples relied only on sacrifices. The author called by scholars today the Deuteronomist, like the Greek Thucydides, invented speeches and omitted positive references to kings he disliked—e.g., Ahab's successful role in the battle at Qargar is ignored—in efforts to enhance his theme. Some of the books are attributed to someone other than the likely author—e.g., Psalms to David, Wisdom to Solomon—which was a common practice in ancient times. By 100 B.C.E., the Hebrew Bible/Old Testament had been translated into Greek, the Septuagint, increasingly the language of educated Jews. That version differs in significant aspects from the Dead Sea Scrolls and the earliest Hebrew text (Masoretic) which suggests someone kept tinkering with and adding things (e.g., the Book of Jeremiah gets longer). [24]

---

[24] The Dead Sea Scrolls contain all the books of the Hebrew Bible/Old Testament except Esther. As a result of the discovery of those writings, scholars now have four editions of Exodus, of varying lengths, and can observe when insertions of Isaiah have occurred.

Religious leaders today often see the major thrust of the Hebrew Bible/ Old Testament as the story of a healthy relationship with God bringing a fresh understanding of one's situation, one's suffering. Thus the Exodus becomes a metaphor about release from whatever makes one's life miserable. The Exile and return fit the same theme. With this view, the God of the Hebrew Bible/Old Testament comes down out of the sky and becomes a comfort when bad things happen. Whether that is a satisfactory outcome of a large, massive even, writing adventure probably depends on what the Thoughtful expected.

**Love. Christian Scripture/New Testament.**

The second part of scripture, the Christian scripture/New Testament, is all about Jesus. From Paul, through the gospels, to the other writings, the effects of Jesus on his followers are the focus.

Mark's gospel establishes a basic framework of organizing the events of Jesus' life and death into a coherent story. However, it is unclear, and probably can't be made clear, whether Mark creates some events to show Jesus' actions were fulfilling ancient prophecies—Mark was writing to convince listeners and readers Jesus was the Messiah—or if Jesus intentionally acted so as to fulfill those prophecies. For instance, the entrance in Jerusalem riding on a colt parallels Hebrew Bible/Old Testament material (Zechariah 9:9). Were Jesus' last words on the cross, as written in Mark's gospel, ("My God, my God, why have you forsaken me?" (Mark 15:34)), something he really said, a lament from Psalm 22:1, or did Mark use that Psalm in order to complete the story he was telling? Jesus teaches and heals, is seen as the Messiah—though he constantly asks people who call him that to remain silent—and discusses the Kingdom of God. Mark's theme is to be a follower of Jesus will involve suffering. Moreover, there does not seem to be any ultimate reward or victory for this suffering. Jesus may die feeling forsaken and no details of any resurrection are included. Perhaps the odd ending, quitting in mid-sentence, was designed to give hope but generally the gospel is not upbeat.

Matthew's gospel, written about 85, seeks to show Jesus is the fulfillment of all that the Hebrew Bible/Old Testament had predicted about the

Messiah. As the Kingdom of God still had not appeared, and it is not clear Matthew thinks it will anytime soon, the gospel is directed to the body of believers—Matthew, uniquely, uses the word "church". He prescribes how the followers are to behave and how to spread Jesus' message, be disciples. Long the most popular gospel for this teaching about discipleship, Matthew gets pride of place in the Christian scripture/New Testament, even though it is not the earliest writing or even the earliest gospel. This gospel most clearly ties together the 2 sections of scripture, the Hebrew Bible/Old Testament and Christian scripture/New Testament.

Also writing about 85, Luke was the best writer among the evangelists, and his gospel has the clearest theme. Combined with the Acts of the Apostles, also written by Luke, his gospel tells the story of the new understanding of the Jewish religion, as captured by Jesus, to all the world, symbolized by its appearance in the city of Rome, the capital of the world. Like Matthew, Luke is moving the Jesus movement into an organization that will later be called the church and pushing the end time into a distant future.

John's gospel has its own twist and resembles the other three only vaguely. Called the "spiritual gospel," John's writing lets theology override any historical basis, and, maybe as a result, the gospel is fairly disjointed. After Jesus' death, his message was preached and, in the process, changed. When those homilies were gathered and written down is anybody's guess, which may account for the unevenness of the gospel's final version. While Jesus performs a few miracles and travels a bit, the theme of the gospel is a series of "I am" speeches. They are long, set-pieces which expound on who Jesus was. A listener/reader of John's gospel might conclude Jesus is God, which would be a mistake; that view was coming to the fore in the Jesus movement.

The relationship of the gospels to each other is odd. Mark is very barebones, no nativity or resurrection stories. The general thrust is Jesus' disciples never quite caught on to what he was doing, and Mark's ending with Jesus' questioning God strongly implies, perhaps unintentionally, Jesus was a failure. Fifteen years later, Matthew and Luke wrote their gospels, using Mark as the skeleton for longer writings. Matthew and Luke add (different) nativity stories and have (different) Resurrection appearances. Another ten years later, John wrote a gospel which varies in almost every way from the other three. Jesus speaks in long discourses, and the focus is not on Jesus' message of the Kingdom of God, but on what Jesus himself was—in some circles he had become divine by the year 95, something John maybe sought to resist. The portrayal of Jesus, as the reader moves from Mark to John is of a figure more in control of events, less a human being, more god-like. Finally, some scholars think Mark is a complete piece of fiction, at least in its factual rather than metaphorical sense, which means the reliance of Luke and Matthew makes them untrustworthy as well. Ah, the joys of scholarship.

All of this knowledge has been grist for scholars over the last two centuries, and an example of the scholarly process in this area can be found, beginning in the 1980s, when a group, mostly professors, met regularly to discuss which sayings attributed to Jesus were in fact his and which were later additions by his followers. Called the "Jesus Seminar," the group developed several rules/guidelines and, after discussion and debate, voted. They used four categories: Jesus said it, he probably said it, he probably did not say it, and no way. The resulting book, *The Five Gospels* was printed in various colors to illustrate the voting results. One conclusion of the group was only one saying in the entire gospel of John was uttered by Jesus, and it might not be in the original writing but be a later insert by a copyist (John 4:44)[25] The Jesus Seminar removed much theological and literary overlay from Jesus' words, leaving a starker, more historically realistic, individual. Their conclusions have not gone unchallenged, however; indeed much other work is a reaction to the conclusions of the Jesus Seminar.

The gospels tell how Jesus affected particular communities and what they understood about him. Because John and the Synoptics are included in Christian scripture/New Testament, the listener/reader makes a connection they deal with the same figure, Jesus, yet if they were not so situated, a listener/reader could be excused for not seeing such a connection; the stories differ greatly. The gospels, theological writings attempting to convey

---

[25] Robert W. Funk et al., *The Five Gospels* (Macmillan, 1993). "Five" gospels are included because the members of the seminar included *The Gospel of Thomas*, a writing that wasn't included in the Bible but which they find a valuable, and early, source about Jesus.

religious meaning, were not intended to be historically accurate. And they aren't.

While all four gospels do seem to be part of the same story, the differing mixtures of theology and oral tradition in each produce dramatically different works. Thus the gospels are partly about the religion of Jesus—the Kingdom of God material—and partly about Jesus himself—his unique status as Son of God and what that meant. All the gospels end with Jesus' death or resurrection but what to make of it is left to the listener/reader. Most of the remaining works of the Christian scripture/New Testament deal with the meaning of the Resurrection and its relation to salvation, whether of the individual or the group. Lots of possible themes are bouncing around in the Christian scripture/New Testament, and Christianity has responded with many denominations (over 30,000 world-wide at last count). The Thoughtful are left with the knowledge the gospels have differing themes, and scholars, as exemplified by the Jesus Seminar, have distilled the story into a few basics, much more barebones than the Thoughtful believed.

The overall theme of the Christian scripture/New Testament is God is love and Jesus shows what that means. Acceptance of those ideas leads to a new understanding of the world—a resurrection if you will—and a better ability to cope individually and collectively with the unfairness of that world.

## Conclusion.

The Thoughtful can now understand the Bible is a source but not a simple source for Christianity. Its importance has led to it being manipulated and misused as well as honored and respected. What the Bible is and what it contains is both a factual problem and a theological one. Certainty has not been achieved, at least for most in the Thoughtful mold, and never will be. However, for the Thoughtful most of the disagreements mentioned in this chapter are not so earth-shaking as to bring down the edifice of Christianity. Inconsistencies, if not exactly abounding, are not rare, especially in the

Christian scripture/New Testament. None need be a deal-breaker for a Thoughtful believer, but all point to the uncertainties of the biblical text. One can look to the Bible for the Word of God, but not the words of God. Too many problems.

The Thoughtful may react to this wealth of possible interpretation with a welter of opinions. Complete disregard of it all as bunk is one reaction to the discovery of the variety of options present, especially in the Christian scripture/New Testament. At the other extreme, one can select one of those options, usually some version with a definition of salvation, declare it Truth and quit worrying. Perhaps the presence of multiple gospels or two creation stories or two histories of Israel resembles the multiple biographies of Abraham Lincoln; when one cannot "know" something, approaching it from different angles leads to more understanding. A more likely scenario is confusion. As the end time receded into the future, now a quite distant future, and modern science precludes any final judgment and resurrection, at least in any literal sense, the Thoughtful stick to the here and now. The Bible posits that a right relationship with God—love God and do the right thing—brings salvation, a feeling of contentment, spiritual health. Caring for and helping others will flow from that state. The religion of and about Jesus suggests a major result will be comfort in times of troubles, also a theme of the Hebrew Bible/Old Testament.

# CONCLUSION

Where are we? What to do?

For many Thoughtful, believers or skeptics, Christianity gets difficult when, as a result of scholarly work, scripture starts falling apart. The Thoughtful, even if not raised in the Christian tradition, have absorbed enough of the stories to think Christianity is based on historical events. As this book shows, scripture is a pretty shaky basis to argue for the historicity of much of the Christian story, though some history is present. The gospels turn out not to be biographies, and the historical books of the Hebrew Bible/ Old Testament have lots of holes. Many writings do not accurately report events or jibe with archaeology. Some stories are created out of wholly new cloth. Many are metaphorical. Inconsistencies abound. Some Thoughtful come to a place where disbelief is an option that looks attractive, and they decide to chuck the whole thing. However, others find some value in the tradition and realize despite their rejection of simplistic literalism, they are tied, however tenuously, to the scriptural stories. Now, cast adrift, they must move to more sophisticated readings of scripture and different understanding of Christianity. For centuries believers accepted scripture (though maybe not literally) because it was traditional and it explained the past adequately; there was no alternative. But today with science uncovering more and more about life, the Thoughtful realize scripture can be seen as an effort to understand the experience of God, and it should be taken as such. The Bible is not a history of the world nor even the Israelite and Christian portions of it.

The history of Christianity poses yet another problem. Certainly "killing for Christ" has occurred—and not just once but repeatedly and in large numbers—which is a problem for a religion that espouses loving one's neighbor and forgiving one's enemies. Then there is the rampant ambition, careerism, and general tawdriness of the lives of too many leading figures of the church—popes who were unpopely, monks who were unmonkly, television evangelists who couldn't keep their pants up or their hands out of the till. Finally, a distressing reality is the dislike, distrust, yes, even hatred, found among and between the various branches of Christendom. Some Protestants see Roman Catholics as slaves to unthinking tradition. A visitor to the church of the Holy Sepulchre in Jerusalem can witness four denominations holding services in the same building simultaneously and in an obvious competition to be the loudest. Why can't at least the professional church folk love their neighbors? If they cannot, how can the rest of us even aspire to such a worthy view?

American culture is suffused with Christian ideas and practices, although perhaps less than it was in the past, and the result is often troubling to the Thoughtful. Even the skeptical Thoughtful have difficulties ignoring various messages associated with Christmas. Politicians routinely invoke God, and letters to the editor often decry society's failure to honor Jesus' teachings (which, to the writers, explains all current woes). The issue of treatment of homosexuals is permeated with Christian talk which can only surprise someone ignorant of U.S. religious history. Peer group pressure is strong; even many who are not strongly connected to any denomination claim otherwise. Surveys usually produce numbers of respondents avowing church attendance which do not correlate at all with counts produced by the churches. Whether the U.S. is, or ever was, a "Christian nation" is open to debate but Christianity, often in a very watered-down form, permeates the culture, which is often not a Christianity attractive to the Thoughtful.

Today nothing puts the Thoughtful off more than a conversation/confrontation with someone about "What do you believe?" or "Are you saved?" Certainly, Christian history is filled with disputes about beliefs—what is orthodox—and the nasty consequences of being caught on the wrong side of an issue. However, at no time have all Christians agreed about any belief or doctrine, as this book makes abundantly clear. And it does not appear they ever will. Arguing about beliefs became the issue when the church adopted creeds and doctrines, though it appears Jesus did not concern himself with such matters. If Truth exists in this area, Christians seem unable to find it; Plato's image of the myth of the cave with its vision of a reality, an eternal and absolute Truth, needs to be discarded. Thoughtfuls, quit worrying about beliefs.

A standard criticism of contemporary Christianity comes from those who are exposed to the material of this book. "If X didn't really happen, why don't the clergy preach and teach in ways to disabuse us of believing in X?" As this book has argued, belief in facts is not crucial to the Christian experience; transforming lives is the object. Clergy, therefore, feel little need to make the faithful *au currant* in historical, archaeological, and exegetical research as such material will rarely change lives, except when someone cannot accept such new ideas and departs the building—a negative result to the clergy.[1] If transforming lives is the object, Christianity must seek to appeal to the heart, but the early Greek thinkers in the church also sought to make it attractive to the head. Maybe that was a bad idea

A related statement is "If Y, as described in scripture, did not really happen, how can you trust anything in the Bible?"[2] The Thoughtful recognize this as the "slippery slope" problem; once going down that hill, where or how can you stop? This attitude is related to the either/or development stage discussed in Chapter 2. While the Thoughtful are not particularly perturbed by the slippery slope style of argument, it is difficult to explain to the many who aren't Thoughtful, because this is usually a place where discussion or argument is futile and not rewarding to the participants. Let sleeping dogs lie. Especially if waking them would lead to consequences not particularly Christian.

It might be easier to approach the issue of belief by adopting Socrates' position of not knowing Truth but only knowing what is false. The easy

---

[1] For a list of stuff that the Thoughtful may wish they had been told, see Oliver Thomas, *10 Things Your Minister Wants To Tell You (But Can't, Because He Needs the Job)* (St. Martin's 2007)

[2] Christopher Hitchins in *God is not Great* (Twelve, 2007) presents his atheistic arguments and argues the gospels must have literal truth or be a fraud.

ones— "the sun revolves around the earth" variety—have become so commonplace the Thoughtful often forget things were not always such. In matters Christian, it is a bit harder to find agreed-upon wrong answers. The Thoughtful probably reject a literalist approach to the Bible or that every word in the Bible is fully inspired— "plenary"—even though not all Christians would accept those rejections. Do evil things to others before they do them to you—an adage sometimes found among the ancient Greeks—would find nearly universal rejection. Maybe some Thoughtful understand Pascal's wager and choose to believe. For the Thoughtful it is easiest to agree Truth is unknowable so those clamoring for it are wrong. Beyond that statement, lack of certainty prevails.

The truth is: all things in the past are subject to probabilities. It is very unlikely, but not totally out of the question, the world was flooded in Noah's time, but it is very, very probable a fellow named "Jesus" wandered around Galilee and was later executed by the Roman government. These sort of things fall into categories of probability in the same way stories as those about King Arthur and Queen Elizabeth I. Some verge on the fantastic and some are probable. One seeks more information, picks and chooses, maybe makes a judgment, and forms an opinion. It is just the reality the religious story of the Bible is somehow more important than English history, at least to non-English historians.

In addition to the problems of certainty, the Thoughtful now appreciate, as many folk have difficulty dealing with concepts, the early church quickly moved to stories and visual representations. Thus "patience" could be discussed by relating the life of a particular saint or biblical character (Job, for example) or illustrated by the painting of that individual. Of course, this approach had risks as many folk worshipped the saint or character rather than understanding and practicing the underlying concept. Certainly many Christians, in the past and present, have taken their notion of God from art, and Michelangelo's Sistine Chapel ceiling probably looms large. Perhaps for this reason Judaism and Islam ban representational art. The Eastern Christian tradition fought about this issue early on but the West, at least until the Reformation, accepted art in all its forms as beneficial to the faith experience. Today, Protestant denominations have varying attitudes to such art, with some banning it completely and others accepting it in limited amounts. All of this matter is connected to the developmental stages discussed in Chapter 2, and the Thoughtful can appreciate now why such issues exist in Christianity. This issue is not, however, a dispute of much relevance to the Thoughtful.

A theme of this book has been that things are not as they are often seem and life is complex. The Thoughtful can accept that a man named Jesus had a particularly good, maybe unique, grasp of the idea of God and lived and taught in ways that convinced some a new world, a Kingdom of God, was beginning. When that new world did not sweep the world, hopes for its eventual success were pushed into the future, even into an afterlife, and the church was born. Maybe all ideas need a community or an institution, such as the church, to protect and develop them, but the Thoughtful can be forgiven if they find many later developments of Christian history, especially in the church, to be distasteful. However, this book has sought to show most "oddities," were natural and logical developments, based upon prior understandings and the nature of the audience. For example, the Trinity grew out of efforts to describe Jesus as divine, which in turn grew out of feelings anyone as unusual as he could only be described as a god. The Inquisition, awful and immoral as its excesses were, evolved from a desire to insure all humans had the opportunity to inhabit the Kingdom of God. At many, perhaps most, times, some nasty people exploited aspects of Christianity for their own purposes but the Thoughtful recognize this matter as a common human failing that need not discredit the basic idea. All of these issues do not invalidate the core ideas of Christianity but do serve as a caution about being too certain in one's faith. Certainty too often brings hatred, tragedy, and a host of other evils.

What to do in the face of such problems?

Lower the expectations. Unfortunately, for the Thoughtful, they know someone who proclaims "When I found Jesus, he cured my cancer." And, of course, the gospel stories of Jesus calming the storm, healing lepers, curing blindness, and so forth, lend credence to the idea Christianity, or perhaps many religions, claims great benefits, tangible benefits, for believers. The Thoughtful don't see things that way. Perhaps, an idea that is more acceptable is faith won't calm the stormy waters but will give an inner calm that makes the waters seem less violent—a "peace of God that surpasseth all human understanding." Most of the world's religions, at heart, suggest "going with the flow," "getting in sync with things," leads to a more contented life.

Therefore, for the Thoughtful, whether spiritual or religious, a good first step would be to forget the various images of God they have acquired. Whether from the Sistine Chapel ceiling, the comics page of the newspaper, or the vocabulary one hears from television preachers, all images bother the Thoughtful. Many Americans still have the understandings of their teen years even though they would find it foolish they would accept ideas about child raising or maybe sex from their past. Along this line many believers see Jesus as God, a position traditionally rejected as Docetism because it raises unfortunate questions as to why he did not heal everyone, or speak Chinese, or bring world peace. Still others talk of God as a spirit, which raises the old dualism of materialism/spiritualism which many Thoughtful both accept, because it fits a traditional view of the Western intellect, and reject, because it is rejected by current science. The Thoughtful even have trouble talking about God in any way that implies an active involvement by that deity in the world. A new take on Christianity involves shedding lots of baggage and accepting that language is inadequate in this matter. The notion human concepts do not adequately describe God (apopbatic theology) takes some getting used to.

"God," thus becomes a word used to describe the idea, the feeling, the effort, when one seeks to be a "better" person, to help another, to think beyond one's self. For too long, the notion of "God" has been portrayed as an entity, a person even, that, the Thoughtful reflect, looks a lot like the Greek god Zeus. (Even ancient Greek philosophers ultimately rejected anthropomorphic portrayals of the deity.) The New Atheists are tilting against windmills, are knocking down strawmen, as far as the Thoughtful believer is concerned, because God has become an ineffable present, not a supernatural being; a mystery, not an intellectual system. While evolutionary psychologists and biologists might call this matter an "instinct" developed to ensure the survival of the species or one's genes, is probably unprovable. And, so what?

Some seek an experience to the effect there is something that encompasses all of creation but it is so wholly transcendent as to be ungraspable. If the Thoughtful choose to pursue, work, and exercise discipline on this topic (more than one hour per week in a building), they might conclude religion is not a set of doctrines or a litany of beliefs, but experience a breakdown of thought, an awareness of the unknowability of God, an abdication of the intellect. At this point a common position for the Thoughtful is to declare an interest in "spirituality," but not "religion." While the words are not precise, such a statement often appears to mean "religion" is organized religion, the churches, the denominations, while "spirituality" involves a belief "something" greater than us is involved in the world; a "something" that may give some solace in hard times and a meaning to life in good times. Some take this interest in spirituality seriously, studying things to deepen and widen their understanding, think often about the consequences of their position, and join with others in examining the options. A twenty-first century movement for the spiritually inclined is often called the "emergent church," which means small groups, often meeting in someone's home, with no creeds, no affiliation with any denomination. However, many interested in spirituality go no further than to assert their spiritual interest and enjoy pop culture that skims over the surface (think television and self-help books). Seeking after spirituality is usually an individual quest, one that does not involve working with or helping others, and it often peters out after the initial enthusiasm wears off.

Perhaps talk about God can be forgone. Writers often leave the notion, the idea, the discussion of God as a mystery, the "ground of being." [3] Perhaps the Thoughtful should too. Arguing about definitions may entertain phi-

---

[3] The term is from Paul Tillich, *Systematic Theology* (U. of Chicago Press, Chicago, 1951), vol. 1, 156. A mid-twentieth-century existentialist theologian, Tillich is very abstract. Perhaps "ground of being" can be interpreted as "God is the basis for all things."

losophers and logicians but most of the rest of us have to get on with our lives. This approach involves a shift in thinking away from a view of God as the great chess player in the sky which is something else the Thoughtful can appreciate and accept. Almost a millennium ago, Thomas Aquinas suggested the nature of God was unknowable, at least in this life.

Besides spirituality, another approach is often used to describe one's life as a "journey" because one sees and learns new things constantly, maybe never arriving at a destination, a conclusion, a definitive end. Martin Buber, a twentieth-century philosopher, wrote every journey has a secret destination of which one is unaware. With the old rules of behavior or belief based upon scripture discredited and a belief in knowability discarded, the journey is guided by the insights of Jesus: love your neighbors and do the right thing. However, even those minimal themes are not clear as "love" can mean many things and lots of discussion and dispute. Nonetheless, some consensus exists over how to love (serve) a neighbor and what the "right thing" might be. And an absence of certainty is always as good quality. Whether those in the pews know it or not, this is the theme of many sermons. Maybe combining the two approaches by acting with compassion and having an interior spirituality is the way to go.

What can be surprising about seeing life as a religious journey with constantly shifting understandings is how many others are on the same journey, usually at different stages. The ideas of developmental stages, discussed in chapter 2, make sense as the Thoughtful can understand why literalists remain literalistic. Does that make someone who has moved past literalism—and most who have were once literalists themselves—superior? If one does calculus, is one better than someone who cannot master algebra? Or, are professional athletes superior to the rest of us? As individuals we all have strengths and weaknesses but as humans we are all equal. One benefit of joining a community comes with the sharing of experiences on the journey. The Thoughtful now realize it is easier to resist feelings of superiority or snobbism ("We're further along on our journey than you, simple literalist.") following the discovery someone else is "further along" than the Thoughtful are. (However, one is wise to defer to a mathematical judgment by the calculus master and let one's child imitate the moves of the pro athlete. Is religion the same?) For the Thoughtful, churchgoers have often been seen as a unified body with the same beliefs and answers. Tain't so, McGee.

Maybe a part of this new approach is to shift interest from the individual to the community, from "me" to "we." Historically, the focus of scripture was on collectivities, Israel for the Hebrew Bible/Old Testament, the church for Christian scripture/New Testament. Today for many believers, perhaps most, Christianity is a religion of comfort and consolation for the individual. When disaster—illness, accident—strikes, believing God is there, listening, caring, maybe aiding, makes the whole thing bearable, maybe worthwhile. For some, not personally suffering, the opportunity to joint with their fellows to help others, be they the local homeless, the victims of a hurricane, or the distant sufferers of AIDS is a good thing. Christian leaders throughout the centuries have argued against being a "solitary Christian" as that condition is not truly being a Christian. (Even monks, initially solitary beings in the desert, were soon gathered into communities.) Today, to the Thoughtful, most of Jesus' message—love your neighbor—can be acted upon without becoming a member of any denomination or sect or calling oneself "Christian." Tolerance, forgiveness, selflessness, all make for a better world and perhaps a healthier spiritual life. However, finding fellowship in a community of people committed to Jesus' message might bring other, bigger results. In such circumstances, the whole is greater than the sum of the parts.

How does this approach work? Being part of a community permits one to work on disaster relief, something usually unavailable to the individual. And who will visit when one is old and alone? A community is always available to help celebrate accomplishments and lend support in time of trouble. Peer group pressure (for lack of a better term) might push one to be a more honest business person, to work at a homeless shelter, to live a life like "good people." If belief is pretty much irrelevant, behavior might be the important aspect of life. Indeed, perhaps faith is a practice, not a system of beliefs; a commitment, not an argument. (Again, look at Chapter 2.)

No afterlife as reward, but consolation in one's time of trouble, doing good for others, fellowship with similar souls, being drawn out of oneself occasionally—is this result enough to justify participation in a church? Maybe not when one is young, healthy, sound, and busy. Probably yes when age, illness, and troubles are more prevalent and time passes slowly. So, joining up is a selfish act? Perhaps. Just as mission work or responding to God increasingly draws one out of one's self, worship can let the individual join in a greater body. Light, smell, music, all can let the believer cease thinking selfishly, at least for a few moments, and enter into something greater, even if it is a mystery as to what that something is. Thinking of one's self all the time may not be healthy, and certainly is boring.

The point is?

If the God the Thoughtful can accept is not the personal, supernatural God of so much Christian history, but a mystery beyond thinking, is this God distinctively Christian? For some, no; for others, Jesus' insights resonate so perfectly other paths need not be sought. Where do the Thoughtful land? Perhaps the Thoughtful now understand the Christian life, or journey, is not about obtaining an afterlife, at least in any literal sense. Salvation—a good relationship with God, spiritual health—may be acquired but concerns with heaven can be forgotten. Moreover, religion turns out to require hard work, persistence, discipline. "I've got my hands full in this life. I'll let God worry about the afterlife." is a position the Thoughtful can adopt comfortably. Whether God is distinctively Christian becomes irrelevant. The scripture story is open to the interpretation that a power exists that works to defy the forces of destruction, oppression, and injustice. For some Thoughtful, at this point the issue becomes the existence of God. Despite the destruction of entire forests to make paper, the existence or nonexistence of God remains unproven, and unprovable.

Maybe these issues point to the idea of not referring to God in a gendered way. Called "political correctness" by some, the result of a more neutral language is a step towards getting away from the Sistine Chapel ceiling image of God. As soon as God is called "he" or "she," it becomes difficult to avoid conjuring up a human image, a personality. As this book has attempted to show, maybe God is not a supernatural being in the sky or anything similar. And maybe God is not an all-powerful creator but something totally different. The language of gender makes jettisoning those older notions more difficult.

With these views, what then is off the table? Probably for many, the most important religious belief is about eternal life, at least as it is commonly understood. Leaving aside images of standing on clouds playing harps, one cannot, in honesty, imagine an eternal life that would be other than boring. A common response is to say God can create an eternal life beyond our imagination. OK, maybe that works for you. Also, the modern scientific view of the world has no place for such an idea. The idea, moreover, one gets a reward—heaven—for good behavior or proper belief is preposterous, more worthy of ancient Egyptians. Many Christians, finally, see eternal life as a merging of one's self into the notion of the deity—a proper relationship, a healthy spiritual life—which can occur here and now.

As to Jesus, the Thoughtful can consider him as a human who demonstrated what God looks like or how God would have lived. Someone said "Jesus was the best photograph of God we have." Behavior and understanding, not certain beliefs, define the Christian, but that behavior doesn't earn or merit any reward; one does it because "it is just the right thing to do"—no reason or power causes it. The message comes down to us from Jesus is that our faith is to be shown in our actions, in what we do, and is to love (serve) our neighbors, forgive our enemies, and seek to do the right thing. While Thoughtful skeptics can reject the mythology of Christianity, the basic insights discussed in this book are a bit more difficult to ignore. While rejecting historical Christianity, Thoughtful skeptics still follow the ethical and moral teachings of the tradition. Unfortunately, this approach may lead to a lack of self-examination (no growth) and an acquiescence in the status quo of society, especially as to society's disadvantaged, the outcasts, and the marginalized. By accepting the basic insights of Christianity, many Thoughtful believers understand living selflessly and compassionately gives the experience of transcendence, the experience of God.

For the Thoughtful who were raised in the Christian tradition, dealing with the ideas implanted in their youth is a challenge. For Protestants the Bible was (apparently) taught as literally true, or close to literally true, and letting go of that is difficult. Roman Catholics, on the other hand, were not explicitly told to observe scripture literally so much as to obey the dictates of the representatives of the church who explained scripture in ways that implied literal truth. However, in both cases they usually were living in the Christian tradition—engaging in charitable acts, trying to live a morally decent lives. Abandonment of attachment to a denomination did not bring a significant change to their lives as their actions often continued as they had. What was lost was the presence of a community and, in many cases, that loss was a relief. Eventually, the Thoughtful may come to the realization membership in a group has its advantages. Then the issue becomes whether it should be a religious or a secular organization. For many, perhaps most, Christian thinkers there is no such thing as a solitary Christian; Christianity requires community or fellowship, to use their preferred term. Getting repetitious, isn't it?

To conclude, what is a "Christian?" At its simplest, the definition means someone who accepts Jesus was Christ. What is "Christ?" A Greek word meaning "Messiah." So what is "Messiah?" In the Hebrew Bible/Old Testament it meant "the anointed one." Not getting anywhere? By Jesus' time Messiah usually meant a leader or leaders (two in some view) who would lead people to regain past glories, maybe political (power), maybe religious (purity). Jesus' followers morphed those ideas into one who gave a new understanding of life. For those early Christians, Jesus was ushering in the "Kingdom of God," by which they meant a world operating by divine rules of behavior, such as forgiveness and service. Thus a Christian becomes one who has a relationship with God whereby life is lived in accordance with Christian tradition. That conclusion is both more and less than the Thoughtful probably thought before reading this book.

# APPENDICES

## *Western Church Developments*

The following chart gives a visual representation of the development of Western Christianity through the Reformation. The time scale is not uniform, the first 100 years and last 40 years have disproportionate space. The width of the various bands does not attempt to correspond to the population of believers, e.g., the band of the split of the Western and Eastern branches about 1000 is not reflective of the size of each group, if such size could be calculated (which is doubtful).

Christianity emerged about 100, separate from Judaism, and was the result of a mix of Jewish religious traditions and Greek philosophy. The circle encompassing Jesus, Paul, and the Jesus people, represents the formative era and details are lacking as to many of the developments; think of the circle as a cloud through which we can see only dimly until about the year 100. The dotted line from 100 to 300 suggests, in the absence of a governing structure and creeds, that the boundaries of Christianity were vague.

When Constantine converted in the fourth century, the elite of the Roman Empire followed him into the fold, bringing their Greek education with them. As a result, much squabbling occurred as the Greek-educated churchmen (and almost all were men) sought to bring order and rationality to their faith. A series of councils met to define the "proper" understandings of Christianity and drafted creeds incorporating their beliefs. Loosely called "Nicene," the resulting church had imperial support. Many, especially in Asia and Africa, could not accept the creedal results, particularly as to the nature of Jesus, and they went their own ways. Thereafter, the imperial church slowly drifted into a Eastern and Western division, something seen as permanent in 1054.

The focus of the latter part of this book is the Western church, an institution increasingly dominated by the pope; it also began to fuss about proper doctrine and practices, with heresies resulting, the most famous being those of John Hus in Bohemia and John Wycliffe in England. These actions further narrowed the church's boundaries until 1517 when Luther, quickly followed by other reformers, blew up the edifice. Another circle, think cloud, and lots of confusion until about 1560 when five major branches of Western Christianity emerged. Those branches, which continue to produce separate groups, cover the variety of Western Christians today.

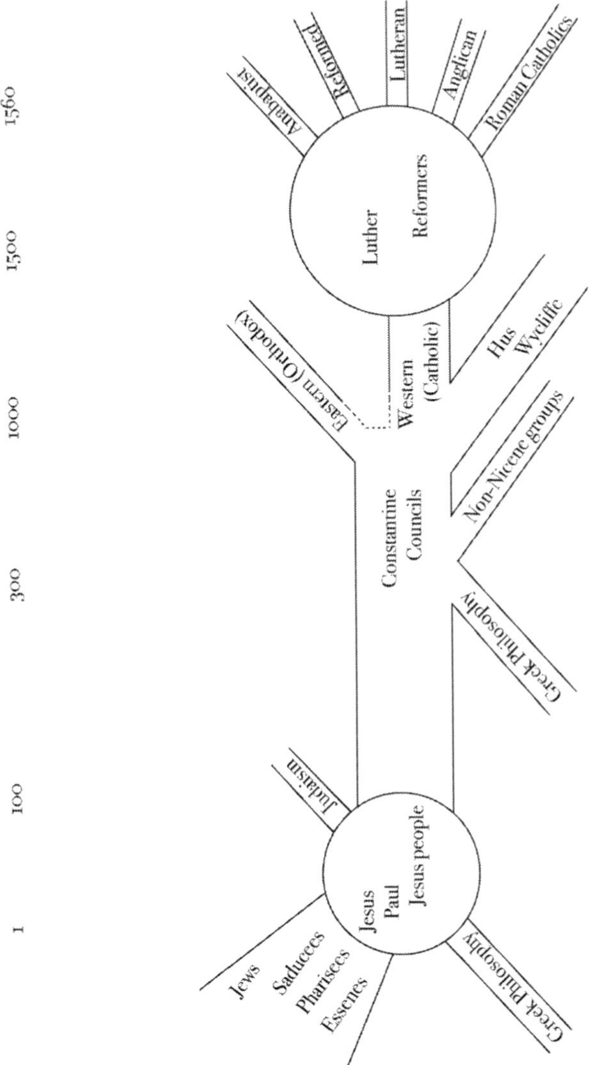

1
100
300
1000
1500
1560
Jews
Saducees
Pharisees
Essenes
Jesus
Paul
Jesus people
Greek Philosophy
Judaism
Constantine
Councils
Greek Philosophy
Non-Nicene groups
Eastern (Orthodox)
Western
(Catholic)
Hus
Wycliffe
Luther
Reformers
Anabaptist
Reformed
Lutheran
Anglican
Roman Catholics

MAP 1

# TOPOGRAPHY OF PALESTINE

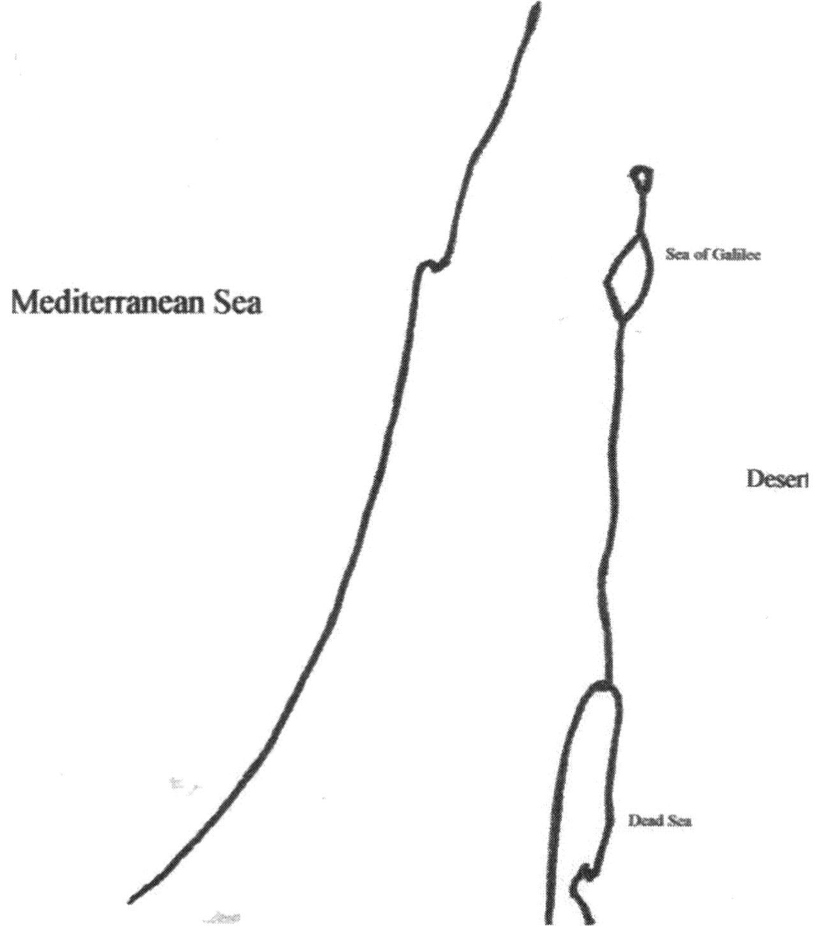

MAP 2

# PALESTINE
# IN
# HEBREW BIBLE/OLD TESTAMENT TIMES

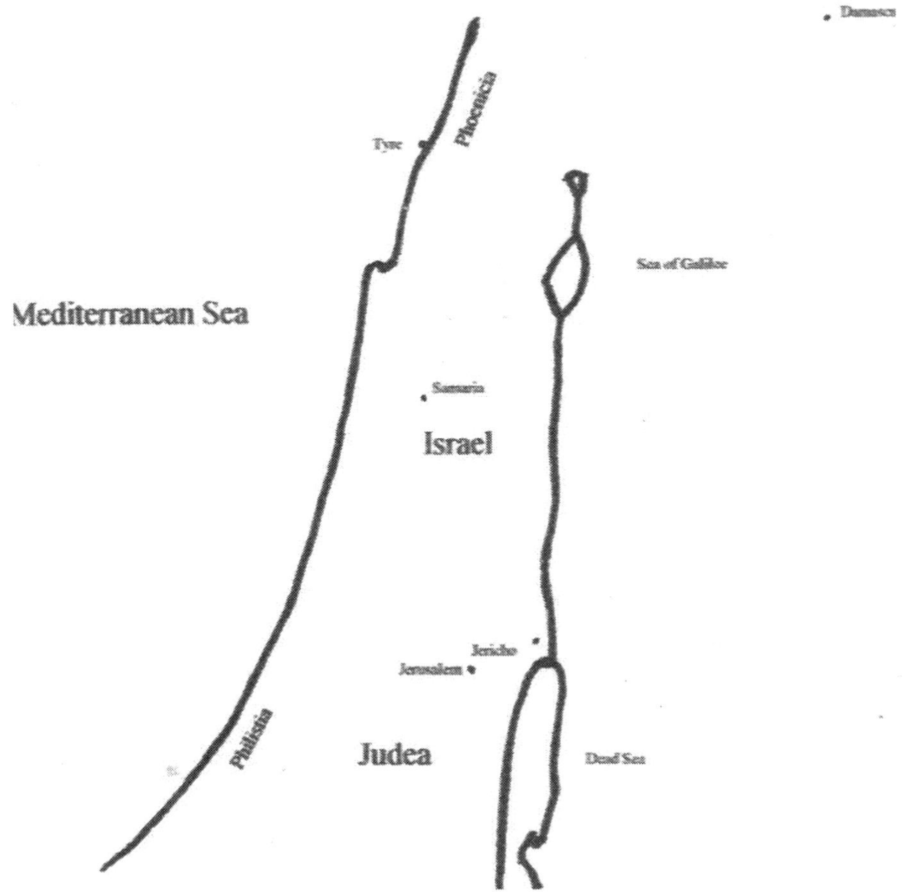

MAP 3

# PALESTINE
# IN
# CHRISTIAN SCRIPTURE/NEW TESTAMENT TIMES

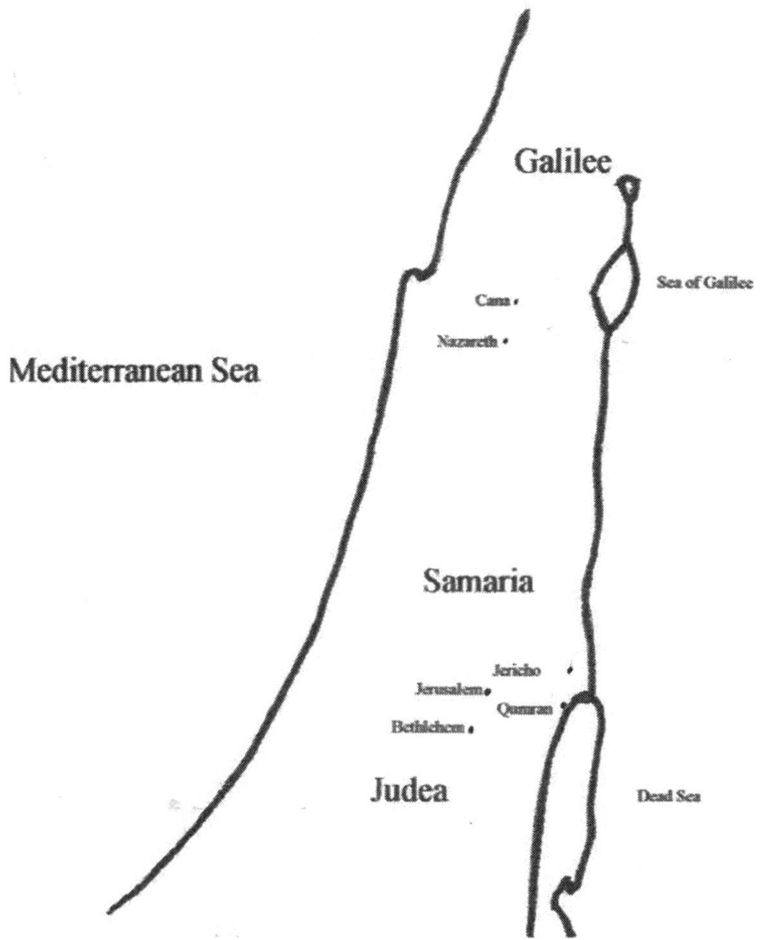

# CHRONOLOGY

## *History of Israel*

(All dates except for Augustus are B.C.E.)

| | ELSEWHERE | PALESTINE |
|---|---|---|
| **B.C.E./B.C.** | | |
| | writing in Mesopotamia<br>Bronze Age begins<br>Egypt united under one ruler | |
| **3000** | | |
| **2500** | Egyptian pyramids | |
| **2000** | | |
| | Hittite empire (1800 – 1200)<br>Hammurapi's law code | |
| **1500** | | patriarchs (?) |
| | | Egypt conquers Palestine |
| | Akenaten pharaoh (1352 – 36)<br>"Israelites" mentioned<br>in Egyptian stele (1309) | Exodus (?) |

| | | |
|---|---|---|
| | Trojan War | |
| | Philistines settle coast | David (?) |
| | Iron Age begins | Solomon (?) |
| | | First Temple built |
| **1000** | | |
| | | Two Kingdoms (928) |
| | | Israel Judah |
| | Assyrian empire (1114 – 612) | |
| | | Omni (882 – 71) |
| | Homer (c. 800) | Ahab (873 – 52) |
| | | Prophets appear |
| | | disappear (722) |
| | | Josiah's reforms (632) |
| | Babylonian empire (612 – 539) | Exile (586) |
| | Persian empire (539 – 333) | Return (538) |
| | Persia-Greek wars | Second Temple (520) |
| **500** | | |
| | Plato in Athens | |
| | Alexander the Great (336 – 23) | Alexander the Great |
| | Hellenistic kingdoms | Ptolemies (312 – 198) |
| | Rome-Carthage wars | Seleucids (198 – 67) |
| | | Macabee revolt (167) |
| | | Hasmonean Kingdom (165 – 3) |
| | | Dead Sea Scrolls created |
| | | Rome (63) |
| | Augustus emperor (30 B.C.E.-14 C.E.) | Herod the Great (37 – 4 ) |
| | | Jesus born (4) |

# *Early Christianity*

**C.E./A.D.**

| | MEDITERRANEAN WORLD | CHRISTIANITY |
|---|---|---|
| | Augustus (30 B.C.E. – 14 C.E.) | Jesus executed (30) |
| | | Paul's letters (40s & 50s) |
| | Nero (54 – 68) | Persecution in Rome (64) |
| | | Jewish Revolt (66 – 73) |
| | | Temple destroyed (70) |
| | | Gospel of Mark |
| | | Gospel of Luke |
| | | Gospel of Matthew |
| | | Gospel of John |
| | Trajan (98 – 117) | Revelation |
| **100** | | |
| | | Second Jewish Revolt (132 – 5) |
| | Era of Good Emperors | Marcion (170) |
| | | Local persecutions |
| **200** | | |
| **300** | | |
| | Diocletian emperor (284 – 305) | The Great Persecution |
| | Constantine emperor (423 – 37) | Constantine converts (313) |
| | | Council of Nicaea (325) |
| | Julian (360 – 2) last non-Christian emperor | Earliest complete Bible |
| | | New Testament as we know it listed (376) |

# *Christian History*

| | EUROPEAN EVENTS | CHRISTIANITY/CHURCH |
|---|---|---|
| **400** | | Vulgate Translation |
| | | Augustine (396 – 430) |
| | Visigoths capture Rome (410) | |
| | Vandals capture Rome (455) | Councils (Christianity divides) |
| **500** | | |
| | | Monte Cassino founded (529) |
| | | Pope Gregory (590 – 604) |
| **600** | Muhammad (578 – 632) | Conversion of England begun |
| | Arabs conquer Jerusalem (638) | |
| **700** | | |
| | Battle of Tours (732) | |
| **800** | Charlemagne | |
| | Vikings | |
| **900** | | |
| | | Cluny Abbey founded (910) |
| | | Christianity spreads in eastern Europe |
| **1000** | | East-West divide "final" (1054) |
| | Norman Conquest (1066) | Investiture Controversy (1077) |
| | | First Crusade (1095) |
| **1100** | | |
| | | Second Lateran Council (1139) |

| | | |
|---|---|---|
| | | Gothic architecture appears |
| | | Era of cathedral building |
| 1200 | | Pope Innocent III (1198 – 1215) |
| | | Francis of Assisi (1181 – 1226) |
| | Magna Carta (1215) | |
| 1300 | Dante (1265 -1321) | Babylonian Captivity (1309 – 78) |
| | | Schism (1378) |
| | | John Wycliffe (1320 – 84) |
| 1400 | | Three popes |
| | | Council of Constance (1417) |
| | Joan of Arc (1431) | |
| | Constantinople conquered by Turks (1453) | Guttenberg Bible (1455) |
| 1500 | Copernicus (1473 – 1543) | Luther posts 95 theses (1517) |
| | | Henry VIII breaks with Rome (1531) |
| | | Council of Trent (1545 – 63) |
| 1600 | | |
| | | King James Bible (1611) |
| | Thirty Years' War (1620-1648) | |
| 1700 | | |
| | Isaac Newton (1642 – 1726) | |
| | | First Great Awakening (1740s) |
| | American Revolution | John Wesley (1703 – 91) |
| 1800 | French Revolution | Growth of Methodists and Baptists in U.S. |

| | | |
|---|---|---|
| | Darwin's *Origin of the Species* (1859) | Slavery divides U.S. |
| **1900** | | Pentecostalism begins |
| | World War I (1913 -18) | *The Fundamentals (1910 – 15)* |
| | World War II (1939 – 45) | Billy Graham's ministry |
| | | Ecumenical movement |
| **2000** | | Culture War begins |

# BIBLIOGRAPHY


Adams, John, *History of the Principal Republic of the World: A Defense of the Constitutions of Government of the The United States of America* (1794).

Adams, Marilyn McCord, *Horrendous Evil and the Goodness of God* (Cornell University Press, 1999).

Amit, Yairah, *In Praise of Editing the Hebrew Bible: Collected Essays in Retrospect* (Sheffield Phoenix, 2012).

Aslan, Reza, *Zealot: The Life and Times of Jesus of Nazareth* (Random House, 2013)

Barnes, Julian, *History of the World in 10 ½ Chapters* (Vintage, 1989).

Barr, James, *History and Ideology in the Old Testament: Biblical Studies at the End of a Millennium* (Oxford University Press, 2000).

Bass, Diane Butler, *A People's History of Christianity* (HarperOne, 2009).

Bauckham, Richard, *Jesus and the Eyewitnesses: The Gospels as Eyewitness Testimony* (Eerdmans, 2006).

Benson, Herbert, J.A. Dusek, J.B. Sherwood, P. Lam, C.F. Bethea, W. Carpenter, S. Levitsky, P.C. Hill, D.W. Clem, Jr., M.K. Jain, D. Drumel, S.L. Kopecky, P.S. Mueller, D. Maret, S. Robbins, and P.L. Hibberd, "Study of the Therapeutic Effects of Intercessory Prayer…. "*American Heart Journal* 151 no. 4 (April 2006) 934-42.

Best, Joel, *Damned Lies and Statistics* (University of California Press, 2001).

Borg, Marcus, *Conflict, Holiness and Politics in the Teachings of Jesus* (Mellen, 1984).

Borg, Marcus, *Jesus* (HarperOne, 2006).

Borg, Marcus, *Meeting Jesus Again for the First Time* (HarperSanFrancisco, 1994).

Boyer, Peter J., "The Big Tent", The New Yorker, August 15, 2005, 47-50.

Brown, Raymond E., *An Introduction to the New Testament* (Doubleday 1997).

Brown, Raymond E., Joseph A. Fitzmyer, Roland E. Murphy, eds., *The New Jerome Biblical Commentary* (Prentice, Hall, 1990).

Brown, Raymond E., *The Birth of the Messiah* (Doubleday, 1993).

*Catechism of the Catholic Church,* (Doubleday, 1995).

Chilton, Bruce, *Rabbi Jesus* (Doubleday, 2000).

Clark, Norman, *Deliver Us From Evil* (Norton, 1976).

Cohen, J.M., trans., *The Life of Saint Teresa of Avila by Herself* (Penguin, 1957).

Conn, Robert, *All That's Left Unsaid/What You Didn't Learn in Sunday School* (unpublished manuscript).

Coogan, Michael D., ed., *The Oxford History of the Biblical World* (Oxford University Press, 1992).

Crossan, J.D., "Why Jesus Didn't Marry," www.beliefnet.com/story/135/Entertainment/Movies/The-Da-Vinci-Code/Why-Jesus-Didn't-Marry.aspx, accessed August 20, 2013.

Crossan, J.D., and Jonathan L. Reed, *In Search of Paul* (HarperSanFrancisco, 2004).

Crossan, J.D., *Jesus, A Revolutionary Biography* (HarperOne, 1994).

Crossan, J.D., *The Historical Jesus* (HarperSanFrancisco, 1991).

D'Antionio, William V., James D. Davidson, Dean R. Hoge, and Katherine Meyer, *American Catholics: Gender, Generation, and Commitment* (AltaMira, 2001)

Dalrymple, William, "Homer in India," *The New Yorker,* Nov. 20, 2006, 52.

Davies, Philip R., *Scribes and Schools: The Canonization of the Hebrew Scriptures* (Westminster John Knox Press, 1996).

Dawkins, Richard, *The God Delusion* (Houghton Mifflin, 2008).

Dawkins, Richard, *The Greatest Show on Earth* (Free Press, 2009).

Dennett, Daniel C., *Breaking the Spell* (Viking, 2006).

Easton, S.C., and H. Wieruszowski, *The Era of Charlemagne* (Van Nostrand, 1961).

Ehrman, Bart D., *Misquoting Jesus* (Harper/San Francisco, 2005).

Ehrman, Bart D., *The New Testament,* (Oxford University Press, 2000)

Elias, Norbert, *The Civilizing Process* (Blackwell, 2000).

Elkind, David, "Quantity Conception in College Students," *Journal of Social Psychology* 57 (1962) 459-65.

Erikson, Erik, *Young Man Luther* (Norton, 1958).

Eusebius, *Ecclesiastical History*, translated by J.E.L. Oulton, (Harvard University Press, 1964), Book VI .

F. Scott Fitzgerald, "The Crack-Up," *Esquire*, February, 1936.

F. Scott Fitzgerald, *The Crack-Up with other Unpublished Pieces, Note-Books and Unpublished Letters*, edited by Edmund Wilson (New Directions, 1945).

Finke, Roger, and Rodney Stark, *The Churching of America, 1776-1990* (Rutgers University Press, 1992).

Flynn, James, *What is Intelligence?* (Cambridge, 2007).

Fox, Robin Lane, *Pagans and Christians* (Knopf, 1989).

Fox, Robin Lane, *The Unauthorized Version: Truth and Fiction in the Bible* (Knopf, 1992).

Freeman, Charles, *A New History of Early Christianity* (Yale, 2009).

Frick, Frank, *A Journey Through the Hebrew Scriptures* (Harcourt Brace, 1995).

Funk, Robert W., Roy W. Hoover, and The Jesus Seminar, *The Five Gospels* (Macmillan, 1993).

Garfinkel, Yosef, "The Birth and Death of Biblical Minimalism," *Biblical Archaeological Review,* 77 no. 3 (2011) 46-53, 78.

Gibbs, Nancy, and Richard N. Ostling, "God's Billy Pulpit," *Time* 142 (1993) 70-8.

Giberson, Karl, and Randall J. Stephens, *The Anointed: Evangelical Truth in a Secular Age* (Harvard University Press, 2011).

Graham, Billy, *Death and Life After* (W. Publishing Group, 1987).

Guelzo, Allen, *Abraham Lincoln: Redeemer President* (Erdmans, 1998).

Hardon, John, *The Catholic Catechism* (Doubleday, 1975).

Heidel, Alexander, *The Babylonian Genesis: The Story of Creation,* (University of Chicago Press, 1951).

Hitchins, Christopher, *God is not Great* (Twelve, 2007).

Hoffmeier, James, "Out of Egypt," *Biblical Archaeological Review* 33 (2007) 36-41, 77.

Holmes, David L., *The Faiths of the Founding Fathers* (Oxford, 2006),

Hoover, Roy W., "How the Books of the New Testament Were Chosen," *Bible Review* 9 (1993) 44-7.

Hopkins, Keith, *A World Full of Gods* (Plume, 2001).

Hultgren, Arland J., *The Rise of Normative Christianity* (Fortress, 1994).

Hunter, James Davison, and Alan Wolfe, *Is There a Culture War?* (Brookings Institute Press, 2005).

Johnson, Luke Timothy, *The Real Jesus* (HarperSanFrancisco, 1996).

Kahneman, Daniel, *Thinking Fast and Slow* (Farrar, Straus, and Girous, 2011).

Kee, Howard Clark, "The Gospel According to Matthew" in *The Interpreter's One-Volume Commentary on the Bible,* edited by Charles M. Laymon, 609-43 (Abingdon, 1971) .

Knight, Douglas A., and Amy-Jill Levine, *The Meaning of the Bible* (HarperOne, 2011).

Kohlbert, L., and R. Mayer, "Development as the Aim of Education," *Harvard Educational Review* 41 (1972) 449-96.

Kosmin, Barry A., and Ariela Keysar, "American Religious Identification Survey" (Program on Public Values, 2009). www.americanreligionsurvey-aris.org (accessed August 23, 2013.)

Kosmin, Barry A., and Seymour P. Lachman, *One Nation Under God: Religion in Contemporary American Society* (Harmony Books, 1993).

Kugel, James L., *How to Read the Bible* (Free Press, 2007).

Kugel, James L., *The Bible as It Was* (Harvard University Press, 1997).

Kuhn, D., J. Langer, L. Kohlberg, and N.S. Haan, "The Development of Formal Operations in Logical and Moral Judgment," *Genetics Psychology Monographs* 95 (1977) 95, 97-188.

Kuhn, Deanna, "How Well Do Jurors Reason," *Current Directions in Psychological Science* 5 (1994) 289- 96.

Latourette, Kenneth Scott, *A History of Christianity* (HarperSanFrancisco, 1975).

Leonard, Bill J., *Baptists in America* (Columbia University Press, 2005).

MacCulloch, Diamaid, *Christianity: The First Three Thousand Years* (Viking, 2009).

Mack, Burton, *Myth of Innocence: Mark and Christian Origins* (Fortress, 1988).

Mackey, James P., *Jesus: The Man and the Myth* (SCM, 1979).

Mason, Herbert, trans., *The Epic of Gilgamesh* (Mentor, 1972).

McRaney, David, *You Are Not So Smart* (Gotham Books, 2011).

Meacham, Jon, "God, Satan, and Katrina," *Newsweek*, March 20, 2006, 53.

Meier, John P., *A Marginal Jew* (Doubleday, 1991).

Mendels, Doron, "Why Paul Went West," *Biblical Archaeological Review* 37 (2011) 49-54, 68.

Moore, Christopher, *Lamb, The Gospel According to Biff, Christ's Childhood Pal* (HarperCollins, 2002).

Newman, William M., and Peter L. Halverson, *Atlas of American Religion* (AltaMira, 2002).

Nicolson, Adam, *God's Secretaries: The Making of the King James Bible* (Harper Collins, 2003).

Niebuhr, Gustav, "Hell Is Getting A Makeover From Catholics; Jesuits Call It a Painful State But Not a Sulfurous Place, The New York Times, http://www.nytimes.com/1999/09/18/arts/hell-getting-makeover-catholics-jesuits-call-it-painful-state-but-not-sulfurous.html?pagewanted=all&src=pm.

Ogden, Daniel, *Magic, Witchcraft, and Ghosts in Greek and Roman Worlds* (Oxford, 2002).

Origen, *Commentary of John*, 10.4.

Origen, *Contra Celsum*, 1.28, 32.

*Origen: Homilies on Luke, Fragments on Luke*, translated and edited by Joseph T. Lienhard (Catholic University of America Press, 1996).

Parker, Andrew, *The Genesis Enigma: Why the Bible is Scientifically Accurate* (Dutton, 2009).

Perry, Jr., William G, *Forms of Intellectual and Ethical Development in the College Years* (Holt, Rinehart, 1968).

Pew Forum on Religion & Public Life, *U.S. Religious Landscape Survey* (2008). www.pewforum.org/pdf/report-religious-landscape-study-full.pdf, accessed August 28, 2013.

Philostratus, *Life of Apollonius*.

Pilch, John J., *A Cultural Handbook to the Bible* (Eerdmans, 2012).

Pinker, Steven, *The Better Angels of Our Nature: Why Violence has Declined* (Viking, 2011).

Plummer, Martin, and Brian King, *Beyond Coincidence* (St. Martin, 2005).

Pope, Harrison G., M.B. Poliakoff, M.P. Parker, M. Boynes, and J. Hudson, "Is dissociative amnesia a culture-bound syndrome? Findings from a survey of historical literature," *Psychological Medicine* 37 (2007) 225-33.

Prothero, Stephen, *American Jesus* (Farrar, Straus and Giroux, 2003).

Pullman, Philip, *The Good Man Jesus and the Scoundrel Christ* (Canongate Books, 2007).

Putnam, Robert D., and David E. Campbell, *American Grace* (Simon and Schuster, 2010).

Rahner, Karl, *The Content of Faith* (Crossroad 1993).

Redmount, Carol A., "Bitter Lives: Israel in and out of Egypt," in *The Oxford History of the Biblical World,* edited by Michael D. Cogan, (Oxford University Press, 1998) 79-122.

Robertson, Pat, *The Inspirational Writings of Pat Robertson* (Inspirational Press, 1989).

Robinson, James M., Paul Hoffman, John S. Kloppenborg, and Milton C. Moreland, *The Critical Edition of Q* (Fortress, 2000).

Rorabaugh, W.J., *The Alcoholic Republic: An American Tradition* (New York, Oxford University Press, 1979).

Rossing, Barbara, *The Rapture Exposed* (Westview, 2004).

Sasson, Jack, "Should Cheeseburgers be Kosher?" *Bible Review* December, 19 (2003) 40-3, 50-1.

Schaberg, Jane, *The Illegitimacy of Jesus* (Sheffield Phoenix Press, 2006).

Schillebeeckx, Edward, *Jesus An Experiment in Christology* (Seabury Press, 1979).

Schussler Fiorenza, Elizabeth, *In Memory of Her* (Crossroad, 1983).

Sides, Ronald J., *The Scandal of the Evangelical Conscience* (Baker, 2005).

Sidonius, *The Letters of Sidonius*, translated by O.M. Dalton (Clarendon, 1915).

Smith, Page, *The Rise of Industrial America* (McGraw-Hill, New York, 1984).

Southern, R.W., *Western Society and the Church in the Middle Ages* (Penguin, 1970).

Spong, John Selby, *Rescuing the Bible from Fundamentalism* (HarperSanFrancisco, 1991).

Spong, John Shelby, *Born of a Woman* (HarperSanFrancisco, 1992).

Spong, John Shelby, *Jesus for the Non-Religious* (HarperOne, 2007).

Stark, Rodney, *The Rise of Christianity: A Sociologist Reconsiders History* (Princeton University Press, 1996).

Steiner, Wendy, *The Scandal of Pleasure: Art in an Age of Fundamentalism* (University of Chicago Press, 1995).

Stone, Barton W., "A Short History of the Life of Barton W. Stone Written by Himself," in Sydney E. Ahlstrom, *A Religious History of the American People* (Yale University Press, 1972) 434-435, originally published in *Voices from Cane Ridge*, edited by Rhodes Thompson, (Bethany Press, 1954).

Tertullian, *Apologeticus*, translated by T.R. Gover, (Harvard University Press, 1960).

Theissen, Gerd, and Annette Merz, *The Historical Jesus* (Fortress, 1998).

Thomas, Oliver, *10 Things Your Minister Wants To Tell You (But Can't, Because He Needs the Job)* (St. Martin's, 2007).

Thompson, T.L., *The Bible in History: How Writers Create a Past* (Jonathon Cape, 1998).

Thuesen, Peter J., *In Discordance with the Scripture: American Protestant Battles over Translating the Bible* (Oxford UP, 1999).

Tillich, Paul, *Systematic Theology* (University of Chicago Press, 1951).

Tilly, Charles, *Why?* (Princeton University Press, 2006).

Tuckett, Christopher, *Reading the New Testament: Methods of Interpretation* (Fortress, 1987)

Vermes, Geza, *The Complete Dead Sea Scrolls in English* (Penguin, 2004).

Vermes, Geza, *The Resurrection* (Doubleday, 2008)

Wheelan, Charles, *Naked Statistics* (Norton, 2013).

Wieseltier, Leon, "The God Genome," review of *Breaking the Spell* by Daniel Dennett, *The New York Times Book Review*, February 19, 2006, 12.

Wills, Garry, *What Jesus m*eant (Viking, 2006).

Wills, Gary, *What Paul meant* (Viking, 2006).

Wills, Gary, *Why Priests? A Failed Tradition* (Viking, 2013).

Wright, Lawrence, *Remembering Satan* (Knopf, 1994).

Wright, N.T., *The Resurrection of the Son of God* (Fortress, 2003).

Wright, Robert, *The Evolution of God* (Little, Brown, 2009).

www.gallup.com/poll/154799/americans-including-catholics-say-birth-control-morally.asp (accessed August 20, 2013).

www.philamuseum.org/collections/permanent/51449.html (accessed August 20, 2013).

www.religions.pewforum.org/pdf/report2-religious-landscape-study-full.pdf (accessed August 20, 2013).

Yanko-Hombach, Valentina, Allan S. Gilbert, Nicolae Panin, and Pavel M. Dolukhanov, *The Black Sea Flood Question: Changes in Coastline, Climate and Human Settlement* (Springer-Verlag, 2007).

# INDEX

Made in the USA
Charleston, SC
01 July 2014